THE

C TRILOGY

A Complete Library for C Programmers

Dedication

To my wife Kim, without whose love and respect, I would be nothing.

Acknowledgments

I would like to thank Lattice Inc. and Microsoft Corp. for the use of their superbly designed C compilers. I would also like to thank Dr. Chand of Bentley College for his support and guidance.

THE

C TRILOGY

A Complete Library for C Programmers

ERIC P. BLOOM

TAB TAB BOOKS Inc.

Blue Ridge Summit, PA 17214

FIRST EDITION
FIRST PRINTING

Library of Congress Cataloging in Publication Data

Bloom, Eric P.
The C Trilogy.

Includes index.
1. C (Computer program language)   I. Title.
QZ76.73.C15B56 1987   004.13′3   87-10006
ISBN 0-8306-7890-5
ISBN 0-8306-2890-8 (pbk.)

Questions regarding the content of this book
should be addressed to:

Reader Inquiry Branch
Editorial Department
TAB BOOKS Inc.
P.O. Box 40
Blue Ridge Summit, PA 17214

Contents

Introduction

The C Trilogy has been designed to assist the programming neophyte, the seasoned computer professional, and all those who fall somewhere between these two polarized extremes. As the title suggests, this book is divided into three related, but distinctly different parts.

PART I is a language tutorial designed to take a would-be C programmer by the hand and lead him (or her) through the maze of functions, rules, and idiosyncrasies that make C a versatile but sometimes hostile language. Additionally, because of its intricate level of detail, it may assist seasoned C programmers in conceptualizing and digesting those one or two concepts that have thus far eluded personal clarification.

PART II is a generalized C user's reference manual. All too often, a software manufacturer creates an ingenious software compiler or application that contains the latest state-of-the-art algorithms, and then falls short in creating nontechnical, user-oriented software documentation. This section attempts to complement, but certainly not replace, these manufacturer supplied C reference manuals by providing less technically orientated explanations in a reference manual format. These explanations will hopefully provide you with the insight needed to understand the more sophisticated manufacturer documentation. I strongly suggest that you investigate the use of a statement or function using the following steps:

1. Read the function (or statement) explanation that is provided within your manufacturer-supplied documentation. If additional clarification is required, proceed to step 2.

2. Read the appropriate one page explanation provided within Part II of this book. If additional clarification is still needed, proceed to step 3.

3. Turn to the tutorial explanation of that topic within Part I of this book.

PART III is a potpourri of ready-to-use functions. These functions can generally be grouped into the following categories:

Chapter 16—Printer Output Functions
Chapter 17—String Manipulation Functions
Chapter 18—Data Input Functions
Chapter 19—Array Manipulation Functions
Chapter 20—Measurement Conversion Functions
Chapter 21—Date Manipulation Functions
Chapter 22—Screen Output and Video Functions
Chapter 23—Simple Mathematical Functions

This third section may be used in three primary ways. First, you may purchase a diskette from TAB BOOKS Inc. containing these source code libraries. Second, you may create your own library by manually typing in appropriate functions. Third, you may use these functions for reference when writing your own functions.

1

The Basics of Programming

Welcome to the C Trilogy. This introductory chapter provides a brief overview of program design, the compilation and linkage process, and various structured programming concepts.

PROGRAM DESIGN

The development of a program requires more then just sitting down and typing in the code. It requires preparation by analyzing what the program should do, how it should be structured and how it should be implemented. To this end, this chapter discusses the program development process that should be followed to help ensure the successful implementation of both stand-alone programs and entire applications.

The program development process is divided into many steps. They are conceptualization, functional design, technical design, programming, implementation, and maintenance.

Program Conceptualization

Any program begins as an idea. In this stage, the originator of the idea, if time allows, tends to play mental "what if" games in an effort to consolidate and refine the program's size and function. After these mental exercises, if the program still seems worthwhile, "back of the envelope" analysis then begins. In this step, the originator is trying to place his thoughts on paper. To this end, he starts scratching out notes, report formats, input screens, or just lines and arrows alluding to the flow of data. Once, these notes are reasonably complete and the program is conceptually designed in the mind of the author, it is time to employ a more formalized and structured design approach. This next step is the functional design phase.

Functional Design

The functional design phase is the process of formalizing the user's requirements and developing functional documentation. All programs, regardless of their application, whether it be financial, scientific, or process control, can be described in terms of their inputs, processes, and outputs. Inputs are the pieces of information entered into a program. Outputs are the reports, files, screens, and other results that are sent from the program to the users. Processes are the step by step instructions used to transform these inputs into outputs. When defining these functional segments, the analyst should first define the program outputs, then decide what program inputs are needed to create those outputs, and finally, develop the process needed to transform the inputs into the outputs. To this end, many techniques have been developed to assist in this design process. The techniques that shall be briefly introduced in this chapter are program logic flowcharts, data dictionaries, decision trees, and decision tables.

Program Logic Flowcharts

Flowcharts are a series of lines, boxes, and circles that graphically represent the logical process contained within a program. This technique is used to assist the analyst in describing the program in a way that is easily understood and simple to create and modify. The symbols employed by the flowcharting process are shown below.

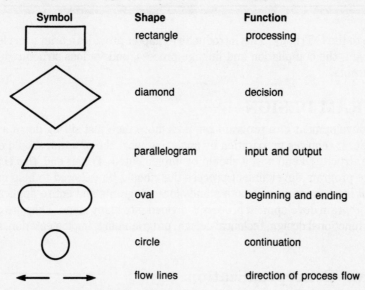

Symbol	Shape	Function
	rectangle	processing
	diamond	decision
	parallelogram	input and output
	oval	beginning and ending
	circle	continuation
	flow lines	direction of process flow

Fig. 1

The flowchart shown in Fig. 1-2 is the representation of a report program similar to the one discussed in this chapter. In this logic-flowchart example, the files are opened and a record is read from the file. If a record is retrieved, it is formatted and written to the file, and another record is read. This process continues until an end of file condition is reached. At that time, the files are closed and the program ends.

This technique can be used to illustrate complex logic in a very simple way. This is shown in Fig. 1-3, which describes the process needed to calculate an employee's gross pay. In the gross pay calculation flowchart, two pay related questions are asked.

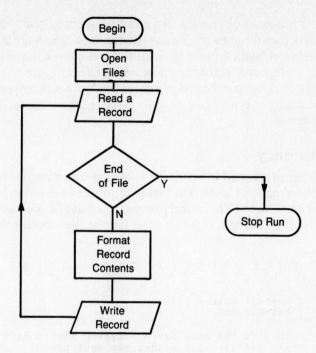

Fig. 1-2.

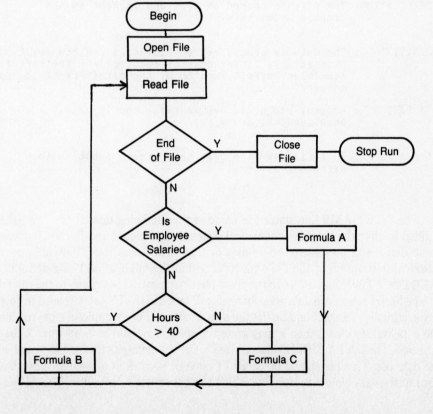

Fig. 1-3.

The first assesses if an employee is payed on an hourly or salaried basis. If the employee is salaried, then the gross pay is calculated as the hourly wage times 40 regardless of the number of hours actually worked. If the employee is not salaried, hence hourly, a second question is asked regarding the number of hours worked. If the answer is 40 or less, the gross pay is calculated as the hourly wage times the hours worked. Otherwise, the employee is payed for 40 hours at the regular wage and time and a half for all hours over 40.

Data Dictionary

Data dictionaries are used to define the information contained within a data file. This tool is divided into two parts. The first part provides a description of the file including a list of its elements. The second part contains detailed information about each field. Figure 1-4 is an example of a fact sheet used to describe each data file.

```
        F I L E   D E S C R I P T I O N   S H E E T

FILE NAME    : Payroll Master File
FILE ID      : PAYMAST.DAT

DESCRIPTION  : This is the main payroll system master file
               and contains all needed employee payroll information.

FILE LOCATION: The file is stored on tape and is kept in the
               computer room safe.

SECURITY     : The data is considered confidencial and company
               proprietary. It may only be removed from the safe for
               scheduled payroll runs or by the signiture of the payroll
               manager.

DATA FIELDS· : emp_no, emp_name, emp_address, hourly_wage,
               no_of_deduct, gross_pay

MISC         : This file is also used as the main input to the
               personnel system.
```

Fig. 1-4.

The FILE NAME line states the name of the file being described. The FILE ID is filled in after the program's technical design is completed and the file is given the name that it will be referred to on disk or tape. The DESCRIPTION field provides a textual description of the file's function within the application being defined. The FILE LOCATION line refers to the file's physical location in regard to the disk drive or tape library where the data actually resides. The SECURITY entry is used to describe any security issues surrounding the file's information. For example, if a payroll master file is being described, then it may state the specific people or departments that can access it. The DATA FIELDS area is used to list the elements that are included within the data file. This list should be carefully entered because it is used as a cross reference to the data element information that shall shortly be described. The MISC area is used to place other information that is of specific interest and does not fit neatly into any of the other categories.

Figure 1-5 is the data element description for the EMP-NO field. The data element field is comprised of seven specific categories. The ELEMENT NAME is the connection to the file description sheets, and is also the name that should be used to describe the data field in the program's DATA DIVISION. The ELEMENT TITLE is a two or three word description of the data field. Generally, the words used in this title coincide with the abbreviations used in the element name. For example, as shown below, EMP-NO has a title of "Employee Name."

```
          E L E M E N T    D E S C R I P T I O N    S H E E T


ELEMENT NAME     : emp_no
ELEMENT TITLE    : Employee Number
SIZE AND FORMAT  : char emp_no[6]

DESCRIPTION      : This is the employee identification number used
                   by the payroll system to uniquely identify each
                   employee

SOURCE           : A number is assigned by personnel to each employee
                   at the time of hire.

UPDATE RULES     : This number should never be changed during the
                   employee's employment with the company and should
                   not be re-used after the employee's termination.

ALIASES          : Badge Number, Payroll Check ID Number
```

Fig. 1-5.

The SIZE AND FORMAT line describes the element's length and type in C data type definition format. This format is described in detail within Chapters 3 and 14. The DESCRIPTION is used to explain the element's function or usage within the application. SOURCE is used to describe the location or process from which the data was originally created. This may be a vendor's invoice, the accounting department's control handbook, or it may be automatically generated by the computer. The UPDATE RULES category specifies the rules and procedures that involve the modification and deletion of the element once it is originally entered into the system. The ALIASES section lists other names for the same element. For example, an employee number is often referred to as a badge number because it is displayed on the employee identification badges.

When applications require many data files, there are usually some data elements contained in more than one file. When this is the case, it is suggested to maintain two separate alphabetic lists. One list should contain the file description sheets and the other should contain the element description sheets. This will save the step of rewritting the element information over and over when it pops up in many files. Additionally, a cross reference from the element description sheets to the data file description can be easily maintained by adding one more category to the former element sheets. This category would list the data files in which the element was used.

Decision Trees

A decision tree is a technique used to define and document the possible options associated with a given situation. One nicety of this definition process is that it is very easy to conceptualize and can therefore be instantly understood by non-technical users. The decision tree below can be used to illustrate the gross pay calculation previously defined during the flowcharting discussion.

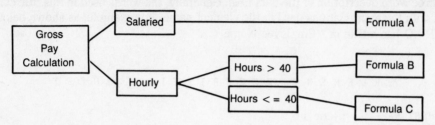

Fig. 1-6.

The decision tree begins with a block, stating the problem or question being addressed. Stemming out from the block are two branches indicating the two possible answers to the question being asked, namely, "Is the employee compensated on a salaried or hourly basis?" If salaried, the tree ends and the appropriate gross pay calculation is displayed. If however, the employee is paid hourly, a second decision is reached which further divides the branch into two new lines. This block and its newly formed branches are called an event fork showing that one question has been answered but another has yet to be addressed. As with the original branches, each option is marked with its specific criteria and corresponding gross pay calculation.

Decision Tables

Decision tables are yet another way to describe the alternatives associated with a given decision. In this technique, two lists are developed. The first is called a condition list and contains the criteria that must be evaluated. These questions must be answerable with either a "yes" or a "no." The second list contains the possible actions that could be taken. The process used to connect the questions to the actions can most easily be explained through illustration. Shown below is a decision table again outlining the gross pay calculation example.

Condition List:			
Is the employee payed by salary	Y	N	N
Is hours worked greater than 40		Y	N
Is hours worked less than or equal to 40		N	Y
Action List:			
Formula A	X		
Formula B		X	
Formula C			X

Fig. 1-7.

Each question places answers on one or more of three vertical columns. Each of these columns is associated with a particular action as is specified by an "X" in the action's specific row. The first gross pay calculation has an "X" in the first vertical column, therefore, if the answers in column one match the answers for a given employee, then the first formula should be used. For example, if the employee being analyzed was not on a salary and worked 35 hours, the first question is answered "N," the second is answered "Y" and the third is answered "N." These three responses match the second column of the decision table, therefore the calculation "gross__pay = hourly__wage * hours__worked" should be used.

Lastly, note that in the second and third question the first column was left blank. This was done because if the first answer was yes, then the employee was salaried and the number of hours worked has no bearing on the action taken.

Technical Design

Technical design is the process of defining a program's structure and detailed logic. To effectively describe this logic, the program being discussed should be divided into bite-size sections called modules. Modules are distinct program segments each of which performs a specific function. The program structure is the way in which these modules interrelate. Detailed logic outlines the steps and algorithms that must be performed within each module to complete its logical function.

Like the design step, this process also contains formalized techniques to assist in the process. The techniques that shall be discussed here are HIPO, pseudocode, and program flowcharts.

HIPO Charts

The word HIPO stands for Hierarcical Input Process Output technique. This method is comprised of two parts. The first part is the development of a hierarchical structure chart that arranges the program modules in a top-down fashion. The structure chart for a payroll check writing report is shown below.

Fig. 1-8.

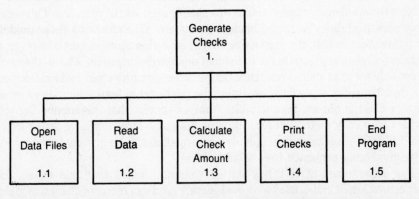

This structure chart illustrates the modules contained within a check generation program. The top module is Generate Checks which is used to control the five subordinate level modules. These modules are Open Files, Read Data, Calculate Check Amounts, Print Checks, and End Program. When the program is executed, Generate

Checks calls the Open Files module. When complete, the program reads a record from the data file, calculates the amount to be payed, prints the check and goes back to module three to retrieve another record. This looping process will continue until the input file is out of records and the sixth module is called to close the files and end the program.

There are times when a single level of module detail will not adequately describe the program's breakdown. In these cases, subordinate modules can be further divided as shown below.

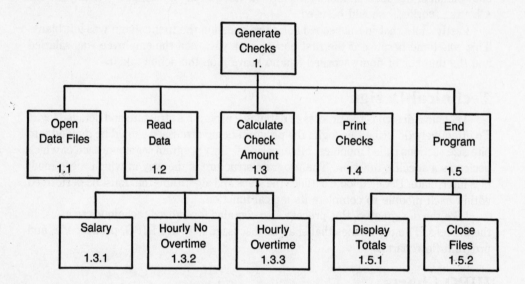

Fig. 1-9.

An additional level of detail has been added to modules 1.3 and 1.5. These new levels were designed to provide a finer level of program detail. Remember, these specifications will be used by the programmer as the blueprint of a program's structure. Therefore, the better the design specifications, the easier it is for the programmer.

Note the numbering sequence that was used to identify the modules. This sequence allows each module to be traced back to its owner. When viewing these modules in a structure chart format, the numbering may seem rather unimportant. However, these numbers will also be placed in the individual module descriptions. There, the numbers will not only serve as a cross reference between the structure chart and module descriptions, but that will also assist in assessing the relationship between modules when the structure chart is not easily accessible. Another service that this numbering scheme provides is an easy method of locating a module on a large complex structure chart. Even if a chart has hundreds of modules, any module can be quickly found by following its numbering sequence from level to level.

The second part of HIPO is the IPO charts. Recall that this stands for Input/Process/Output and is used to provide detailed information about each module that was identified in the structure chart. Shown in Fig. 1-10 is the IPO chart associated with module 1.3 in the second structure chart example.

The IPO chart displayed in Fig. 1-10 is divided into many parts. The SYSTEM NAME is used to place the name of the application being designed. In this case, the

```
                        I P O   C H A R T

    SYSTEM NAME    : Payroll        PREPARED BY  : E. Bloom
    PROGRAM NAME   : PRLOO9.C       DATE         : 8/30/85
    MODULE NAME    : Get Check Amount  APPROVED BY : E. Wells
    MODULE NUMBER  : 1.3


    CALLED BY : 1. Create Checks    IT CALLS : 1.3.1 Salaried
                                               1.3.2 Hourly No Overtime
                                               1.3.3 Hourly With Overtime


    INPUTS : Hourly-wage, Salary-type,  OUTPUTS : Gross-pay
             Gross-Pay, Hours-worked


    DESCRIPTION : This Module decides which gross pay calculation should
                  be used and calls the appropriate module.


    PROCESS     : If Salary-type = 'salaried'
                      Then do module 1.3.1
                  Else
                      If Hours-worked <= 40
                          Then do module 1.3.2
                      Else
                          Do module 1.3.3


    LOCAL DATA ELEMENTS : None
```

Fig. 1-10.

program being designed is part of the payroll system. PROGRAM NAME is used to record the name of the program being written. The MODULE NAME and MODULE NUMBER are the cross reference to the structure chart. These two fields should be filled out identically to that in the structure chart. The PREPARED BY area specifies the person who completed the IPO form. The DATE field may contain either the date the chart was originally prepared or the date that it was approved. The particular date used will depend on the customs and style of the data processing department doing the work. In some places, both dates are required and another date field is added to the form.

The next section of the IPO chart describes how the module relates to other modules. The CALLED BY area lists the names and numbers of the modules that call the module being defined. The section IT CALLS states its subordinate modules. The INPUT and OUTPUT blocks list the variables that are passed to and from the module during processing.

The last chart section explains the processes that will be performed within the module. The DESCRIPTION area provides a textual description of the modules process. The PROCESS area describes the needed module logic in a C-like format. This near C description is called Structured English and can later be easily transformed into code, thus assisting the programmer in writing the internal program logic. The LOCAL DATA ELEMENTS field is used to list those local variables which are only referenced within the module and are not passed from place to place. Lastly, the MISC section is used to place pertinent information that does not neatly fit into any other category.

PSEUDOCODE

Pseudocode is a tool used to design and later document the processes within a module. This is done by using regular English words, within a C-like format. The difference between this process and the structured English previously mentioned is that this includes all programming steps needed to execute the module and not just selected pieces of logic. In fact, the format of the pseudocode used on the design of a given application is dictated by the language in which the application will be programmed. However, because pseudocode is so close to the actual program coding, most programmers dislike it. The general feeling among most programmers is that is the text being written is almost the actual program, so why not just write the actual code? Below is an example of the pseudocode for a small report program.

```
Start:   Open Master File for input
         Open Report File for output
         Set record flag to NO
         Read report master file, at end set record flag to Yes
         If record Flag is equal to No
            Perform Loop until record flag is NO
         Close master file and report file
         Stop run

Loop :   Move master file data to report record
         Write report record to report file
         Read master file, at end move NO to record flag
```

Fig. 1-11.

There are three types of commands being used above. They are functional, conditional logic, and repetition. The functional commands are executed in sequence and perform specific functions like opening and closing files, moving values from variable to variable, and mathematics. The "if" commands perform conditional logic, function calls allow subroutining, and "for," "while" and "do/while" facilitate looping. As shall be seen in Chapter 7, these three functions are very closely tied to structured programming ideologies.

PROGRAMMING

The programming phase consists of three steps; writing the source code and preliminary testing.

Writing The Source Code

There are two basic ways in which programs are actually written and entered into the computer. The first method is to write the program out by hand on either plain lined paper or on some type of special coding form, and keying in the entire program. Second, as programmers become more experienced, they tend to try to type the program directly into the computer without first writing on paper. The success of this second method is solely based on the talent of the programmer and the complexity of the application being developed. In either case, proper design specifications greatly assist in the process.

Preliminary Testing

During the programming and compilation process there are two basic types of programming bugs that can and usually do occur. They are syntactical errors and logical errors. Syntax errors are easy to find because the program listing that is created during the compilation process tells the programmer exactly where the error occurred and provide some explanation of the problem. These errors are caused by statements that are not in the correct C format. For example, the statement "whiile (x < 1)" will cause an error because "whiile" is not a valid statement and therefore cannot be understood by the compiler.

Once the program being written is free of syntactical problems, logical errors must be identified and corrected. Logical errors are mistakes in the way the program processes the data. These errors are much more difficult to find and may periodically turn up after months or even years, depending on the complexity of the program and the thoroughness of the testing process. To identify these errors, the programmer should develop a small set of test data. This data should contain information that is representative of that used in the application as well as information with out-of-range values and invalid formats. The valid data will assist in the testing of the program's processing logic and the invalid information will test the program's error checking capabilities.

Program Implementation and Maintenance

The implementation of a program or system is the final step in the software development process. This step is comprised of final testing, implementation, and program maintenance.

The Final Testing and Implementation Process

Once the program is completed and seemingly ready for production, it should go through one more rounds of testing. When possible, these tests should not be performed by the program's author. The person who wrote the program tests it to see if it works. Others test a program to find the errors. It is this difference in mental attitude that helps to provide a more thorough and complete test. Also, the programmer has presumably tested the program prior to implementation, and may therefore take a second round of testing less seriously than a newcomer to the process.

A very common practice in testing new programs is to develop a testing team. This team usually consists of the program's author, a fellow programmer and someone who will use the program once it is implemented. The program's author is present only to provide technical background about the program's development. The testing is performed by the second programmer and the user.

This team approach seems to work well because the second programmer can evaluate the program's technical aspects without being hindered by a pride of authorship, and the user has the application knowledge to analyze the program's functional merit. Also, the user has a strong vested interest in that he or she will have to rely on the ability and correctness of this program for the foreseen future.

There are many techniques that can be used to test programs. Three of the most common are parallel testing, prior testing and simulation testing. Parallel testing is the process of running two systems simultaneously. Using this technique requires continuing the old methods and also taking on the task of doing it the new way. This additional responsibility may just be running another report over the weekend or it may mean manually inputting data into two systems. Once complete, the outputs of the two systems are compared. If the results are the same, or at least reconcilable, then the new system continues and the old mode of operation is discontinued. If the test results are unsatisfactory, it's back to work, to discuss the problems and make the appropriate changes.

Parallel testing sounds good in theory, but in actuality, it can sometimes be impractical or even impossible to perform, due to a lack of the resources needed to do twice the work or the inability to capture the data in two places at once. Therefore, two alternate approaches were developed that can be performed by just the testing team. The first of these techniques is called prior testing. This process uses the same principles as parallel testing except it uses data from past months. For example, if a new payroll system is being installed in November, establish the test files as of a few months before, say March. Then, enter April's actual data and compare the test reports to the actual April numbers. Continue this process through the October data, and if all looks good, go with only the new system in November.

The third testing process is similar to the second, except that the test data is strictly simulated. This alternative will not produce as thorough a test. However, if the test data is selected carefully, it should suffice. To implement a system using this test method, the files being used by the old programs are copied and converted to the new format, and on an appropriate day, the old method is turned off and the the new method is turned on.

Program Maintenance

Regardless of the implementation method used to operationalize the new program or system, there is usually a need for maintenance programming. Maintenance programming becomes necessary for many reasons. Errors may be found in the code that must be corrected. Company policies or procedures may change. Growing firms may outgrow current systems or enhancements may be made to meet new business challenges. Whatever the reason, this task can be made easier if the software being written is well documented, written in a clear, concise, structured format, and carefully modified, so as not to violate structured principles or outdate the documentation.

THE COMPILATION PROCESS

Once the source code is written and typed into the computer, it must be translated from a human readable format into computer readable form. This translation process is known as compilation, and is illustrated in Fig. 1-12.

To compile a program, the programmer must execute the C compiler and specify the name of the program to be transformed. This process leaves the input source code unchanged, and creates two outputs; a program listing and a file containing the program object code. The program listing is different from the source code listing because it contains information about the compilation, including the number of errors, the error locations, a variable cross reference list and other similar information that can be used in the program debugging process. The object code is the source code in a computer readable format (binary). Like many other languages, the C compilation process

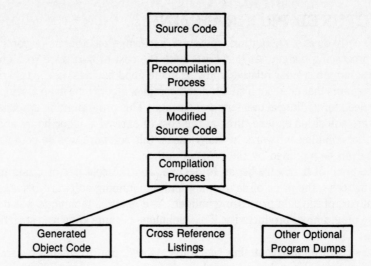

Fig. 1-12.

is performed in two main stages. The first stage is called precompilation which modifies the source code as specified by the compiler directives discussed in Chapters 12 and 15. The second step is the actual compilation, which reads the modified source code, analyzes its syntax for errors, and generates the compiled object code.

After the compilation process is complete, there is one more step that must be performed before the program can be executed. This step is program linkage. The linkage process is illustrated below.

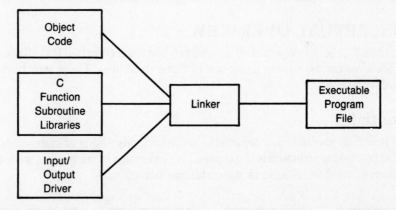

Fig. 1-13.

The linkage process connects all the various processes needed to successfully execute the program, and places them together in one file. In the linkage example shown above, there are three files being consolidated. The first file is the program's object code. The second file contains the object code from a function library like those provided in Part III of this book. The input/output driver is required by any executing program, regardless of the language in which it was written. This routine connects the program's logic to the terminals, disk drives, and other input or output devices. The particular linker you use will dictate whether this device driver is automatically called in during the linkage process or if it must be explicitly stated.

STRUCTURED PROGRAMMING

In the early days of computing, computer hardware was the major contributor to the data processing budget. At that time, with the cost of hardware so high and the cost of programming labor relatively low, it made good business sense to write applications programs that used sophisticated and complex algorithms in an attempt to minimize the need for additional memory and storage. This programming emphasis saved on hardware aquisition expenditures at the cost of extensive labor hours and the development of complex software. In many cases, this software was so complex that it could not even be modified by the original author.

As the price of hardware began to decline, and the cost per programming hour began to increase, the price of developing and maintaining software became a more significant part of the data processing budget. As a result, a technique was developed to improve programmer productivity. This technique became known as structured programming.

When structured programming was implemented, improvements became noticeable in many areas. First, because of the self-documenting nature of structured programming, programs became easier to read and thereby easier to enhance or modify. Second, since the program's structure was generally the same from program to program, less time was spent in the program design phase. Also, because of a common formalized structure, many programs could be created just by copying and modifying previously written programs. This was especially seen in regard to programs that generated reports. Third, due to the module-like nature of structured programs, they were easier to test and debug. Lastly, as a result of the previously discussed benefits, the software being developed was more reliable and had a longer production life.

A CONCEPTUAL OVERVIEW

Conceptually, the developers of structured programming theorized that all programming procedures can be written using one of three structures. These structures are; sequential, if-then-else and do-while.

Sequential

The flowchart shown below depicts the sequential processing of statements. The sequential processing structure is the consecutive execution of statements without the interruption of conditional logic or unconditional branching.

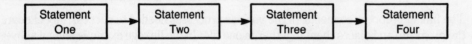

Fig. 1-14.

An example of sequentially processed statements is shown below.

```
salary = hourly_wage * 40;
total_salary += salary;
printf("\n Employee Salary is %f",salary);
```

Fig. 1-15.

There are very few programs that use only sequentially processed statements. What is very common however, is to have a group of statements much like those shown above, incorporated into if-then-else logic, or within a do-while looping structures.

If-Then-Else

The if-then-else structure is a very powerful and flexible part of the C language and is essential in the development of most business application programs. Its function is to define the program's logic and cause the execution of selected statements based on specified criteria. In other words, if a particular condition is met, then perform a function or group of functions, else, if the condition is not met, perform a different set of functions. The figure below represents if-then-else logic.

Fig. 1-16.

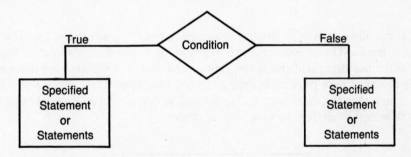

Within the C language, this if-then-else structure is performed by the if statement. Even though C does not use the word then in the if statement format, it logically implys its function by the statements that are placed directly after the conditional expression. An example of an if condition is shown below.

Fig. 1-17.

```
if ( strcmp(pay_type,"salaried") == 0 )
      salary_count +=1;
else
      hourly_count +=1;
```

A value of 1 will be added to salary_count if pay_type is equal to salaried. Otherwise, 1 will be added to the hourly employee counter hourly_count. Note that both these add statements will never be executed for the same employee. Therefore, this relationship is always an either/or scenario.

Do-While

The last of the structured constructs is the Do-While format. This format is used for looping and instructs the computer to do these statements while a particular condition is true. Figure 1-18 is a flowchart representing the Do-While process.

Note that in the do-while flowchart that the specified statements are always executed at least once, then the condition is checked to see if the loop should continue. This processing order will have ramifications from a C perspective in regard to how and when the loop is processed. Figure 1-19 displays this looping process.

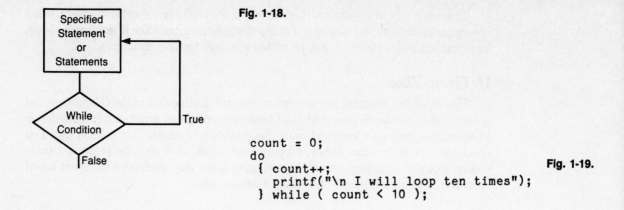

Fig. 1-18.

```
count = 0;
do
  { count++;
    printf("\n I will loop ten times");
  } while ( count < 10 );
```

Fig. 1-19.

C also allows two other structured looping options. These options are the while and for statements. The while statement is very similar to the do/while shown in Fig. 1-19, the difference being that the statements contained within the while are not automatically executed once prior to assessing the test condition. Thus, if the test condition is not met, then the statements within the while loop will not be executed at all. Below is a flowchart depicting the while looping process

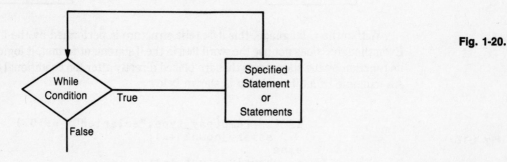

Fig. 1-20.

and the following code lists an actual while statement.

Fig. 1-21.

```
int count = 0;

while ( count < 10 )
  { printf("\n I will also print 10 times");
    count++;
  }
```

The for statement is yet another variation on the do/while structure. The for statement is designed to loop a specified number of times based on an incremented counter. Figure 1-22 describes this looping algorithm and Fig. 1-23 is an actual C for statement.

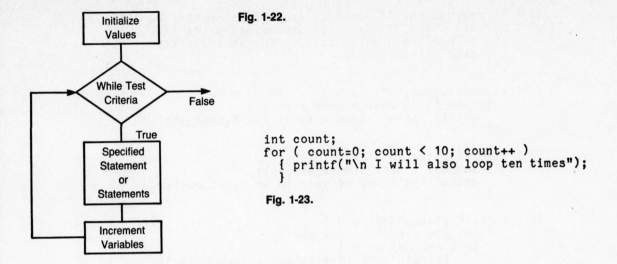

Fig. 1-22.

```
int count;
for ( count=0; count < 10; count++ )
   { printf("\n I will also loop ten times");
   }
```

Fig. 1-23.

TOP-DOWN DEVELOPMENT

As research of structured analysis continued, it was discovered that because of the modular structure caused by the use of only sequential, if-then-else, and do-while processes, any program, regardless of its application, could be written from the first instruction, straight to the bottom without having to rework previously entered statements. Therefore, the program could be tested during the coding phase each time logical groups of modules were added. Thus, the name Top-Down development was coined. To illustrate this phenomena, consider the development process used to create the simple menu driven date manipulation program listed in Fig. 1-24. Note that the date manipulation techniques used in this example are included in the Chapter 21 date library.

Fig. 1-24.

```
#include <stdio.h>

main()
{ menu();
}

Menu()
{ char option[2];
  char date_string[12];
  char day[10];
  int int_day;
  long int long_day;
  long int date_4();

  do
   { printf("\n\n\n\n\n");
     printf("\n            1. Julian Date");
     printf("\n            2. Day of the Year");
     printf("\n            3. Leap year");
     printf("\n            4. Day of Week");
     printf("\n            Q. Quit program");
     printf("\n\n                      Enter option : ");
     gets(option);
```

```
            if ( strcmp(option,"1") == 0 || strcmp(option,"2") == 0 ||
                 strcmp(option,"3") == 0 || strcmp(option,"4") == 0 )
                { printf("\n\n Enter date in format MM/DD/YYYY : ");
                  gets(date_string);
                }

            if ( strcmp(option,"1") == 0 )
                { long_day = date_4(date_string);
                  printf("\n\n Julian date is %ld ",long_day);
                }

            if ( strcmp(option,"2") == 0 )
                { int_day = date_5(date_string);
                  printf("\n\n Day of year is %d ",int_day);
                }

            if ( strcmp(option,"3") == 0 )
                { int_day = date_6(date_string);
                  if ( int_day == 0 )
                     printf("\n\n This is not a leap year ");
                  else
                     printf("\n\n This is a leap year");
                }

            if ( strcmp(option,"4") == 0 )
                { int_day = date_7(date_string);
                  if ( int_day == 0 ) strcpy(day,"Sunday");
                  if ( int_day == 1 ) strcpy(day,"Monday");
                  if ( int_day == 2 ) strcpy(day,"Tuesday");
                  if ( int_day == 3 ) strcpy(day,"Wednesday");
                  if ( int_day == 4 ) strcpy(day,"Thursday");
                  if ( int_day == 5 ) strcpy(day,"Friday");
                  if ( int_day == 6 ) strcpy(day,"Saterday");

                  printf("\n\n Day of the week is %s",day);
                }

    } while ( strcmp(option,"Q") != 0 );
}


 /* ********************************************************************
  * Function name  : date_4
  *
  * Description    : This function converts the date from a format of
  *                  MM/DD/YYYY to its julian equivilant.
  *
  * Variables      : d_in - The variables contains the date that is
  *                         passed to the function for conversion to
  *                         its julian date.
  *
  *                  julian - This long integer variable contains the
  *                           numeric julian value that is returned to
  *                           the calling function.
  *
  ***********************
  * 0123456789          *
  * MM/DD/YYYY input     *
  *********************/
```

18

```c
long int date_4(d_in)
 char *d_in;
{ int in_year, in_month, in_day;
  int cent, cent_y, month, year, out_day;
  long int long_day, temp_long;
  *(d_in+2) = '\0';
  *(d_in+5) = '\0';
  in_year  = i_convert(d_in+6);
  in_month = i_convert(d_in);
  in_day   = i_convert(d_in+3);

  if ( in_month > 2 )
    { month = in_month - 3;
      year  = in_year;
    }
  else
    { month = in_month + 9;
      year = in_year - 1;
    }
  temp_long = 146097;
  cent   = year / 100;
  cent_y = year - ( cent * 100 );
  long_day = temp_long * cent / 4;
  long_day = long_day + 1461.0 * cent_y / 4;
  long_day = long_day  + ( 153 * month + 2 ) / 5;
  long_day = long_day + in_day;

  return(long_day);
}

/* *******************************************************************
 * Function name  : date_5
 *
 * Description    : This function receives a date in the format
 *                  MM/DD/YYYY and returns its daily position within
 *                  within the year. For example, February 5th is
 *                  the 36th day of the year.
 *
 * Variables      : d_in - The variables contains the date that is
 *                         passed to the function for conversion to
 *                         its julian date.
 *
 *                  out_day - This long integer variable contains the
 *                            numeric value that is returned to
 *                            the calling function.
 *
 ***********************
 * 0123456789          *
 * MM/DD/YYYY input    *
 ***********************/
date_5(d_in)
 char *d_in;
{ int in_year, in_month, in_day;
  int cent, cent_y, month, year, out_day, leap_year;
  long int long_day;
  *(d_in+2) = '\0';
  *(d_in+5) = '\0';
  in_year  = i_convert(d_in+6);
```

```
    in_month  = i_convert(d_in);
    in_day    = i_convert(d_in+3);

    long_day = ( 3055.0 * ( in_months + 2 ) / 100 ) -91;
    out_day = long_day;

    if ( in_month > 2 )
      { leap_year = 0;
        if (( in_year % 4 )   == 0 ) leap_year = 1;
        if (( in_year % 100 ) == 0 ) leap_year = 0;
        if (( in_year % 400 ) == 0 ) leap_year = 1;
        out_day = out_day - 2 + leap_year;
      }
    out_day += in_day;
    return(out_day);
}

/* ********************************************************************
 * Function name   : date_6
 *
 * Description     : This function receives a date in the format
 *                   MM/DD/YYYY and returns a 0 if the year is not a
 *                   leap year and a 1 if the year is a leap year.
 *
 * Variables       : d_in - The variables contains the date that is
 *                          passed to the function for conversion to
 *                          its julian date.
 *
 *                   leap-year - This integer variable contains the
 *                               numeric value that is returned to
 *                               the calling function.
 *
 ***********************
 * 0123456789          *
 * MM/DD/YYYY input    *
 ***********************/
date_6(d_in)
 char *d_in;
{ int in_year, in_month, in_day;
  int leap_year;
  *(d_in+2) = '\0';
  *(d_in+5) = '\0';
  in_year   = i_convert(d_in+6);
  in_month  = i_convert(d_in);
  in_day    = i_convert(d_in+3);

  leap_year = 0;
  if (( in_year % 4 )   == 0 ) leap_year = 1;
  if (( in_year % 100 ) == 0 ) leap_year = 0;
  if (( in_year % 400 ) == 0 ) leap_year = 1;
  return(leap_year);
}

/* ********************************************************************
 * Function name   : date_7
 *
 * Description     : This function receives a date in the format
 *                   MM/DD/YYYY and returns its daily position within
```

```
*                    within the week. For example, Dec. 5, 1986 fell on
*                    a friday, therefore this function will return a 5.
*                    ( 0=Sun, 1=Mon, 2=Tue, 3=Wed, 4=Thu, 5=Fri, 6=Sat )
*
* Variables        : d_in - The variables contains the date that is
*                           passed to the function for conversion to
*                           its julian date.
*
*                    out_day - This integer variable contains the numeric
*                              value standing for the day of the week
*                              that is returned to the calling function.
*
***********************
* 0123456789          *
* MM/DD/YYYY input     *
***********************/
date_7(d_in)
 char *d_in;
{ int in_year, in_month, in_day;
  int cent, cent_y, month, year, out_day;
  long int long_day;
  *(d_in+2) = '\0';
  *(d_in+5) = '\0';
  in_year   = i_convert(d_in+6);
  in_month  = i_convert(d_in);
  in_day    = i_convert(d_in+3);

  if ( in_month > 2 )
    { month = in_month - 2;
      year  = in_year;
    }
  else
    { month = in_month + 10;
      year = in_year - 1;
    }
  cent   = year / 100;
  cent_y = year - ( cent * 100 );
  long_day = ( 13 * month - 1 ) / 5;
  long_day = long_day + in_day + cent_y + ( cent_y/4 );
  long_day = long_day  + ( cent/4 ) - cent - cent + 77;
  long_day = long_day - 7 * ( long_day / 7 );
  out_day = long_day;

  return(out_day);
}
```

This sample program consists of a user menu with four date options and "Q" to quit (exit the program). These options ask the user to input a date in the format "MM/DD/YYYY" and the appropriate date related information is returned. The first option returns a unique julian value uniquely identifying that day, month and year. The second option returns the day of the year, for example, February 10th would be day 41. The third option states whether the year being analyzed is a leap year, and the fourth option returns the day of the week on which that date fell. When this program was being designed, the HIPO structure chart shown in Fig. 1-25 was developed.

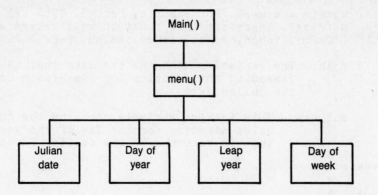

Fig. 1-25.

When the date manipulation program was developed, the main() and menu() functions were developed and tested with the program in the status shown below.

Fig. 1-26.

```c
#include <stdio.h>

main()
{ menu();
}

Menu()
{ char option[2];
  char date_string[12];
  char day[10];
  int int_day;
  long int long_day;
  long int date_4();

  do
  { printf("\n\n\n\n\n");
    printf("\n          1. Julian Date");
    printf("\n          2. Day of the Year");
    printf("\n          3. Leap year");
    printf("\n          4. Day of Week");
    printf("\n          Q. Quit program");
    printf("\n\n                    Enter option : ");
    gets(option);

    if ( strcmp(option,"1") == 0 || strcmp(option,"2") == 0 ||
         strcmp(option,"3") == 0 || strcmp(option,"4") == 0 )
           { printf("\n\n Enter date in format MM/DD/YYYY : ")
             gets(date_string);
           }

    if ( strcmp(option,"1") == 0 )
           { long_day = date_4(date_string);
             printf("\n\n Julian date is %ld ",long_day);
           }
```

```
        if ( strcmp(option,"2") == 0 )
            { int_day = date_5(date_string);
              printf("\n\n Day of year is %d ",int_day);
            }

        if ( strcmp(option,"3") == 0 )
            { int_day = date_6(date_string);
              if ( int_day == 0 )
                  printf("\n\n This is not a leap year ");
              else
                  printf("\n\n This is a leap year");
            }

        if ( strcmp(option,"4") == 0 )
            { int_day = date_7(date_string);
              if ( int_day == 0 ) strcpy(day,"Sunday");
              if ( int_day == 1 ) strcpy(day,"Monday");
              if ( int_day == 2 ) strcpy(day,"Tuesday");
              if ( int_day == 3 ) strcpy(day,"Wednesday");
              if ( int_day == 4 ) strcpy(day,"Thursday");
              if ( int_day == 5 ) strcpy(day,"Friday");
              if ( int_day == 6 ) strcpy(day,"Saterday");

              printf("\n\n Day of the week is %s",day);
            }

    } while ( strcmp(option,"Q") != 0 );
}

/* Julian Date Calculation */
date_4(d_in)
 char *d_in;
{ long int long_return;
  long_return = 123456;
  return(long_return);
}


/* Day of Year Calculation */
date_5(d_in)
 char *d_in;
{ return(123);
}

/* Leap Year Calculation */
date_5(d_in)
 char *d_in;
{ return(0);
}

/* Day of Week Calculation */
date_5(d_in)
 char *d_in;
{ return(2);
}

    return(long_day);
}
```

Once the program as shown in Fig. 1-26 was tested, functions date__4 and date__5 were added and debugged. At that point in time the program was in the state exhibited below.

Fig. 1-27.

```
#include <stdio.h>

main()
{ menu();
}

Menu()
{ char option[2];
  char date_string[12];
  char day[10];
  int int_day;
  long int long_day;
  long int date_4();

  do
   { printf("\n\n\n\n\n");
     printf("\n          1. Julian Date.");
     printf("\n          2. Day of the Year");
     printf("\n          3. Leap year");
     printf("\n          4. Day of Week");
     printf("\n          Q. Quit program");
     printf("\n\n                          Enter option : ");
     gets(option);

     if ( strcmp(option,"1") == 0 || strcmp(option,"2") == 0 ||
          strcmp(option,"3") == 0 || strcmp(option,"4") == 0 )
         { printf("\n\n Enter date in format MM/DD/YYYY : ");
           gets(date_string);
         }

     if ( strcmp(option,"1") == 0 )
         { long_day = date_4(date_string);
           printf("\n\n Julian date is %ld ",long_day);
         }

     if ( strcmp(option,"2") == 0 )
         { int_day = date_5(date_string);
           printf("\n\n Day of year is %d ",int_day);
         }

     if ( strcmp(option,"3") == 0 )
         { int_day = date_6(date_string);
           if ( int_day == 0 )
               printf("\n\n This is not a leap year ");
           else
               printf("\n\n This is a leap year");
         }

     if ( strcmp(option,"4") == 0 )
         { int_day = date_7(date_string);
           if ( int_day == 0 ) strcpy(day,"Sunday");
```

```
                        if ( int_day == 1 ) strcpy(day,"Monday");
                        if ( int_day == 2 ) strcpy(day,"Tuesday");
                        if ( int_day == 3 ) strcpy(day,"Wednesday");
                        if ( int_day == 4 ) strcpy(day,"Thursday");
                        if ( int_day == 5 ) strcpy(day,"Friday");
                        if ( int_day == 6 ) strcpy(day,"Saterday");

                        printf("\n\n Day of the week is %s",day);
                }
        } while ( strcmp(option,"Q") != 0 );
}
/* ********************************************************************
 * Function name  : date_4
 *
 * Description    : This function converts the date from a format of
 *                  MM/DD/YYYY to its julian equivilant.
 *
 * Variables      : d_in - The variables contains the date that is
 *                         passed to the function for conversion to
 *                         its julian date.
 *
 *                  julian - This long integer variable contains the
 *                           numeric julian value that is returned to
 *                           the calling function.
 *
 ***********************
 * 0123456789          *
 * MM/DD/YYYY input    *
 ***********************/
long int date_4(d_in)
 char *d_in;
{ int in_year, in_month, in_day;
  int cent, cent_y, month, year, out_day;
  long int long_day, temp_long;
  *(d_in+2) = '\0';
  *(d_in+5) = '\0';
  in_year   = i_convert(d_in+6);
  in_month  = i_convert(d_in);
  in_day    = i_convert(d_in+3);

  if ( in_month > 2 )
    { month = in_month - 3;
      year  = in_year;
    }
  else
    { month = in_month + 9;
      year = in_year - 1;
    }
  temp_long = 146097;
  cent   = year / 100;
  cent_y = year - ( cent * 100 );
  long_day = temp_long * cent / 4;
  long_day = long_day + 1461.0 * cent_y / 4;
  long_day = long_day  + ( 153 * month + 2 ) / 5;
  long_day = long_day + in_day;
  return(long_day);
}
```

```
/* ***********************************************************************
 * Function name  : date_5
 *
 * Description     : This function receives a date in the format
 *                   MM/DD/YYYY and returns its daily position within
 *                   within the year. For example, February 5th is
 *                   the 36th day of the year.
 *
 * Variables       : d_in - The variables contains the date that is
 *                   passed to the function for conversion to
 *                   its julian date.
 *
 *                   out_day - This long integer variable contains the
 *                   numeric value that is returned to
 *                   the calling function.
 *
 ***********************
 * 0123456789          *
 * MM/DD/YYYY input    *
 ***********************/
date_5(d_in)
 char *d_in;
{ int in_year, in_month, in_day;
  int cent, cent_y, month, year, out_day, leap_year;
  long int long_day;
  *(d_in+2) = '\0';
  *(d_in+5) = '\0';
  in_year   = i_convert(d_in+6);
  in_month  = i_convert(d_in);
  in_day    = i_convert(d_in+3);

  long_day = ( 3055.0 * ( in_months + 2 ) / 100 ) -91;
  out_day = long_day;

  if ( in_month > 2 )
    { leap_year = 0;
      if (( in_year % 4 )   == 0 ) leap_year = 1;
      if (( in_year % 100 ) == 0 ) leap_year = 0;
      if (( in_year % 400 ) == 0 ) leap_year = 1;
      out_day = out_day - 2 + leap_year;
    }
  out_day += in_day;
  return(out_day);
}

/* Leap Year Calculation */
date_6(d_in)
 char *d_in;
{ return(0);
}
/* Day of Week Calculation */
date_6(d_in)
 char *d_in;
{ return(2);
}
```

The program as seen in Fig. 1-27 can be compiled, linked, and executed. As a result, the functions or modules that have been written can be completely tested and left alone. Thus, as new modules are added, only these newly added segments must be reviewed. This divide-and-conquer strategy makes it much easier to identify and correct programming errors.

The Use of the GOTO Statement

Over the years there has been much debate over the use of the goto statement in structured programming environment. Many industry specialists believe that this statement has no place in modern programming and should be avoided under all circumstances. The other school of thought believes that goto provides a needed function and may be used if it does not hurt a program's readability and self-documenting nature. In the final analysis, however, the rules for using the goto statement will differ from company to company. Remember that the goal is not to avoid goto statements, but to write programs that are as clear, reliable, and self-documenting as possible.

PART I

THE C PRIMER

2

Getting Started with C

This chapter is designed to begin you on your voyage through the C language. By the end of the chapter, you will have an understanding of many C concepts and statements and will have the knowledge needed to write simple programs.

WRITING A PROGRAM

The only real way to learn a programming language is to write programs. Therefore, let's write a very simple program, and expand upon it as new topics are discussed. The program that will be written adds two numbers together and prints their total on the terminal. Let's begin by writing a program that will display the words. "This program adds up two numbers." The program that does this is shown below:

```
main( )
{ printf("This program adds up two numbers");
}
```

This short program brings forward many key points that are typical of all C program, regardless of their size. First, note that the program begins with the word "main" followed by a set of parentheses. Their combination, namely "main( )", states that the lines which are listed below it within the brackets are part of a function called main. The concept of a function will be fully explained in Chapter 6, but for now, consider it to be a group of related C statements that perform a specified task. The parentheses following the function's name are used to pass data values called parameters to the function. Even when there is no data to be passed, as is the case with main( ), the parentheses are still required. Second, note that the statements, or in this case a single statement, within main( ) are enclosed within opening and closing curly brackets. These brackets signify the beginning and ending boundaries of the main( ) function. As shall be seen in later chapters, these brackets signify statement blocks and are required by all functions. Lastly, C, unlike most other programming languages, is case sensitive and suggests that all statement and function names by typed in lower case. For example, printf( ) and PRINTF( ) are not considered equal and the function must be called using lower case letters, if that is how it was originally defined.

All C programs are, or should be, divided into functions which are executed when they are referenced within other functions. This referencing is done by placing a function's name within another function. For example, when looking at main( ), we see that another function called printf( ) is contained within the main brackets. This reference of printf( ) will cause printf( ) to execute, thus printing the words "This program adds up 2 numbers" on the screen. This process of executing functions from within other functions does however cause a small problem over which function is executed first. To solve this problem, C requires all programs to have a function named main( ) and by default, this function is executed first.

Once again, let's turn turn our attention to printf( ). This function, as you can well imagine, stands for "print function" and instructs the computer to display the words contained within the quotation marks on the screen. The function printf( ) is a standard library print routine that is supplied with virtually all C compilers. When examining this function, there are three key points that should be noted. First, note that quotation marks are used to specify which characters are to be printed to the terminal. Second, note that like main( ), printf( ) is followed be both opening and closing parentheses. These required parentheses contain the character string that is to be printed to the screen and is actually the parameter that is passed from main( ) to printf( ). Lastly, note that the call to printf( ) ends with a semicolon. This semicolon is called a statement terminator and must be placed at the end of all C function calls (function references) and all other C statements.

Now that we can write a small C program, let's expand the program to include some additional C code. This program is shown below:

```
main( )
{ int a, c;
int b = 5;

a = 10;
c = a + b;

printf("The sum of variables A and B is %d",c);
}
```

This second program unfolds many new attributes of the C language. Lets start by looking at the statement int, which stands for integer and is used to declare a, b and c as variables which may only contain integer values. Shown in Table 2-1 is a list of all standard variable data definition types. The variable type int as well as the other variable type definitions, will be discussed in depth in Chapter 3.

Table 2-1.

Data Definition	Data Type
char	character
double	double precision floating point
float	floating point
int	decimal signed integer
long	long signed integer
short	short signed integer
unsigned	unsigned decimal integer

Now examine the first int statements in our second program. The first int states that a and c are integer variables. The second int statement defines variable b in a similar fashion. This int, however, has one additional component. This component is the " = 5 " clause. The equal sign followed by a 5 (or what ever value the variable being assigned should have) initializes the variable being defined, namely "b", to a value of five. This procedure may also be used to initalize variables to a value of zero. Unlike many other programming languages, C will not allow you to make the assumption that the initial value of a variable is zero. Therefore, if a variable needs a beginning zero value, as would a counter or totaler, for example, then you must explicitly assign a zero to that variable. If it is initially a zero without being assigned that value, it is purely by coincidence and not by convention. Even worse, it may be a zero today and another value tomorrow, causing inconsistent results. Therefore, if a variable is not initialized within its data type declaration statement, as is the case with a, it is often initialized shortly afterwards. This initialization process is also discussed in Chapter 3.

Once again, looking at our second program, let,s analyze the statement "c = a + b;". This is one of the many types of mathematical expressions that will be discussed within the next few chapters. This statement adds together the values contained within variables a and b and places the total in variable c. This mathematical statement is divided into three basic parts; the variable receiving the calculation, which is c, the equal sign which causes c to be assigned to the value calculated in the equation, and the equation. In this example, the equation variables a and b are separated by a plus sign. As you might expect, the plus sign denotes addition. Thus, since a has a value of 10 and b has a value 5, c will be assigned a value of 15.

When looking at the printf() function in our second program, notice that some changes were also made within the parenthesis. First, note that a %d was added within the double quotes. This %d performs a special task and is used within many standard C functions. Its purpose is to specify the type of variable being referenced (int, float, etc.) within the function and is additionally used in printf() to show where the referenced variable should be placed within the printed string. A list of the variable identifiers and their corresponding variable types is shown below.

Table 2-2.

Data Definition	"%" Code
char	%s
double	%lf
float	%f
int	%d
long	%ld

hexadecimal value %x . scient.note %e
octal value %o

33

In the second program, the %d is being used in the printf( ) function to state that c is an integer variable and that its value should be placed on the screen after the word "is", as shown below:

The sum of variables A and B is 15

The second addition to the printf( ) is the "\n" clause at the beginning of the words to be printed. This clause instructs the computer to go to a new line before printing the rest of the text. An example usage of the \n clause is shown below:

```
main()
{ printf("\nThis is line 1 \n This is line 2 \n This is line 3");
}
```

The result of the program lines above is:

```
This is line 1
This is line 2
This is line 3
```

To more completely understand the use of the %d clause within the the printf( ) function, examine the program lines shown below:

```
main()
{ int a, c;
 int b = 5;

 a = 10;
 c = a + b;

 printf("The values of variables A,B and C are %d, %d and %d "a,b,c);
}
```

In this example, a, b and c are given the value of 1, 2 and 3 respectively, then these variables are printed to the terminal via a printf( ) function. Note that unlike the printf( ) function in our second program, this example has three %d clauses and three corresponding variable names. The output of this program is shown below:

The values of variables A,B and C are 10, 5 and 15

Now that we have completed work on our first C program, it is time for documentation. Documentation may be placed directly within the program by placing it between the comment compiler directives. These directives are "/*" to mark the beginning of a comment and "*/" to denote the end of the comment area and the continuation of C source code. Figure 2-1 shows how a program can be documented.

```
*****************************************************************
* Program Name : Fig2_1
* Author       : Eric P. Bloom
* Description  : This Program adds up two numbers and prints
*                the total on the screen.
******************************************************************/

main()
  {int a,c;
   int b = 5;

   a = 10;
   c = a + b; /* This line calculates the sum to be printed */

   printf("The values of variables A, B, and C are %d, %d, and %d " a,b,c);
```

Fig. 2-1.

As a final thought, over the years of documenting programs written in C and other languages, programmers have sought to develop techniques that would make their internal program documentation easy to find and read. As a result, many programmer try to highlight their comments by using one of the formats shown below.

Example 1.
```
j++;            /* on same line as a statement */
```

Example 2.
```
/* Outlining a Group of comment lines by
 * placing asterisks at the beginning of
 * each commented line.
 */
```

Example 3.
```
/*
 Just using the beginning and ending
 indicators with no additional asterisk
 blocking
*/
```

Fig. 2-2.

Example 4.
```
/*****************************************
 * Outlining the comments within a four *
 * sided asterisk box                   *
 *****************************************/
```

Example 5.
```
/* Outlining each line of the comments */
/* with its own beginning and ending   */
/* comment indicators                  */
```

3

Data Types and Arithmetic Operators

This chapter explains and illustrates the various C data definition types. Additionally, it provides an indepth discussion of C's wide range of arithmetic operators.

VARIABLES AND CONSTANTS

As a new programmer, the first conceptual hurdle that must be overcome is the concept of constants and variables. Variables are labels which represent locations in the computer's memory. For example, when you define a variable by entering int a;, as was done in chapter two, you are actually reserving a place in memory that can be referenced through a variable named a. Therefore, variable a may only contain integer values that can physically fit in that reserved memory location. Additionally, because the value within a memory location can change, the value of variable a can be changed. A constant, unlike a variable, does not point to a location in memory, it is just a specified value. For example, the number 7 is a constant, and as you can see, the value 7 by definition will never have any other value.

The founders of C developed a concept which closely parallels this idea of variables and constants. This is the concept of *lvalues* and *rvalues* standing for left value and right value respectively. These values allude to the type of values that can be on each side of an equation.

Lvalues are variables that are associated with memory locations and may therefore receive a value. Note that this concept of receiving a value alludes to being on the left side of the equal sign within an equation. For example, in the equation "a = b + 7," "a" will receive the value of the expression "b + 7." Note also, that the "a" variable is on the left side of the equal sign, thus, the term lvalue is coined. Rvalues are constants, functions and other entities that may only reside on the right side of the equal sign. For example, the equation "7 = x + 1" does not make sense because

7 cannot be set to the value of "x + 1." Remember that in C, this equation is not solving the value of "x," it is trying to set the number 7 equal to the value of the arithmetic expression "x + 1." This inability of the number 7 causes it and all constants to be rvalues because they cannot logically be placed on the left of the equal sign. The table below provides a list of valid rvalue and lvalue types.

Table 3-1.

Type	Lvalue	Rvalue
Variables	yes	yes
Constants	no	yes
Functions	no	yes
Math expressions	no	yes

Valid Variable Name Formats

When choosing the names of program variables, there are many things that must be considered: name syntax, reserved words, function names, capitalization of letters, and documentation.

The C language, like all languages, has certain rules that must be followed when constructing a variable's name. These rules specify what characters may be used within the name, how the name must begin and its minimum and maximum length. In C's case, variable names may contain letters, numbers, and underlines "__." However, they must begin with either an underline or a letter. Additionally, the length of a variable is categorized in two ways, *total length* and *significant length*. Generally, variable names may have a total length of up to thirty characters. However, the compiler only uses the first six to eight characters and considers any additional letters to be purely documentational. This split rule gives you the flexibility to use long meaningful names, but requires you to make the first part of that name unique.

Reserved words are words like "if", "int", "double", and "while" that have special meaning to the compiler. These words should not be used as variable names because it may confuse programmers who must later modify your program. Also, in most instances, a compilation error will occur if you try to use one of these words as a variable.

Function names should also never be used as the name of a variable. Even though this dual naming concept will in many cases compile and execute, it is an extremely poor programming practice and can greatly degrade your program's readability. It may also cause future syntax errors if the program is modified in a way that places the variable name and its identically named function in the same program area.

The capitalization of letters within variable names must be carefully employed. Remember, the C language is case sensitive. For example, total, Total, and TOTAL are viewed by C as three different and distinct variables. It is strongly suggested within the programming industry that all variables by written using only lowercase letters, saving uppercase (capital letters) for special situations, such as within compiler directives.

The last variable naming topic is the documentation value that can be realized by using useful, descriptive names that help to explain how that variable is being used. For example, cash__ytd may be the variable used to hold the amount of cash that has been received this year to date. However, remember the rules on variable length. The variables total__cash__ytd (total cash year to date) and total__cash__mtd (total cash month to date) are both seen by the compiler as total__ca and are therefore considered the same variable. To keep your names documented and unique, place the variable's distinguishing feature first. For example, rename total__cash__ytd and total__cash__mtd to ytd__total__cash and mtd__total__cash, thus making then ytd__tota and mtd__tota to the compiler. The table below lists examples of both valid and invalid variable names.

Table 3-2.

Valid Names	Invalid Names
count	1__name
total__pay	name − 1
name__1	total__pay
last__name	last name
Help__flag	123
f100__type	100__type
__my__var	

Variable Data Types

As we now know, variable names are actually pointers, or labels so to speak, of specified locations in memory. Now let's talk about the format of these locations. Logically, a memory location on the IBM-PC is nothing more than sixteen on/off switches collectively called two "bytes" and individually called "bits." It is up to the software to interpret the meaning of these bits. Therefore, in an attempt to maximize C's flexibility, as is done with many programming languages, you are given many options of how to store the data in these memory areas. This is where variable data types come into play. When you define a variable as an int, float or other data type, you are actually specifying how the data associated with that variable should be stored in memory. Table 3-3 lists the standard variable data types.

Table 3-3.

Data Definition	Data Type
char	character
double	double precision floating point
float	floating point
int	decimal signed integer
long	long signed integer
short	short signed integer
unsigned	unsigned decimal integer

The int Data Type

The int data type states that the variable being defined may only contain integer values ranging from − 32,768 to 32,767. Mathematically speaking, an integer is a numeric value which may contain a negative sign and does not have a decimal part. For example, 10 and − 10 are valid integer values but 5.2 is not an integer because of the .2 decimal component. In fact, if you try to move the number 5.2 to an integer variable, the .2 will be truncated and the number will be stored as 5 with the .2 being permanently discarded. Table 3-4 lists both valid and invalid integer values.

Table 3-4.

Valid Integers	Invalid Integers
0	.5
5	12.34
10	50000
−15	

The next question at hand, is why the −32,768 to 32,767 range of allowed values. Remember, the IBM-PC is a sixteen bit machine and there are only 65,536 (2 to the 16th power) possible combinations of 16 on-or-off switches. You do however have many options that allow you to easily overcome this limitation. These options are to use the "unsigned int" or long int data types if you wish to stay with an integer data type or float and double if you are willing to move to a floating point format. These other data types will soon be discussed.

One advantage of integer numbers is the relative ease with which you can print the octal (base 8) and hexadecimal (base 16) equivalents of a decimal (base 10) number. These alternative numbering systems are very commonly used in the computer world because they can be easily converted to binary (base 2) which is the numbering system ultimately used by all computers. An octal equivalent of a decimal number can be displayed by replacing the letter "d" after the "%" within the printf( ) function with the letter "o." Alternatively, a decimal's hexadecimal equivalent may be displayed using the "printf( )" function by replacing the "d" after the "%" with the letter "x." Examples of these alternate print types can be found below.

Program :
```
main()
{ int a_variable
  a_variable = 45;

  printf("\nThese are values of %d", a_variable)'
  printf("\n    This is decimal       = %d", a_variable);
  printf("\n    This is octal         = %o", a_variable);
  printf("\n    This is hexadecimal   = %x", a_variable);
}
```

Program Output :
```
These are values of 45
    This is decimal     = 45
    This is octal       = 55
    this is hexadecimal = 2d
```

Fig. 3-1.

This numeric conversion may also be done in reverse, that is to say, from an octal or hexadecimal value to decimal. As shown in Fig. 3-2, if a zero "0" is placed before the number being assigned, the assigned number will be construed as an octal value. Alternatively, a number may be defined as hexadecimal by placing a 0x before the number being assigned.

```
Program :          main()
                   { int a_variable

                     a_variable = 055;
                     printf("\n Decimal is = %d from octal input", a_variable);

                     a_variable = 055;          x ?
                     printf("\n Decimal is = %d from hex input", a_variable);
                   }


Program Output :   Decimal is = 45 from octal input
                   Decimal is = 85 from hex input
```

Fig. 3-2.

The float Data Type

The float data type states that the variable being defined may contain floating point numeric variables. Floating point numbers are values which may optionally contain whole numbers, decimal values or both. Additionally, variables defined using as float variables can contain values in scientific notation. Table 3-5 lists examples of valid floating point numbers.

Valid Floats
0
5
−10.5
1.234e6
1.234e-3

Table 3-5.

Floating point variables may be assigned a value in either standard numeric format (123.45) or in scientific notation (1.2345e2). If the later is used, then the correct format is the mantissa (1.2345), followed by the letter "e", followed by the appropriate exponent (2). Figure 3-3 illustrates these two options. Additionally, like integers, floating point numbers may be displayed via the "printf( )" function. To print floating point numbers in a standard notation format use %f and use %e for scientific notation. This printf( ) usage is also shown below.

```
Program :          main()
                   { float a_variable;

                     a_variable = 12.6e5;
                     printf("\n\nValue entered");
                     printf("\n     The value is %f",a_variable);
                     printf("\n     The value is %e",a_variable);

                     a_variable = 12.345;
                     printf("\n\nValue entered");
                     printf("\n     The value is %f",a_variable);
                     printf("\n     The value is %e",a_variable);
                   }
```

Fig. 3-3.

```
Program Output :    Value entered
                        The value is 1260000.000000
                        The value is 1.260000e+06
```
Fig. 3-3 (cont.)
```
                    Value entered
                        The value is 12.345000
                        The value is 1.234500e+1
```

The double Data Type

The double data type stands for double precision floating point and is essentially just a large float. To achieve this larger size, the compiler stores the variable's value in two memory locations instead of one, hence, the term double precision. From a programming perspective, with the exception of the ability to hold large numbers, a double and a float can be treated as the same. In fact, many compilers automatically place floating point numbers in memory using the double precision format. Even though these two data types are very similar, do not use them interchangeably. The problem is that rounding and truncation errors may occur. An example usage of the double data type is shown below.

Fig. 3-4.

```
Program :         main()
                  { double a_variable;              %lf

                      a_variable = 12.6e5;
                      printf("\n\nValue entered");
                      printf("\n     The value is %f",a_variable);
                      printf("\n     The value is %e",a_variable);

                      a_variable = 12.345;
                      printf("\n\nValue entered");
                      printf("\n     The value is %f",a_variable);
                      printf("\n     The value is %e",a_variable);
                  }
```

```
Program Output :   Value entered
                       The value is 1260000.000000
                       The value is 1.260000e+06

                   Value entered
                       The value is 12.345000
                       The value is 1.234500e+1
```

The long Data Type Prefix

The long data type prefix can be placed before int and float and instructs the compiler to store the specified variable across two memory locations instead of one, thus doubling its size. In fact, a double data type is actually a long float. Very often, however, when the word long is followed by a variable name and no data type is specified, then this technique is used, the default long data type is an int. Therefore, long a_variable and long int a_variable can be considered equivalent expressions. As previously discussed, remember that the valid "int" values ranged from −32,768 to 32,767. When an integer is stored over two memory locations instead of one, the possible range of numbers expands to a range of −2,147,483,648 to 2,147,483,647. These is however a drawback to using "long int". This disadvantage is that it requires twice as much memory space. Therefore, if memory size is a critical concern in your application, then you should use this feature sparingly. Figure 3-5 illustrates the use of the long data type prefix.

Program :

```
main()
{ long int a_variable;
  long b_variable;

  a_variable = 100;
  printf("\n\nValue entered");
  printf("\n      The value is %d",a_variable);
  printf("\n      The value is %ld",a_variable);

  b_variable = 75;
  printf("\n\nValue entered");
  printf("\n      The value is %d",b_variable);
  printf("\n      The value is %ld",b_variable);
}
```

Fig. 3-5.

Program Output :

```
Value entered
      The value is 100
      The value is 100

Value entered
      The value is 75
      The value is 75
```

The short Data Type

The short data type refers specifically to integers and in fact is an abbreviation of short int which is also valid. The idea behind a short integer is that you can store a number in one half of a memory location allowing two numbers to be stored in one physical memory address, thus saving memory space. On the IBM-PC however, as you can well imagine, this would only allow for very small numbers. Therefore, most PC based compilers treat a short integer like a regular int. As a result, short integers are primarily seen on PC's when the software has either come from or is going to a mainframe computer. The use of the short data type is illustrated below.

Program :

```
main()
{ short int a_variable;
  short b_variable;

  a_variable = 100;
  printf("\n\nValue entered");
  printf("\n      The value is %d",a_variable);
  printf("\n      The value is %ld",a_variable);

  b_variable = 75;
  printf("\n\nValue entered");
  printf("\n      The value is %d",b_variable);
  printf("\n      The value is %ld",b_variable);
}
```

Fig. 3-6.

```
                    Value entered
                       The value is 100
                       The value is 100

                    Value entered
                       The value is 75
                       The value is 75
```

Fig. 3-6. (cont.)

The unsigned Data Type

The unsigned data type also refers specifically to integers and is actually short for unsigned int which may also be used. If you recall from the section on integers, a regular integer value may range from −32,768 to 32,767. This was because the IBM-PC, is a sixteen bit machine, meaning that each memory location contains sixteen on/off switches called bits. These 16 bits can only combine to form 65,536 possible combinations of on/off. Integers divide this range of possible values into three parts; 32,768 combinations to stand for negative numbers, one combination to stand for zero and 32,767 combinations for positive numbers. However, if the compiler knows that there will not be any negative numbers (thus all being positive), then it can use 65,535 on/off combinations to represent positive numbers and as before, one combination to represent zero. This shifting of numeric values makes the valid numbering range 0 to 65,535. The use of the "unsigned" integer data type is illustrated below.

Program :

```
main()
{ unsigned int a_variable;
  unsigned b_variable;

  a_variable = 100;
  printf("\n\nValue entered");
  printf("\n      The value is %d",a_variable);
  printf("\n      The value is %ld",a_variable);

  b_variable = 75;
  printf("\n\nValue entered");
  printf("\n      The value is %d",b_variable);
  printf("\n      The value is %ld",b_variable);
}
```

Fig. 3-7.

Program Output :

```
                    Value entered
                       The value is 100
                       The value is 100

                    Value entered
                       The value is 75
                       The value is 75
```

The char Data Type

The char data type is used to store a single alphanumeric character like "A", "x", "1" and "?". As shall be seen in later chapters, these character fields can be grouped together into strings of characters called arrays. These arrays can then in turn be used to store names, addresses and other similar alphabetic data.

Technically speaking, a character variable contains the ASCII numeric equivalent of the character being stored. For example, the character "S" is represented by the number 83 and the character "1" is represented by an ASCII value of 49. ASCII stands for American Standard Code of Information Interchange and is used in computers to numerically identify the valid computer character set. In simpler terms, consider ASCII to be a coding system similar to Morse Code, but instead of dots and dashes, it uses zeros and ones. So as you can see, an integer value of 1 and the ASCII code associated with the character "1" are not the same. This concept shall be become more obvious after reviewing the following program.

Program :

```
main()
{ char a_char;

    a_char = 'S';
    printf("\n\nValue entered");
    printf("\n       The value is %c",a_char);

    a_char = '\123';
    printf("\n\nValue entered");
    printf("\n       The value is %c",a_char);

    a_char = 83;
    printf("\n\nValue entered");
    printf("\n       The value is %c",a_char);

}
```

Fig. 3-8.

Program Output :

```
Value entered
        The value is S

Value entered
        The value is S

Value entered
        The value is S
```

As with all variable data types, you must have the ability to assign it a value and print out that entered data. Data may be moved into a char variable in four primary ways: constant, octal constant, decimal value, and octal value. A constant value is moved to a character variable by placing that character within single quotes (a_char = 'S';). An octal constant is moved to a character variable by placing a backslash followed by the octal value of the appropriate character within single quotes (a_char = '\123';). An integer may also be used to specify the appropriate character by moving the character's decimal character value to the char variable (a_char = 83;). Lastly, an octal variable may be used to set a character variable by passing the appropriate octal value (a_char = 0123;). From a data output perspective, the variable within a char data type variable can be printed using the printf() function by placing a %c in the print mask and the variable name to be printed in the printf() argument list.

ARITHMETIC EXPRESSIONS AND OPERATORS

Like all programming languages, C has the ability to perform mathematical tasks by combining numeric variables and arithmetic operators into mathematic expressions. The numeric variables are defined using the various numeric data types previously discussed. The arithmetic operators are the symbols like "+" and "−" which tell the compiler which mathematic process to perform. These operators are broken down into three types: standard expressions, unary expressions, and increment/decrement expressions. These operator types will be discussed in the next section.

Standard Expressions

There are five standard arithmetic expressions. They are; "+", "−", "*", "/" and "%" standing for addition, subtraction, multiplication, division, and remainder respectively. The table below lists some examples of the operators and the outcome of their equations.

Table 3-6.

Expression	Before a b c	After a b c
a = b + c	1 2 3	5 2 3
a = b − c	1 2 3	−1 2 3
a = b * c	1 2 3	6 2 3
a = b / c	1 4 2	2 4 2
a = b % c	1 9 5	4 9 5

When reviewing the examples in Table 3-6, you'll see the percent "%" operator. This operator does not calculate a percent. Its purpose is to calculate the remainder that would be generated if two integers (those on the left and right of the percent sign) were divided. For example, given the equation "a = 3 % 2;", "a" would be given a value of 1. The following program illustrates some examples of this operator.

Fig. 3-9.

Program :
```
main()
{ int a;
  int b = 3;
  int c = 2;

  a = b % c;

  printf("\n Remander is = %d",a);

  a = 8 % 5;
  printf("\n Remander is = %d",a);

  a = 4 % c;
  printf("\n Remander is = %d",a);

  a = 8 % b;
  printf("\n Remander is = %d",a);
}
```

Program Output :
```
Remainder is = 1
Remainder is = 3
Remainder is = 0
Remainder is = 2
```

When combining these operators into a single formula, care should be taken to assure that the mathematical processes are performed in the expected order. C evaluates mathematic equations in a way that is consistent with mathematic principles of precedence. This precedence first processes expressions within parentheses left to right, then multiplication and division left to right, then addition from left to right. For example, the equation a = 1 + 2 * 3 will give a a value of 7. First the 2 and 3 are multiplied, giving a value of 6, then 1 is added to 6 making a total of 7. Therefore, a = 1 + 2 * 3 and a = 1 + (2 * 3) are equivalent expressions. If however, you wish to add the 1 and 2 first and then multiply the sum by three, the equation should be written a = (1 + 2) * 3. The general rule regarding when to use these parentheses is to always use them, thus forcing the proper order of operation, and as a by-product improving the formula's documentation. The table below lists example formulas and displays their expected result.

Table 3-7.

Expression	Result
a = (1 + 2) * 3	9
a = 1 + 2 * 3	7
a = 1 + (2 * 3)	7
a = 2 * (1 + 1) / 2	2
a = 1 + (2 + 6) / 4	3

Unary Expressions

Unary expressions perform the same processes as the standard arithmetic operators previously mentioned. The difference is in their format, ease of typing, and most importantly, the creation of more efficient compiled object code. These unary operations and their standard arithmetic equivalents are listed below.

Table 3-8.

Unary	Standard
a + = b	a = a + b
a + = 2	a = a + 2
a * = 3	a = a * 3
a - = c	a = a - c
a % = b	a = a % b
a / = b	a = a / b
a / = 4	a = a / 4

As can be seen, a unary equation is comprised of three primary parts; the variable being calculated, the unary operator and the ending variable or constant. The variable being calculated is on the left of the operator. The unary operator specifies the process that is to be performed and the variable or constant on the right is the value being used to complete the equation. At first glance, these unary operators seem to be more trouble than they are worth, but they were incorporated into the language for a specific purpose. This purpose is the generation of more efficient compiled machine code. More efficient code can be created, because the use of a unary operator signifies to the compiler that only one operation will be performed within the equation and that the first variable will be receiving the calculated value. This information allows the compiler to optimize the way it performs the mathematic process, thus generating less machine instructions.

Increment/Decrement Expressions

The increment and decrement operators are yet another attempt to assist the compiler in the generation of machine code. These operators are + + and − −. The + + causes its associated variable to be incremented by 1, thus making $a = a + 1$ and $a + +$ equivalent equations. This operator however, has one additional feature. As you review various C programs, you will see that sometimes the + + is before the variable being incremented and sometimes it is after the variable. When the + + is before the variable, the increment is performed prior to the execution of the statement or function in which the variable resides. When the + + is after the variable, the increment is performed after its associated statement or function is performed. For example, in Fig. 3-10, a is set to an initial value of 1 prior to each printf( ) function call. Additionally, note that in the first printf( ) the + + is before variable a and in the second printf( ) the + + is after its associated variable.

Program :
```
main()
{ int a;

    a = 1;
    printf("\n A has a value of %d with ++ before the a",++a);

    a = 1;
    printf("\n A has a value of %d with ++ after the a",a++);
}
```

Program Output :
```
A has a value of 2 with ++ before the a
A has a value of 1 with ++ after the a
```

Fig. 3-10.

The decrement operator − − acts exactly like the + + operator, with the one exception that it subtracts one from its associated variable's value. Figure 3-11 illustrates the use of this operator.

Program :
```
main()
{ int a;

    a = 1;
    printf("\n A has a value of %d with -- before the a",--a);

    a = 1;
    printf("\n A has a value of %d with -- after the a",a--);
}
```

Program Output :
```
A has a value of 0 with -- before the a
A has a value of 1 with -- after the a
```

Fig. 3-11.

To sum up the three types of arithmetic operators, Table 3-9 shows all three operator types and, where applicable, highlights equivalent expressions.

Unary	Standard	Increment/Decrement
a += b	a = a + b	
a += 1	a = a + 1	a++
a *= 3	a = a * 3	
a - = 1	a = a - 1	a--
a %= b	a = a % b	
a /= b	a = a / b	
a /= 4	a = a / 4	

Table 3-9.

4

Control Statements

All the programs that have thus far been listed and explained have begun executing at the first encountered statement or function and have continued executing, line by line, until each line has been executed once, until the program ended. This type of program is an excellent vehicle to illustrate the usage of a particular statement, function, or operator, but they are not very realistic in regard to the functionality that would be required from even the simplest of programs. The creation of these more complex programs however, require the ability to optionally execute statements based on some specified criteria. As well as, have the ability to optionally repeat the execution of selected statements when performing reiterative processes. This chapter will explain the statements needed to perform these complicated tasks.

This chapter has been divided into three parts, coinciding with the three types of control statements. These types are conditional logic, looping, and transfer of control.

CONDITIONAL LOGIC

Conditional logic is the ability to appropriately respond to specified circumstances. In a programming context, this means that the program being executed can determine what tasks to perform by assessing what needs to be done. That is to say, if the test criteria is met, certain statements will be executed. Conversely, if the test is not met, other statements, if present, will be executed. Figure 4-1 illustrates this concept.

In Fig. 4-1, the user is being asked to enter the type of pay to be calculated. If the person is payed hourly, the user is asked to enter the hourly rate of pay and the number of hours worked. Once this is entered, the program calculates the gross pay amount. If the person being payed is a salaried employee, the user is just asked to enter the hourly rate. Once this is entered, the program calculates the gross pay based on an assumed forty hours worked. Then, regardless of the payment type, the gross pay amount is displayed to the user.

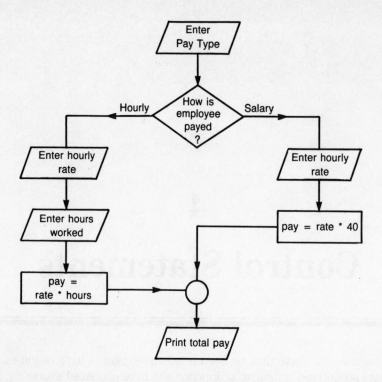

Fig. 4-1.

Now that we have seen and discussed this procedure from a conceptual viewpoint, lets reshape Fig. 4-1 from a flowchart format into one that looks more program-like. This reworked format is shown below in Fig. 4-2.

```
Enter employee's pay type

If the pay type is salaried ( code is 'S' )
   Enter hourly rate
   Gross pay = hourly rate * 40 ( hours )
Else
   Enter hourly rate
   Enter hours worked
   Gross pay = hourly rate * hours worked

Print gross pay
```

Fig. 4-2.

In this format, note that the first statement is testing for the salaried pay type, and the next statements are the activities to be performed if the entered employee is salaried. Then comes the word "else" followed by the activities to be executed if the employee is hourly. This example parallels the format and structure of the if statement, which is C's primary tool for facilitating conditional logic.

Now that we have seen two conceptual views of the pay calculation, lets move to the actual C program that will perform it, which appears on the next page.

```
            main()
            { char pay_type;
              float hours;
              float rate;
              float grosspay;

              printf("\n Enter pay type ( S=salaried, H=hourly) : ");
              scanf("%c",&pay_type);

              if ( pay_type == 'S' )
                { printf("\n Enter hourly rate : ");
                  scanf("%f",&rate);
                  grosspay = rate * 40;
                }
              else
                { printf("\n Enter hourly rate : ");
                  scanf("%f",&rate);
                  printf("\n Enter hours worked : ");
                  scanf("%f",&hours);
                  grosspay = rate * hours;
                }

              printf("\n\n  Gross pay is = %.2f",grosspay);
            }
```

Program Output :   Ex. A)   Enter pay type (S=salaried, H=hourly) : S

                                     Enter hourly rate : 10

                                     Gross pay is = 400.00

                        Ex. B)   Enter pay type (S=salaried, H=hourly) : H

                                     Enter hourly rate : 7.50

                                     Enter hours worked : 10

                                     Gross pay is = 75.00

Fig. 4-3.

The if Statement

The if statement is divided into three sections: conditional logic, positive statements, and else statements. The word "if" begins the conditional logic section and is followed by the conditions to be examined. Next are the positive statements. These statements are the commands that should be executed if the conditions are met. The optional else statement or statements that begin with the word "else" and are only executed when the conditions are not met. The if statement format is shown below.

```
            if ( condition )
                 statement or statement block
            else
                 statement or statement block
```

Fig. 4-4.

and the conditional symbols that may be used to define the if logic are shown below.

Symbolic Meaning

==	Equal to
>	Greater than
<	Less than
!=	Not equal to
>=	Greater than or equal to
<=	Less than or equal to

Fig. 4-5.

Some if statement examples are shown below.

```
Ex. 1   if ( hours_worded > 40 ) overtime(emp_no);

Ex. 2   if ( hours_worked > 40 )
          overtime(emp_no);
        else
          regular(emp_no);

Ex. 3   if ( employee_status == 'A')
          ;
        else
          error_flay = 'Y';

Ex. 4   if ( employee_status == 'A' )
          { active(emp_no);
            status_indicator = 'A';
            ++employee_count;
          }
        else  ++error_count
          error_par(emp_no);


Ex. 5   if ( a )
          printf("\n A has a non-zero value");
        else
          printf("\n A has a value of zero");
```

Fig. 4-6.

The first if statement in Fig. 4-6 above checks to see if hours_worked is greater than 40. If it is, the condition is satisfied and overtime() is executed. If hours_worked is less than or equal to 40, the if condition is not met, overtime() is not executed and program control is passed to the next sequential statement.

The second if statement example is very similar to the first. The difference is that an else clause has been added. This else clause states that if the specified condition (hours_worked > 40) is not true then execute reg_time().

The third if statement tests for employees with a status code if "A" for active. This line states that if an employee is active, do nothing. This is done by placing a semicolon after the if condition with no corresponding statement, thus serving as a place holder prior to the else clause. In context, the underlying logic is to do nothing if the employee is active but to set an error flag to "Y" if the employee is not active.

The fourth example in Fig. 4-6 contains two new aspects of the if statement. First is the option of executing many statements after the conditional logic and else clauses. When exercising this option, note that the statements are enclosed within brackets. These enclosed statements are collectively called a statement block. This block informs the compiler that all of the statements within it are to be executed based on the outcome of its associated if statement. The statement block concept will be seen again when we discuss looping techniques later in this chapter. The second new aspect of the fourth example is the format that should be followed when using multi-line if statements. This format is designed to ease readability by vertically lining up the words if and else and evenly indenting the condition logic and statements being executed. Also, it is important to remember that a semicolon must be placed at the end of each executable statement within the if.

The fifth and final example in Fig. 4-6 illustrates a new key concept. The if conditions that we have thus far discussed, like "a = = b" and "a < b | | b > c" performs an evaluation. Once evaluated, the expression produces a zero value if the expression is false and a non-zero value if the condition is true. It is this zero/non-zero value that is used by the "if" statement to assess the condition's outcome. Therefore, since the "if" statement only requires the presents of a numeric value, you may optionally replace the test expression with an integer variable. This action will cause the "if" statement to assess the variable's value using the same zero/non-zero criteria.

Multi if Conditions

There are many occasions where a single if condition cannot completely decide a course of action to be taken. To fill this void, the & & and | | operators allow for more advanced logic. The operator & & stands for and, while | | stands for or. See the examples of these conditional operators below.

```
if ( hours > 40 && pay_type == 'H' ) overtime_flag = 'Y';

if ( net_pay < 0 || net_pay > 10000 )
        error(emp_no);

if  ( employee_status = 'A' || ( employee_status == 'L'
        && pay_indicator == 'Y' )
            cut_check(emp_no,net_pay);
```

Fig. 4-7.

The first statement in Fig. 4-7 above uses the & & clause to connect two conditions. This clause states that both conditions must be met for the condition to be true. The second if example uses the | | option. This connector specifies that only one of the conditions must be met for the if to be true.

The third if statement example contains both & & and | | operators. In this case, similar to mathematical expressions, there is an order of operation. This order dictates that conditions within parentheses are considered first, then & &, then | |. What this means is that in the statement if (a = = a & & b = = b | | c = = c) conditions a and b are processed first and then the outcome of a and b is compared to c. In effect, either a and b must be true or c must be true. The adding of parentheses however, could change this scenario. In the statement if (a= =a && (b= =b || c= =c)), the condition a must be true and either b or c must also be true. Therefore, in the third if example, the result of (employee_status = = 'L' && pay_indicator = = 'Y') is first decided and then the outcome is compared to employee_status = 'A'. Also note that because & & is processed before | |,this statement would have executed the same way either with or without the parentheses. Including the parentheses, however, is a good programming practice because it clearly documents the way the if statement will be executed.

Nested if Statements

C has the ability to define and interpret complex logic by placing if statements within if statements. This "if within an if" is called nesting. The following shows a nested if example.

```
if ( pay_type == 'H' )
    if ( hours_worked > 40 )
        regular_hours( emp_no );
    else
        overtime( emp_no );
else
    salaried_emp( emp_no );
```

Fig. 4-8.

In Fig. 4-8 above, there is an if statement contained within an if statement. The first if asks if the employee pay type is hourly. If the pay type is not hourly, then the else statement is used and salaried_emp() is executed. If the employee is hourly, then a second question is asked pertaining to the number of hours worked. Remember, the inner if will only be reached when pay type is hourly. This inner if statement will call regular_hours() if the employee worked forty hours or less and overtime() if more then forty hours were worked. Below is a flowchart of the nested if logic from Fig. 4-8.

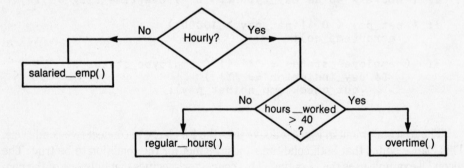

Fig. 4-9.

Tandem if Statements

There are times when it is required to ask a group of related questions. An example of this is a program to calculate the number of employees making $5,000 to $10,000, $10,001 to $15,000, and so on up to $100,000. There are two programming methods that can be employed to calculate the answer. The first method is to type twenty single line if statements as shown in part A of Fig. 4-10 below. The second way to calculate the answer is to use tandem if statements as shown in part B of Fig. 4-10.

```
Part A:    if ( salary >=  5000 && SALARY < 10000 ) ++salary5;
           if ( salary >= 10000 && SALARY < 10000 ) ++salary10;
           if ( salary >= 15000 && SALARY < 15000 ) ++salary15;
           if ( salary >= 20000 && SALARY < 20000 ) ++salary20;
           if ( salary >= 25000 && SALARY < 25000 ) ++salary25;
                            •                •                •
                            •                •                •
                            •                •                •
           if ( salary >= 95000 && SALARY < 95000 ) ++salary95;
```

Fig. 4-10.

```
Part B:    if ( salary < 10000 )
               ++salary5;
           else if ( salary < 15000 )
               ++salary10;
           else if ( salary < 20000 )
               ++salary15;
           else if ( salary < 25000 )
               ++salary20;
             •         •         •
             •         •         •
             •         •         •
           else if ( salary < 100000 )
               ++salary95;
```

The statements of both parts of Fig. 4-10 will provide the same answer. The questions are: "How long will it take to process?", and "How self-documenting is the procedure?" In this case, both part A and part B are self-documenting. The difference lies in the processing time needed to run the program. When part A is executed, all twenty individual if statements will always be executed. Additionally, each if statement has two conditions that must be examined (a greater than and a less than condition). In part B, the entire procedure ends when the a conditional statement is finally met. This means that all twenty questions are not always asked. Additionally, each question only contains one condition, again minimizing the needed processing.

Additional if statement examples are provided below.

```
           if ( error_flag == 'Y' ) error(emp_no);

           if ( emp_stat == 'A' ) ++active_count;
```

Fig. 4-11.

```
           if ( job_class == '1' || job_class == '2' )
               { ++mgr_count;
                 printf("\n %s is a manager",emp_name);
               }
           else
               ++support_count;
```

The switch Statement

The tandem "if" process previously discussed, is so commonly used that the developers of C designed the "switch" statement to specifically interpret that type of conditional logic. The format of this statement is shown below.

```
switch ( expression )
    {
    case value1:
        program statement;
        . . .
        break;

    case value2:
        program statement;
        . . .
        break;

    case value-n:
        program statement;
        . . .
        break;

    default:
        program statement;
        . . .
        break;
```

Fig. 4-12.

The switch statement is divided into three basic parts; the word "switch" followed by the expression to be tested, the case sections, and the default section. The expression following the word "switch" contains the value to be assessed by the case test expression. The case section is comprised of the word case, followed by the value to be compared with the value in the switch clause, that being followed by the statements to be executed if these two values match. The default section contains statements that are to be executed if none of the case test conditions are satisfied. An example of this statement can be seen below.

Program :
```
main()
    { char operator;
    float num_1;
    float num_2;

    printf("\n\nEnter formula : ");
    scanf("%f %c %f",&num_1,&operator,&num_2);

    switch( operator )
        {
        case '+':
            printf("\n\n  Answer is %.2f", ( num_1 + num_2 ) );
            break;

        case '-':
            printf("\n\n  Answer is %.2f", ( num_1 - num_2 ) );
            break;
```

Fig. 4-13.

```
            case '*':
                printf("\n\n  Answer is %.2f", ( num_1 * num_2 ) );
                break;

            case '/':
                printf("\n\n  Answer is %.2f", ( num_1 / num_2 ) );
                break;

            default:
                printf("\n\n  Unknown operation");
        }
    }
```

Fig. 4-13. (cont.)

Program Output :

Ex. A)   Enter formula : 10*3

               Answer is 30.00

Ex. B)   Enter formula : 15.5-4

               Answer is 11.50

The program in Fig. 4-13 is an elementary calculator that performs addition, subtraction, multiplication and division. Note that the second input variable (operator) within the scanf() function receives the symbol of the operation to be performed. This symbol, as specified in the switch expression is then compared with the case values. If a match is made, the appropriate mathematical process is performed. However, if no match can be found, then the statements following the default label are performed.

Once again, review the switch statement example in Fig. 4-13. Now however, turn your attention to the word break contained within each of the case and default statement list. The break statement is discussed in depth later in the chapter. Its purpose is to instruct the computer to exit the statement in which it is contained. In the case of the switch statement, break causes switch to be exited and program control to be passed to the next sequential statement.

The Conditional Operator

The conditional operator is one of the most cryptic features of the C language. Its function is to perform an if-then-else type procedure and it is formatted in the following manner.

condition ? expression1 : expression2

The condition is usually a relational test like "a>b". This expression, as discussed in reference to the if statement, produces a value of zero if the expression is false and a non-zero value if the condition is true. A true response causes the expression immediately after the question mark to be evaluated. If the relational test is false, the expression after the colon is evaluated. The program in Fig. 4-14 on the next page illustrates the use of this operator.

57

```
Program :    main()
             { int a;
               int b;
               int c;
               int d;

               a = 1;
               b = 2;

               c = a < b ? 1 : 0;
               printf("\nAnswer is %d",c);

               c = a == b ? 1 : 0;
               printf("\nAnswer is %d",c);

               c = ( (a>b) ? 1 : 0 );
               printf("\nAnswer is %d",c);

               d = 1;
               c = ( d ? 1 : 0 );
               printf("\nAnswer is %d",c);
             }
```

Fig. 4-14.

Program Output :   Answer is 1
                    Answer is 0
                    Answer is 0
                    Answer is 1

Above, there are four conditional operator examples. In the first example, a is less then b, thus c is set to the value following the question mark, namely 1. In the second example, "a" is not equal to b, so c is set to the value after the colon, which is zero. In the third example, note that parentheses were added. These parentheses are not required as previously seen, however, they greatly assist in the readability of the statement. The forth and last example has a slightly different twist. This twist is the use of variable d. Remember, a relational test expression (a = = b) returns either a zero or non-zero value. It is this value that is then used by the operational operator. Therefore, because the syntax of the conditional operator only requires the presents of a zero or non-zero value, you may optionally use an integer variable at that location. This technique will cause the operator to assess the variable's value using the same zero/non-zero criteria.

LOOPING

The ability to repeat the execution of selected program statements is a fundamental feature of all computers. It is this ability that allows programmers to write routines that perform reiterative tasks. For example, a company may have thousands of employees. Therefore, it prints thousands of payroll checks. The program which prints these checks reexecutes the same statements when processing each check. Without this reiterative feature (also known as looping), the programmer would be forced to write thousands of check printing routines, one for each check. As you can imagine, this could make a program prohibitively large.

The C language provides three statements which can perform this vital looping function. They are while, do/while, and for. A small program that illustrates these statements is listed below.

Program :
```
main()
{ int x;

    printf("\n\n The while loop");
    x=1;
    while ( x <= 3 )
     { printf("\n    X has a value of %d",x);
       x++;
     }

    printf("\n\n The do/while loop");
    x=1;
    do
       { printf("\n    X has a value of %d",x);
         x++;
       } while ( x <= 3 );

    printf("\n\n The for loop");
    for (x=1; x <= 3; x++ )
       { printf("\n    X has a value of %d",x);
       }
}
```

Fig. 4-15.

Program Output :
```
            The While loop
                x has a value of 1
                x has a value of 2
                x has a value of 3

            The do/While loop
                x has a value of 1
                x has a value of 2
                x has a value of 3

            The for loop
                x has a value of 1
                x has a value of 2
                x has a value of 3
```

The while Statement

The while statement is designed to repeatedly execute a statement or statements based on a specified test condition. The format of this statement is shown below.

Fig. 4-16.

```
            while ( test expression )
                statement or statement block
```

The while statement is divided into three parts; the word "while", the condition being tested and the statement or statements being executed.

The following provides an example of the while looping process.

```
Program :    main()
             { int input;
               int count = 1;
               long int total = 1;

               printf("\n Enter a number for factorial : ");
               scanf("%d",&input);

               while ( input >= count )
                { total *= count;
                  printf("\n     Factorial of %d is %ld",count,total);
                  ++count;
                }
             }
```

Fig. 4-17.

```
Program Output :   Enter a number for factorial :
                       Factorial of 1 is 1
                       Factorial of 2 is 2
                       Factorial of 3 is 6
                       Factorial of 4 is 24
                       Factorial of 5 is 120
                       Factorial of 6 is 720
                       Factorial of 7 is 5040
                       Factorial of 8 is 40320
                       Factorial of 9 is 362880
                       Factorial of 10 is 3628800
```

The while statement shown above typifies how this statement is used. Note that it begins with the word "while" followed by the expression "(input < = counter)". This expression is the condition that is tested prior to each reiteration of the statement below it. The proper form of this expression is identical to that used within the if statement test criteria previously mentioned. If the test is true (a non-zero value is produced), the looping process continues. If the test proves to be false (a zero value is produced), the looping ends, and program control is passed to the next sequential C statement.

Lets now turn our attention to the statements within the while loop that are being reiterated. First, note (within Fig. 4-17) that the indented statements are enclosed within brackets. Like the if statement previously mentioned, while only associates itself with the one C statement or function call below it. Therefore, if more than one statement is to be contained within the loop, all looping statements must be placed within a statement block. This block instructs the while statement to incorporate the entire blocked group within the loop. It is these brackets that define the beginning and end of the block. Examine the various while statement examples below.

```
x = 10;
while ( x )
  printf("\n X has a value of %d",x--);

x = 1;
while ( x <= 10 )
  { printf("\n X has a value of %d",x);
    x++
  }
```

Fig. 4-18.

The do/while Statement

The do/while statement is very similar to while, the difference being when the test condition is evaluated. Recall that while examines the test criteria prior to each execution of the looping statement or statements. The do/while statement assesses the test criteria after each reiteration of the looping statement. This distinction may seem trivial, but it causes a key side effect on the statements being executed. This effect is that unlike the statements in while, the statements in the do/while are always executed at least once. Remember, the test condition is assessed after the loop has executed. Therefore, if the criteria in the test is not met, the loop will not execute a second time. The format of this statement is shown below.

Fig. 4-19.

```
do
    statement or statement block
while ( test expression );
```

This statement is divided into four parts; the word "do", the statement or statement block to be executed, the word "while" and the condition to be tested. An example of the do/while statement is shown below.

```
Program :  main()
           { int input;
             int count = 1;
             long int total = 1;

             printf("\n Enter a number for factorial : ");
             scanf("%d",&input);

             do
               { total *= count;
                 printf("\n    Factorial of %d is %ld",count,total);
                 ++count;
               } while ( input >= count );
           }
```

```
Program Output :  Enter a number for factorial :
                      Factorial of 1 is 1
                      Factorial of 2 is 2
                      Factorial of 3 is 6
                      Factorial of 4 is 24
                      Factorial of 5 is 120
                      Factorial of 6 is 720
                      Factorial of 7 is 5040
                      Factorial of 8 is 40320
                      Factorial of 9 is 362880
                      Factorial of 10 is 3628800
```

Fig. 4-20.

When reviewing the program above, take special note of the word "do", the placement of the statement block, and the word "while" followed by its associated test criteria. The statement begins with do, and as you can see, it is the only word on the line. This convention is not a language syntax rule, but is generally done to maximize program readability. That line is followed by the statements to be looped. Like the while statement, if more than one statement or function call is to be looped, then they must be enclosed within brackets, thus creating a statement block. After the looping portion, comes the word "while" and the test criteria. Finally, note that unlike while, this statement must be terminated by placing a semicolon after the test criteria's closing parentheses. The following provides some additional do/while examples.

```
x = 10;
do
   printf("\n X has a value of %d",x--);
   while ( x );

x = 1;
   { printf("\n X has a value of %d",x);
   x++
   } while ( x <= 10 );
```

Fig. 4-21.

The for Statement

The for statement is the last of the looping statements and is designed differently than while and do/while. This statement is primarily used to loop a specified number of times, based on the incrementation of a counter variable. The format of this statement is shown below.

```
for ( initalization; test condition; incrementation )
   statement of statement block
```

Fig. 4-22.

The for statement is divided into five basic parts, the word "for", initialization, test criteria, incrementation, and the statements to be looped. An example of this statement is shown below.

```
Program :   main()
            { int input;
              int count = 1;
              long int total = 1;

              printf("\n Enter a number for factorial : ");
              scanf("%d",&input);

              for ( count = 1; input >= count; ++count )
                 { total *= count;
                   printf("\n    Factorial of %d is %ld",count,total);
                 }
            }
```

Fig. 4-23.

```
Program Output :   Enter a number for factorial :
                   Factorial of 1 is 1
                   Factorial of 2 is 2
                   Factorial of 3 is 6
```

Fig. 4-23. (cont.)

```
Factorial of 4 is 24
Factorial of 5 is 120
Factorial of 6 is 720
Factorial of 7 is 5040
Factorial of 8 is 40320
Factorial of 9 is 362880
Factorial of 10 is 3628800
```

This statement begins with the word "for", followed by three control areas enclosed within parentheses, being followed by the statement of statement block to be reiterated. The three sections within the parentheses are for initialization of the appropriate variables, the test condition that is assessed to see if the loop should continue to reiterate and the statement which increments the counter variable. For example, in Fig. 4-23, the three enclosed areas are thus explained. The phrase "count = 0;" is initializing the counter variable to zero. The phrase "count < = input;" is testing to see if the loop should continue to reiterate, and finally, the phrase "count + +" is incrementing the "count" variable by one after each execution of the loop, thus bringing it closer to satisfying the test criteria. Lastly, like while and do/while, a single statement may be repeated by just placing it after the word "for", or alternately, many statements may be reiterated by placing them within a statement block. The following provides additional "for" statement examples.

Fig. 4-24.

```
for ( x=10; x > 0; x-- )
   printf("\n X has a value of %d",x);

for ( x=1; x <= 10; x++ )
   { printf("\n X has a value of %d",x);
   }
```

Nested Loops

There are times when automating a procedure, that the programmer must place a loop within a loop. This loop-in-a-loop is called, as you may expect, a nested loop. When this procedure is used, the inner loop processes to completion during each reiteration of the outer loop. This looping process is illustrated in Fig. 4-25.

The program in Fig. 4-25 has a for statement within a for statement and uses two variables; outer and inner, both of which loop within their respective "for" statements. Note that each time the outer loop increments, the inner loop processes to completion.

Fig. 4-25.

```
Program :   main()
            { int outer;
              int inner;

              for ( outer = 0; outer < 3; ++outer )
                { printf("\n Outer loop -> %d",outer);
                  for ( inner = 0; inner < 4; ++inner )
                    { printf("\n   Inner loop -> %d",inner);
                    }
                }
            }
```

Fig. 4-25. (cont.)

```
Program Output :   Outer loop -> 0
                       Inner loop -> 0
                       Inner loop -> 1
                       Inner loop -> 2
                       Inner loop -> 3

                   Outer loop -> 1
                       Inner loop -> 0
                       Inner loop -> 1
                       Inner loop -> 2
                       Inner loop -> 3

                   Outer loop -> 2
                       Inner loop -> 0
                       Inner loop -> 1
                       Inner loop -> 2
                       Inner loop -> 3
```

Figure 4-26 also dramatizes the nested loop concept by printing a picture of a right angle triangle. The inner loop is repeating based on the value of the counter in the outer loop (look in the test criteria section in the inner loop for clarification). Also, note that once again, the inner loop processes to completion during each reiteration of the outer loop.

```
Program :   main()
            { int outer;
              int inner;

              for ( outer = 1; outer <= 10; ++outer )
                { for ( inner = 1; inner <= outer; ++inner )
                    { printf("*");
                    }
                  printf("\n");
                }
            }
```

Fig. 4-26.

```
Program Output :   *
                   **
                   ***
                   ****
                   *****
                   ******
                   *******
                   ********
                   *********
                   **********
```

Associated Looping Statements

There are two other C statements which are associated with the looping process, but do not perform looping functions. These statements are break and continue. The break statement is used to immediately terminate the looping process, regardless of the looping test criteria. Figure 4-27 illustrates this statement by listing a program containing two loops and the program's respective output. The first loop is a single "for" statement containing a "printf( )" function which displays the counter's value. In contrast, the second "for" loop is identical with the exception of an "if" statement causing the loop to "break" when the counter is equal to 3. Note that when reviewing the output of this program, the first loop repeats 5 times and the second loop repeats 3 times, thus indicating that the break statement does in fact end execution of the loop.

Fig. 4-27.

```
Program :    main()
             { int count;

               printf("\n\n First loop");
               for ( count = 1; count <= 5; count++)
                 { printf("\n    Count is %d",count);
                 }

               printf("\n\n Second loop");
               for ( count = 1; count <= 5; count++)
               { printf("\n    Count is %d",count);
                 if ( count == 3 ) break;
               }
             }
```

```
Program Output :   First loop
                       Count is 1
                       Count is 2
                       Count is 3
                       Count is 4
                       Count is 5

                   Second loop
                       Count is 1
                       Count is 2
                       Count is 3
```

The continue statement performs a function that is similar, but not identical, to break. This statement causes the statements within a looping control block to skip a reiteration. The following illustrates this process.

Fig. 4-28.

```
Program :    main()
             { int count;

               printf("\n\n First loop");
               for ( count = 1; count <= 5; count++)
                 { printf("\n    Count is %d",count);
                 }

               printf("\n\n Second loop");
               for ( count = 1; count <= 5; count++)
                 { if ( count == 3 ) continue;
                   printf("\n    Count is %d",count);
                 }
             }
```

65

Program Output :
```
                 First loop
                   Count is 1
                   Count is 2
                   Count is 3
                   Count is 4
                   Count is 5

                 Second loop
                   Count is 1
                   Count is 2
                   Count is 4
                   Count is 5
```

Fig. 4-28. (cont.)

When viewing the output of Fig. 4-28, note that the phrase "count is 3" is missing from the second loop, but count 4 and 5 are present. This skipped reiteration is the work of the continue statement. Within the program, the statement "if (count = = 3) continue;" is contained in the second for loop. This statement instructs the program to execute the continue statement when the counter variable is equal to 3. This continue statement instructs the computer to skip the execution of all the remaining statements within the loop's control block and to proceed directly to the next loop reiteration. Thus, the printf() function call has skipped.

One final clarification of the continue statement should be made. This clarification is that the continue statement only suppresses the execution of statements that are after the word "continue". The statements before it within the loop will still execute. For example, in Fig. 4-29 the for loop contains two printf() function calls separated by a continue statement. As you can see by reviewing the program's output, the first printf() always executes and the second one is never called.

Program :
```
          main()
          { int count;

              printf("\n\n First loop");
              for ( count = 1; count <= 5; count++)
                { printf("\n    Count is %d",count);
                }

              printf("\n\n Second loop");
              for ( count = 1; count <= 5; count++)
              { if ( count == 3 ) continue;
                  printf("\n    Count is %d",count);
              }
          }
```

Fig. 4-29.

Program Output :
```
                 This is the first printf()
                 This is the first printf()
                 This is the first printf()
                 This is the first printf()
                 This is the first printf()
```

THE goto STATEMENT: TRANSFERRING CONTROL

The goto statement is used to permanently transfer control from the statement being executed to a specified label name somewhere else within the function.

Since the concept of structured programming was introduced as a method of standardized programming techniques, the goto statement has somewhat fallen from grace. As was discussed in Chapter 1, structured programming relies heavily on subroutining through function calls as the preferred branching process. However, goto is still a commonly used programming option. Its format is shown below.

Fig. 4-30.

```
goto label-name;
```

The goto statement consists of two parts; the word "goto" and a label name. For the statement to function correctly, the specified label name must exist in a valid format somewhere within the same function as the goto. Figure 4-31 shown below illustrates the use of the goto statement, and illustrates the classic justification for using the goto statement.

Program :
```
main()
{ int outer;
  int inner;

  for ( outer=1; outer < 5; outer++ )
    { for ( inner=1; inner < 5; inner++ )
        { printf("\n Outer is %d, inner is %d",outer, inner);
          if ( outer == 3 && inner == 3 ) goto skipout;
        }
    }
 skipout:
   printf("\n I skipped out");
}
```

Program Output :
```
Outer is 1, inner is 1
Outer is 1, inner is 2
Outer is 1, inner is 3
Outer is 1, inner is 4
Outer is 2, inner is 1
Outer is 2, inner is 2
Outer is 2, inner is 3
Outer is 2, inner is 4
Outer is 3, inner is 1
Outer is 3, inner is 2
Outer is 3, inner is 3
I skipped out
```

Fig. 4-31.

Within the first program example, the goto statement is contained within the nested loop. When both looping counters have a value of 3, the loops will be exited via the goto statement, with program control being passed directly to the label statement placed below the loop. This program in itself is not very useful. However, it illustrates a simple and efficient way to exit from the depths of a nested loop. The program in Fig. 4-32 exits the looping process by a more structured approach, by using two break statements and the assistance of an if statement and an additional variable. Note that both techniques will get the job done, but the program using the goto is a tad more efficient (It uses fewer program statements and one less variable) and is easier to read. This situation, however, is the exception rather than the rule. Thus, for many reasons, the goto statement should be used with discretion.

Program :

```
main()
  { int outer;
    int inner;
    int flag = 0;

    for ( outer=1; outer < 5; outer++ )
      { for ( inner=1; inner < 5; inner++ )
          { printf("\n Outer is %d, inner is %d",outer, inner);
            if ( outer == 3 && inner == 3 )
              { flag = 1;
                break;
              }
          }
        if ( flag == 1 ) break;
      }
    printf("\n I skipped out");
  }
```

Fig. 4-32.

Program Output :

```
Outer is 1, inner is 1
Outer is 1, inner is 2
Outer is 1, inner is 3
Outer is 1, inner is 4
Outer is 2, inner is 1
Outer is 2, inner is 2
Outer is 2, inner is 3
Outer is 2, inner is 4
Outer is 3, inner is 1
Outer is 3, inner is 2
Outer is 3, inner is 3
I skipped out
```

5

Arrays and
Character Strings

An array is a collection of related data items stored under a common name. These arrays, also known as tables, may contain the days of the week, months of the year, a list of valid employee numbers or any other group of related information. This chapter discusses the role that these arrays can play as a programming tool. This discussion will include: the validation of data entry, statistical manipulation, character array manipulation, and other specific techniques and procedures that can be easily incorporated into any application.

NUMERIC ARRAYS

Data can be loaded into a table in one of two ways: as part of the array definition process or by assigning it the appropriate value during the execution of the program. Both of these methods are equally popular. In fact, the method chosen for loading an array is usually dictated by the ultimate use of the array and the type of data within it, rather than programming style. In most cases, if the information placed in the table does not change from day to day, such as the number of days in each month, the data can be permanently placed in the program within the array definition statement, as shown below.

There are a few key points of the example below that should be discussed. First, note that the variable name "months" was followed by "[]". These braces state that the

```
main()
{ static int months[] = { 31,28,31,30,31,30,31,31,30,31,30,31 };
  int count;
  for ( count=0; count <= 11; count++ )
    printf("\n [%d] = %d",count,months[count]);
}
```

variable being defined is an array. Second, note that the array definition is followed by an equal sign and a list of numbers enclosed within brackets. When this loading procedure is used, the size of the array is automatically calculated by the compiler by counting the number of array elements listed between the brackets. Figure 5-2 illustrates conceptually how the array elements defined in Fig. 5-1 are viewed within the computer's memory. When reviewing this figure, take special notice that the array begins at position [0], not [1], therefore, the value for January will be in "month[0]", February will be in months[1] and so on.

months[0]	31
months[1]	28
months[2]	31
months[3]	30
months[4]	31
months[5]	30
months[6]	31
months[7]	31
months[8]	30
months[9]	31
months[10]	30
months[11]	31

Fig. 5-2.

Let's now turn our attention back to the "printf( )" function in Fig. 5-1. The array months[ ] is being subscripted by the variable count, causing the array to be written as months[count]. This procedure will cause the printf() function to print the contents of a particular location of the months[ ] array as specified by the value of the variable count. For example, if count has a value of 3, then months[count] translates to months[3], thus printing April's value of 30.

Figure 5-3 is an expanded version of the program previously discussed in Fig. 5-1. Note that this program includes the printing of headings and the numbers of the associated memory locations being printed. It contains one new major point of interest.

```
Program :  main()
           { static int months[] = { 31,28,31,30,31,30,31,31,30,31,30,31 };
             int count;
             printf("\n     Month     No. of Days");
             printf("\n     -----     -----------");
             for ( count=0; count <= 11; count++ )
             printf("\n        %d            %d",count+1,months[count]);
           }
```

Fig. 5-3.

Fig. 5-3. (cont.)

Program Output:	Month	No. of Days
	-----	------------
	1	31
	2	28
	3	31
	4	30
	5	31
	6	30
	7	31
	8	31
	9	30
	10	31
	11	30
	12	31

The printf( ) function within the for loop was modified. This modification took out the open and close brackets from around the %d associated with count, deleted the equal sign, and most importantly, changed the first printed value from count to count + 1. By temporarily adding 1 to the value of count prior to printing, the month's number (1 = January, 2 = February, etc.) and its corresponding numbers line up.

The second array loading option, mentioned earlier, reads the information from a data file or from the user's keyboard. This process is primarily used in applications that should not have the information permanently written into the program. For example, a payroll system may contain thirty programs that use employee status information. If all thirty programs had the employee information explicitly written into them, then the addition of a new employee would cause all the programs to be edited and recompiled. However, if these programs read the codes from a small sequential disk file into memory, then only the small file would require modification. The program listed in Fig. 5-4 shows how an array can be loaded from the keyboard. Loading an array from a file will be discussed in Chapter 9 on file input and output.

Program :
```
      main()
      { int months[12];
        int count;

        for ( count=0; count <= 11; count++ )
          { printf("\nEnter value of month %d : ",count+1);
            scanf("%d",&months[count]);
          }
        printf("\n    Month  No. of Days");
        printf("\n    -----  ------------");
        for ( count=0; count <= 11; count++ )
          printf("\n      %d          %d",count+1,months[count]);
      }
```

Program Output:
```
      Enter value of month 1 : 31
      Enter value of month 2 : 28
      Enter value of month 3 : 31
      Enter value of month 4 : 30
      Enter value of month 5 : 31
      Enter value of month 6 : 30
```

Fig. 5-4.

```
Enter value of month 7 : 31
Enter value of month 8 : 31
Enter value of month 9 : 30
Enter value of month 10 : 31
Enter value of month 11 : 30
Enter value of month 12 : 31
   Month    No. of Days
   -----    -----------
     1          31
     2          28
     3          31
     4          30
     5          31
     6          30
     7          31
     8          31
     9          30
    10          31
    11          30
    12          31
```

Fig. 5-4. (cont.)

When reviewing Fig. 5-4, note that a second for loop has been added. This loop causes the phase "Enter value of month : " to be displayed, and allows the user, via a scanf( ) function, to enter the number of days in each month. Also note that the word static and the twelve monthly values were deleted from the int statement where months[ ] was defined. Additionally, the number 12 was placed within the array brackets. This 12 specifies that array months[ ] will be 12 members long, with array locations ranging from 0 to 11. Remember, when to array values where listed within the int statement, the 12 was not needed because the compiler could figure out the appropriate array size by counting the number of elements.

Figure 5-5 converts the previously explained array examples into a useful date validation routine. This program asks the user to enter a date in a specified format, assesses its value and displays a message stating if the entered date was valid or invalid. One caution however, if you try to use this program as a real application, a leap year was used when developing the validation logic in an attempt to simplify the example.

```
Program :   main()
            { static int months[] = { 31,28,31,30,31,30,31,31,30,31,30,31 };
              int count;
              int month;
              int day;
              int year;
              char dummy;

              printf("\n Enter date in format MM/DD/YY : ");
              scanf("%d%c%d%c%d",&month,&dummy,&day,&dummy,&year);

              if ( day >= 1 && day <= months[month-1] )
                  printf("\n     Date is valid");
              else
                  printf("\n     Date is not valid");
            }
```

Fig. 5-5.

Program Output: Run 1.   Enter date in format MM/DD/YY : 12/23/86

                                        Date is valid

                     Run 2.   Enter date in format MM/DD/YY : 02/31/86

                                        Date is not valid

                     Run 3.   Enter date in format MM/DD/YY : 06/06/87

                                        Date is valid

Fig. 5-5. (cont.)

The next programming example, shown in Fig. 5-6, allows a teacher to enter student grades. Then, once the grades are entered, the program calculates and prints the average grade value. This program in itself is only marginally useful, but it illustrates how arrays can be used to analyze and manipulate numerically oriented statistical data.

Program :
```
main()
{ int grades[30];
  int count;
  int total = 0;
  int ave_grade;

  for ( count=0; count <= 11; count++ )
    { printf("\nEnter grade for student number %d : ",count+1);
      scanf("%d",&grades[count]);
      if ( grades[count] == -1 ) break;
    }
  for ( count=0; grades[count] != -1; count++ )
    { total += grades[count];
    }
  ave_grade = total / count;
  printf("\n Average is = %d",ave_grade);
}
```

Program Output:
```
Enter grade for student number 1 : 100
Enter grade for student number 1 : 90
Enter grade for student number 1 : 80
Enter grade for student number 1 : 85
Enter grade for student number 1 : 95
Average is = 90
```

Fig. 5-6.

The grading program listed above is divided into four parts; variable initialization, data entry, array manipulation and final calculation with output. Take special note of the array manipulation section (the second for loop). This for statement is analyzing the contents of the grades[] array by summing the grades in preparation for calculating an average.

Figure 5-7 is a little more complex than the example in Fig. 5-6. This program also allows for the input of student grades, but also calculates the maximum grade, minimum grade, and arithmetic mean.

Program :
```
main()
    { int grades[30];
      int count;
      int total = 0;
      int ave_grade;
      int mean_val;
      int max_val;
      int min_val;

      for ( count=0; count <= 11; count++ )
        { printf("\nEnter grade for student number %d : ",count+1);
          scanf("%d",&grades[count]);
          if ( grades[count] == -1 ) break;
        }
      max_val = grades[0];
      min_val = grades[0];
      for ( count=0; grades[count] != -1; count++ )
        { total += grades[count];
          if ( max_val < grades[count] ) max_val = grades[count];
          if ( min_val > grades[count] ) min_val = grades[count];
        }

      ave_grade = total / count;
      mean_val = ( max_val + min_val ) / 2;

      printf("\n Average is = %d",ave_grade);
      printf("\n Maximum is = %d",max_val);
      printf("\n Minimum is = %d",min_val);
      printf("\n Mean    is = %d",mean_val);
    }
```

Program Output:
```
Enter grade for student number 1 : 100
Enter grade for student number 1 : 90
Enter grade for student number 1 : 80
Enter grade for student number 1 : 85
Enter grade for student number 1 : 95
Average is = 90
Maximum is = 100
Minimum is = 80
Mean    is = 90
```

Fig. 5-7.

CHARACTER ARRAYS

Arrays are very commonly used in C to store ASCII character strings, such as names and addresses. Unlike many other computer programming languages, C requires the programmer to treat character strings as a characters array and not as a single variable. This seemingly small difference in representation has a dramatic effect in the way alphabetic data is stored, accessed, and modified.

Lets begin our discussion on the use of character strings by going back to our first C program, again shown in Fig. 5-8.

Fig. 5-8.

```
main()
{ Printf("Hi there");
}
```

Recall from the previous discussion that the phrase "Hi there" is called a character string and must be enclosed within double quotes. These double quotes perform
two main functions. First, and most obvious, they specify the beginning and ending
points of the string. Second, it instructs the compiler to place a special character at
the end of the string, called a null string terminator. Remember, in C a character string
is just an array of individual letters. The null terminator specifies where these letters
end. Let's now modify Fig. 5-8 in an attempt to better analyze the null terminator concept. This reworked program is shown below.

Fig. 5-9.

```
main()
{ static char a_string[] = { "Hi there" };

    printf("\n %s",a_string);

}
```

This reworded program assigns the value "Hi there" to a character array string
called a_string. Then the printf() function prints the value contained within a_string,
namely, "Hi there". Also note that when using the printf( ) function to print character
strings, the symbol %s is used to denote the printing of a string. Now let's once again
expand the program to shed further light on the character manipulation process.

Program :
```
main()
{ static char a_string[] = { "Hi there" };
    int count;

    printf("%s",a_string);

    for ( count = 0; count < 9; count++ )
        printf("\n a_string[%d] = %c = %d"
            ,count,a_string[count], a_string[count] );

}
```

Fig. 5-10.

Program Output:
```
Hi there
    a_string[0] = H = 72
    a_string[1] = i = 105
    a_string[2] =   = 32
    a_string[3] = t = 116
    a_string[4] = h = 104
    a_string[5] = e = 101
    a_string[6] = r = 114
    a_string[7] = e = 101
    a_string[8] =   = 0
```

The second expanded program contains an additional routine which prints the value
of each individual memory location within the a_string array. When reviewing this program, pay close attention to the new printf() function. In particular, note that three values

are being printed: count, which is the variable used as the array subscript, and the character and ASCII decimal values of the array contents. As you can see, the ASCII value of a__string[8] is zero. This zero value is the null terminator specifying the end of the string. The other numeric values are the ASCII equivalents of the characters on the associated line.

Calculating String Length

The program shown in Fig. 5-11 calculates the size of a character string (also known as a string array or character array) and typifies how these strings must be handled. Don't worry. All C compilers provide prewritten functions that copy, compare, test, and manipulate this type of data.

```
Program :  main()
           { static char a_string[15] = {"aaaaaaaa"};
             int the_len;

             the_len = length(a_string);
             printf("\n The length of a_string is %d",the_len);
           }

           int length(s1)
              char s1[];
           { int x = 0;
             while ( s1[x] )
                 ++x;
             return(x);
           }
```

Fig. 5-11.

Program Output: The length of a_string is 8

The use of the while statement in this program is particularly noteworthy. It is constructed in a manner that it increments the variable "count" until the referenced array location contains a value of ' \ 0'. This value, as you recall, is called a string terminator and signifies the end of the character string. Without this terminator, the length testing will read past the end of the array and access whatever values happen to be in the next sequential memory location. As you can well imagine, this error could, and probably will, produce inconsistent and often strange results.

The '\0' notation is comprised of three basic parts; the single quotation marks, the backslash, and the zero. The backslash states that the number which is placed after it is the ASCII value of the character to be referenced. The zero is the number following the backslash. Therefore, the expression ' \ 0' is a representation of the character which has an ASCII value of zero. This character is the null string terminator. Lastly, the single quotation mark can best be explained by comparing it with the double quotation mark. The double quotation as previously discussed, is used to enclose characters strings literals and instructs the compiler to place a null terminator at the end of the string. The single quotation mark also encloses a character or group of characters, but is does not instruct the compiler to place a null after the string.

The standard C function which performs this task is named "strlen( )" and is shown below.

Program :
```
main()
{ static char a_string[15] = {"aaaaaaaa"};
  int the_len;

  the_len = strlen(a_string);
  printf("\n The length of a_string is %d",the_len);
}
```

Fig. 5-12.

Program Output: `The length of a_string is 8`

Comparing String Equality

Character strings can not be compared in the same manner as variables are compared, namely a__string == b__string. Strings must be compared by assessing the equality of each pair of corresponding array locations. Figure 5-13 illustrates this process.

Program :
```
main()
{ char a_string[15];
  char b_string[15];
  int x;

  scanf("%s",a_string);
  scanf("%s",b_string);

  if ( equals(a_string,b_string) == 0 )
      printf("\n Strings are equal");
  else
      printf("\n Strings are not equal");
}

int equals(s1,s2)
char s1[], s2[];
{ int x = 0;
  while ( s1[x] == s2[x] )
    if ( s1[x++] == '\0' )·return(0);
  return(s1[x] - s2[x]);
}
```

Fig. 5-13.

Program Output:
Run 1.
```
Hello
Hi
 Strings are not equal
```

Run 2.
```
Hello
Hello
 Strings are equal
```

Run 3.
```
Hello
Hellox
 Strings are not equal
```

77

As with string length, don't worry, all compilers provide a built in function to perform this task.

Figure 5-13 brings forward a C feature that has thus far only been mentioned in passing. This facility is the creation and execution of a function. A function is a group of associated statements grouped under a common name. For example, when you say use the command printf("Hello");, you are actually running a group of C statements collectively bundled under the name printf(). This concept is completely discussed in Chapter 8, but for now, it is only important to know that when the function equals() is called in Fig. 5-13, the value of a__string and b__string are passed to variables s1 and s2 respectively, and that the return statement passes a numeric value from the equals() function, back to the main program.

Within the equals() function, each array location in s1[] is compared to the corresponding array location in s2[]. If the two locations are equal, the while statement within which the comparison is being made will continue to process. During the reiteration of this loop, the if statement within the loop increments the counter x and tests for a null terminator. If s1[x] is null, then the two strings are equal and a zero value is returned to the main program, thus signifying equality. Remember, since you are still within the loop, s2[x] must also be equal to '\0' because the looping criteria states that the two locations must be equal. Also, since they are equal to this point, and they have both ended, as specified by the null terminators, then the two arrays must contain identical information. If the two locations do not match, then the loop will be terminated and the return statement below the loop will be executed. This return will perform two activities. First, it will subtract the ASCII value of s2[x] from the ASCII value of s1[x]. Second, the value just calculated will be passed back to the main program, and because it is a nonzero value, it will signify that the strings are not equal. This ASCII subtraction performs an interesting byproduct. If the calculated return value is positive, then s1[] is greater then s2[]. Conversely, if the returned value is negative, then s1[] is less then s2[]. This greater-than/less-than byproduct is illustrated below.

```
Program :   main()
            { static char a_string[15] = {"string-a"};
              static char b_string[15] = {"string-b"};
              static char c_string[15] = {"string-c"};
              static char d_string[15] = {"string-d"};
              int x;

              x = equals(a_string,b_string);
              printf("\n equals function returned a value of ==> %d",x);

              x = equals(b_string,a_string);
              printf("\n equals function returned a value of ==> %d",x);

              x = equals(a_string,d_string);
              printf("\n equals function returned a value of ==> %d",x);

              x = equals(a_string,a_string);
              printf("\n equals function returned a value of ==> %d",x);

            }
```

Fig. 5-14.

```
                    int equals(s1,s2)
                      char s1[], s2[];

                    { int x = 0;
                      while ( s1[x] == s2[x] )
                        if ( s1[x++] == '\0' ) return(0);
                      return(s1[x] - s2[x]);
                    }
```

Fig. 5-14. (cont.)

Program Output:
```
equals function returned a value of ==> -1
equals function returned a value of ==> 1
equals function returned a value of ==> -3
equals function returned a value of ==> 0
```

The standard C function which performs this task is named "strcmp( )" and is shown below.

Program :
```
main()
{ char a_string[15];
  char b_string[15];
  int x;

  scanf("%s",a_string);
  scanf("%s",b_string);

  if ( strcmp(a_string,b_string) == 0 )
      printf("\n Strings are equal");
  else
      printf("\n Strings are not equal");
}
```

Fig. 5-15.

Program Output:

Run 1.
```
Hello
Hi
 Strings are not equal
```

Run 2.
```
Hello
Hello
 Strings are equal
```

Run 3.
```
Hello
Hellox
 Strings are not equal
```

Copying a Character String

String copying, like string equality testing, may also not be performed by using a simple assignment operator. This task also requires each element of the array to be individually copied from the old array to the appropriate location in the new array. Figure 5-16 illustrates this process.

```
Program :  main()
           { static char a_string[15] = {"aaaaaaaa"};
             static char b_string[15] = {"bbb"};

             copy(a_string,b_string);
             printf("\n a_string = %s,   b_string = %s",a_string,b_string);
           }

           void copy(s1,s2)
            char s1[], s2[];

           { int x = 0;
             while ( s1[x] = s2[x++] )
               ;
           }
```

Program Output: a_string = bbb, b_string = bbb

Fig. 5-16.

Figure 5-16 begins by defining and initializing two character strings, one with a value of "aaaaaaaa" and the other with a value of "bbb". Then, the function copy() is called, thus transferring control to that function. Note that here, as in Fig. 5-12, the string arrays a_string and b_string are then passed to arrays s1[] and s2[] respectively. Once passed, the variable x is defined, and a while loop is entered. This while loop appears unfinished, but in fact, it is performing the entire string copy. Note that the test expression within the parentheses is actually an assignment operator = and not the equality test operator = =. Also note that variable x is being incremented within the assignment. This combination allows three crucial things to happen at once. First, the loop will continue to loop until s2[x] has a value of zero, the value of a null terminator which also happens to signify the end of the string to be copied. Second, while the loop is waiting for the zero value, it is copying each encountered s1[x] array to the corresponding s2[x] location. Third and last, after the s2[x] value is moved to s1[x] and the expression is tested for a null terminator, the + + adds 1 to x, thus moving to the next array location.

The standard C function which performs this task is named strcpy() and is shown below.

```
Program :  main()
           { static char a_string[15] = {"aaaaaaaa"};
             static char b_string[15] = {"bbb"};

             strcpy(a_string,b_string);
             printf("\n a_string = %s,   b_string = %s",a_string,b_string);
           }
```

Program Output: a_string = bbb, b_string = bbb

Fig. 5-17.

Concatenating Two Strings

Thus far, we have discussed the comparison and copying of strings, now lets discuss their concatenation, that is to say, adding the value of one string array to the end of another. The following figure illustrates how this is performed.

Program :
```
main()
{ static char a_string[15] = {"aaaa"};
  static char b_string[15] = {"bbb"};

  concat(a_string,b_string);
  printf("\n a_string = %s,   b_string = %s",a_string,b_string);
}

void concat(s1,s2)
  char s1[], s2[];

{ int x = 0;
  int y = 0;

  while ( s1[x++] )
    ;
  x--;

  while ( s1[x++] = s2[y++] )
    ;
}
```

Fig. 5-18.

Program Output: a_string = aaaabbb, b_string = bbb

The program in Fig. 5-18 begins in a manner similar to string comparison and copying. However, the difference is the calling and execution of the concat function. This concatenation begins by defining and initializing the variables x and y. x will be used to subscript s1[] and y will be used to subscript s2[]. Once defined, the first while statement will scan the s1[] array in search of its null terminator. When reached, the value of x will contain a value that is one greater than the location of the null terminator within the array. This is the case, because x is automatically incremented after the while test criteria is evaluated as specified by the + + operator. Therefore, 1 must be subtracted from the x to assure that the null value is overwritten by the first character of the array being added. Lastly, the second while loop copies the s2[] characters to the end of s1[] using a process similar to that discussed for string copying.

The standard C function which performs this task is named strcat() and is shown below.

Fig. 5-19.

Program :
```
main()
{ static char a_string[15] = {"aaaa"};
  static char b_string[15] = {"bbb"};

  strcat(a_string,b_string);
  printf("\n a_string = %s,   b_string = %s",a_string,b_string);
}
```

Program Output: a_string = aaaabbb, b_string = bbb

6

Structures

From our discussion of arrays in Chapter 5, we learned of a way to group together related elements of data. C provides yet another facility called structures to perform this task. In this case however, unlike arrays, structures have the ability to bring together data of different data types, data sizes, and even data arrays. To illustrate the use of structures, two primary examples will be used, the first is the definition of a date, and the second is the definition of a structure within a structure.

DEFINING STRUCTURES

To begin our discussion, the program shown below uses a struct statement to define the format of a date. Once defined, this date variable will be given a value and printed to the screen via a printf() function.

```
Program : main()
          {
          struct date_format
            { int month;
              int day;
              int year;
            };

          struct date_format date;

          date.month = 4;
          date.day   = 9;
          date.year  = 1987;

          printf("\n Month is = %d",date.month);
          printf("\n Day is   = %d",date.day);
```

Fig. 6-1.

```
                    printf("\n Year is  = %d",date.year);
              }
```

Fig. 6-1. (cont.)

Program Output: Month is = 4
                      Day is   = 9
                      Year is = 1987

The structure programming example shown in Fig. 6-1 is divided into four parts: the structure definition, structure allocation, variable assignment, and printing of defined values. The first section begins with the word "struct" and is explained in the first structure format shown below.

Fig. 6-2.

```
struct template-name
  { data-type data-name;
    date-type date-name;
       . . .
    date-type date-name;
  };
```

The struct statement stands for structure and begins as you would expect, with the word "struct", followed by the name of the structure being defined. This name is then followed by the definition of the variables to be contained within the structure. For example, in Fig. 6-1, the structure is named date_format and contains the three integer variables named month, day, and year. Also note that this variable list is contained within brackets and is followed by an ending semicolon. This punctuation is required and is considered to be part of the format.

Before moving on to the second struct statement in Fig. 6-1, let's examine the purpose of the first struct. The first struct did not create a usable data area or allocate memory for the variables month, day, and year. This first statement only defined the format (also known as a template) by which a structure may be defined. The second struct statement, then uses this template to state that a structure called date should be created and allocated memory space, based on the format of date_format which has been previously defined. Thus, in Fig. 6-1, the date structure has the same format as the date_format structure template. The difference is that date is associated with actual memory locations and can be used to store data, while date_format is just a structure template from which usable structures may be defined. The format of this second struct statement is shown below.

Fig. 6-3.

```
struct template-name structure-name, structure-name ...
```

As shown in the second struct format, it begins with the word "struct", followed by the name of the structure format (also known as a structure template), which is followed by the name or names of the structure or structures to be defined.

So far in Fig. 6-1 we have defined a structure format named date__format and a us-able structure named date. Now, let's look at the usage of the variables within the date structure. First, you must understand that the variables defined within a structure must always be referenced in association with its structure. This association is made by pre-fixing the variable name with its structure name, followed by a period ("structure__name.variable__name"). For example, in Fig. 6-1, the month, day and year variables are prefixed with date., making then date.month, date.day and date.year respec-tively. Other than this required prefix however, it may be used like and regular non-structured variable.

Now that we have completed discussion of the structure definition process used in Fig. 6-1, let's discuss an alternative definition process. This alternative is shown below.

Program :
```
main()
{
   struct date_format
      { int month;
        int day;
        int year;
      } date;

   date.month = 4;
   date.day   = 9;
   date.year  = 1987;

   printf("\n Month is = %d",date.month);
   printf("\n Day is   = %d",date.day);
   printf("\n Year is  = %d",date.year);

}
```

Fig. 6-4.

Program Output:
```
Month is = 4
Day is   = 9
Year is  = 1987
```

The alternative structure definition process used in Fig. 6-4 combines the two struct formats used in Fig. 6-1 into one statement. Note that within this combined definition, the date structure (the structure that actually has associated memory locations) is named after the closing bracket of the variable name list and before the ending semicolon of the struct statement. This format is commonly used when the defined structure tem-plate is only used in association with one memory allocated structure. The format of this struct statement is shown in Fig. 6-5.

```
struct template-name
   { data-type data-name;
     date-type date-name;
        . . .
     date-type date-name;
   } structure-name;
```

Fig. 6-5.

INITIALIZING STRUCTURES

Structures may be initialized in two main ways, the first of which you have already seen in Figs. 6-1 and 6-4, by the use of an assignment operator ("date.month = 9;"). The second initialization process is shown below.

Fig. 6-6.

```
Program :   main()
            {
              struct date_format
               { int month;
                 int day;
                 int year;
               };

              static struct date_format date = { 4, 9, 1987 };

              printf("\n Month is = %d",date.month);
              printf("\n Day is   = %d",date.day);
              printf("\n Year is  = %d",date.year);

            }
```

```
Program Output:   Month is = 4
                  Day is   = 9
                  Year is  = 1987
```

The structure initialization example in Fig. 6-6 differs from the other structure program examples in three ways: first, the word "static" was placed before the struct statement. Second, the numbers 9, 4, and 1987 are listed after the word "date" following an equal sign. Note that the numbers are in the same order as the structure's variable list. This consistency must be used to assure that the C compiler places the correct value in each variable. Also note that this initialization format is similar to that used when initializing arrays and regular variables. Lastly, notice that the three assignment statements used in Figs. 6-1 and 6-4 have been deleted. This deletion was essential because the structure was defined as static and thus its contents need not be set because the structure has already been initialized to its appropriate values.

As an additional point, this initialization process can also be employed when used on the alternative structure definition process shown in Fig. 6-4. This alternative process is shown below.

Fig. 6-7.

```
Program :   main()
            {
              static struct date_format
               { int month;
                 int day;
                 int year;
               } date = { 4, 9, 1987 };

              printf("\n Month is = %d",date.month);
              printf("\n Day is   = %d",date.day);
              printf("\n Year is  = %d",date.year);
            }
```

Fig. 6-7. (cont.)

Program Output:
```
Month is = 4
Day is   = 9
Year is  = 1987
```

Now that we have discussed and examined various structure definition alternatives, Fig. 6-8 provides a programming example of how structures may be effectively used. In fact, to assist in contrasting the use of regular and structured variables, Fig. 6-8 is a rework of the date validation program discussed in Fig. 5-5.

Program :
```
    main()
    { static int months[] = { 31,28,31,30,31,30,31,31,30,31,30,31 };
      int count;
      char dummy;

      struct date_format
       { int month;
         int day;
         int year;
       };

      struct date_format date;

      printf("\n Enter date in format MM/DD/YY : ");
      scanf("%d%c%d%c%d",&date.month,&dummy,&date.day,&dummy,&date.year)

      if ( date.day >= 1 && date.day <= months[date.month-1] )
          printf("\n     Date is valid");
      else
          printf("\n     Date is not valid");
    }
```

Program Output:
```
    Enter date in format MM/DD/YY : 12/23/86
            Data is valid

    Enter date in format MM/DD/YY : 12/33/86
            Date is not valid
```

Fig. 6-8.

ARRAYS OF STRUCTURES

Now that we have discussed the use of arrays and the use of structures, let's discuss arrays of structures. Figure 6-9 illustrates this concept by asking the user to enter five names and birthdays, facilitates their input, and then prints out a formatted list.

Program :
```
    main()
    { int count;
      char dummy;
      int no_names;

      struct date_format
        { char name[15];
          int month;
```

Fig. 6-9.

```
        int day;
        int year;
      } date[5];

  for ( count=0; count < 5; count++ )
    { printf("\n Enter Last Name : ");
      scanf("%s",&date[count].name);

      printf("\n Enter date in format MM/DD/YY : ");
      scanf("%d%c%d%c%d",&date[count].month,&dummy,
          &date[count].day,&dummy,&date[count].year);
    }

  printf("\n\n    Names and Birthday");
  printf("\n    -------------------");

  for ( count=0; count < 5; count++ )
    { printf("\n %s      %d/%d/%d",date[count].name,
        date[count].month, date[count].day, date[count].year);
    }
}
```

Fig. 6-9. (cont.)   **Program Output:** Enter last name : Bloom
                               Enter data in format MM/DD/YY : 06/06/87
                               Enter last name : Tanner
                               Enter data in format MM/DD/YY : 04/09/87
                               Enter last name : Wells
                               Enter data in format MM/DD/YY : 07/08/83
                               Enter last name : Tobin
                               Enter data in format MM/DD/YY : 10/06/88
                               Enter last name : Gasman
                               Enter data in format MM/DD/YY : 03/05/87

                          Names and Birthday

                          Bloom   06/06/87
                          Tanner   4/9/87
                          Wells   7/8/83
                          Tobin   10/6/88
                          Gasman   3/5/87

The program in Fig. 6-9 defines a structure template named date_format, which in turn is used to define the date structure. This process, as you may recall, looks similar to the process used in Fig. 6-4. This example, however, has one additional attribute. Like the definition of a character string, the [10] states that the entity being suffixed is an array. It just so happens that in this case, it is a structure and not on individual variable. Next, the user is asked to enter five sets of names and dates by a combination of printf() and scanf() functions. Take special note that within the scanf() function, the month variable is referenced as date[count].month. The variable within the braces, like all other arrays, specifies which date array location should be referenced. Figure 6-10 illustrates how an array of structures is stored within memory.

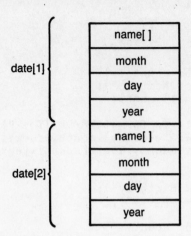

Fig. 6-10.

STRUCTURES WITHIN STRUCTURES

There are times when it is advantageous to place structures within structures. The date structure previously discussed, is the classic example used to illustrate this concept. Like many applications, the program listed in Fig. 6-11 has two dates associated with an individual name, namely, birthday, and wedding anniversary.

Program :
```
main()
    {
    struct date_format
      { int month;
        int day;
        int year;
      };

    struct info_format
      { char name[20];
        struct date_format birth;
        struct date_format wedding;
      } info;

    strcpy(info.name,"Kim S. Bloom");

    info.birth.month = 4;
    info.birth.day   = 9;
    info.birth.year  = 1958;

    info.wedding.month = 11;
    info.wedding.day   = 2;
    info.wedding.year  = 1980;

    printf("\n Name : %s",info.name);
    printf("\n   Birth   : %d/%d/%d",info.birth.month,
           info.birth.day, info.birth.year);

    printf("\n   Wedding : %d/%d/%d",info.wedding.month,
           info.wedding.day, info.wedding.year);

    }
```

Fig. 6-11.

Fig. 6-11. (cont.)

Program Output : Name : Kim S. Bloom
                    Birth   : 4/9/1958
                    Wedding : 11 /2/1980

Figure 6-11 begins by defining a structure template called date—format. Once defined, the program then defines a second structure template named info—format. In this case, however, the word "info" is placed after the structure variable list, thus assigning space in memory as discussed earlier in the chapter. The variable list within the second structure contains the character variable name and two date—format structures named birth and wedding, representing the person's birthday and wedding anniversary respectively.

Now that the variables and structures have been defined, note the way in which the variables within the structure are referenced. The name variable, as you would expect from prior discussion, is referenced by prefixing it with the name of the structure in which it resides, namely, info. Remember, the structure's contents are always associated with info and not info—format. Now take special notice of how the date variables are referenced. As an example, the birthday's month field is written as info.birth.month. The word info refers to the main structure, birth refers to the structure defined within info using the date—format template, and month is the variable's name. After a quick examination, you will see that this naming convention typifies the process used for referencing the other date variables.

ARRAYS WITHIN STRUCTURES

The program in Fig. 6-12 provides an example of how to define and use arrays that are placed within structures. The structure info contains the integer array grades[ ]. This array may be used like any non-structured variable array, with the exception that like all structure variables, it must be prefixed with the name of its associated structure. For example, in Fig. 6-12, grades[ ] is always referenced as info.grades[ ].

Fig. 6-12.

Program :
```
main()
{ int count;

    struct info_format
      { char name[20];
        int grades[5];
      } info;

    printf("\n Enter name : ");
    scanf("%s",info.name);
for ( count=0; count<5; count++ )
  { printf("\n Enter grade %d : ",count);
    scanf("%d",&info.grades[count]);
  }

printf("\n\n Grades for %s are \n",info.name);
for ( count=0; count<5; count++ )
  { printf("\n   Grade %d = %d: ",count,info.grades[count]);
  }
}
```

Fig. 6-12. (cont.)

```
Program Output :   Enter name : Bloom
                   Enter grade 0 : 100
                   Enter grade 1 : 95
                   Enter grade 2 : 80
                   Enter grade 3 : 90
                   Enter grade 4 : 85

                   Grades for Bloom are :

                   Grade 0 = 100
                   Grade 1 = 95
                   Grade 2 = 80
                   Grade 3 = 90
                   Grade 4 = 85
```

Figure 6-13 shows how this array and structure is stored within memory. When reviewing this conceptual view, note that the name[] string is an array and is stored in the same manner as grades[].

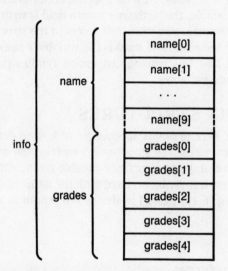

Fig. 6-13.

ARRAYS OF STRUCTURES CONTAINING ARRAYS

When discussing various structure and array usages, it is inevitable that someone will be forced to place an array of variables within an array of structures. To perform this task, you must define the structure to be an array, as well as the appropriate variables as arrays as shown in Fig. 6-14.

```
main()
{ int bigloop;
  int count;

  struct info_format
  { char name[20];
    int grades[5];
  } info[5];
```

Fig. 6-14.

```
      for ( bigloop=0; bigloop<3; bigloop++ )
        { printf("\n Enter name : ");
          scanf("%s",info[bigloop].name);

          for ( count=0; count<5; count++ )
            { printf("\n Enter grade %d : ",count);
              scanf("%d",&info[bigloop].grades[count]);
            }
        }

      for ( bigloop=0; bigloop<3; bigloop++ )
        { printf("\n\n Grades for %s are : \n",info[bigloop].name);
          for ( count=0; count<5; count++ )
            { printf("\n        Grade %d = %d: ",count,info[bigloop].grades
            }
        }
    }
```

Fig. 6-14.

Figure 6-14 begins by defining two integer variables, bigloop and count. The variable bigloop will be used to subscript the structure info. The variable count, as before, will be used to subscript the grades[ ] array. Next, the info structure is defined as an array by placing "info[ ]" after the structure's variable list. Once the variable and array definitions are complete, the program loops three times, asking the user to enter a name and five associated grades. Note that within this loop, names[ ] is referenced as info[bigloop].names, and the grades[ ] array is referenced as info[bigloop].grades[count], thus in both cases stating which array location within "info" is being referenced. Additionally, in the case of grades[ ], the array is further defined by the use of count.

This double array definition process is stored in memory in the form shown in Fig. 6-15 on the next page.

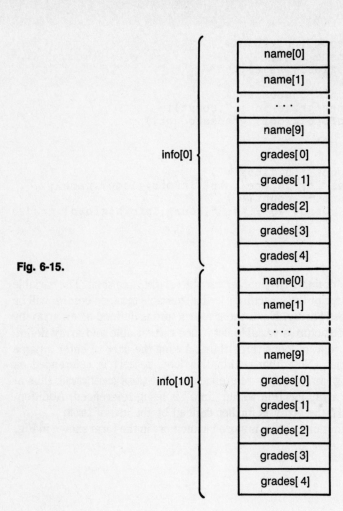

Fig. 6-15.

7
Pointers

This chapter discusses a feature of C which not only distinguishes it from virtually all other high level programming languages, but also provides it with incredible power and flexibility. This feature is the use of pointers. These pointers can assist in the manipulation of arrays, the passing of data between functions, the definition of complex data structures, and the tracking of allocated computer memory.

To understand this feature, you must first understand the concept of indirection. Indirection can best be explained by using the nontechnical example of a telephone book. The friend you are calling does not physically live in the book. However, the telephone book provides you with the address and phone number where your friend can be found. Therefore, the phone book is acting as a pointer to your friend. In C, a pointer performs a similar function. A pointer variable contains the memory location where its associated data actually resides. Figure 7-1 illustrates this concept.

Fig. 7-1.

Memory Location	Name	Conceptual View
5	char__pointer	location 1d
1d	char__variable	value X

Note that char__pointer is actually located in memory location 5 and char__variable is actually located in memory location 1d. Furthermore, note that char__variable has a value of x and char__pointer has a value of 1d. This 1d, as can be seen in the diagram, specifies where the value of char__variable can be found, namely, location 1d. This process in a C program can be seen in Fig. 7-2.

Program :

```
main()
{ char *char_pointer;
  char char_variable;

  char_variable = 'x';
  char_pointer = &char_variable;

  printf("\n The pointer value of char_pointer is %x",char_pointer);
  printf("\n The value of char_pointer is %c",*char_pointer);
  printf("\n The value of char_variable is %c",char_variable);
}
```

Fig. 7-2.

Program Output :
```
The pointer value of char_pointer is 1d
The value of char_pointer is x
The value of char_variable is x
```

Like Fig. 7-1, Fig. 7-2 contains a character variable and a pointer to a character variable. As you may surmise, the asterisk in the char statement that prefixes char_pointer instructs the compiler to treat its associated variable as a pointer and not a regular variable. This is an important distinction, because character data and pointers are stored differently in memory. In some cases, they even require different amounts of memory space. As a result, an attempt to incorrectly use their data types could cause very strange results. Once defined, char_variable is set to a value of x and the pointer char_pointer is given the memory address of where char_variable is stored. This is done by placing an ampersand (&) before char_variable in the assignment statement. The ampersand is called the address operator and instructs the compiler to pass the address, not the value, of the variable being prefixed. Therefore, once these two statements are executed, char_variable will contain a value of x and char_pointer will contain the address of the memory location associated with char_variable.

To prove and further illustrate this point, three printf( ) function calls are used. The first printf( ) statement prints the memory location where x resides, namely, location 1d. The second printf( ) function prints the value of char_varaible, which is the value x. Lastly, the third printf( ) function prints the indirect value of char_pointer which is also x.

There is one last point that is of the utmost importance when reviewing this program and all other programs that use pointers. This point is that all pointers are not the same. Namely, a pointer that points to a char variable, must be defined as a char and a pointer that points to an int or double should be defined as an int pointer or double pointer respectively. For example, the pointer used to reference char char_pointer must be defined as char *pointer, a pointer to int an_integer must be defined as int *pointer.

Figure 7-3 expands the first pointer example and sheds additional light on the use of pointers.

Program :

```
main()
{ char *char_pointer;
  char char_variable;
  char val_of_x;

  val_of_x = 'x';
```

Fig. 7-3.

```
                       char_pointer = &val_of_x;
                       char_variable = *char_pointer;
Fig. 7-3. (cont.)       printf("\n The value of char_variable is %c",char_variable);
                    }
```

Program Output : The value of char_variable is x

The program above begins in a manner similar to Fig. 7-1, by defining a character variable and a pointer to a character variable. From there, a third variable named val_of_x is also defined. This variable, as you may expect, is set to a value of x immediately after being defined. The next line, char_pointer = &val_of_x, causes the address of val_of_x to be passed to the pointer value char_pointer. Then, in the statement char_variable = *char_pointer, char_variable is set to the value contained in the memory location specified by char_pointer which in fact is the value x. Remember, the asterisk before char_pointer causes the indirection to val_of_x. If the asterisk was not present, then char_variable would be set equal to the value in char_pointer which is the address of val_of_x. This accidental error is shown below.

Program :
```
main()
{ char *char_pointer;
  char char_variable;
  char val_of_x;

  val_of_x = 'x';

  char_pointer = &val_of_x;
  char_variable = char_pointer;

  printf("\n The value of char_variable is %c",char_variable);
  printf("\n The value of char_variable is %x",char_variable);
}
```

Program Output :
```
The value of char_variable is
The value of char_variable is 20
```

Fig. 7-4.

The errored program in Fig. 7-4 incorrectly passes a character pointer to a non-pointer variable in the statement char_variable = char_pointer. This program moves the contents of char_pointer and not the indirect value of char_pointer to char_variable. As shown in the output of the program, you can see that the ASCII value is nonprintable, thus it could not possibly be x.

Up to now, pointers have been used in cooperation with regular variables. As can be seen below, pointer values can be passed from pointer to pointer.

Program :
```
          main()
          { char *point_1;
            char *point_2;
            char var_1;
            char var_2;
```

Fig. 7-5.

95

```
    var_1 = 'x';

    point_1 = &var_1;
    point_2 = point_1;

    var_2 = *point_2;
```

Fig. 7-5. (cont.)

```
    printf("\n The value of var_1 is %c",var_1);
    printf("\n The value of var_2 is %c",var_2);
    printf("\n The indirect value of point_1 is %c",*point_1);
    printf("\n The indirect value of point_2 is %c",*point_2);
    printf("\n The address value of point_1 is %d",point_1);
    printf("\n The address value of point_2 is %d",point_2);
}
```

Program Output :
```
            The value of var_1 is x
            The value of var_2 is x
            The indirect value of point_1 is x
            The indirect value of point_2 is x
            The address value of point_1 is 33
            The address value of point_2 is 33
```

The program in Fig. 7-5 set var__1 to a value of x and sets pointer point__1 to the address of var__1. Then, the statement point__2 = point__1 makes point__2 point to the same location as point__1. Next, now that pointer point__2 points to variable var__1, the statement var__2 = *point__2 gives var__2 the value of x. This four statement scenario is proven by the ending printf( ) calls. In particular, note that the contents of both variables is x, that both pointers contain the same indirect value of x (Remember, they both point to var__1), and as shown by the last two printed lines, both pointers point to the same indirect memory location.

The program in Fig. 7-6 displays yet another introductory pointer program. This program, however, illustrates that many pointers can point to the same memory location and can thus all be initialized at one time.

Program :
```
            main()
            { char *point_1;
              char *point_2;
              char *point_3;
              char *point_4;
              char *point_5;
              char char_variable;

              point_1 = &char_variable;
              point_2 = &char_variable;
              point_3 = &char_variable;
              point_4 = &char_variable;
              point_5 = &char_variable;

              char_variable = 'x';

              printf("\n The indirect value of point_1 is %c",*point_1);
              printf("\n The indirect value of point_2 is %c",*point_2);
```

Fig. 7-6.

```
                    printf("\n The indirect value of point_3 is %c",*point_3);
                    printf("\n The indirect value of point_4 is %c",*point_4);
                    printf("\n The indirect value of point_5 is %c",*point_5);
                }
```

Fig. 7-6. (cont.)

Program Output : The indirect value of point_1 is x
                  The indirect value of point_2 is x
                  The indirect value of point_3 is x
                  The indirect value of point_4 is x
                  The indirect value of point_5 is x

In Fig. 7-6, all five pointers are directed to the memory location associated with char__variable. Thus, when char__variable is set to x, the indirect value of all five pointers is also set to x.

POINTERS AND ARRAYS

Array manipulation is one of the most common uses of pointers. They are often used for this purpose for three reasons: program efficiency, ease of writing, and C snob appeal. Program efficiency can be improved because compilers tend to generate better machine code from pointer notation then from array notation. This advantage however, is starting to diminish as compiler optimization techniques improve. In fact, many compilers automatically convert array notation to pointer notation during the compilation process. The second reason people use pointers is that, as shall soon be seen, the notation is easier to type. The third reason for using pointers in general and especially with arrays, is C snob appeal. This idea is that if you are not going to take advantage of C's strengths and format, then why use C at all?

In Fig. 7-7 there are print statements, the first prints the value of the first alphabet[ ] array location, namely the value a. The second printf( ) function prints the contents of the memory location where the a value previously printed physically resides. Note that in both sets, the same value is printed, thus proving the equivalency of the two notations.

Program :
```
main()
{ static char alphabet [] = {"abcdefghijklmnopqrstuvwxyz"};
  int count;

  count = 0;

  printf("\n Value of grades[0] = %c",alphabet[0]);
  printf("\n Value of *grades   = %c",*alphabet);

  printf("\n Pointer to grades[0] is address  %d",&alphabet[0]);
  printf("\n Pointer to grades is address     %d",alphabet);
}
```

Program Output : Value of grades[0] = a
                  Value of *grades   = a
                  Pointer to grades[0] is address   15
                  Pointer to grades is address   15

Fig. 7-7.

Figure 7-8 expands on the previous example by adding a loop to print the alphabet in both standard and pointer notation.

```
main()
{ static char alphabet [] = {"abcdefghijklmnopqrstuvwxyz"};
  int count;

  count = 0;

  printf("\n Letters of the Alphabet");
  printf("\n -----------------------");
  for ( count = 0; count < 26; count++ )
    printf("\n        %c          %c",
         alphabet[count], *(alphabet + count) );
}
```

Fig. 7-8.

The example in Fig. 7-9 introduces a new concept called pointer arithmetic. This process allows you to move from array location to array location by incrementing or decrementing a pointer's value. In this program, c__pointer is being given the starting address of the alphabet array in the statement c__pointer = alphabet. This is needed, because if you modify the pointer value within alphabet then you will lose the starting position of the alphabet array. Also, many compilers will give an error or warning if you attempt to modify that value. Next, after printing the words "The alphabet", the while loop causes the repeated execution of printf(). Within this function, the clause *(c__pointer + +) is referencing the memory location to be printed and is then incrementing c__pointer, causing it to point to the next array location.

```
main()
{ static char alphabet [] = {"abcdefghijklmnopqrstuvwxyz"};
  char *c_pointer;

  c_pointer = alphabet;

  printf("\n The Alphabet : ");

  while ( *c_pointer )
    { printf("%c", *(c_pointer++) );
    }
}
```

Fig. 7-9.

To further illustrate this process, Fig. 7-10 not only prints the alphabet array, but prints its associated memory addresses. Note that the pointer value within c__pointer is incremented by 1 after each reiteration of the loop.

```
main()
{ static char alphabet [] = {"abcdefghijklmnopqrstuvwxyz"};
  char *c_pointer;

  c_pointer = alphabet;

  printf("\n The Alphabet");
  printf("\n ------------");
```

Fig. 7-10.

Fig. 7-10. (cont.)

```
        while ( *c_pointer )
          { printf("\n      %c  %d", *(c_pointer), c_pointer++ );
          }
    }
```

As you may expect, a pointer value may also be decremented using the "– –" operator. This process is shown in Fig. 7-11. Figure 7-11 performs two types of pointer arithmetic. First, in the statement c_pointer = alphabet + 25, c-pointer is being pointed to the location that is 25 memory locations after the beginning of the alphabet, namely the location of z. The second type of pointer arithmetic is employing the – – to move the pointer back one memory location with each loop reiteration.

Fig. 7-11.

```
main()
{ static char alphabet [] = {"abcdefghijklmnopqrstuvwxyz"};
  char *c_pointer;

  c_pointer = alphabet + 25;

  printf("\n The Alphabet");
  printf("\n ------------");

  do
    { printf("\n      %c  %d", *(c_pointer), c_pointer-- );
    } while ( c_pointer >= alphabet );
}
```

POINTERS TO STRUCTURES

Thus far, we have discussed how pointers can be used to manipulate regular variables and arrays. As shall soon be seen, pointers may be used in the processing of structures. An example of this manipulation can be found in Fig. 7-12, which begins by defining the date_format structure template using the struct format shown in Fig. 6-2 of Chapter 6.

Fig. 7-12.

```
Program :   main()
            {
                struct date_format
                  { int month;
                    int day;
                    int year;
                  };

                struct date_format date, *date_pointer;
                date_pointer = &date;

                date_pointer->month = 4;
                date_pointer->day   = 9;
                date_pointer->year   = 1987;
```

```
      printf("\n Month is = %d",date_pointer->month);
      printf("\n Day is   = %d",date_pointer->day);
      printf("\n Year is  = %d",date_pointer->year);
   }
```

Fig. 7-12. (cont.)

Program Output :   Month is = 4
                        Day is   = 9
                        Year is = 1987

Once defined, a second struct statement defines a usable structure named "date" and a pointer to the date structure named *date__pointer. When defining a pointer to a structure, it is imperative that the pointer being defined is not only defined within a struct statement, but that it is defined using the same structure template as the structure it will be referencing. In the case of Fig. 7-12, note that both date and date__pointer are defined using the date__format template. Once defined, like other pointers, date__pointer must be passed the address of the structure it will be defined. Next, note the format that is used to reference the month variable. This format is the pointer name, followed by – >, which is followed by the variable being referenced. Therefore, the statement date.month = 4 can be written in the format date__pointer – >month = 4.

As discussed in previous chapters, C supports the concept of arrays or structures. Therefore, since pointers can be used interchangeably with standard array notation, array structures may also be referenced through pointers in a manner similar to the process used to reference variables and arrays. Figure 7-13 illustrates this concept.

Program :

```
   main()
   { int count;
     char dummy;
     int no_names;

     struct date_format
       { char name[15];
         int month;
         int day;
         int year;
       } date[5];

     struct date_format *date_pointer;
     date_pointer = &date;

     for ( count=0; count < 5; count++ )
       { printf("\n Enter Last Name : ");
         scanf("%s",&(date_pointer + count )->name);

         printf("\n Enter date in format MM/DD/YY : ");
         scanf("%d%c%d%c%d",&( date_pointer + count )->month,&dummy,
            &( date_pointer + count )->day,&dummy,
            &( date_pointer + count )->year);
       }

     printf("\n\n   Names and Birthday");
     printf("\n   -------------------");
```

Fig. 7-13.

```
    for ( count=0; count < 5; count++ )
    { printf("\n  %s      %d/%d/%d",( date_pointer + count )->name,
        ( date_pointer + count )->month,
        ( date_pointer + count )->day,
        ( date_pointer + count )->year);
    }
}
```

Program Output :   Enter Last Name : Bloom
                         Enter date in format MM/DD/YY : 01/01/87
                         Enter Last Name : Tanner
                         Enter date in format MM/DD/YY : 02/02/87
                         Enter Last Name : Wells
Fig. 7-13. (cont.)   Enter date in format MM/DD/YY : 03/03/87
                         Enter Last Name : Gagne
                         Enter date in format MM/DD/YY : 04/04/87
                         Enter Last Name : Kalish
                         Enter date in format MM/DD/YY : 05/05/87

                          Names and Birthday

                          Bloom   1/1/87
                          Tanner   2/2/87
                          Wells   3/3/87
                          Gagne   4/4/87
                          Kalish   5/5/87

The program in Fig. 7-13 is a rewording of the array program shown in Fig. 6-9, and is explained in Chapter 6. When reviewing this figure, take special note as to how the structure's array locations are referenced. For example, the month variable is referenced as (date__pointer + count)- >month. This format encloses the pointer name and offset, date__pointer and count respectively, within the parentheses to assure that the compiler correctly understands the order of operations. This is followed by the – > operator and the structure variable being referenced.

8

Functions

Thus far, functions have been used and manipulated as needed to illustrate other topics, but as promised within those illustrations, functions will now be discussed in length.

A function is nothing more than a label which allows a defined list of statements to be grouped under a common name, thus allowing these statements to be executed simply by referencing the specified label. To illustrate this process, let's once again turn to our first C program re-listed below.

```
Main()
{ Printf("Hello There");
}
```

Fig. 8-1.

This program brings forward some key points that have not as of yet been discussed. First, note that the program begins with the word "main" followed by a set of empty parentheses. This combination, namely main(), states that the lines listed below it within the brackets, are part of a function called main. The parentheses are used to pass data values called parameters from function to function. Even when there is no data to be passed, as is the case with main(), the parentheses are still required.

All C programs are, or should be, divided into these functions which are executed when their name is referenced within other functions. This referencing concept can be seen by reviewing the way in which the "printf( )" function was executed in Fig. 8-1.

This process of executing functions within other functions however, causes the small problem of which function should be executed first. Therefore, to alleviate this problem, C requires all programs to have a function called main( ), and by default, this function is automatically executed first.

CALLING FUNCTIONS

Now let's turn our attention to the printf() function call in main() of Fig. 8-1. When reviewing this function call, there are three points that should be noted. First, note that quotation marks are used to specify which characters are to be printed to the terminal. Second, note that like main(), printf() is followed by opening and closing parentheses. These parentheses contain the string to be passed from main() to printf(). Lastly, the printf() function call ends with a semicolon. This semicolon is not part of the function call. It is just a statement terminator like that at the end of all C statements. As shall be seen in Figs. 8-2 through 8-4, functions are often called within statements, mathematical formulas and even within other functions. In these cases, the semicolon is placed at the end of the line and not at the end of the function call.

The figure below illustrates how functions can be called from within C statements.

```
Program :  main()
           { static char a_string[] = {"Hello there"};
             static char b_string[] = {"Hello there"};

             if ( strcmp(a_string, b_string) == 0 )
                 printf("\n The two strings are equal");
             else
                 printf("\n The two strings are not equal");
           }
```

Fig. 8-2.

```
Program Output :  The two strings are equal
```

The program above employs the strcmp() function which compares the equality of character strings. (This function is discussed in length within Chapter 5.) Note that this function is called from within an if statement. When this technique is used, the value returned by the function and not the function itself, is used by the if statement. For example, in Fig. 8-2, character strings a__string and b__string are compared. Since they have equal values, strcmp() returns a zero (stating equality). It is this zero that is used for comparison in the if statement.

The following illustrates how a function may be called from within a mathematical formula.

```
Program :  #include "c:\lc\math.h"

           main()
           { double x;
             double y;
             double z;

             x = 9.0;
             y = 10.0;

             z = sqrt(x) + y;

             printf("\n The value is %4.2f",z);
           }
```

Fig. 8-3.

```
Program Output :  The value is 13.00
```

The program defines the variables x, y, and z. Once defined, the variable x is set to a value of 9, y is set to a value of 10, and z is set equal to the square of x plus the value of y. This program has three noteworthy points. First, note the presence of the #include statement. This statement is called a compiler directive and is discussed fully in Chapter 11. For now, however, just consider it to be a requirement of the square root function. Second, note that x and y were set to the values 9.0 and 10.0, not 9 and 10. This is floating point format and not an an integer. Remember, C is very particular in regard to the format of data variable values. Without the .0, the 9 and 10 would be construed as integers and would be incorrectly placed in "x" and "y". Lastly, and most important to this discussion, the formula uses the square root value within the assignment of z.

As previously mentioned, functions may be called from within functions. This process is illustrated below.

```
Program :  main()
           { static char a_string[] = {"Hello there"};

             printf("\n a_string is %d characters long",strlen(a_string) );
           }
```

Program Output : a_string is 11 characters long   Fig. 8-4.

As in Figs. 8-2 and 8-3, when a function is called from within a function, the return value of the inner function is used by the outer function. For example, in Fig. 8-4, the strlen() function is called from within a printf() function. The strlen() function calculates the number of characters in a character string and returns that calculated value. The printf() function then displays this returned value on the screen as shown in the program's output.

PASSING AND RECEIVING PARAMETERS

Thus far, we have discussed how values are passed to functions. Now let's discuss how the functions being called deal with these passed values. A simple example of this process is shown below.

```
Program :   main()
            { int x;

              x = 3;

              square(x);
            }
            square(a)
            int a;
            { int b;
              b = a * a;
              printf("\n The square of %d is %d", a, b);
            }
```

Fig. 8-5.

Program Output : The square of 3 is 9

104

The program listed in Fig. 8-5, defines and calls a function named square( ), which calculates and prints the square of a number. When reviewing this function, note the way in which variables a and b are defined. In particular, note that a is defined before the function's open bracket and that b is defined after the opening bracket. This placement states that a is a variable into which a parameter is passed. The variable b on the other hand, is called an automatic variable and instructs the compiler that b will only be used within the function. Now, let's modify our program to multiply two numbers together and print the calculated value. This modified program is shown below.

Program :

```
main()
{ int x;
  int y;

  x = 2;
  y = 3;

  times(x,y);
}

times(a,b)
int a;
int b;
{ int c;
  c = a * b;
  printf("\n The product of %d times %d is %d", a, b, c);
}
```

Fig 8-6.

Program Output : The product of 2 and 3 is 6

The program in Fig. 8-6 defines and calls the times( ) function. This function accepts two integer parameters, multiplies them together and prints the total. As shown in the program, each passed parameter has a variable into which it can be placed. Also, note that these parameters are passed positionally, this meaning, that the first passed parameter is placed in the first listed, the second parameter is placed in the second variable, and so on. In the case of the times( ) function in Fig. 8-6 for example, the value of x will be passed into variable a and the value of y is placed in variable b.

This concept of positionally passed values has one additional component. This component is the consistency of the data types of the values being passed. For example, in Fig. 8-6, both x and a are defined as integers. This data type consistency is required. Without it, the called function would not know the format of the incoming data, and could not interpret it correctly. Figure 8-7 further illustrates this concept of data type consistency.

Program :
```
main()
{ int    an_int;
  double a_double;
  long   a_long_int;
  char   a_char;
```

Fig. 8-7.

```
                an_int = 1;
                a_double = 2;
                a_long_int = 3;
                a_char = 'A';

                dummy(an_int, a_double, a_long_int, a_char);
        }

        dummy(a, b, c, d)
          int a;
          double b;
          long c;
          char d;
        {
          printf("\n The integer   is %d", a);
          printf("\n The double    is %f", b);
          printf("\n The long      is %ld", c);
          printf("\n The character is %c", d);
        }
```

Fig. 8-7. (cont.)

```
Program Output :   The integer   is 1
                   The double    is 2
                   The long      is 3
                   The character is A
```

RETURN VALUES

Figure 8-8 is a modification of the program in Fig. 8-6. This modification moved the printf( ) function out of times( ) and placed it in main( ). Also, it placed a return statement in the times( ) function. This statement will pass the value contained within it, namely c, back to the equation where times( ) was called. This process will instruct the compiler to give the times( ) function the variable-like property of containing a value. This value will be the value of the variable in the return statement.

```
Program :   main()
            { int x;
              int y;
              int z;

              x = 2;
              y = 3;

              z = times(x,y);
              printf("\n The product of %d times %d is %d", x, y, z);
            }

            int times(a,b)
              int a;
              int b;
            { int c;
              c = a * b;
              return (c);
            }
```

Program Output : The product of 2 times 3 is 6   **Fig. 8-8.**

For example, in Fig. 8-6, both x and a are defined as integers. This data type consistency is required. Without it, the called function would not know the format of the incoming data, and could not interpret it correctly. Figure 8-7 further illustrates this concept of data type consistency.

Now that we have discussed the process of returning values from a function, there is an additional type of required data consistency. This requirement is between the data type of the value in the "return" statement and the data type of the function. This consistency is illustrated in Fig. 8-9.

```
Program :  main()
           { int x;
             double y;
             double square();

             x = 4.0;

             y = square(x);
             printf("\n The square of %d is %4.2f", x, y);
           }

           double square(a)
            int a;
           { double b;
             b = a * a;
             return(b);
           }
```

Program Output : The square of 4 is 16.00

There are two types of consistency being employed in Fig. 8-9. The first was previously discussed and deals with the passing of parameters. Note that the value being passed, namely x, and the variable into which x will be received, namely a, are both defined as integers. The second data consistency involves the process used to return a value from the called function. This consistency is in four areas, two being within the calling function and two being within the function being called. Within the calling function, namely main(), there are two double data type definitions. The first (double y), defines the data type of the variable that will be receiving the returned value of the square() function. The second double statement states that the function square will be returning a value defined as a double. Turning to the square() function itself, note that the name is prefixed by the data type that it shall return, and lastly, in the statement double b, b is being defined as a double. The variable b is referenced in the return statement.

Figure 8-10 further illustrates this required return value data type consistency.

```
Program :  main()
           { int a;

             double d;
             double dbl_function();

             int i;
             int int_function();
```

```
        a = 5;

        d = dbl_function(a);
        printf("\n The double function returned a %f", d);

        i = int_function(a);
        printf("\n The double function returned a %d", i);
    }

    double dbl_function(x)
     int x;
    { double y;
      y = x * 3.14;
      return(y);
    }

    int int_function(x)
     int x;
    { int y;
      y = x * 3.14;
      return(y);
    }
```

Fig. 8-10. (cont.)

Program Output :   The double function returned a 15.7000000
                    The double function returned a 15

PASSING ARRAYS

Like regular variables, arrays may also be passed to a function. This array passing, however, is different from that done with regular variables. With regular variables, the value of the specified variable is passed, with arrays, the address of the first array memory location is passed, namely, an array pointer. Once passed to the function, you may manipulate that array using either array or pointer notation. As a first example of this process, Fig. 8-11 passes a character array to the function length(). This function is similar to the strlen() function supplied on most compilers and illustrates how to receive an array pointer in a way that facilitates the use of standard array notation.

```
Program : main()
        { static char a_string[15] = {"Hi There"};
          int the_len;

          the_len = length(a_string);
          printf("\n The length of a_string is %d",the_len);
        }

        int length(s1)
         char s1[];
        { int x = 0;
          while ( s1[x] )
          ++x;
          return(x);
        } ,
```

Program Output : The length of a_string is 8

Fig. 8-11.

The program listed in Fig. 8-11 is discussed at length in Chapter 5, but briefly, it counts the number of characters in a character array by searching for its ending string terminator. In this program, the starting address of the a_string character array is passed to length( ) in the statement the_len = length(a_string). Remember, as discussed in Chapter 7, when an array's name is used without a suffixed [ ], the name is considered a pointer to the array's first location. Within the called function length( ), an array named s1[ ] is positioned to receive the pointer and establish the array within the function. Once defined, it may be used like any other array. One note of caution, however. Because the array address was passed, and not the array values, you are accessing the same memory area as the original array, and therefore, any changes that are made to the passed array are permanently changed in the original array.

Figure 8-12, shown below, performs the same task as that discussed in Fig. 8-11, except that length( ) is using pointer instead of array notation.

Program :
```
main()
{ static char a_string[15] = {"Hi There"};
  int the_len;

  the_len = length(a_string);
  printf("\n The length of a_string is %d",the_len);
}
```

Fig. 8-12.
```
int length(s1)
 char *s1;
{ int x = 0;
  while ( *s1++ )
  ++x;
  return(x);
}
```

Program Output : `The length of a_string is 8`

In Fig. 8-12 the process used to call functions is identical with that used in Fig. 8-11. The difference is completely within the length( ) function. Note that within length( ), the pointer received from a_string[ ] is placed in a character pointer defined as char *s1. Once defined as a pointer, the array may be manipulated using pointer notation.

If you wish, you may define the incoming pointer as an array for documentation purposes, then pass the array address to a pointer and use pointer notation. This notation combination is shown below.

Program :
```
main()
{ static char a_string[15] = {"Hi There"};
  int the_len;

  the_len = length(a_string);
  printf("\n The length of a_string is %d",the_len);
}
```

Fig. 8-13.
```
int length(s1)
 char s1[];
{ char *s_point;
  int x = 0;
```

```
            s_point = s1;
            while ( *s_point++ )
            ++x;
            return(x);
        }
```

Fig. 8-13. (cont.)

Program Output : The length of a_string is 8

GLOBAL VARIABLES

There are times when it is necessary to reference the same variable from within many functions. A classic case of this need is the line counter in a report program. These variables are known as global variables and are defined by placing the variable's definition before the main() function. An example of this can be seen below.

Program :
```
int line_count = 0;

main()
{ print1();
  print2();
  print3();
  print4();
  print5();
}

print1()
{ line_count++;
  printf("\n This is print1, line_count is %d",line_count);
}

print2()
{ line_count++;
  printf("\n This is print2, line_count is %d",line_count);
}

print3()
{ line_count++;
  printf("\n This is print3, line_count is %d",line_count);
}

print4()
{ line_count++;
  printf("\n This is print4, line_count is %d",line_count);
}

print5()
{ line_count++;
  printf("\n This is print5, line_count is %d",line_count);
}
```

Program Output : This is print1, line_count is 1
            This is print2, line_count is 2
            This is print3, line_count is 3
            This is print4, line_count is 4
            This is print5, line_count is 5

Fig. 8-14.

In Fig. 8-14 the integer variable line__count is defined prior to the beginning of the main() function. This simple action of not placing a variable within a particular function makes it usable by all functions. To illustrate this point, main() calls five functions, each of which increments line__count and prints its value on the screen. As you can see, line__count is not defined within any of these functions and keeps its value as it moves from function to function.

AUTOMATIC AND STATIC VARIABLES

By a quick review of the programming examples in this and other chapters, you will see that some variable definitions begin with the word static and some do not. Those variables defined by using the static statement are called static variables. Variables defined without the static statement are considered to be automatic variables. Automatic variables may be defined by prefixing the data definition with the word "auto". However, because auto is the default, you do not have to specify it in that way.

During program execution, automatic variables are created and allocated memory when the function in which they reside is executed. When the function is terminated, the memory associated with these variables is released. Hence, in a manner of speaking, the variables disappear. This automatic creation and deletion of variables facilitates an efficient use of memory because only the variables currently in use require space. The drawbacks of this process are that the variables must be created and initialized each time its function is called, and additionally, because the variable is being recreated, it loses its prior value.

Static variables are not created and deleted along with their host functions. If a variable is defined as static, its memory space is allocated and initialized when the program begins, and remains in memory until the program terminates. The advantage of this approach is that since the memory space associated with the variable is not lost, when the function is called a second time, the variable's value from the prior execution is still present. The major drawbacks of static variables are that they take up memory space for the entire execution of the program and their values are only reinitialized once. Therefore, if the first execution of the function modifies its value, the second execution of that function will begin with modified data.

Figure 8-15 illustrates the difference between these two variable types. Variable stat__var, a static variable, held its value from execution to execution. auto__var, an automatic variable, was continually reinitialized.

Fig. 8-15.

```
Program :   main()
            { int count;
              for (count = 0; count < 5; count++)
                { printf("\n\n Loop %d",count);
                  loop_function();
                }
            }

            loop_function()
            { static int stat_var = 0;
              int auto_var = 0;

              stat_var++;
              auto_var++;
```

```
            printf("\n     The stat_var variable = %d",stat_var);
            printf("\n     The auto_var variable = %d",auto_var);
        }
```

Program Output :   Loop 0
                       The stat_var variable = 1
                       The auto_var variable = 1

                   Loop 1
                       The stat_var variable = 2
                       The auto_var variable = 1

Fig. 8-15.   (cont.)

                   Loop 2
                       The stat_var variable = 3
                       The auto_var variable = 1

                   Loop 3
                       The stat_var variable = 4
                       The auto_var variable = 1

                   Loop 4
                       The stat_var variable = 5
                       The auto_var variable = 1

PARAMETER PASSING BY VALUE AND ADDRESS

All data that is passed from one function to another is passed in one of two ways, by value or by address. When a parameter is passed by value, the actual value of the variable is sent. When a parameter is passed by address, a pointer is passed stating where in memory the needed value can be found. The process and implications of these two different methods is shown below.

Program :   main()
```
        { int a_variable;
          int *a_pointer;
          int b_variable;

          a_variable = 10;
          b_variable = 10;
          a_pointer = &a_variable;

          dummy(a_pointer, b_variable);
```

Fig. 8-16.

```
          printf("\n A_variable has a value of %d",a_variable);
          printf("\n B_variable has a value of %d",b_variable);
        }

        dummy(a_point, b_var)
         int *a_point;
         int b_var;
        { *a_point = 5;
          b_var = 5;
        }
```

Fig. 8-16. (cont.)

Program Output : `A_variable has a value of 5`
`B_variable has a value of 10`

As shown in Fig. 8-16, two parameters are being passed to the function called dummy( ). The first is a pointer and the second is a regular variable. When a regular variable is passed, C automatically sets up a memory location for the received value in the format specified in the parameter definition. Therefore, since this received value resides in its own memory location, changes to this value do not affect the original variable. When a pointer is passed, as is the case with a_pointer, the called function accesses the variable using the same memory locations as the original pointer. Therefore, changes made to a variable within the called function permanently effect the value of the variable in the calling function.

9

Input and Output

All of the programs that have been discussed in prior chapters received their input from the keyboard, via the scanf( ) function, and displayed their output on the screen using printf( ). These abilities are fine for some software projects. However, most applications require the additional ability of accessing and manipulating data stored on floppy disks or other storage media. As you may expect, C provides this ability. However, unlike most other programming languages, C does not contain any input/output statements like read, write, input, print or display. All I/O is performed by calling functions similar to scanf( ) and printf( ) that are supplied by the compiler manufacturer.

Let's begin our discussion of program input and output by analyzing the functions that we are most familiar with, scanf( ) and printf( ).

THE printf( ) FUNCTION

The printf( ) function is used to display text and variable values on the screen or other specified output device. The format of this function is shown below.

```
printf(print-mask, varaible-list)
```

Fig. 9-1.

The printf( ) function is divided into three parts; the word "printf", the print mask, and if applicable, the list of variables to be printed. The print mask is an intertwined combination of the text that will be printed as shown in the mask and variable definition types. As shall soon be seen, these definition types are used to specify the data type of the variable being printed, as well as their location within the surrounding text. The variable list is the list of variables to be printed in accordance with the variable definition types in the print mask. Figure 9-2 is an example of the printf( ) function.

Fig. 9-2.

```
Program :  main()
           { int x = 5;
             printf("\n The variable x has a value of %d",x);
           }
```

Program Output : The variable x has a value of 5

The program in Fig. 9-2 brings forth many key points about the printf( ) function, namely, the \n, %d, the text within the double quotes, and the x variable placed after the closing quote and comma. The \n is called an escape sequence and causes the text following it to begin on a new line. Figure 9-3 further illustrates this process.

```
Program :  main()
           { printf("\n x \n xx \n xxx \n xxxx \n xxxxx");
           }
```

Fig. 9-3.

```
Program Output :    *
                    **
                    ***
                    ****
                    *****
```

As can be seen when reviewing the program output in Fig. 9-3, each time a \n was encountered, the X's began printing on a new line. Without the \n values, the X's would just print horizontally on one line. The \n is not the only escape sequence option. Other additional options are shown in the table below.

Type	Sequence
Backslash	\ \
Backspace	\ b
Bit pattern	\ ddd
Carriage return	\ r
Form feed	\ f
Horizontal tab	\ t
New line	\ n
Single quote	\ '

Table 9-1.

Figure 9-4 illustrates the use of other selected escape sequence characters.

Fig. 9-4.

```
Program :  main()
           { printf("\n tab \t tab \t tab \t tab");
             printf("\n backslash \\ backslash \\ backslash");
             printf("\n quote \' quote \' quote \'");
           }
```

```
Program Output :   tab      tab       tab        tab
                   backslash \ backslash \ backslash
                   quote ' quote ' qoute
```

Looking back to Fig. 9-2, the %d is called a data type identifier. This identifier serves two purposes. First, it identifies the data type of its associated variable. Second, it states where that variable's values should be printed. Figure 9-5 further illustrates this concept.

Fig. 9-5.

Program :

```
main()
{ int    i = 1;
  float  f = 2.0;
  char   c = 'A';

  printf("\nThe integer is %d, float is %f, character is %c",i,f,c);
}
```

Program Output : `The integer is 1, float is 2.0000000, character is A`

In Fig. 9-5, three variables are defined: i as an integer, f as a floating point and c as a character. When reviewing this program, take special note that these variables were printed in the order that they were listed within the function. Also, the data type identifiers within the print mask are placed in the same order as the variable list. As you can see, %d is used for integers, %f is used for floating points, and %c is used for characters. A complete list of these symbols can be found in the table below.

Character	Purpose
c	Prints the value of a character
d	Prints the decimal value of an integer number
e	Prints a number in an exponential notation format
f	Prints a floating point number in floating point format
g	Prints a floating point number in either 'e' or 'f' format based on the number being printed
o	Prints the octal value of an integer number
u	Prints the value of an unsigned integer
x	Prints the hexadecimal value of an integer number

Table 9-2.

THE scanf( ) FUNCTION

The scanf( ) function is used to input data from the keyboard or other specified input device and place this entered value in the appropriate variable or variables. The format of this function is shown below.

`scanf(input_control_list, variable_list)`

Fig. 9-6.

The scanf( ) function is divided into three primary parts: the word "scanf", the input control list, and the variable list. The control list contains the data type identifiers associated with the variables being read. The variable list contains the list of these variables. Figure 9-7 provides an example of this function.

The program listed in Fig. 9-7 asks the user to input a date, and then prints that date back to the screen. The display to the user is done by the printf( ) function that has already been discussed, and the date input was done via a scanf( ). The input control list in the scanf( ), namely %d/%d/%d, states that three integer values will be entered as specified by the three %d clauses. The slashes between the %d clauses further state that the entered numbers will be delimited by backslashes. The variable list after the control list defines the memory address of the variables into which these integer values should be placed. Remember from Chapter 8 that integers are passed by value, and therefore their original values cannot be modified. Thus, by placing an ampersand before the variable, you are passing the variable's memory address to scanf() and not its value. Once it has this address, scanf() can then modify the variable's value by setting it equal to the value entered from the keyboard.

Program :

```
main()
{ int year;
  int month;
  int day;

  printf("\n Enter the date in the format MM/DD/YY : ");
  scanf("%d/%d/%d",&month, &day, &year);

  printf("\n Date is %d:%d:%d",month,day,year);
}
```

Fig. 9-7.

Program Output :

```
Enter the date in the format MM/DD/YY : 12/23/87

Date is 12/23/87
```

Like the printf() function, scanf() must specify the data type of the variables being entered. These data types are specified using the same % identifiers as printf() and are listed in Table 9-2.

When defining the input control list, you should take special notice as to where you place spaces, dashes, and other characters. These non-data-type identifiers are construed as field delimiters by some compilers and can produce unexpected results. In all cases however, a space is considered a delimiter. For example, in Fig. 9-8, last name and first name end up in different variables because they were entered with a space between them.

Program :

```
main()
{ int age;
  char f_name[10];
  char l_name[10];

  printf("\n   Enter name : ");
  scanf("%s %s",f_name, l_name);
  printf("\n   Your first name is %s",f_name);
  printf("\n   Your last age is   %s",l_name);
}
```

Fig. 9-8.

Program Output :

```
Enter Name : Eric Bloom

Your first name is Eric
Your last name is  Bloom
```

Thus far, all of the programs that have been discussed in this and prior chapters have used the scanf() function for input and the printf() function for output. These functions, as we have learned, facilitate the input and output of integers, strings, and other data types. They are not, however, the only input option. There is another class of less sophisticated functions that receives or sends one character of data at a time, thus allowing you the ability to write your own input and output routines and have full control over your input and output procedures. These functions are getch(), which gets a character from the keyboard or other designated input device, and putch(), which puts (or writes) a single character on the screen.

THE putch() FUNCTION

The putch() function is used to output a character to the screen. The format of this function is shown below.

```
putch ( integer-value )
```

Fig. 9-9.

This function consists of two parts: the word "putch" and the integer variable or integer constant containing the ASCII value of the character to be printed. Examples of this process are shown below.

```
Program :  main()
           { int x;
             x = 65;

             putch(x);
             putch(66);
           }
```

Fig. 9-10.

Program Output : AB

The program listed in Fig. 9-10 contains two putch() functions. The first prints the letter "A", which has an ASCII value of 65, and illustrates how a variable can be used to specify the character being output. The second putch() function illustrates how an integer constant can be passed, causing the letter "B" to print.

```
Program :  main()
           { char a_char;
             a_char = 'Y';

             putch(a_char);
             putch('Z');
           }
```

Fig. 9-11.

Program Output : YZ

Figure 9-11 above shows a trick that can be used to print character values on the screen. To understand this trick, you must understand that integers and characters are treated very similarly by C. In fact, characters are stored in memory as numbers.

These numbers are the ASCII value associated with the character being stored. Therefore, as seen in Fig. 9-11, you may pass character values to the putch( ) function and it will work correctly. A word of caution however, when using this technique. Read your compiler's documentation to be sure that characters and integers are stored in identical formats.

In Fig. 9-11, the first putch( ) function call prints the value "Y" as specified by a_char. The second putch( ) function prints the letter "Z" as specified by the character constant passed as a parameter.

Now that we have seen the putch( ) function work on the output of individual characters, let's employ it to print the character string as shown below.

Program :
```
main()
{ static char a_string[] = {"Hello there "};
  char *a_pointer;

  a_pointer = a_string;

  while ( *a_pointer )
   { putch(*a_pointer++);
   }
}
```

Program Output : Hello There

In Fig. 9-12, the putch( ) function is placed within a loop. This loop causes putch( ) to continue to execute until the null indicator at the end of a_string is reached. Remember—the + + in *a_pointer + + is performing pointer arithmetic, thus moving the pointer to the next memory location after the current value is printed.

THE getch( ) FUNCTION

The getch( ) function is used to get a single character from the keyboard and place the ASCII value associated with that character into an integer variable. The format of this function is shown below.

Fig. 9-13.

```
                        int-varaible = getch();
```

The getch( ) function is extremely simple in format. In fact, it just consists of the function name, preceded by the variable into which the retrieved character should be placed. Figure 9-14 below provides a first example of this function.

Program :
```
main()
{ int an_int;

  an_int = getch();
  putch( an_int);
}
```
Fig. 9-14.

Program Output : A

119

The program in Fig. 9-14 defines an__int as an integer variable, gets a character from the keyboard via the getch( ) function, and then prints that character on the screen by use of putch( ). Note that when reviewing the output of this program, there is only one character printed. This is caused because the getch( ) function only reads a character from the keyboard, and does not automatically echo that character to the screen. Therefore, the putch( ) function is needed to allow the user to view the entered keystrokes. Figure 9-15 expands on this procedure and illustrates how an entire character string can be entered using these two single character functions.

```
Program :   main()
            { char a_string[20];
              char *a_pointer;

              a_pointer = &a_string;

              do
                { *a_pointer = getch();
                  putch(*a_pointer);
                } while ( *a_pointer++ != '\15' );

              a_pointer--;
              *a_pointer = '\0';

              printf("\n\n a_string = %s", a_string);
            }

Program Output :  Hello There

                  a_string = Hello There
```

Fig. 9-15.

In Fig. 9-15, the getch( ) statement is placed within a do/while loop. This loop will continue to execute until the carriage return key (\ 15) is hit. At this time, one is subtracted from the pointer in the statement a__pointer− −; and the \ 15 is replaced with a null \ 0. Lastly, a printf( ) function is called just to illustrate that the input process worked correctly.

DATA REDIRECTION

The MS-DOS environment has two processes that allow you to redirect a program's input and output from the keyboard and screen defaults to other specified programs and devices. These processes are called piping and filtering. Piping lets you read or write data to or from a file without changing the program. Filtering allows you to specify that the output from program should be used as the input of another program.

Piping

If you wish to write the output of your program to a data file, attached printer, or other appropriate device, you may do so by placing a greater-than sign (>) after the program name whose output is being redirected, and following that sign by the device or file name that is to receive the data. Table 9-3 lists and explains various piping alternatives.

Table 9-3.

Command	Effect
dir > xyz	Writes a directory to file xyz
file1 > prog1	Uses file1 as input to program prog1
file1 < sort > file2	Sorts file1 and places the output in file2

Filtering

Filtering is the process of using the output of one program as the input of another program. This process is performed by placing a | symbol between the two programs being employed. Table 9-4 lists and explains various filtering examples.

Command	Effect
dir ¦ sort	Prints a directory in sorted order
prog1 ¦ prog2	Uses prog1 as input to program prog2
dir ¦ sort > file1	Writes a sorted directory to file file1

Table 9-4.

SPECIAL FILE HANDLING COMMANDS

There are many applications which require the ability to read, write, and manipulate data files in ways that can not be easily handled using piping techniques. As a result, virtually all C compilers come equipped with predefined functions to facilitate data manipulation.

The fopen( ) Function

When attempting to manipulate data within a file, you must first tell the program what file is to be accessed and the type of processing that will be performed on that file. This information is provided by the fopen( ) function. The format of this function is shown below.

Fig. 9-16.

```
file-pointer = fopen(file-name, file-mode )
```

This function is divided into four parts, the word "fopen", standing for file open, the name of the file to be opened, the mode of the file (read, write, append, etc.), and the pointer variable that will be used to identify the file in all file related procedures. An example of this function is shown below.

Fig. 9-17.

```
#include "stdio.h"
FILE *input_file, *fopen();
*input_file = fopen("infile.dat,"r");
    • • •
    • • •
fclose(input_file);
```

The partial program listed in Fig. 9-17 consists of four lines: the #include statement, FILE statement, fopen( ) function, and fclose( ) function. The #include statement is a compiler directive (discussed in Chapter 11) which causes the file stdio.h to be included in your compiled program. This file contains all the standard input and output definitions needed to access files. The file stdio.h is called a header file and is also discussed in Chapter 11. The FILE statement is defined within this stdio.h file and is used to declare the file pointer's data type and the date type of the fopen( ) function's return value. The fopen( ) function actually opens the file, sets up the internal file data buffers, and returns a pointer stating where the file information and buffers can be found. This returned pointer value is then placed in the file variable input__file. Lastly, the fclose( ) function is used to close the file which has previously been opened.

The fgets( ) Function

The fgets( ) function is used to retrieve information from an open file and place the retrieved data in a specified variable. The format of this function is shown in Fig. 9-18.

$$fgets(\ string,\ size,\ file\text{-}pointer\ )$$

Fig. 9-18.

The fgets( ) function is divided into four parts, the word "fgets", the name of the character string array that will be receiving the data, the number of characters to be retrieved and the file pointer identifying which file should be read. The use of this function is illustrated in Fig. 9-19. As can be seen, this program reads a file named data9.dat and prints the retrieved data on the screen.

The fgets( ) function in Fig. 9-19 is instructing the compiler to read 10 characters from the file associated with file pointer input__file, and place the retrieved characters in the character string a__string.

```
Program :  #include "c:\lc\stdio.h"

           main()
           { FILE *input_file, *fopen();
             char a_string[11];

             input_file = fopen("data9.dat","r");

             while ( fgets(a_string, 11, input_file) != NULL )
                 printf("\ndata is ==> %s",a_string);

             close(input_file);

           }
```

Fig. 9-19.

```
Program Output :  1234567890
                  abcdefghij
                  klmnopqrst
```

The fputs( ) Function

The fputs( ) function is used to place data in a file. The format of this function is shown below.

$$fputf(\ string,\ file\text{-}pointer\ )$$

Fig. 9-20.

The fputf() function is divided into three parts, the word "fputf", the name of the variable string to be printed and the pointer value associated with the file being written. Figure 9-21 lists a program that illustrates the use of this function. This listed program receives input from the screen via a scanf() function and writes the entered data in a file.

```
Program :    #include "c:\lc\stdio.h"

             main()
             { FILE *output_file, *fopen();
               char a_string[11];

               output_file = fopen("data9.dat","w");

               printf("\n Enter name : ");
               scanf("%s",a_string);
               while ( strcmp(a_string,"end") != 0 )
                 { fputs(a_string, output_file);
                   printf("\n Enter name : ");
                   scanf("%s",a_string);
                 }
               close(output_file);
             }

Program Output :   Enter name : Bloom
                   Enter name : Tanner
                   Enter name : Wells
                   Enter name : Gagne
                   Enter name : Kalish
```

The fscanf() and fprintf() Functions

The fscanf() and printf() file manipulation functions are very similar to their keyboard and screen counterparts, except that fscanf() and fprintf() receive and send their data to and from a specified data file. Examples of these functions can be found below.

```
fprintf(out_file, "Hello There ");
fprintf(out_file, "The answer is %d", x);
fprintf(out_file, "%f plus %f is %f", x, y, z);

fscanf(in_file,"%s",a_string);
fscanf(in_file,"%f%s",a_float, a_string);
```

The fgetc() and fputc() Functions

The fgetc() and fputc() file functions are also very similar to their interactive partners, namely getch() and putch(). The difference is that fgetc() and fputc() require an additional parameter that specifies the file that should be accessed. As with all file manipulation functions, the file being referenced by this pointer must be opened in an appropriate file mode using the fopen() function. For example, a fputc() function call, which writes a character to a file, can not be used on a file that was opened for read only access. Examples of this functions are given below.

```
fgets(a_string, 7, file_pointer);
fgets(b_string, 4, in_file);

fputs(a_string, file_pointer );
fputs(b_string, file_pointer );
```

Fig. 9-23.

The fclose() Function

Once you have finished the processing of a particular file, that file should be closed by calling the fclose() function. This function consists of the word "fclose", followed by the file pointer associated with the file to be closed. An example of this function can be seen below.

```
fclose(input_file);
```

Fig. 9-24.

If by chance you forget to close your files, they will be automatically be closed when the program terminates. This automatic file closing process will work, but is considered to be a poor programming practice.

The stdin, stdout, and stderr File Channels

When a C program is executed, three file channels are automatically opened. These files are stdin, stdout, and stderr. First, stdin is the standard input file which defaults to the keyboard. Second, stdout is the standard output channel which defaults to the screen. Lastly, stderr is the standard error message area and is where most of the error messages are printed. This third file is also sent to the screen.

It is this concept of standard input and standard output that facilitates the use of the piping and filtering techniques previously discussed. In fact, because stdin and stdout are considered files, you may use any of your file manipulation functions like fscanf() and fputc() to perform keyboard input or screen output simply by using the words "stdin" and "stdout" as your file pointer. Examples of this process are shown below.

```
fprintf(stdout, "Hello There ");
fprintf(stdout, "The answer is %d", x);
fprintf(stdout "%f plus %f is %f", x, y, z);

fscanf(stdin, "%s",a_string);
fscanf(stdin, "%f%s",a_float, a_string);
```

Fig. 9-25.

SPECIAL IBM PC INPUTS AND OUTPUTS

One advantage of writing software for a particular computer or class of computers is that you can capitalize on the particular attributes of the machine being used. In particular, we will be discussing screen formatting, the input of function keys and printer commands.

Formatting Screen Outputs

Screen attributes like reverse video, screen brightness, and background color, as well as cursor placement and screen clearing, can be controlled in two ways. The first way is by using assembly language subroutines to access and modify the area in memory that stores screen information. This method is very complicated and is outside the scope of this book. The second method can be performed using the printf( ) function to pass special video control commands to the screen. In fact, Chapter 22 of this book provides ready-to-use functions for performing this process. To explain this procedure, let's examine the clear screen function shown below.

Fig. 9-26.

```
e_screen()
{ printf("%c"[2J", '\33');
}
```

The printf( ) function in Fig. 9-26 sends a stream of characters to the screen. Note, that the first character of this stream is a \33, and is defined as a character (c) in the print mask. This \33, is the octal ASCII value for the escape key. This escape character informs the screen that the characters which follow are screen instructions and should not be printed on the screen. The characters which follow the escape character are [2J which together form the screen clear command. Then, once the command is completed, the screen automatically reverts back to character printing mode. For a list of additional screen command strings, refer to Chapter 22.

Printer Output

Like video screens, most PC printers can receive and interpret commands from your program by sending escape sequences similar to those discussed for screens. This process is illustrated below.

Fig. 9-27.

```
ds_off()
{ FILE *prn_file, *fopen();
  prn_file = fopen("prn","w");
  fprintf(prn_file,"%cH", '\033');
  fclose(prn_file);
}
```

The function shown in Fig. 9-27 is designed for an EPSON FX100 printer and is using an escape sequence command that instructs the printer to turn off double strike printing mode, which presumably has been previously turned on. When reviewing this function, note that an fopen( ) function is being employed to open a file called prn. This file name is a key word, and stands for the printer port on the back of your PC. Therefore, when you send the escape sequence via an fprintf( ) function call to the file, you are actually sending it out the printer port to the printer. As an additional note, you may also use this printer/file technique to send text and graphical data to your printer. Lastly, like all opened files, you should call an fclose( ) function to close the file when you are done printing.

Figure 9-28 shows the printer command stream that is used to set an EPSON FX100 printer into compressed printing mode. Note that in this case, however, an escape character is not used, just the octal value 22. Printers, unlike screens, often have some commands that do not contain escape characters. This can be done, as long as the first character in the command sequence is not a printable character.

```
comp_off()
{ FILE *prn_file, *fopen();
  prn_file = fopen("prn","w");
  fprintf(prn_file,"%c", '\022');
  fclose(prn_file);
}
```

Fig. 9-28.

One note of caution when using these printer command strings. Each printer manufacturer uses its own set of escape command strings. Therefore, refer to your printer's reference manual for the correct command formats.

Lastly, the two printer functions just discussed, as well as many others, can be found in Chapter 16.

Function Key Input

When you press a function key on your PC keyboard, you are causing two characters to be sent to your program. The first character is a null \0, which signifies that a function key or other special key was hit. The second character specifies which key was entered. Table 9-5 lists the function keys and their associated transmitted characters. As you can see when reviewing this list, that the alt keys and arrow keys also employ this two part character code.

Second ASCII code	Key
3	Null
15	Shift tab
16-25	Alt - Q,W,E,R,T,Y,U,I,O,P
30-38	Alt - A,S,D,F,G,H,J,K,L
44-50	Alt - Z,X,C,V,B,N,M
59-68	F1 - F10
71	Home
72	Cursor up
73	Pg Up
75	Cursor left
77	Cursor right
79	End
80	Cursor down
81	Pg Dn
82	Ins
83	Del
84-93	Shift F1 - F10
94-103	Ctrl F1 - F10
104-113	Alt F1 - F10
114	Ctrl - PrtSc
115	Previous Word
116	Next word
117	Ctrl - end
118	Ctrl - PgDn
119	Ctrl - Home
120-131	Alt - 1,2,3,4,5,6,7,8,9,0,-,=
132	Ctrl - PgUp

Table 9-5.

When analyzing the program in Fig. 9-29, note that a getch( ) function call places the first received character into the variable char__1. If that character is a null, the function what__key( ) is called. Otherwise, a message prints on the screen stating that the entered key was not a special key. If what__key( ) is called, the second character is pulled from the buffer and placed in variable char__2, which is then compared against the octal value of various ASCII characters. If a match is made, the appropriate message is printed. This example in Fig. 9-29 searches for the function keys F1 through F10 and for the four arrow keys. It could however, be easily expanded to include the other special keys listed in Table 9-5.

Program :
```
main()
{ char char_1;

   printf("\n Hit a function key : ");
   char_1 = getch();

   if ( char_1 != '\0' )
     printf("\n\n That was not a function key");
   else
     what_key();
}

what_key()
{ char char_2;

   char_2 = getch();

   if ( char_2 == '\073') printf(" ==> You hit the F1 key");
   if ( char_2 == '\074') printf(" ==> You hit the F2 key");
   if ( char_2 == '\075') printf(" ==> You hit the F3 key");
   if ( char_2 == '\076') printf(" ==> You hit the F4 key");
   if ( char_2 == '\077') printf(" ==> You hit the F5 key");
   if ( char_2 == '\100') printf(" ==> You hit the F6 key");
   if ( char_2 == '\101') printf(" ==> You hit the F7 key");
   if ( char_2 == '\102') printf(" ==> You hit the F8 key");
   if ( char_2 == '\103') printf(" ==> You hit the F9 key");
   if ( char_2 == '\104') printf(" ==> You hit the F10 key");

   if ( char_2 == '\110') printf(" ==> You hit the up arrow");
   if ( char_2 == '\113') printf(" ==> You hit the left arrow");
   if ( char_2 == '\115') printf(" ==> You hit the right arrow");
   if ( char_2 == '\120') printf(" ==> You hit the down arrow");
}
```

Program Output : Hit a function key :

             You hit the up arrow

Fig. 9-29.

10

Bitwise Operations

When the C language was initially designed and developed, it was earmarked for use as a way of developing operating systems and other system level applications. As a result, it was given the ability to analyze and manipulate the individual bits within a given memory location. This chapter discusses the various operators associated with this feature and provides insight into their usage. Table 10-1 lists these bit manipulation commands, called bitwise operators.

Operator	Name
&	AND Operator
¦	Inclusive OR Operator
^	Exclusive OR Operator
~	Ones complement Operator
< <	Shift Left Operator
> >	Shift Right Operator

Table 10-1.

The bitwise operators may be used on any integer variable. That is to say, on any variable defined using int, short, long, or unsigned. Also, with the exception of the ones compliment operator ~, they may be used in a unary or binary equation, such as x & = y and x = x & y, respectively.

THE BITWISE AND OPERATOR

The bitwise operator (&) is used to combine two lists of bits, using the same boolean principles as the && operator used in if statements. In particular, the condition is only true (a value of 1), if both compared bit values are true. Otherwise, the outcome is false (a value of zero). Table 10-2 shows the true/false alternatives.

Table 10-2.

Bit 1	Bit 2	Outcome
0	0	0
0	1	0
1	0	0
1	1	1

The program listed in Fig. 10-1 illustrates the use of the AND operator. When reviewing this program, just concentrate on the statements within main( ). The bit__print( ) function will be explained later in the chapter during the discussion of bit fields. In particular, within main( ), note the statement int__value = int__value & −50;. This statement is instructing the compiler to compare the bits in int__value with the bit placement associated with the number −50. The outcome of this comparison is then placed back within int__value.

Program :

Fig. 10-1.

```
main()
{ int int_value = 50;

    printf("\n                        Bitwise AND    ");
    printf("\n");
    bit_print(int_value);
    bit_print(-50);
    printf("\n                        ----------------");
    int_value = int_value & -50;
    bit_print(int_value);
}

bit_print(value_in)
 int value_in;
{ struct bit_mask
    { unsigned bit_1   :1;
      unsigned bit_2   :1;
      unsigned bit_3   :1;
      unsigned bit_4   :1;
      unsigned bit_5   :1;
      unsigned bit_6   :1;
      unsigned bit_7   :1;
      unsigned bit_8   :1;
      unsigned bit_9   :1;
      unsigned bit_10 :1;
      unsigned bit_11 :1;
      unsigned bit_12 :1;
      unsigned bit_13 :1;
      unsigned bit_14 :1;
      unsigned bit_15 :1;
      unsigned bit_16 :1;
    };

    union
      { struct bit_mask bits;
        int int_mask;
      } bit_union;

    bit_union.int_mask = value_in;
```

129

```
        printf("\n bit mask is : ");
        printf("%d",bit_union.bits.bit_1);
        printf("%d",bit_union.bits.bit_2);
        printf("%d",bit_union.bits.bit_3);
        printf("%d",bit_union.bits.bit_4);
        printf("%d",bit_union.bits.bit_5);
        printf("%d",bit_union.bits.bit_6);
        printf("%d",bit_union.bits.bit_7);
        printf("%d",bit_union.bits.bit_8);
        printf("%d",bit_union.bits.bit_9);
        printf("%d",bit_union.bits.bit_10);
        printf("%d",bit_union.bits.bit_11);
        printf("%d",bit_union.bits.bit_12);
        printf("%d",bit_union.bits.bit_13);
        printf("%d",bit_union.bits.bit_14);
        printf("%d",bit_union.bits.bit_15);
        printf("%d",bit_union.bits.bit_16);
}
```

Fig. 10-1. (cont.)

Program Output :   Bitwise AND

```
bit mask is : 0000000000110010
bit mask is : 1111111111001110
               -----------------
bit mask is : 0000000000000010
```

When reviewing the output from this process, as shown by the use of the bit__print function, only one bit combination proved to be true (both bits had a value of 1), all other bit pairs were either 0 and 1, 1 and 0 or 0 and 0. These pairs, as shown in Table 10-2 are not construed as true and produce a 0 value.

THE INCLUSIVE OR OPERATOR

The inclusive OR operator (¦) also compares two fields of bits, but in this case, using an OR condition similar to the ¦¦ operator used in if statements. Table 10-3 provides a list of the possible OR comparison alternatives.

Bit 1	Bit 2	Outcome
0	0	0
0	1	1
1	0	1
1	1	1

Table 10-3.

The program shown in Fig. 10-2 is similar to that used when explaining the AND operator. In this case however, note that the OR operator is now being used in the statement int__value = int__value ¦ −50 within the main() function.

When reviewing the output produced by the program in Fig. 10-2, note that only the rightmost bit combination was false (both bits had a 0 value) and resulted in a 0 value. All the other combinations contained at least one 1 value.

Program : `main()`

```
{ int int_value = 50;

    printf("\n                       Inclusive OR    ");
    printf("\n");
    bit_print(int_value);
    bit_print(-50);
    printf("\n                       ----------------");
    int_value = int_value | -50;
    bit_print(int_value);
}

    bit_print(value_in)
     int value_in;
    { struct bit_mask
        { unsigned bit_1   :1;
          unsigned bit_2   :1;
          unsigned bit_3   :1;
          unsigned bit_4   :1;
          unsigned bit_5   :1;
          unsigned bit_6   :1;
          unsigned bit_7   :1;
          unsigned bit_8   :1;
          unsigned bit_9   :1;
          unsigned bit_10 :1;
          unsigned bit_11 :1;
          unsigned bit_12 :1;
          unsigned bit_13 :1;
          unsigned bit_14 :1;
          unsigned bit_15 :1;
          unsigned bit_16 :1;
        };

    union
      { struct bit_mask bits;
        int int_mask;
      } bit_union;

    bit_union.int_mask = value_in;

    printf("\n bit mask is : ");
    printf("%d",bit_union.bits.bit_1);
    printf("%d",bit_union.bits.bit_2);
    printf("%d",bit_union.bits.bit_3);
    printf("%d",bit_union.bits.bit_4);
    printf("%d",bit_union.bits.bit_5);
    printf("%d",bit_union.bits.bit_6);
    printf("%d",bit_union.bits.bit_7);
    printf("%d",bit_union.bits.bit_8);
    printf("%d",bit_union.bits.bit_9);
    printf("%d",bit_union.bits.bit_10);
    printf("%d",bit_union.bits.bit_11);
    printf("%d",bit_union.bits.bit_12);
    printf("%d",bit_union.bits.bit_13);
    printf("%d",bit_union.bits.bit_14);
    printf("%d",bit_union.bits.bit_15);
    printf("%d",bit_union.bits.bit_16);
}
```

Fig. 10-2.

```
bit mask is : 0000000000110010
bit mask is : 1111111111001110
               ----------------
bit mask is : 1111111111111110
```

Fig. 10-2. (cont.)

The Exclusive OR Operator

The exclusive OR operator (^) is similar to the inclusive OR ¦ operator with the exception that only one, but not both, of the bits being compared must be true (a 1 value). A list of the possible comparative outcomes are shown in Table 10-4.

Bit 1	Bit 2	Outcome
0	0	0
0	1	1
1	0	1
1	1	0

Table 10-4.

Like the prior operator, the program and program output in Fig. 10-3 illustrates the use and output of the exclusive OR operator.

When reviewing the output of Fig. 10-3, note that the bit combinations which contained both a 0 and a 1 proved to be true and thus produced a 1 value. However, the bit pairs that were both of the same type proved false and a 0 value resulted.

Program :

```
main()
{ int int_value = 50;

    printf("\n                    Exclusive OR    ");
    printf("\n");
    bit_print(int_value);
    bit_print(-50);
    printf("\n                    ------------------");
    int_value = int_value ^ -50;
    bit_print(int_value);
}

bit_print(value_in)
  int value_in;
{ struct bit_mask
    { unsigned bit_1   :1;
      unsigned bit_2   :1;
      unsigned bit_3   :1;
      unsigned bit_4   :1;
      unsigned bit_5   :1;
      unsigned bit_6   :1;
      unsigned bit_7   :1;
      unsigned bit_8   :1;
      unsigned bit_9   :1;
```

Fig. 10-3.

```
                         unsigned bit_10 :1;
                         unsigned bit_11 :1;
                         unsigned bit_12 :1;
                         unsigned bit_13 :1;
                         unsigned bit_14 :1;
                         unsigned bit_15 :1;
                         unsigned bit_16 :1;
                    };

                union
                   { struct bit_mask bits;
                     int int_mask;
                   } bit_union;

                bit_union.int_mask = value_in;

                printf("\n bit mask is : ");
                printf("%d",bit_union.bits.bit_1);
                printf("%d",bit_union.bits.bit_2);
                printf("%d",bit_union.bits.bit_3);
                printf("%d",bit_union.bits.bit_4);
                printf("%d",bit_union.bits.bit_5);
                printf("%d",bit_union.bits.bit_6);
                printf("%d",bit_union.bits.bit_7);
                printf("%d",bit_union.bits.bit_8);
                printf("%d",bit_union.bits.bit_9);
                printf("%d",bit_union.bits.bit_10);
                printf("%d",bit_union.bits.bit_11);
                printf("%d",bit_union.bits.bit_12);
                printf("%d",bit_union.bits.bit_13);
                printf("%d",bit_union.bits.bit_14);
                printf("%d",bit_union.bits.bit_15);
                printf("%d",bit_union.bits.bit_16);
           }
```

Fig. 10-3. (cont.)

Program Output :

                              Exclusive OR

```
bit mask is : 0000000000110010
bit mask is : 1111111111001110
              -----------------
bit mask is : 1111111111111100
```

THE ONES COMPLEMENT OPERATOR

The ones compliment operator ($\sim$) is used to change all the 1 values to 0 and all the 0 values to 1, thus "flip-flopping" the values. An example of this process can be seen in Fig. 10-4.

When reviewing Fig. 10-4, take special note of the statement int_value = $\sim$int_value within main( ). This statement instructs the computer to invert the bits in variable int_value and place this inverted bit pattern back in variable int_value. Additionally, when reviewing the output of Fig. 10-4, note that all of the 0 values have become 1 and all the 1 values have become 0.

133

```
Program :   main()
            { int int_value = 50;

                printf("\n                      Ones Complement ");
                printf("\n");
                bit_print(int_value);
                printf("\n                      ----------------");
                int_value = ~int_value;
                bit_print(int_value);
            }

            bit_print(value_in)
             int value_in;
            { struct bit_mask
                { unsigned bit_1  :1;
                  unsigned bit_2  :1;
                  unsigned bit_3  :1;
                  unsigned bit_4  :1;
                  unsigned bit_5  :1;
                  unsigned bit_6  :1;
                  unsigned bit_7  :1;
                  unsigned bit_8  :1;
                  unsigned bit_9  :1;
                  unsigned bit_10 :1;
                  unsigned bit_11 :1;
                  unsigned bit_12 :1;
                  unsigned bit_13 :1;
                  unsigned bit_14 :1;
                  unsigned bit_15 :1;
                  unsigned bit_16 :1;
                };

                union
                  { struct bit_mask bits;
                    int int_mask;
                  } bit_union;

                    bit_union.int_mask = value_in;

                    printf("\n bit mask is : ");
                    printf("%d",bit_union.bits.bit_1);
                    printf("%d",bit_union.bits.bit_2);
                    printf("%d",bit_union.bits.bit_3);
                    printf("%d",bit_union.bits.bit_4);
                    printf("%d",bit_union.bits.bit_5);
                    printf("%d",bit_union.bits.bit_6);
                    printf("%d",bit_union.bits.bit_7);
                    printf("%d",bit_union.bits.bit_8);
                    printf("%d",bit_union.bits.bit_9);
                    printf("%d",bit_union.bits.bit_10);
                    printf("%d",bit_union.bits.bit_11);
                    printf("%d",bit_union.bits.bit_12);
                    printf("%d",bit_union.bits.bit_13);
                    printf("%d",bit_union.bits.bit_14);
                    printf("%d",bit_union.bits.bit_15);
                    printf("%d",bit_union.bits.bit_16);
                }
```

Fig. 10-4.

Program Output :   Ones Complement

Fig. 10-4. (cont.)

```
bit mask is : 0000000000110010
                ----------------
bit mask is : 1111111111001101
```

THE SHIFT LEFT OPERATOR

The shift left operator (<<) causes the bits within the variable to be shifted to the left a specified number of characters. Figure 10-5 illustrates the use of this operator.

Program :

```
main()
{ int int_value = 50;

    printf("\n                    Shift Left  ");
    printf("\n");
    bit_print(int_value);
    printf("\n                -----------------");
    int_value = int_value << 2;
    bit_print(int_value);
    printf("\n                -----------------");
    int_value = int_value << 3;
    bit_print(int_value);
}

bit_print(value_in)
 int value_in;
{ struct bit_mask
    { unsigned bit_1    :1;
      unsigned bit_2    :1;
      unsigned bit_3    :1;
      unsigned bit_4    :1;
      unsigned bit_5    :1;
      unsigned bit_6    :1;
      unsigned bit_7    :1;
      unsigned bit_8    :1;
      unsigned bit_9    :1;
      unsigned bit_10   :1;
      unsigned bit_11   :1;
      unsigned bit_12   :1;
      unsigned bit_13   :1;
      unsigned bit_14   :1;
      unsigned bit_15   :1;
      unsigned bit_16   :1;
    };

    union
      { struct bit_mask bits;
        int int_mask;
      } bit_union;

    bit_union.int_mask = value_in;

    printf("\n bit mask is : ");
    printf("%d",bit_union.bits.bit_1);
    printf("%d",bit_union.bits.bit_2);
```

Fig. 10-5.

```
        printf("%d",bit_union.bits.bit_3);
        printf("%d",bit_union.bits.bit_4);
        printf("%d",bit_union.bits.bit_5);
        printf("%d",bit_union.bits.bit_6);
        printf("%d",bit_union.bits.bit_7);
        printf("%d",bit_union.bits.bit_8);
        printf("%d",bit_union.bits.bit_9);
        printf("%d",bit_union.bits.bit_10);
        printf("%d",bit_union.bits.bit_11);
        printf("%d",bit_union.bits.bit_12);
        printf("%d",bit_union.bits.bit_13);
        printf("%d",bit_union.bits.bit_14);
        printf("%d",bit_union.bits.bit_15);
        printf("%d",bit_union.bits.bit_16);
    }
```

Fig. 10-5. (cont.)

Program Output : Shift Left

```
bit mask is : 0000000000110010
              ------------------
bit mask is : 0000000011001000
              ------------------
bit mask is : 0000011001000000
```

When reviewing the program listed in Fig. 10-5, you will see that the bit shifting is performed twice. The first shift, performed in the statement int_value = int_value < < 2, causes the sixteen bits originally in int_value to move two places to the left. When this shift is performed, the two leftmost bits are shifted out the left side of the variable and are lost. Also notice that the two bit places on the right that were left vacant by the shift were filled with zeros. The second shift left statement moves the bits three more places to the left, again causing the three leftmost bits to be lost, the remaining bits to be shifted three positions, and the vacated bit locations to be filled with zeros.

THE SHIFT RIGHT OPERATOR

The shift right operator (>>) causes the bits within the variable to be shifted to the right a specified number of characters. Figure 10-6 illustrates the use of this operator. In general, it is identical in operation to the shift left operator.

Program :
```
main()
{ int int_value = 50;

    printf("\n                      Shift Right ");
    printf("\n");
    bit_print(int_value);
    printf("\n                      ----------------");
    int_value = int_value >> 2;
    bit_print(int_value);
    printf("\n                      ----------------");
    int_value = int_value >> 3;
    bit_print(int_value);
}
```

Fig. 10-6.

```
            bit_print(value_in)
             int value_in;
            { struct bit_mask
                { unsigned bit_1  :1;
                  unsigned bit_2  :1;
                  unsigned bit_3  :1;
                  unsigned bit_4  :1;
                  unsigned bit_5  :1;
                  unsigned bit_6  :1;
                  unsigned bit_7  :1;
                  unsigned bit_8  :1;
                  unsigned bit_9  :1;
                  unsigned bit_10 :1;
                  unsigned bit_11 :1;
                  unsigned bit_12 :1;
                  unsigned bit_13 :1;
                  unsigned bit_14 :1;
                  unsigned bit_15 :1;
                  unsigned bit_16 :1;
                };

              union
                { struct bit_mask bits;
                  int int_mask;
                } bit_union;

              bit_union.int_mask = value_in;

              printf("\n bit mask is : ");
              printf("%d",bit_union.bits.bit_1);
              printf("%d",bit_union.bits.bit_2);
              printf("%d",bit_union.bits.bit_3);
              printf("%d",bit_union.bits.bit_4);
              printf("%d",bit_union.bits.bit_5);
              printf("%d",bit_union.bits.bit_6);
              printf("%d",bit_union.bits.bit_7);
              printf("%d",bit_union.bits.bit_8);
              printf("%d",bit_union.bits.bit_9);
              printf("%d",bit_union.bits.bit_10);
              printf("%d",bit_union.bits.bit_11);
              printf("%d",bit_union.bits.bit_12);
              printf("%d",bit_union.bits.bit_13);
              printf("%d",bit_union.bits.bit_14);
              printf("%d",bit_union.bits.bit_15);
              printf("%d",bit_union.bits.bit_16);
            }
```

Fig. 10-6. (cont.)

```
Program Output :                 Shift Right

       bit mask is : 0000000000110010
                     ----------------
       bit mask is : 0000000000001100
                     ----------------
       bit mask is : 0000000000000001
```

137

BIT FIELDS

The bitwise operators that have thus far been discussed have caused a particular process to be performed on all sixteen bits within the variable. There are times, however, when you only want to manipulate selected bits within a variable. Likewise, there are occasions when because of memory constraints, you may be forced to place your data in memory in the most compact way possible. Both of these situations can be addressed through the use of bit fields. A bit field is a structure that is used to assign variable names to the bits contained within a variable. An example of this process is shown below.

Program :
```
main()
{ struct date_format
    { unsigned day    :5;
      unsigned month  :4;
      unsigned year   :7;
    } date;

    date.day = 31;
    date.month = 12;
    date.year = 87;

    printf("\n The month is = %d",date.month);
    printf("\n The day   is = %d",date.day);
    printf("\n The year  is = %d",date.year);
}
```

Fig. 10-7.

Program Output :
```
The month is = 12
The day   is = 31
The year  is = 87
```

When reviewing the program in Fig. 10-7, note that the definition of the day, month, and year include a colon, followed by an integer number. The colon signifies that the variable being suffixed is a bit field and not a regular variable. The number following the colon specifies the number of bits contained within the field. For example, the month variable is defined by the statement unsigned month :4;, stating that month is an unsigned integer that will be stored using four bits. Remember, however, that a four bit field can only contain a range of sixteen numbers, namely, 0 through 15. This limitation is acceptable, however, since there are only 12 months. Next, notice that the three bit fields defined in the date_format structure add up to 16 bits, or one memory location. This memory location is conceptually shown below.

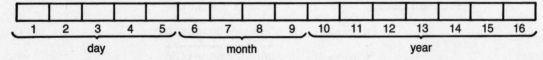

Fig. 10-8.

As you can see when reviewing Fig. 10-8, the 16 bits within the displayed byte are divided into three parts; 5 bits for day, 4 bits for month, and 7 bits for the year.

11

The C Precompiler

Unlike most programming languages, the C compilation process is performed in two steps. The first step adjusts and modifies the source code based on specific instructions called compiler directives that are inserted into the source code by the programmer. These directives all begin with a number sign (#) and will be discussed at length within this chapter. The second step of the compilation process reads this modified source code and performs traditional compilation activities.

THE #define DIRECTIVE

The #define directive serves two purposes. First, it allows you to assign symbolic names to program constants, thus improving program readability. Second, it provides the ability to define small function-like procedures called macros. These two uses will be discussed below.

Simple Text Replacement

One of the most common uses of the #define directive is to perform simple text replacement through the use of symbolic names. For example, the statement

#define TRUE 1

states that the word TRUE has a symbolic value equaling the number 1. Therefore, during precompilation, all occurrences of the word TRUE are replaced with a 1.

The #define directive can also be used to alter the format of the C language. For example, if you wish to add the word THEN to your if statements, place the word LET before your assignment statements, and change the equality operator (= =) to the word EQUALS, you may do so using the process shown in Fig. 11-1.

```
#define EQUALS ==
#define THEN
#define LET

main()
{ int a_number;

  LET a_number = 5;

  if ( a_number EQUALS 5 )
  THEN printf("\n\n The number equals 5");

  if ( a_number EQUALS 6 )
  THEN printf("\n\n The number equals 6");
}
```

Fig. 11-1.

When reviewing the program in Fig. 11-1, note that there are three #define statements. The first statement assigns the word EQUALS a value of = =, causing the precompiler to replace EQUALS with = = during precompilation. The second and third #define statement set the words THEN and LET equal to space, thus telling the compiler to replace those words with spaces. In effect, this procedure is instructing the compiler to delete them for the source code prior to compilation.

Even though the #define directive can be used to alter the appearance of C statements, as shown in Fig. 11-1, this activity is frowned upon. If you are going to program in C, then make your programs look like C and not like some other language.

Defining Macros

The #define directive can also be used to define small function-like procedures called macros. An example of this process is shown below.

```
#define TIMES_TWO(x) ( x * 2 )

main()
{ int a_number;
  int b_number;

  a_number = 5;
  b_number = TIMES_TWO(a_number);

  printf("\n b_number has a value of %d, b_number);
}
```

Fig. 11-2.

The #define statement in Fig. 11-2 defines a macro called times-two. Its purpose, as you may expect, is to take a number and multiply it by the value 2. When precompiling the statement referencing this macro, namely

$$b\text{-}number = times\_\_two(a\_\_number)$$

is passed through precompilation, it will be converted to

$$b\text{-}number = a\_\_number * 2$$

thus replacing the macro call with the macro's process as specified within the parentheses of the #define statement.

Lastly, note that the transformation of (x * 2) to

$$a\_number * 2$$

was made by associating the x parameter in the #define statement, with the a__number parameter in the macro call. To expand this macro call transformation, Fig. 11-3 defines a macro using two parameters.

```
#define multiply(x,y) ( x * y )

main()
{ int a_number;
  int b_number;
  int c_number;

  a_number = 2;
  b_number = 3;
  c_number = multiply(a_number, b_number)
  printf("\n %d times %d is %d", a_number, b_number, c_number);
}
```

As shown in Fig. 11-3, the multiply macro uses two variables x and y. Also note that two variables are used when referencing multiply, namely a__variable and b__variable. When this program is precompiled, the C source code will be modified from

$$c\_number = multiply(a\_variable, b\_variable)$$

to the statement

$$c\_number = a\_variable * b\_variable$$

thus, associating a__variable with x and b__variable with y.

The last #define example is shown in Fig. 11-4 and contains an added twist. This twist is that rather than defining a formula, as previously discussed, the #define directive is defining an if condition using the equation operator.

```
#define is_int(x) ( ( x >= '0' && x <= '9' ) ? 1: 0 )

main()
{ char a_character;

  a_character = '4';
  if ( is_int(a_character) )
      printf("\n a_character is not an integer");
  else
      printf("\, a_character is an integer");
```

The is__int macro, defined in Fig. 11-4, tests to see if the character in a__character is a numeric digit. Like previous examples, the passed parameter, namely a__character, is used to replace the x variable in the macro formula, from the statement

$$if(is\_int(a\_character))$$

to the statement

$$if ((a\_variable >\ = \text{'0'} \&\& a\_variable <\ = \text{'9'}) ? 1 : 0).$$

It is this transformed line, that will actually be compiled into executable code.

Like all programming options, the use of #define macros has advantages and disadvantages. The advantages are that hard-to-type procedures, like that used in Fig. 11-4 can be written and debugged once, and then referenced as needed throughout the rest of the program. Also, because macros can be given descriptive names, it improves the readability of the program. Lastly, macros do not require the processing overhead associated with functions. As a result, they are processed more efficiently. The disadvantages are three fold. First, if macros are not referenced correctly, the source code that is transformed by the precompiler may be modified incorrectly. Even worse, these errors cannot be seen when reading the original source code, making it harder to debug. Second, because the macro is actually copied into the source code each time it is referenced, if used very often, it can expand the size of your executable code, hence requiring more computer resources to store and execute. Lastly, unlike functions, the variable's name, and not the variable's value are passed to the macro. Therefore, if you attempt to pass a parameter in the form of an expression (for example $x + 5$), the expression, and not the value of the expression will be placed in the precompiled source code. For example, the #define statement

$$\#define\ TIMES\_TWO(\ x * 2\ )$$

when referenced by the statement

$$c\_number = TIMES\_TWO(\ a\_variable\ +\ 5)$$

will generate a source code statement of

$$c\_variable = a\_variable + 5 * 2$$

and not the expected result of the value of a__variable plus 5.

THE #include DIRECTIVE

The #include directive is used to instruct the preprocesser to read the C code contained within a specified file (known as a header file), and place its contents within the program being compiled. For example, once you have written a list of #define macros and symbolic names, like those previously discussed, you may place these definitions in their own file and have them automatically called into your C program during precompilation. The advantage of the technique is that since your #define directives can be centrally located, and need not be actually placed in each program, it becomes easy to modify your definitions, because you only have to make the change in one place. Figure 11-5 lists an example file that may be referenced by an #include directive.

Fig. 11-5.

```
A>type mydefs.h

#define NULL '\0'
#define TRUE 1
#define FALSE 0
#define EOF -1
```

When reviewing the definition file in Fig. 11-5, note that the file name mydefs.h ends with an extension of .h. This .h stands for "header file". It is not required, but it is considered a standard convention within the industry. In fact, when you buy a C compiler, it comes with various definition header files which use the .h naming convention. Additionally, note that the file does not contain any procedural statements like for and while. By convention, header files should only be used for the definition of #define macros, external variables, and symbolic names. Figure 11-6 illustrates how the #include statement is used to reference the mydefs.h file.

Fig. 11-6.

```
#include <mydefs.h>

main()
{ char a_character;

    a_character = '4';
    if ( is_int(a_character) == TRUE )
        printf("\n a_character is an integer");

    if ( is_int(a_character) == FALSE )
        printf("\n a_character is not an integer");
```

When the program in Fig. 11-6 is pre-compiled, it will first be transformed into the program shown in Fig. 11-7. When reviewing this modified program, note that the #include directive is gone and the symbols TRUE and FALSE were replaced by the symbolic values as specified in the header file mydefs.h.

Fig. 11-7.

```
main()
{ char a_character;

    a_character = '4';
    if ( is_int(a_character) == 1 )
        printf("\n a_character is an integer");

    if ( is_int(a_character) == 0 )
        printf("\n a_character is not an integer");
```

CONDITIONAL DIRECTIVES

In addition to having the ability to symbolically modify your source code via the #define and #include directives, you may also employ conditional logic. This logic, can

143

be used to decide which #define and #include directives are used by the precompiler, and even which sections of your source code are compiled. The directives which facilitate these conditional options are discussed below.

The #ifdef Directive

The #ifdef directive instructs the precompiler to conditionally compile statements of other directives based on whether a specified name has been defined by a #define directive. An example of this process is shown below.

```
#ifdef TESTRUN
    #define TESTFLAG 1
    printf("\n This is a test");
#endif
```
Fig. 11-8.

The partial program shown in Fig. 11-8 checks to see if the symbolic name TESTRUN has been defined via a #define directive. If it has, the two lines below it are used. If not, the two lines below it are not used. Additionally, note that the #ifdef directive ends with #endif. The #endif statement is required when using any of the conditional directives and signifies the end of the conditional expression.

The #ifndef Directive

The #ifndef directive instructs the precompiler to conditionally use statements of directives based on whether a specified identifier has not been defined by a #define directive. In fact, this directive is the opposite of the #ifdef directive. The example below illustrates the use of this directive.

```
#ifndef TESTRUN
    #define TESTFLAG 0
    printf("\n This is not a test");
#endif
```
Fig. 11-9.

When reviewing the program in Fig. 11-9, note that the lines between the #ifndef directive and its associated #endif directive will only be executed if TESTRUN has not been defined via a #define directive.

The #if Directive

The #if directive provides the ability to compile or not compile sections of source code and directives based on the value of a specified symbolic name. If the symbolic name being tested has a value of zero, the expression is considered false. If the symbolic name has a non-zero value, then it is considered true. The following example illustrates the use of this directive.

```
#if TESTRUN
    #define TESTFLAG 1
    printf("\n This is a test");
#endif
```
Fig. 11-10.

When reviewing this program, note that the lines between #if and its associated #endif directive will only be executed if TESTRUN has a non-zero value.

The #else Directive

The #else compiler directive is used to provide the #if, #ifdef and #ifndef directives with an if-then-else capability. This directive is optional, and should only be used when it will be containing associated lines. Also note that this directive does not take the place of an #endif. The #endif is still required, and must be placed after the #else directive if one is present. The use of this function is illustrated below.

Fig. 11-11.

```
#if TESTRUN
  #define TESTFLAG 1
  printf("\n This is a test");
#else
  #define TESTFLAG 0
  prinf("\n This is not a test");
#endif
```

When reviewing the partial program in Fig. 11-11, note that the #else directive was placed after the conditional directive and before the #endif. Also note that the lines within the conditional expression are indented in a manner similar to that used with the if statement. This format is not required, but it helps make the program more readable.

The #undef Directive

The #undef directive is used to undefine a symbolic name or define macro that has previously been defined using the #define directive. An example of the #undef directive is shown in Fig. 11-12.

When reviewing the partial program in Fig. 11-12, note that the word TRUE was assigned a value of 1, then TRUE became unassigned by executing the #undef command.

Fig. 11-12.

```
#define TRUE
  . . .
  . . .
#undef TRUE
```

145

PART II

THE
C
REFERENCE
MANUAL

12

Language Operators

+	—	Addition Operator
–	—	Subtraction Operator
*	—	Multiplication Operator
/	—	Division Operator
%	—	Remainder Operator
++	—	Incremental Operator
– –	—	Decremental Operator
=	—	Assignment Operator
+=	—	Addition Assignment Operator
–=	—	Subtraction Assignment Operator
*=	—	Multiplication Assignment Operator
/=	—	Division Assignment Operator
%=	—	Remainder Assignment Operator
*	—	Indirection Operator
&	—	Address Operator
[]	—	Array Operator
.	—	Structure Identification Operator
–>	—	Structure Identification Operator
&&	—	Logical AND Operator
!!	—	Logical OR Operator
<	—	Less Than Operator
>	—	Greater Than Operator
<=	—	Less Than or Equal to Operator
>=	—	Greater Than or Equal to Operator
==	—	Equal to Operator
!=	—	Not Equal to Operator
?:	—	If Operator

Name : + addition operator

Function : The purpose of this operator is to add two numerically defined variables or constants.

Example Setup : int a,b,c;
a = 1;
b = 2;

Examples :

c = a + b;	Result, c is set to 3
c = a + 5;	Result, c is set to 6
c = 5 + b;	Result, c is set to 7
c = power (a + b);	Result, c is set to the power of 3 (a + b)

Rules :

1) The values being added must be numeric variables, constants or numeric returns from user or compiler defined functions.
2) Valid values must be placed on both the left and right side of the addition operator as shown above in the example.
3) When adding variables of different storage types (ie., int, double, float, etc.) the data is converted to the highest ranking operand as illustrated in Appendix B.
4) When addition is used in conjunction with other arithmetic operators, C follows the specific rules of precedence outlined in Appendix A.

Name : – subtraction operator

Function : The purpose of this operator is to subtract the value of one numerically defined variable or constant from another.

Example Setup : int a,b,c;
a = 7;
b = 2;

Examples :

c = a − b;	Result, c is set to 5
c = a − 5;	Result, c is set to 2
c = 5 − b;	Result, c is set to 3
c = power (a − b);	Result, c is set to the power of 5 (a − b)

Rules :
1) The values being subtracted must be numeric variables, constants, or numeric returns from user or compiler defined functions.
2) Valid values must be placed on both the left and right side of the subtraction operator as shown above in the example.
3) When subtracting variables of different storage types (ie., int, double, float, etc.) the data is converted to the highest ranking operand as illustrated in Appendix B.
4) When subtraction is used in conjunction with other arithmetic operators, C follows the specific rules of precedence outlined in Appendix A.

*

Name : * multiplication operator

Function : The purpose of this operator is to multiply together two numerically defined variables or constants

Example Setup : int a,b,c;
a = 3;
b = 2;

Examples :

c = a * b;	Result, c is set to 6
c = a * 4;	Result, c is set to 12
c = 6 * b;	Result, c is set to 12
c = power (a*b);	Result, c is set to the power of 6 (a * b)

Rules :
1) The values being multiplied must be numeric variables, constants, or numeric returns from user or compiler defined functions.
2) Valid values must be placed on both the left and right side of the multiplication operator as shown above in the example.
3) When multiplying variables of different storage types (ie., int, double, float, etc.) the data is converted to the highest ranking operand as illustrated in Appendix B.
4) When multiplication is used in conjunction with other arithmetic operators, C follows the specific rules of precedence outlined in Appendix A.

Name : / division operator

Function : The purpose of this operator is to divide the value of one numerically defined variable or constant into another.

Example Setup : int a,b,c;
a = 2;
b = 6;

Examples : c = a / b;   Result, c is set to 3
c = a / 4;   Result, c is set to 2
c = 12 / b;   Result, c is set to 2
c = power (a/b);   Result, c is set to the power of 3 (a / b)

Rules :
1) The values being divided must be numeric variables, constants, or numeric returns from user or compiler defined functions.
2) Valid values must be placed on both the left and right side of the division operator as shown above in the example.
3) When dividing variables of different storage types (ie., int, double, float, etc.) the data is converted to the highest ranking operand as illustrated in Appendix B.
4) When division is used in conjunction with other arithmetic operators, C follows the specific rules of precedence outlined in Appendix A.

%

Name : % remainder operator

Function : The purpose of the remainder operator is to calculate the remainder that would be caused by the division of two integer variables or constants.

Example Setup : int a,b,c;
a = 2;
b = 5;

Examples : c = a % b;   Result, c is set to 1
c = a % 4;   Result, c is set to 0
c = 12 % b;   Result, c is set to 2
c = power (a%b);   Result, c is set to the power of 1 (a % b)

Rules :
1) The values being divided must be numeric variables, integer constants, or numeric returns from user or compiler defined functions.
2) Valid values must be placed on both the left and right side of the remainder operator as shown above in the example.
3) When dividing variables of different storage types (ie., int, double, float, etc.) the data is converted to the highest ranking operand as illustrated in Appendix B.
4) The remainder may only be placed into a variable defined as an integer. Hence, compilation errors may occur or erroneous results may be produced if the recipient of the % operation is a double or floating point variable.

Name : ++ incremental operator

Function : The function of this operator is to add 1 to a specified numerically defined variable. This operator is generally used to increment counters.

Example Setup : int a,b,c

Examples :
:1) a = 5;	a	is first set to 5
a++;	a	is incremented by 1, giving "a" a value of 6
2) a = 3;	a	is set to a value of 3
++a;	a	is incremented by 1, giving "a" a value of 4
3) a = 3;	a	is set to 3
b = ++a;	b	is set to the value of 4 (3 + 1)

Note that in example 3, a is incremented by 1 before b is set to the value of a. This was done because the ++ operator was placed before the variables being incremented. If the ++ was after the a variable, b would have been given a value of 3 as shown below.

| 4) a = 3; | a | is set to 3 |
| b = a++; | b | is set to 3, the value of a, before it was incremented by 1 |

Note that in example 4, b was set to the value of a before the ++ operator incremented a by 1. This was done because the ++ was placed after the a variable, stating that a should be incremented after the equation has been completed.

Rules :
1) The variable being incremented must be defined as a pointer or a numeric variable.
2) The ++ operator may be placed before or after the variable being incremented. If the ++ is before the variable, then the variable is incremented before the equation or function containing it is executed. If the ++ is placed after the variable, then the variable is incremented after the equation or function is executed.
3) When the ++ operator is used in conjunction with other operators, C follows the specific rules of precedence described in Appendix A.

Name : – – incremental operator

Function : The function of this operator is to subtract 1 from a specified numerically defined variable. This operator is generally used to decrement counters.

Example Setup : int a,b,c

Examples : :1) a = 5;   a   is first set to 5
                  a– –;   a   is decremented by 1, giving "a" a value of 4

           2) a = 3;   a   is set to a value of 3
                  – –a;   a   is decremented by 1, giving "a" a value of 2

           3) a = 3;   a   is set to 3
                  b = – –a;   b   is set to the value of 2 (3 – 1)

Note that in example 3, a is decremented by 1 before b is set to the value of a. This was done because the – – operator was placed before the variables being decremented. If the – – was after the a variable, b would have been given a value of 3 as shown below.

           4) a = 3;   a   is set to 3
                  b = a– –;   b   is set to 3, the value of a, before it was decremented by 1

Note that in example 4, b was set to the value of a before the – – operator decremented a by 1. This occurred because the – – was placed after the a variable, stating that a should be decremented by 1 after the equation has been completed.

Rules : 1) The variable being decremented must be defined as a pointer or a numeric variable.
2) The – – operator may be placed before or after the variable being decremented. If the – – is before the variable, then the variable is decremented before the equation or function containing it is executed. If the – – is placed after the variable, then the variable is decremented after the equation or function is performed.
3) When the – – operator is used in conjunction with other operators, C follows the specific rules of precedence described in Appendix A.

Name : = assignment operator

Function : The assignment operator is used to set a variable to a speci-fied value. Note that this single equal sign operator cannot be used to test for equality. The equality operator is com-posed of two equal signs (= =).

Example Setup : int a,b;

Example :

a = 5;	a is set to a value of 5
b = a;	b is set to the value of "a", namely 5

Rules :
1) The assignment operator goes from right to left. In other words, the value on the left side of the equal sign is set to the value of the variable, function, or constant on the right side of the operator.
2) Constants and functions may not be placed on the left side of the equal sign because they cannot logically be assigned a value.
3) When assignments are made from one variable type to another, the data will be automatically converted to the format of the variable receiving the data. Therefore, given the following formula:

```
int a;
float b = 4.1;
float c = 3.0;

a = b + c;
```

"a" will be given a value of 7 and the .1 will be truncated.

+ =

Name : + = addition assignment operator

Function : The + = operator is a shorthand method of adding the value of a variable or constant to a another variable. The statement a + = 5 would thus be a shortcut for the statement a = a + 5. The two main advantages of this shortcut operation is that it is easier to write and it generates more efficient machine code once compiled.

Example Setup : int a,b;

Examples :

a = 5;	a	is set to a value of 5
a + = 3;	3	is added to a, giving "a" a value of 8
a = 5;	a	is set to a value of 5
b = 2;	b	is set to a value of 2
a + = b;		The value of b (2) is added to a (5), giving "a" a value of 7

Rules :

1) The value on the right side of the + = is added to the value of the variable on the left.
2) Constants and functions may not be placed on the left side of the + = operator because they cannot logically be assigned a value.
3) The right side of the operator may contain constants, functions, or numerically defined variables.
4) The variable on the right side of the operator cannot be a pointer.

Name : – = subtraction assignment operator

Function : The – = operator is a shorthand method of subtracting the value of a variable or constant from another variable. The statement a – = 5 would thus be a shortcut for the statement a = a – 5. The two main advantages of this shortcut operation is that it is easier to write and it generates more efficient machine code once compiled.

Example Setup : int a,b;

Examples :

a = 5;	a is set to a value of 5
a – = 3;	3 is added to a, giving a a value of 2
a = 5;	a is set to a value of 5
b = 2;	b is set to a value of 2
a – = b;	The value of b (2) is subtracted from a (5), giving a a value of 3

Rules :
1) The value on the right side of the – = is subtracted from the value of the variable on the left.
2) Constants and functions may not be placed on the left side of the – = operator because they cannot logically be assigned a value.
3) The right side of the operator may contain constants, functions, or numerically defined variables.
4) The variable on the right side of the operator cannot be a pointer.

✱=

Name : ✱= multiplication assignment operator

Function : The ✱= operator is a shorthand method of multiplying the value of a variable or constant by another variable. The statement a ✱= 5 would thus be a shortcut for the statement a = a ✱ 5. The two main advantages of this shortcut operation is that it is easier to write and it generates more efficient machine code once compiled.

Example Setup : int a,b;

Examples :

a = 5;	a is set to a value of 5
a ✱= 3;	3 is added to a, giving a a value of 15
a = 5;	a is set to a value of 5
b = 2;	b is set to a value of 2
a ✱= b;	The value of b (2) is added to a (5), giving a a value of 10

Rules :

1) The value on the right side of the ✱= is multiplied by the value of the variable on the left, placing the product in the left side variable.
2) Constants and functions may not be placed on the left side of the ✱= operator because they cannot logically be assigned a value.
3) The right side of the operator may contain constants, functions, or numerically defined variables.
4) The variable on the right side of the operator cannot be a pointer.

Name : /= division assignment operator

Function : The /= operator is a shorthand method of dividing the value of a variable or constant into another variable. The statement a /= 5 would thus be a shortcut for the statement a = a / 5. The two main advantages of this shortcut operation is that it is easier to write and it generates more efficient machine code once compiled.

Example Setup : int a,b;
float c;

Examples :

a = 5;	a	is set to a value of 5
a /= 3;	3	is divided to a, giving a a value of 2, remember, a is an integer, therefore the remainder of .5 is truncated.
c = 5;	a	is set to a value of 5
c /= 3;	3	is divided to a, giving a a value of 2.5
c = 5;	c	is set to a value of 5
b = 2;	b	is set to a value of 2
c /= b;		The value of b (2) is divided into b (5), giving c a value of 2.5

Rules :
1) The value on the right side of the /= is divided into the value of the variable on the left.
2) Constants and functions may not be placed on the left side of the /= operator because they cannot logically be assigned a value.
3) The right side of the operator may contain constants, functions, or numerically defined variables.
4) The variable on the right side of the operator cannot be a pointer.

%=

Name : %= remainder assignment operator

Function : The %= operator is a shorthand method of calculating the remainder caused by the division of two integer defined variables or constants. The statement a %= 5 would thus be a shortcut for the statement a = a % 5. The two main advantages of this shortcut operation is that it is easier to write and it generates more efficient machine code once compiled.

Example Setup : int a,b;

Examples :

a = 5;	a	is set to a value of 5
a %= 3;	3	is divided into a, giving a a remainder value of 2
a = 5;	a	is set to a value of 5
b = 2;	b	is set to a value of 2
a %= b;		The values of b (2) is divided into a (5), giving a the remainder value of 1

Rules :
1) The value on the right side of the %= is divided by the value of the variable on the left, placing the remainder from the division in the left side variable.
2) Constants and functions may not be placed on the left side of the %= operator because they cannot logically be assigned a value.
3) The right side of the operator may contain constants, functions, or numerically defined variables.
4) The variable on the right side of the operator cannot be a pointer.

Name : * indirection operator

Function : When a * is placed as the prefix of a pointer variable (ex. *a_variable), the combined expression refers to the value contained at the pointer's address. For example, given the following statement:

int a_variable = 15;

The value of a_variable is 15. However, the expression *a_variable refers to the value contained in memory location 15.

Example Setup : int *a_variable, b_variable;
a_variable = 10;

Example : b_variable = *a_variable;

Rules :
1) This operator may only be used with pointer variables.
2) The * must be on the left side of the pointer variable being indirected.
3) An indirected pointer variable can be used like any regular variable.

&

Name : & address operator

Function : The & operator provides a means of obtaining the memory location of a specified variable. For example, if you wish to obtain the location of variable a__variable, you may do so by referencing the variable as &a__variable. This operator is primarily used to pass the address of a variable to a pointer.

Example Setup : int a__variable, *b__pointer;
a__variable = 5;

Example : b__variable = &a__variable;

In the example above, the address of variable a__variable is being placed in the integer pointer b__pointer.

Rules :
1) The & operator can only be used to reference the address of variables, because only variables have memory addresses. Therefore, since constants, functions, and mathematical formulas are not variables, it would not be logical to try to reference their location. If this is attempted, an error will occur during compilation.
2) The & character must be on the left side and adjacent to the variable being referenced. For example, &a__variable is valid, and & a__variable and a__variable& are not.

Name : [ ] array operator

Function : The [ ] operator indicates that the variable being suffixed is an array. Note that this operator is used when defining the size of a character string. This is the case because C treats a character string like a single dimensional array. For example, char a__variable[11]; states that a__variable is a character string of length 10, plus a one character null terminator. Additionally, note that character string definition is the most common, but not the only use of arrays.

Example : char an__array[15];

Rules :
1) The [ ] characters must immediately follow the variable being suffixed.
2) All character strings are interpreted as one dimensional arrays.
3) A static array may be initialized in the following manner:

static int a__variable[ ] = {1,2,3,4,5};

When using the above array assignment option, the compiler will automatically calculate the size of the array by counting the listing array values.

Name : . structure identification operator

Function : This operator is used to associate a variable with its defined structure.

Example Setup :
```
struct name
{ char last[21];
  char first[21];
  char middle__initial[2];
}
```

Example :
```
strcpy(name.last, "Bloom");
strcpy(name.first, "Eric");
strcpy(name.middle__initial,"P");
```

The strcpy function used in the above example stands for string copy and is used to assign the name values to the various structure components.

Rules : 1) No spaces may be present between the structure name, the period and the variable name.
2) The structure/variable relationship must be explicitly defined as shown above in the struct and cannot be created on-the-fly.
3) name.first and (&name) − >first are equivalent expressions.

Name : – > structure identification operator

Function : This operator is used to associate a variable with its defined structure.

Example Setup :
```
struct name
    {   char last[21];
        char first[21];
        char middle__initial[2];
    }
```

Example :
```
strcpy(name – >last, "Bloom");
strcpy(name – >first, "Eric");
strcpy(name – >middle__initial,"P");
```

Rules :
1) No spaces may be present between the structure name, the – > and the variable name.
2) The structure/variable relationship must be explicitly defined as shown above and cannot be created on-the-fly.
3) name.first and (&name) – >first are equivalent expressions.

&&

Name : && logical AND operator

Function : The && operator specifies the AND requirement within an if statement or other testing area.

Example Setup : int a,b,c,d;

Examples : if (a = = b && c = = d)
if (a = = b && a = = c && a = = d)

The first example shown above states that a must be equal to b and c must be equal to d for the if statement to be true.

Rules : 1) The && characters must be side by side with no spaces or other characters between them.
2) The operators & and && are not the same. The & is a bitwise operator and serves a similar, but very different function.
3) There must be a comparative expression on both the left and right of the && operator.

Name : | | logical OR operator

Function : The | | operator specifies the OR requirement in an if state-ment or other testing area.

Example Setup : int a,b,c,d;

Examples : if (a = = b | | c = = d)
if (a = = b | | a = = c | | a = = d)
The first example shown above, states that a must be equal to b or c must be equal to d for the if statement to be true.

Rules : 1) The | | characters must be side by side with no spaces to other characters between them.
2) The operators | and | | are not the same. The | is a bit-wise operator and serves a similar, but very different function.
3) There must be a comparative expression on both the left and right of the | | operator.

<

Name : < less than operator

Function : This operator compares the value of two expressions. Upon making this comparison, a nonzero is generated if the first operator is less than the second. If not, a zero value is produced. As shown below, when incorporated in an if statement, a nonzero value is construed as true and a zero value is construed as false.

Example Setup : int a,b;

Examples :

a = 1;	a	is set to 1
b = 2;	b	is set to 2
if (a < b)		The equation a < b yields a nonzero value, hence, the if expression is true.

: a = 2;	a	is set to 2
b = 1;	b	is set to 1
if (a < b)		The equation a < b yields a zero value, hence, the if expression is false.

Rules :
1) There must be an expression on both the left and right of the < operator.
2) The two variables being compared should be of the same data type. If not, inconsistent results may occur.

Name : > greater than operator

Function : This operator compares the value of two expressions. Upon making this comparison, a nonzero is generated if the first operator is greater than the second. If not, a zero value is produced. As shown below, when incorporated within an "if" statement, a nonzero value is construed as true and a zero value is construed as false.

Example Setup : int a,b;

Example : a = 1;   a   is set to 1
          b = 2;   b   is set to 2
          if (a > b)   The equation a > b yields a zero value, hence, the if expression is false.

        : a = 2;   a   is set to 2
          b = 1;   b   is set to 1
          if (a > b)   The equation a > b yields a nonzero value, hence, the if expression is true.

Rules : 1) There must be an expression on both the left and right of the > operator.
        2) The two variables being compared should be of the same data type. If not, inconsistent results may occur.

$<=$

Name : $<=$ less than or equal to operator

Function : This operator compares the value of two expressions. Upon making this comparison, a nonzero is generated if the first operator is less than or equal to the second. If not, a zero value is produced. As shown below, when incorporated within an if statement, a nonzero value is construed as true and a zero value is construed as false.

Example Setup : int a,b;

Example :

a = 1;	a	is set to 1
b = 1;	b	is set to 1
if (a <= b)		The equation "a <= b" yields a nonzero value, hence, the "if" expression is true.

: a = 1;	a	is set to 1
b = 2;	b	is set to 2
if (a <= b)		The equation a <= b yields a nonzero value, hence, the "if" expression is true.

: a = 2;	a	is set to 2
b = 1;	b	is set to 1
if (a <= b)		The equation a <= b yields a zero value, hence, the if expression is false.

Rules :
1) There must be an expression on both the left and right of the $<=$ operator.
2) The two variables being compared should be of the same data type. If not, inconsistent results may occur.
3) The operator must be written as $<=$, the format $=<$ is invalid and will generate a syntax error during compilation.

Name : $>$ = greater than or equal to operator

Function : This operator compares the value of two expressions. Upon making this comparison, a nonzero is generated if the first operator is greater than or equal to the second. If not, a zero value is produced. As shown below, when incorporated within an if statement, a nonzero value is construed as true and a zero value is construed as false.

Example Setup : int a,b;

Example :

a = 1;	a is set to 1
b = 1;	b is set to 1
if (a $>$ = b)	The equation a $>$ = b yields a nonzero value, hence, the if expression is true.

a = 1;	a is set to 1
b = 2;	b is set to 2
if (a $>$ = b)	The equation a $>$ = b yields a zero value, hence, the if expression is false.

a = 2;	a is set to 2
b = 1;	b is set to 1
if (a $>$ = b)	The equation a $>$ = b yields a nonzero value, hence, the if expression is true.

Rules :
1) There must be an expression on both the left and right of the $<$ = operator.
2) The two variables being compared should be of the same data type. If not, inconsistent results may occur.
3) The operator must be written as $>$ =, the format = $>$ is invalid and will generate a syntax error during compilation.

== =

Name : == equal to operator

Function : This operator compares the value of two expressions. Upon making this comparison, a nonzero is generated if the first operator is equal to the second. If not, a zero value is produced. As shown below, when incorporated within an if statement, a nonzero value is construed as true and a zero value is construed as false.

Example Setup : int a,b;

Example : a = 1;   a   is set to 1
b = 1;   b   is set to 1
if (a == b)   The equation a == b yields a nonzero value, hence, the if expression is true.

: a = 1;   a   is set to 1
b = 2;   b   is set to 2
if (a == b)   The equation a == b yields a zero value, hence, the if expression is false.

: a = 2;   a   is set to 2
b = 1;   b   is set to 1
if (a == b)   The equation a == b yields a zero value, hence, the if expression is false.

Rules : 1) There must be an expression on both the left and right of the == operator.
2) The two variables being compared should be of the same data type. If not, inconsistent results may occur.
3) The == and = operators perform totally different functions. The == operator tests for equality between two values. The = operator sets the variable on the left of the operator equal to the value of the variable, function, or constant on the right.

Name : != not equal to operator

Function : This operator compares the value of two expressions. Upon making this comparison, a nonzero is generated if the first operator is not equal to the second. If equal, a zero value is produced. As shown below, when incorporated within an if statement, a nonzero value is construed as true and a zero value is construed as false.

Example Setup : int a,b;

Example :
a = 1;	a	is set to 1
b = 1;	b	is set to 1
if (a != b)		The equation a != b yields a zero value, hence, the if expression is false.

:
a = 1;	a	is set to 1
b = 2;	b	is set to 2
if (a != b)		The equation a != b yields a nonzero value, hence, the if expression is true.

:
a = 2;	a	is set to 2
b = 1;	b	is set to 1
if (a != b)		The equation a != b yields a non-zero value, hence, the if expression is true.

Rules :
1) There must be an expression on both the left and right of the != operator.
2) The two variables being compared should be of the same data type. If not, inconsistent results may occur.
3) The !=, = and ! operators perform totally different functions. The != operator tests for nonequality between two values. The = operator sets the variable on the left of the operator not equal to the value of the variable, function or constant on the right. Lastly, the ! operator deals with the logical negative of a value.

?:

Name : ?: equation operator

Function : This operator is similar to an if/else statement. If the first value or condition produces a nonzero value (true), then the second value is used. If the first value yields a zero value (false), then the third value is used.

Example Setup : int a,b,c,d,e;

Examples :

a = 1;	a	is set to 1
b = 2;	b	is set to 2
c = 3;	c	is set to 3
d = 4;	d	is set to 4
e = (a = = b)?c:d	e	will be set to 4, the value of d because a and b are not equal, hence, the expression a = = b yields a zero value.

: a = 1;	a	is set to 1
b = 2;	b	is set to 2
c = 3;	c	is set to 3
d = 4;	d	is set to 4
e = a?c:d	e	will be set to 3, the value of c because a has a nonzero value.

Rules :
1) The leftmost operand is calculated first. Then, the second or third (but never both) operand is calculated next, based on the outcome of the first.
2) The first operand may be a variable, expression or function. Note, however, that if a constant is placed in the first position, the same result would always be chosen, thus negating the nonchosen option.

Name : & Bitwise AND

Function : This operator is used to AND two bit fields based on the boolean principles shown below in the rules section.

Example Setup : int a;
int b;
int c;
a = 1;
b = 2;

Example : c = a & b

Rules : 1) Bitwise operations may only be performed on variables defined as integers, namely int, long, unsigned and short.
2) The AND operation is performed using the following rules:

Bit 1	Bit 2	Outcome
1	1	1
1	0	0
0	1	0
0	0	0

3) When this operator is used in conjunction with other operators, C follows the specific rules of precedence outlined in Appendix A.

Name : | Bitwise inclusive OR

Function : This operator is used to inclusive OR two bit fields based on the boolean principles shown below in the rules section.

Example Setup : int a;
int b;
int c;
a = 1;
b = 2;

Example : c = a | b

Rules : 1) Bitwise operations may only be performed on variables defined as integers, namely, int, long, unsigned and short.
2) The inclusive OR operation is performed using the following rules:

Bit 1	Bit 2	Outcome
1	1	1
1	0	1
0	1	1
0	0	0

3) When this operator is used in conjunction with other operators, C follows the specific rules of precedence outlined in Appendix A.

Name : ∧ Bitwise exclusive OR

Function : This operator is used to exclusive OR two bit fields based on the boolean principles shown below in the rules section.

Example Setup : int a;
int b;
int c;
a = 1;
b = 2;

Example : c = a ∧ b

Rules : 1) Bitwise operations may only be performed on variables defined as integers, namely, int, long, unsigned and short.
2) The exclusive OR operation is performed using the following rules:

Bit 1	Bit 2	Outcome
1	1	0
1	0	1
0	1	1
0	0	0

3) When this operator is used in conjunction with other operators, C follows the specific rules of precedence outlined in Appendix A.

~

Name : ~ one's complement operator

Function : This operator is used to change all the 1 values to 0 and all the 0 values to 1, thus flip-flopping the bit values.

Example Setup : int a;
int b;
a = 1;

Example : b = ~a

Rules : 1) Bitwise operations may only be performed on variables defined as integers, namely, int, long, unsigned and short.
2) The one's complement operation is performed using the following rules:

Bit 1	Outcome
1	0
0	1

3) When this operator is used in conjunction with other operators, C follows the specific rules of precedence outlined in Appendix A.

Name : < < Bitwise shift left

Function : This operator is used to shift the bits contained within a variable or bit field a specified number of places to the left.

Example Setup : int a;
int b;
int c;
a = 1;
b = 2;

Examples : c = a < < b

shifts bits in a 2 places and places the result in c

c = a < < b

shifts bits in a 2 places to the left and places the result in c

c = a < < 3

shifts bits in a 3 places to the left and places the result in c

Rules : 1) Bitwise operations may only be performed on variables defined as integers, namely, int, long, unsigned and short.
2) The bits which are shifted out the left side of the variable are lost.
3) The spaces left vacant by the bit shifting are zero filled.
4) When this operator is used in conjunction with other operators, C follows the specific rules of precedence outlined in Appendix A.

Name : > > Bitwise shift right

Function: This operator is used to shift the bits contained within a variable or bit field a specified number of places to the right.

Example Setup : int a;
int b;
int c;
a = 1;
b = 2;

Examples : c = a > > b   shifts bits in a 2 places and places the result in c

c = a > > 3   shifts bits in a 3 places to the right and places the result in c

Rules : 1) Bitwise operations may only be performed on variables defined as integers, namely, int, long, unsigned and short.
2) The bits which are shifted out the right side of the variable are lost.
3) The spaces left vacant by the bit shifting are zero filled.
4) When this operator is used in conjunction with other operators, C follows the specific rules of precedence outlined in Appendix A.

Name : & = Bitwise AND

Function : This unary operator is used to AND two bit fields based on the boolean principles shown below in the rules section and place the generated value in the variable on the left side of the operator.

Example Setup : int a;
int b;
a = 1;
b = 2;

Example : b &= a

Rules : 1) Bitwise operations may only be performed on variables defined as integers, namely, int, long, unsigned and short.
2) The AND operation is performed using the following rules:

Bit 1	Bit 2	Outcome
1	1	1
1	0	0
0	1	0
0	0	0

3) When this operator is used in conjunction with other operators, C follows the specific rules of precedence outlined in Appendix A.

|=

Name : |= unary bitwise inclusive OR

Function : This operator is used to inclusive OR two bit fields based on the boolean principles shown below in the rules section and place the generated value in the variable on the left side of the operator.

Example Setup : int a;
int b;
a = 1;
b = 2;

Example : a |= b

Rules : 1) Bitwise operations may only be performed on variables defined as integers, namely int, long, unsigned and short.
2) The inclusive OR operation is performed using the following rules:

Bit 1	Bit 2	Outcome
1	1	1
1	0	1
0	1	1
0	0	0

3) When this operator is used in conjunction with other operators, C follows the specific rules of precedence outlined in Appendix A.

Name : ^=   Unary bitwise exclusive OR

Function : This operator is used to exclusive OR two bit fields based on the boolean principles shown below in the rules section and place the generated value in the variable on the left side of the operator.

Example Setup : int a;
int b;
a = 1;
b = 2;

Example : a ^= b

Rules : 1) Bitwise operations may only be performed on variables defined as integers, namely, int, long, unsigned and short.
2) The exclusive OR operation is performed using the following rules:

Bit 1	Bit 2	Outcome
1	1	0
1	0	1
0	1	1
0	0	0

3) When this operator is used in conjunction with other operators, C follows the specific rules of precedence outlined in Appendix A.

<<=

Name : <<= Unary bitwise shift left

Function : This operator is used to shift the bits contained within a variable or bit field a specified number of places to the left and place the outcome in the variable on the left side of the operator.

Example Setup : int a;
int b;
a = 1;
b = 2;

Examples : a <<= b   shifts bits in a 2 places and places the result in "a"

a <<= 3   shifts bits in "a" 3 places to the left and places the result in a

Rules : 1) Bitwise operations may only be performed on variables defined as integers, namely, int, long, unsigned and short.
2) The bits which are shifted out the left side of the variable are lost.
3) The spaces left vacant by the bit shifting are zero filled.
4) When this operator is used in conjunction with other operators, C follows the specific rules of precedence outlined in Appendix A.

Name : >> =   Unary bitwise shift right

Function : This operator is used to shift the bits contained within a variable or bit field a specified number of places to the right and place the outcome in the variable on the left side of the operator.

Example Setup : int a;
int b;
a = 1;
b = 2;

Examples : a >> = b   shifts bits in a 2 places and places the result in a

a >> = 3   shifts bits in a 3 places to the right and places the result in a

Rules : 1) Bitwise operations may only be performed on variables defined as integers, namely, int, long, unsigned and short
2) The bits which are shifted out the right side of the variable are lost.
3) The spaces left vacant by the bit shifting are zero filled.
4) When this operator is used in conjunction with other operators, C follows the specific rules of precedence outlined in Appendix A.

13

Storage Classes and Data Types

auto	—	automatic storage class
char	—	character data type
double	—	double data type
extern	—	external storage class
FILE	—	data file pointer type
float	—	floating point data type
int	—	integer data type
long	—	long data type prefix
register	—	register storage class
short	—	data type prefix
static	—	static storage class
struct	—	structure storage class
typedef	—	type-definition data type
union	—	union storage class
unsigned	—	unsigned data type

Name	:	auto
Type	:	Storage Class Definition
Syntax	:	auto *variable-type variable-name;*
		auto *variable-type variable-name, variable-name* . . . ;
Function	:	The function of auto is to define a variable as automatic storage class. This means that C will not reserve space for the specified variable at the beginning of the program's execution. Rather, it will dynamically allocate memory space at the time the function containing the element is called.
Examples	:	auto char a__variable[10];
		auto int b__variable, c__variable, d__variable;
Rules	:	1) All locally defined variables default to automatic class unless expressly defined to be otherwise (extern, register, static or typedef).
		2) All data types can be defined as automatic.
		3) Prior to initialization, the value contained within automatic variables should be considered to be garbage (some unknown set on numbers or characters).
		4) Automatic variables are local to the function in which they are defined.
		5) A variable may only be defined as one storage class.

char

Name	:	char character definition
Type	:	Data definition
Syntax	:	char *variable-name*; char *variable-name, variable-name* . . . ; *storage-class* char *variable-name*; *storage-class* char *variable-name, variable-name* . . . ;
Function	:	The char statement states that the listed variables will contain a single ASCII character.
Example	:	char a__variable; char a__variable, b__variable; auto char a__variable; extern char a__variable, b__variable, c__variable;
Rules	:	1) Character variables may be set to a particular value by placing that value in single quotes as shown below:

```
char a__variable;
a__variable = 'x';
```

2) Character variables may be set to non-printing character values (null, escape, line feed, etc.) by placing a backslash and the octal ASCII equivalent of that character in single quotes as shown below:

```
char a__variable;
a__variable = '\33';
```

Octal 33 is escape key ASCII equivalent.

3) Strings of characters may be defined by suffixing the defined variable with an array operator. For example, the following statement defines a character string (array) of 21 characters.

```
char last__name[21];
```

Note that in the above example, that last name would have a maximum length of 20 characters. The last character would be a null terminator, indicating the end of the character string.

Name : double   double floating point

Type : Data definition

Syntax : double *variable-name;*
double *variable-name, variable-name* . . . ;
storage-*class double variable-name;*
storage-*class double variable-name, variable-name* . . . ;

Function : The double statement declares that the listed variables are to be double precision floating point data types.

Example : double a__variable;
double a__variable, b__variable;
auto double a__variable;
extern double a__variable, b__variable, c__variable;

Rules :   1) Double precision floating point variables are two storage locations long (2 bytes), thus allowing for much larger and more precise values.
2) Rounding errors may occur when moving double precision variables to other numerically defined data types.
4) double and long float are equivalent expressions.

extern

Name : extern

Type : Storage Class Definition

Syntax : extern *variable-type variable-name;*
extern *variable-type variable-name, variable-name . . . ;*

Function : The function of extern is to define a variable as external storage class.

Examples : extern char a__variable[10];
extern int b__variable, c__variable, d__variable;

Rules :
1) Variables defined as extern remain in memory until the program ends execution.
2) extern defined variables must also be defined outside the function as an auto class variable.

Name : FILE

Type : Data definition

Syntax : FILE *variable-name;*
FILE *variable-name, variable-name . . . ;*

Function : The FILE data type is used exclusively to define the fopen( ) function and the variables needed to open, reference and close data files.

Example : FILE *input__file, *fopen( );

Rules :
1) The stdio.h leader file must be referenced in order to use the FILE data type. This file is the standard input/output header and is accessed by placing the following line at the beginning of your program:

    #include <stdio.h>

2) The word FILE is almost always printed in uppercase.
3) The particular rules surrounding the FILE statement tend to vary from compiler to compiler.
4) FILE serves as a nice documentation method for stating which variables are file related.

float

Name : float

Type : Data definition

Syntax : float *variable-name;*
float *variable-name, variable-name* . . . ;
storage-class float *variable-name;*
storage-class float *variable-name, variable-name* . . . ;

Function : The float statement declares that the listed variables are to be floating point data types.

Example : float a__variable;
float a__variable, b__variable;
auto float a__variable;
extern float a__variable, b__variable, c__variable;

Rules :
1) Floating point numbers are generally from 6 to 8 digits long and may be expressed in both conventional and exponential notation.
2) Rounding errors may occur when moving float point variables to other numerically defined data types.
3) double and long float are equivalent expressions.

Name : int

Type : Data definition

Syntax : int *variable-name;*
int *variable-name, variable-name* . .
storage-class int *variable-name;*
storage-class int *variable-name, variable-name* . . . ;

Function : The int statement defines the listed variables as integer data types.

Example : int a__variable;
int a__variable, b__variable;
auto int a__variable;
extern int a__variable, b__variable, c__variable;

Rules :
1) Integer numbers may contain values ranging from – 32767 through 32767.

2) Integer type variables may only contain whole numbers.

3) The decimal portion of a number will be truncated when moved to an integer data type variable.

4) The valid range of numbers that can be placed in an integer field can be expanded by declaring it as long or unsigned.

long

Name : long

Type : Data definition

Syntax : long *variable-name;*
long *variable-name, variable-name* . . . ;
long *variable-type variable-name;*
long *variable-type variable-name, variable-name* . . . ;
storage-class long *variable-name;*
storage-class long *variable-name, variable-name* . . . ;
storage-class long *variable-type variable-name;*
storage-class long *variable-type variable-name, variable-name* . . . ;

Function : The long statement defines variables to be twice as long as the normal specified data type (a type of double precision).

Example : long a__variable;
long a__variable, b__variable;
auto long a__variable;
extern long a__variable, b__variable, c__variable;

Rules :
1) A long float is the same as a double.
2) If the word "long" is present with no specified data type, then the variable's data type is assumed to be integer.
3) A long integer may contain values ranging from −2,147,483,647 through 2,147,483,647.
4) The decimal portion of a number will be truncated when moved to an integer data type variable.

Name : register

Type : Storage Class Definition

Syntax : register *variable-type variable-name;*
register *variable-type variable-name, variable-name* . . . ;

Function : Register class variables are stored in the CPU's register list, thus speeding up calculations performed on that variable.

Example : register char a__variable[10]
register int b__variable, c__variable, d__variable;

Rules :
1) If the CPU does not have room to store the register variable then it is automatically converted to auto class.
2) Structures, unions and arrays cannot be defined as register class variables.
3) The address of a register class variable cannot be obtained by the & address variable.
4) A variable may only be defined as one storage class.

short

Name :   short

Type :   Data definition

Syntax :   short *variable-name;*
short *variable-name, variable-name* . . . ;
short *variable-type variable-name;*
short *variable-type variable-name, variable-name* . . . ;
storage-class short *variable-name;*
storage-class short *variable-name, variable-name* . . . ;
storage-class short *variable-type variable-name;*
storage-class short *variable-type variable-name, variable-name* . . . ;

Function :   The short statement defines variables to be a short integer data type.

Example :   short a__variable;
short int a__variable;
short a__variable, b__variable;
auto short a__variable;
extern short a__variable, b__variable, c__variable;

Rules :
1) The word short stands for short integer.
2) If the word "short" is present with no specified data type, then the variable's data type is assumed to be integer.
3) A short integer is stored in half the space of a regular integer. Thus, requiring less memory space, but consequently, it can only hold smaller numbers.
4) Many IBM PC compilers store a short integer in the same manner as a regular integer, namely, in a full word. This is done because in a 16 bit machine, an 8 bit integer only allows for very small numbers. Because of this constraint, short is much more useful on a 32 bit machine.
4) Some compilers allow short data types other than integer, but this is not a standard C feature.
5) If your compiler stores short integers in a full 16 bit word, you may overcome this constraint by using bit fields as discussed in Chapter 11.

Name : static

Type : Storage Class Definition

Syntax : static *variable-type variable-name;*
static *variable-type variable-name, variable-name . . . ;*

Function : The static class is used to allocate a variable's memory space prior to, or at the very beginning of program execution and instructs the compiler to retain that space through the entire execution of the program.

Example : static char a__variable[ ] = "Hi, I'm a static";
static int b__variable = 5;

Rules :
1) The value placed within a static variable can be changed during program execution.
2) Static variables remain in memory throughout the entire execution of the program, thus, permanently taking up storage space.
3) Static variables are generally placed in a special data area and thus do not use space within the program stack.
4) Static variables are assigned their initial values either during compilation or at the very beginning of program execution.
5) Variables may only be defined as one storage class.
6) If a static variable is defined within a function, that variable is not re-initialized each time the function is called. Therefore, if the function modifies the value of a static variable, that modified value will be present in the variable if the function is called a second time.

struct

Name : struct

Type : Storage Class Definition

Syntax :
struct *struct__name* { *member-list* } ;
struct *struct__name* { *member-list* } *a__variable;*
struct *struct__name a__variable;*
struct *struct-name a__variable, b__variable;*

Function : A structure groups together variables under a common structure name.

Examples :

1) struct name {
  char last[10];
  char first[10];
  char middle[10];
 };

2) struct name employee;

3) struct name {
  char last[10];
  char first[10];
  char middle[10];
 } employee;

Rules :

1) As shown above, the member-list, is the set of the variable declarations that are included within the structure template.
2) The semicolon following the member-list's closing bracket is required.
3) A structure declaration is not allocated space in memory until it becomes associated with a structure variable. The association may be defined in one of two ways: First, you may define a structure template (example 1), followed by a structure variable assignment (example 2) or you may incorporate the variable name into the original structure definition (example 3).

Name : typedef

Type : Data definition

Syntax : typedef variable-type variable-name;

Function : typedef is used to define your own data definition types.

Example : typedef long unsigned int lui;
lui a__variable;

Rules :   1) All characters after the word "typedef" and before the last word are considered to be part of the type definition being defined. As shown below,

typedef long unsigned int lui;

typedef is the statement name, long unsigned int is the definition being defined and lui is the new data definition name.

union

Name : union

Type : Storage Class Definition

Syntax : union *union__name* { *member-list* } ;
union *union__name* { *member-list* } *a__variable;*

Function : A union allows you to store various data types within a single memory location.

Examples : 1) union all__types {
char a__character;
int an__integer;
double a__double;
};

Rules : 1) Memory space is reserved based on the largest union data type. In the example shown above, the union would require two bytes to memory storage, because of the a__double floating point variable.
2) A semicolon must be placed after the member list closing bracket.

Name :   unsigned

Type :   Data definition

Syntax :   unsigned *variable-name;*
unsigned *variable-name, variable-name* . . . *;*
unsigned *variable-type variable-name;*
unsigned *variable-type variable-name, variable-name* . . . *;*
storage-class unsigned *variable-name;*
storage-class unsigned *variable-name, variable-name* . . . *;*
storage-class unsigned *variable-type variable-name;*
storage-class unsigned *variable-type variable-name, variable-name* . . . *;*

Function :   The unsigned statement defines variables to be an unsigned integer data type.

Example :   unsigned a__variable;
unsigned int a__variable;
unsigned a__variable, b__variable;
auto unsigned a__variable;
extern unsigned a__variable, b__variable, c__variable;

Rules :   1) The word "unsigned" stands for unsigned integer.
2) An unsigned integer may contain values ranging from 0 to 65,635.
3) Unsigned integer variables may only contain positive values (or zero). Note, that a negative number is moved to an unsigned variable then unpredictable results may occur.

14
Compiler Directives

comment	—	comment directive
#asm	—	assembly language beginning indicator
#define	—	define directive
#else	—	else directive
#endasm	—	end assembly language indicator
#endif	—	end if directive
#if	—	if directive
#ifdef	—	if defined directive
#ifndef	—	if not defined directive
#include	—	include directive
#undef	—	undefine directive

Name : /* */comment

Syntax : /* The comment is placed here */

Function : The comment operator instructs the compiler to ignore the text placed between the beginning and ending comment symbol indicators.

Examples : Comments are generally formatted in the following ways:

1) j + + ; /* on same line as a statement */

2) / *   Outlining a group of comment lines by
        *   placing asterisks at the beginning of
        *   each commented line.
        */

3)   /*
        Just using the beginning and ending
        indicators with no additional asterisk
        blocking
        */

4) / ***** ***
        *   Outlining the comments within a four   *
        *   sided asterisk box.   *
        ***** ** /

5)   /*   Outlining each line of the comments   * /
        /*   with its own beginning and ending   * /
        /*   comment indicators   */

Rules : 1) A comment must begin with a slash, followed by an asterisk.
2) A comment statement must be terminated with an asterisk followed by a slash.
3) A good way to remember the comment syntax is to keep in mind that the asterisk is always on the inside of the comment.

#asm

Name : #asm

Long Name : assembly language beginning indicator

Function : The #asm compiler directive informs the compiler that the lines of code which follow are written in assembly language and not C.

Syntax : #asm
. . .
#endasm

Example : #asm
;
;*assembly language goes here*
;
#endasm

Rules :
1) Compiler directives are not followed by semicolons.
2) The #endasm directive must be placed after the last assembly language statement and before the next C statement.
3) The #asm and #endasm directives are not implemented on all C compilers.
4) Many compilers require the # to be in the first column.
5) The C compiler invokes a preprocessor which scans the source code in search of compiler directives. This preprocessor creates a temporary source code file which reflects the compiler directive. This temporary source code file is then used as the compiler's input file.

Name : #define

Long Name : define expression

Function : The #define compiler directive instructs the C compiler to replace all occurrences of a specified key word, with an associated character string.

Syntax : #define *defined-word expression*

Example :
```
#define BELL printf("%C", '\007)';
#define isblank(x) ((x = = ' ') ? 1 : 0 )
#define TRUE 1
#define FALSE 0
#define EOF −1
```

Rules :
1) Compiler directives are not followed by an ending semicolon.
2) As shown in the first #define example, a single word may be used to represent an entire statement.
3) As shown in the second #define example, the #define directive can be used to define function like procedures. These mini-functions are called "macros".
4) Define macros have an advantage over functions. This advantage, is that during precompilation, the macro is actually placed within the source code at all the locations where the key word is found. Therefore, executing the macro does not require the overhead associated with a function, namely, placing data and program pointers in the push down stack.
5) As shown in the last three #define examples, the #define directive can be used to set a variable equal to a specific value. In the case of TRUE and FALSE, given the values of 1 and 0 respectively, these words are much more self documenting than 0 and 1.
6) General industry conventions dictate that define macros are written in lowercase, and that simple word replacements (TRUE, FALSE, EOF, etc.) are in uppercase. Note that this is not a compiler requirement, just a standard programming practice.
7) When a define macro is passed a variable, as shown in the second #define example, the variable passed to the macro is placed within that macro during the precompilation process. For example, given the macro:

   ```
   #define square(x) ( x * x )
   ```

   as called by:

   ```
   square(a_value);
   ```

   the precompiler would place the equivalent of a_value * a_value in the source code.

#else

Name : #else

Function : The #else compiler directive is used to provide the #if, #indef and # ifndef directives with an if-then-else capability.

Syntax : #else *statement or statements*

Example : #ifdef TESTRUN
    printf("This is a test run");
#else
    printf("This is not a test run");
#endif

Rules :
1) Compiler directives are not followed by an ending semicolon.
2) The #else directive may only be used within the #if, #ifdef, and #ifndef directives.
3) The #else directive is optional and should only be used when it will contain compilable statements.
4) The #else directive does not replace #endif. The #endif is still required and must be placed after the #else directive and its associated statements.

Name : #endasm

Long Name : end assembly language section

Function : The #endasm compiler directive is used to inform the compiler that the assembly language statement section has ended at statements which follow are written in C.

Syntax : #endasm

Example : #asm

   ;

   ; *assembly language source code*

   ;

#endasm

Rules :
1) Compiler directives are not followed by an ending semicolon.
2) The #endasm directive may only be used in conjunction with #asm.
3) All statements placed between #asm and #asmasm are assumed to be assembly language source code.

#endif

Name : #endif

Long Name : end if

Function : This directive is used to signify the end of an #if, #ifdef, or #ifndef directive.

Syntax : #endif

Example : #if TESTRUN
    printf("This is a test");
#endif

Rules : 1) Compiler directives are not followed by an ending semicolon.
2) This #endif directive may only be used in conjunction with #if, #ifdef, and #ifndef.
3) #endif is a required part of the three if directives mentioned above. Note, that if the #endif is not present (assuming a syntax error is not produced), then your entire program will be considered part of the if directive.
4) The #endif directive will only signify the completion of the inner-most if. Thus, when nesting #if/def/ndef directives, you must have an associated #endif for each #if/def/ndef.

Name : #if

Function : The #if directive provides the ability to compile, or not compile sections of the source C code based on the value of a specified expression.

Syntax : #if

Examples : 1) #if TESTRUN
    printf("This is a test");
#else
    printf("this is not a test");
#endif

2) #if TESTRUN
    printf("This is a test");
#endif

Rules : 1) Compiler directives are not followed by an ending semicolon.
2) This directive can only interpret numerically defined constants. Note that the preprocessor is part of the compilation process, therefore, runtime values have not yet been defined.
3) All statements between the #if and the #endif are considered to be part of the #if directive. Hence, if the #endif is inadvertently left out, then your entire program from the #if forward will be compiled based on the outcome of that #if condition.
4) #if has an optional #else modifier.
5) When evaluating #if expressions, a zero is considered false and a nonzero is considered true.

#ifdef

Name : #ifdef

Long Name : if defined

Function : The #ifdef directive instructs the precompiler to conditionally compile statements (or review additional directives) based on if a specified identifier has been defined using #define.

Syntax :
#ifdef *expression-name statements* #endif
#ifdef *expression-name statements* #else *statements* #endif

Examples : 1)
```
#ifdef TESTRUN
    #define TESTFLAG 1
    printf("This is a test");
#else
    #define TESTFLAG 0
    printf("This is not a test");
#endif
```

2)
```
#ifdef TESTRUN
    printf("This is a test");
#endif
```

Rules :
1) Compiler directives are not followed by an ending semicolon.
2) All statements between the #ifdef and the #endif are considered to be part of the #ifdef directive. Hence, if the #endif is inadvertently left out, then your entire program from the #ifdef forward will be compiled based on the outcome of that #ifdef condition.
3) #ifdef has an optional #else modifier.
4) This directive is true if the identifier being tested has previously been defined.
5) #ifdef is false if the identifier being tested has not been previously defined.
6) The #ifdef directive may be nested with other #ifdef, #if, or ifndef directives.

Name : #ifndef

Long Name : if not defined

Function : The #ifndef directive instructs the precompiler to conditionally compile statements (or review additional directives) if a specified identifier has not been defined using #define.

Syntax :
#ifndef *expression-name statements* #endif
#ifndef *expression-name statements* #else statements #endif

Examples : 1)
```
#ifndef TESTRUN
    #define TESTFLAG 0
    printf("This is not a test");
#else
    #define TESTFLAG
    printf("This is a test");
#endif
```

2)
```
#ifndef TRUE
    #define TRUE 1
    #define FALSE 0
#endif
```

Rules : 1) Compiler directives are not followed by an ending semicolon.
2) All statements between the #ifndef and the #endif are considered to be part of the #ifndef directive. Hence, if the #endif is inadvertently left out, then your entire program from the #ifndef forward will be compiled based on the outcome of that #ifndef condition.
3) #ifndef has an optional #else modifier.
4) This directive is true if the identifier being tested has not previously been defined.
5) #ifndef is false if the identifier being tested has been previously defined.
6) The #ifndef directive may be nested with other #ifndef, #if, or ifndef directives.

#include

Name : #include

Long Name : include this source file

Function : The #include directive instructs the compiler to insert the source code contained within a specified file into the program being compiled.

Syntax : #include < *filename.ext* >

Examples : #include < stdio.h >
#include <math.h >

Rules :
1) Compiler directives are not followed by an ending semicolon.
2) The main use of this directive is to load header files into the source code prior to compilation.
3) Header files are generally used to establish define macros and word constants (TRUE, FALSE, EOF, etc.).
4) The file being included into the program must contain valid C source code.
5) It is valid to nest include statements. That is, an #include directive can be placed in a file that was itself included.
6) When nesting #include statements be sure not to cause an endless looping condition.

Name : #undef

Long Name : undefine a defined word or macro

Function : This directive is used to undefine a word or define macro that has previously been defined using the #define directive.

Syntax : #undef *defined-word*
#undef *defined-macro*

Example : #define TRUE
. . .
#undef TRUE

Rules : 1) Compiler directives are not followed by an ending semicolon.
2) In the above example, the word TRUE was assigned a value of 1. That word, then became unassigned by executing the #undef command.

15

Common C
Statements and Functions

abs	—	absolute value	for	—	for statement
acos	—	arc cosine	fprintf	—	file print function
asin	—	arc sine	fputc	—	put character
atan	—	arc tangent	fputs	—	file put string
atof	—	ASCII to floating point	fread	—	file read
atoi	—	ASCII to integer	fscanf	—	file scan function
atol	—	ASCII to logn	fseek	—	file seek
calloc	—	character allocation	ftell	—	file tell
ceil	—	ceiling of a number	fwrite	—	file write
cfree	—	characters free	getc	—	get character
clearerr	—	clear error	getch	—	get character
cos	—	cosine	getchar	—	get character
cosh	—	cosine hyperbolic	goto	—	goto statement
do	—	do statement	if	—	if statement
exit	—	exit statement	isalnum	—	is alphanumeric
exp	—	exponential	isalpha	—	is alpha
fabs	—	float absolute	isascil	—	is ascii
fclose	—	file close	iscntrl	—	is control character
feof	—	file end of file	isdigit	—	is digit
ferror	—	file error	islower	—	is lower case character
fflush	—	file flush	isprint	—	is print character
fgetc	—	file get character	ispunct	—	is punctuation character
fgets	—	file get string	isspace	—	is space character
floor	—	floor of a number	issupper	—	is upper case character
fopen	—	file open	itoa	—	integer to ascii

log	—	logarithm	sscanf	—	string scan function
malloc	—	memory allocation	strcat	—	string concatination
printf	—	print function	strcmp	—	string conpare
putc	—	put character	strcpy	—	string copy
putch	—	put character	strlen	—	string length
putchar	—	put character	strncat	—	string concatenate to length
rand	—	random number	strncmp	—	string compare
realloc	—	reallocate memory	strncpy	—	string copy to a number
remove	—	remove file from disk	switch	—	switch statement
rename	—	rename disk file	tolower	—	to lower case
rewind	—	rewind data file	toupper	—	to upper
scanf	—	scan input function	ungetc	—	unget character
sin	—	sine	unlink	—	unlink file
sinh	—	sine hyperbolic	while	—	while statement
sprintf	—	string print function	exit	—	exit program
srand	—	seeded random number			

abs

Name :	abs
Long Name :	absolute value
Library/Header :	math.h
Function :	The abs function receives an integer value and returns the absolute value of that integer.
Syntax :	ret_value = abs(int_value);
Definitions :	ret_value—This integer variable will contain the integer's absolute value as returned by the function.
	int_value—This integer variable contains the value being passed to the function.

Example Setup :

```
int ret_value;
int int_value;
```

Examples :

```
int_value = 10;
ret_value = abs(int_value);
printf("\n First example = %d",ret_value);

int_value = −5;
ret_value = abs(int_value);
printf("\n Second example = %d",ret_value);
```

Example Output :

```
First Example = 10
Second Example = 5
```

Rules : 1) The math.h header file must be include using the # include compiler directive.

2) The variable being passed to the function, as well as the variable receiving the function's return value must be defined using the int data type.

Name : acos

Long Name : arc cosine

Library/Header : math.h

Function : The acos function receives a variable defined as a double and returns its corresponding arc cosine value.

Syntax : ret__value = acos(double__value);

Definitions : ret__value—This double variable will contain the returned value of the acos function.

double-value—This variable contains the value being passed to the function.

Example Setup : double ret__value;
double double__value;

Examples : double__value = 10;
ret__value = acos(double__value);
printf("\n First example = %f",ret__value);

double__value = −5;
ret__value = acos(double__value);
printf("\n Second example = %f",ret__value);

Rules : 1) The math.h header file must be include using the # include compile directive.
2) The variable being passed to the function, as well as the variable receiving the function's return value must be defined using the double data type.

asin

Name	:	asin
Long Name	:	arc sine
Library/Header	:	math.h
Function	:	The asin function receives a variable defined as a "double" and returns its corresponding arc sine value.
Syntax	:	ret_value = asin(double_value);
Definitions	:	ret_value—This double variable will contain the returned value of the asin function.
		double-value—This variable contains the value being passed to the function.
Example Setup	:	double ret_value; double double_value;

Examples	:	double_value = 10;
		ret_value = asin(double_value);
		printf("\n First example = %f", ret_value);

		double_value = −5;
		ret_value = asin(double_value);
		printf("\n Second example = %f", ret_value);

Example Output	:	First example = 10 Second Example = 5
Rules	:	1) The math.h header file must be include using the # include compiler directive.
		2) The variable being passed to the function, as well as the variable receiving the function's return value must be defined using the double data type.

atan

Name :	atan
Long Name :	arc tangent
Library/Header :	math.h
Function :	The atan function receives a variable defined as a double and returns its corresponding arc tangent value.
Syntax :	ret__value = atan(double__value);
Definitions :	ret__value—This double variable will contain the returned value of the atan function.
	double-value—This variable contains the value being passed to the function.
Example Setup :	double ret__value; double double__value;

Examples :	double__value = 10;
	 ret__value = atan(double__value);
	 printf("\n First example = %f", ret__value);
	
	 double__value = −5;
	 ret__value = atan(double__value);
	 printf("\n Second example = %f",ret__value);

Example Output :	First example = 10 Second Example = 5
Rules :	1) The math.h header file must be include using the # include compile directive. 2) The variable being passed to the function, as well as the variable receiving the function's return value must be defined using the double data type.

atof

Name : atof

Long Name : ASCII to floating point

Library/Header : math.h

Function : The atof function receives a number in ASCII string format and converts it into a double precision floating point number (double).

Syntax : ret__value = atof(string__pointer);

Definitions : ret__value—This double precision floating point variable (double) receives the numeric value returned by the atof function.

string__pointer—This parameter must be a string pointer containing the address of the string to be converted.

Examples Setup : char a__string[ ] = "150";
char b__string[ ] = "−150.25 ";
char c__string[ ] = "1.234e-6";
double a__number;
double b__number;
double c__number;

Example : a__number = atof(a__string);
b__number = atof(b__string);
c__number = atof(c__string);

Rules : 1) The math.h header file must be included using the # include compiler directive.

2) The string__pointer being passed to the function is usually the name of the character array containing the number to be converted without the array bracket notation []. Note that when a character array is used without the array bracket notation, this unsuffixed array name is a pointer containing the address of the memory location in which the first array element resides.

3) The variable which will receive the function's return code must be defined as a double.

4) The string being passed to the function must contain a valid numeric representation. This representation may include the numbers 0 through 9, a period, or exponential notation.

Name : atoi

Long Name : ASCII to integer

Library/Header : math.h

Function : The atoi function receives a number in ASCII format and converts it into an integer value.

Syntax : ret__value = atoi(string__pointer);

Definitions : ret__value—This integer variable (int) receives the numeric value returned by the atoi function.

string__pointer—This parameter must be a string pointer containing the address of the string to be converted.

Examples Setup : char a__string[ ] = "150";
char b__string[ ] = "−150";
int a__number;
int b__number;

Example : a__number = atoi(a__string);
b__number = atoi(b__string);

Rules :
1) The math.h header file must be included using the # include compiler directive.
2) The string__pointer being passed to the function is actually the name of the character array containing the number to be converted without the array bracket notation [ ]. Note that when a character array is used without the array bracket notation, this unsuffixed array name is a pointer containing the address of the memory location in which the first array element resides.
3) The variable which will receive the functions return code must be defined as a int.
4) The string being passed to the function must contain a valid numeric integer representation. This representation may include the numbers 0 through 9 and a minus sign if the value is negative.

atol

Name : atol

Long Name : ASCII to long integer

Library/Header : math.h

Function : The atol function receives a number in ASCII string format and converts it into an long integer value.

Syntax : ret__value = atol(string__pointer);

Definitions : ret__value—This long integer number (long or long int) receives the numeric value returned by the atol function.

string__pointer—This parameter must be a string pointer containing the address of the string to be converted.

Examples Setup : char a__string[ ] = "150";
char b__string[ ] = "−150";
long a__number;
long int b__number;

Example : a__number = atol(a__string);
b__number = atol(b__string);

Rules : 1) The math.h header file must be included using the # include compiler directive.
2) The string__pointer being passed to the function is usually the name of the character array containing the number to be converted without the array bracket notation [ ]. Note, that when a character array is used without the array bracket notation, this unsuffixed array name is a pointer containing the address of the memory location in which the first array element resides.
3) The variable which will receive the functions return code must be defined as a long int or long.
4) The string being passed to the function must contain a valid numeric integer representation. This representation may include the numbers 0 through 9.
5) If the long data type key word is used without any additional clarification, the variable being defined is considered to be a long integer.

Name : calloc

Long Name : character allocation

Function : The calloc function is used to allocate a specified amount of contiguous CPU memory.

Syntax : c__pointer = calloc(no__of__units,unit__size);

Definitions : c__pointer— This is a character pointer that will contain the address of the first allocated memory location.

no__of__units—This is the number of data units you wish to allocate.

unit__size   This is the actual memory size in bytes of the data type, structure or union being allocated space.

Examples :
```
1) char *c__pointer;
     char c__variable;
     c__pointer = calloc ( 250, size of(c__variable);
```

```
2) char *c__pointer;
     struct name {
        char last[10];
        char first[10];
        char middle[10];
     };
     struct name *n__pointer;
     n__pointer = ( struct *)calloc(10,size of(struct name);
```

Rules :
1) The calloc function returns the address of the first allocated memory location. This address, must be saved to use as the base address for accessing the allocated memory.
2) The cfree and free functions use the memory address returned by "calloc" to free space originally reserved by calloc
3) A null value is returned by calloc if the function cannot allocate the requested amount of space.
4) General industry standards suggest that the calloc size parameter should be stated using the size of function as shown in the above example.

5) This function always allocated contiguous memory space. Therefore, the reserved memory area can be accessed through arrays or pointer arithmetic.

6) Many compilers require that when allocating memory space, non char data types, such as integers, structures and union, that the returned calloc value should be cast into the appropriate pointer type. An example of this casting is shown above in the second example.

7) The calloc function is very similar to the malloc function. The main distinction is that calloc can allocate memory for structures of varying date types while malloc generally requires that all allocated space be of one data type.

Name : ceil

Long Name : ceiling of a number

Library/Header : math.h

Function : The ceil function receives double-precision value and returns its ceiling value.

Syntax : ret__value = ceil(double__value);

Definitions : ret__value   This double precision variable will contain the parameter's ceiling value returned by the function.

double__value—This variable contains the value being passed to the function.

Example Setup : double ret__value;
double double__value;

Examples : double__value = 10;
ret__value = abs(double__value);
printf(" \n First example = %f",ret__value);

double__value = 25;
ret__value = ceil(double__value);
printf(" \n Second example = %f",ret__value);

Rules : 1) The math.h header file must be included using the # include compiler directive.
2) The variable being passed to the function, as well as the variable receiving the function's return value must be defined using the double data type.

cfree/free

Name : cfree/free

Long Name : free (deallocate) allocated memory

Function : The cfree and free functions are used to release memory space that was previously allocated through the use of calloc, malloc or realloc.

Syntax : ret__code = cfree(character__pointer);

Definitions : ret__code—This in an integer variable that generally will be given a value of 0 if cfree executed successfully and a -1 if it was unsuccessful.

c__pointer—This is a character pointer that was returned from a memory allocation function and contains the address of the first allocated memory location.

Example :
```
int ret__code;
char *c__pointer;
char c__variable;
c__pointer = calloc(250,size of(c__variable);
. . .
ret__code = cfree(c__pointer);
```

Rules :
1) The syntax examples and rules shown for cfree also apply to free if it exists on your particular compiler.
2) The pointer passed to cfree must be the address returned by a calloc, malloc or realloc function call.
3) Generally, a 0 will be returned if the function executed correctly, otherwise, a -1 is returned to signal an error.
4) If the calloc, malloc or realloc pointer was cast to be a non-character pointer, it must be recast back to a character when passed to cfree.

Name : clearerr/clreer

Long Name : clear error

Library/Header : stdio.h

Function : The clearerr and clreer functions are used to clear the appropriate file error flag.

Syntax : clearerr(file__pointer);

Definition : file__pointer—This is the file pointer that was returned from on fopen function.

Example :
```
FILE *f__pointer;
f__pointer = fopen("data.dat","r");
. . .
clearerr(f__pointer);
```

Rules :
1) The syntax, examples and rules shown for clearerr also apply to clreer if it exists on your particular compiler.
2) When a file error occurs, the file's error flag is activated. From this time forward, an end of file message will be returned from file I/O functions that attempt to access that file until the error is cleared by calling clearerr.
3) The file pointer must be associated with an open data file.

COS

Name : cos

Long Name : cosine

Library/Header : math.h

Function : The cos function receives a variable defined as a double and returns its corresponding arc cosine value.

Syntax : ret__value = cos(double__value);

Definitions : ret__value—This double variable will contain the returned value of the cos function.

double__value—This variable contains the value being passed to the function.

Example Setup : double ret__value;
double double__value;

Example : double__value = 10;
ret__value = cos(double__value);
printf("\n First example = %f",ret__value);
double__value = −5;
ret__value = cos(double__value);
printf("\n Second example = %f",ret__value);

Rules : 1) The math.h header file must be included using the # include compile directive.
2) The variable being passed to the function, as well as the variable receiving the function's return value must be defined using the double data type.

Name : cosh

Long Name : cosine hyperbolic

Library/Header : math.h

Function : The cosh function receives a variable defined as a double and returns its corresponding arc cosine value.

Syntax : ret__value = cosh(double__value);

Definitions : ret__value—This double variable will contain the returned value of the cosh function.

double__value—This variable contains the value being passed to the function.

Example Setup : double ret__value;
double double__value;

Examples : double__value = 10;
ret__value = cosh(double__value);
printf("\n First example = %f",ret__value);

double__value = −5;
ret__value = cosh(double__value);
printf("\nSecond example = %f",ret__value);

Rules : 1) The math.h header file must be include using the # include compiler directive.
2) The variable being passed to the function, as well as the variable receiving the function's return value must be defined using the double data type.

do

Name : do

Function : The do statement and its corresponding while clause is used to repeat the execution of a selected group of statements based on the test criteria within the while statement.

Syntax : do
statement or statement block
while *(test-expression)*;

Definitions : statement—A single C instruction or statement block may be repeated by placing it between the key words do and while.

Statement block—A statement block is a group of one or more C statements contained within block control brackets.

test-expression—The test-expression within the while clause is the criteria used to test if looping should be continued or if the do statement should be exited.

Examples :
1)  ```
    int x = 0;
    do
    printf("\nLets count to 5 : %d", x + +);
    while ( x < 5 );
    ```

2)  ```
    char answer[2];
    do
    { printf(\nEnter Y for yes or N for no: ");
    gets(answer);
    } while (answer[0] != 'Y' && answer[0] != 'N');
    ```

Rules :
1) The statement or statement block within the do loop are always executed at least once.
2) The while condition is evaluated after each execution of the statement or statement block.
3) The statements will continue to execute until the while test-expression returns a zero value.
4) The semicolon after the while test-expression is required.

Name : exit

Function : The exit statement terminates execution of the current program, closes all open files and purges all existing buffers.

Syntax : exit;
exit(integer__value or integer__constant);

Definition : The integer value or constant return value may be passed from the program being terminated to a host program or main function.

Examples : 1) exit;

2) exit(0);
or
exit(1);

3) int ecode;
ecode = 1;
exit(ecode);

Rules : Some compilers require a return code parameter, while others assume a return of 0 if no parameter value is found.

exp

Name : exp

Long Name : exponential value

Library/Header : math.h

Function : The exp function receives a variable defined as a double and returns its corresponding exponential value.

Syntax : ret__value = exp(double__value);

Definitions : ret__value—This double variable will contain the returned value of the exp function.

double-value—This variable contains the value being passed to the function.

Example Setup : double ret__value;
double double__value;

Examples : double__value = 10;
ret__value = exp(double__value);
printf("\n First example = %f",ret__value);

double__value = −5;
ret__value = exp(double__value);
printf("\n Second example = %f",ret__value);

Rules : 1) The math.h header file must be included using the # include compile directive.
2) The variable being passed to the function, as well as the variable receiving the function's return value, must be defined using the double data type.

Name : fabs

Long Name : floating point absolute value

Library/Header : math.h

Function : The fabs function receives a variable defined as a double and returns its corresponding absolute value.

Syntax : ret__value = fabs(double__value);

Definitions : ret__value—This double variable will contain the returned value of the fabs function.

double-value—This variable contains the value being passed to the function.

Example Setup : double ret__value;
double double__value;

Examples : double__value = 10;
ret__value = fabs(double__value);
printf("\n First example = %f",ret__value);

double__value = − 5;
ret__value = fabs(double__value);
printf("\n Second example = %f",ret__value);

Rules : 1) The math.h header file must be included using the # include compile directive.
2) The variable being passed to the function, as well as the variable receiving the function's return value, must be defined using the double data type.

fclose

Name : fclose

Long Name : file close

Library/Header : stdio.h

Function : The fclose function is used to close data files which has previously been opened using the fopen function.

Syntax : ret__value = fclose(f__pointer);

Definitions : ret__value—This integer variable will contain the returned value of the fclose function.

f__pointer—The file pointer is a pointer to an open data file. This variable must have obtained its pointer value from the return of the file open function fopen.

Example :
```
FILE *f__pointer;
int ret__code;
f__pointer = (fopen("data.dat","r");
. . .
ret__code = fclose(f__pointer);
```

Rules :
1) In most compilers, a 0 is returned if the file was successfully closed and a -1 if an error was detected when trying to close.
2) The stdio.h header file must be included in the program using the #include compiler directive.
3) When called, the fclose function will delete the file attributes from the file access table, flush the buffers and free up the file's associated pointers for reuse.
4) Upon program termination, all open files will automatically be closed by the system. However, it is good a programming practice and strongly suggested that you use fclose to close all open files prior to program termination.
5) When checking to see if the fclose function worked correctly, look for a non-zero. Some compilers use 1 and others use -1 to signal success.

Name : feof

Long Name : file—end of file

Library/Header : stdio.h

Function : The feof function is used to test if an input file has been completely read or if data still remains to be processed.

Syntax : ret__value = feof(f__pointer);

Definitions : ret__value—This integer variable will contain the returned value of the feof function.

f__pointer—The file pointer is a pointer to an open data file. This variable must have obtained its pointer value from the return of the file open open function fopen

Example : FILE *f__pointer;
int ret__code;
f__pointer = (fopen
("data.dat","r");
. . .
ret__code = feof(f__pointer);

Rules : 1) In most compilers, a 1 is returned if the file is out of data and a 0 is returned if data still remains to be read.
2) The stdio.h header file must be included in the program using the #include compiler directive.
3) The file pointer must be a valid file pointer associated with an open file.

ferror

Name : ferror

Long Name : file error status

Library/Header : stdio.h

Function : The ferror function is used to return the current error status of a specified file.

Syntax : ret__value = ferror(f__pointer);

Definitions : ret__value—This integer variable will contain the returned value of the ferror function.

f__pointer—The file pointer is a pointer to an open data file. This variable must have obtained its pointer value from the return of the file open open function fopen.

Example :
```
FILE *f__pointer;
int ret__code;
f__pointer = (fopen ("data.dat","r");
. . .
ret__code = ferror(f__pointer);
```

Rules :
1) In most compilers, a nonzero is returned if the file contains an error and a 0 is returned if no error has yet been detected.
2) The stdio.h header file must be included in the program using the # include compiler directive.
3) The file pointer must be a valid file pointer associated with an open file.

Name : fflush

Long Name : file—flush buffer

Library/Header : stdio.h

Function : The fflush function causes the data contained within the file buffer to be written to disk.

Syntax : fflush(f__pointer);

Definition : f__pointer—The file pointer is a pointer to an open data file. This variable must have obtained its pointer value from the return of the file open open function fopen

Example :
```
FILE *f__pointer;
int ret__code;
f__pointer = (fopen ("data.dat","r");
. . .
ret__code = fflush(f__pointer);
```

Rules :
1) The stdio.h header file must be included in the program using the #include compiler directive.
2) The file pointer must be a valid file pointer associated with an open file.
3) This function may only be used on files opened for output.

fgetc

Name : fgetc

Long Name : file—get character

Library/Header : stdio.h

Function : The fgetc function is used to retrieve a single character from a specified data file.

Syntax : int__variable = fgetc(f__pointer);

Definitions : int__variable—This variable is defined as an int and will be given the return value of the fgetc function. This return will be the ASCII value of the character read from the file or a −1 if an end of file or error condition is found.

f__pointer—The file pointer is a pointer to an open data file. This variable must have obtained its pointer value from the return of the file open function fopen.

Examples : FILE *f__pointer;
int ret__code;
f__pointer = (fopen ("data.dat","r");
. . .
int__variable = fgetc(f__pointer);

Rules : 1) The stdio.h header file must be included in the program using the #include compiler directive.
2) The file pointer must be a valid file pointer associated with an open file.
3) fgets is a function. Its define macro equivalent is the getc function.

Name : fgets

Long Name : file—get ASCII string

Library/Header : stdio.h

Function : The fgets function reads an ASCII character string from a specified data file.

Syntax : s__pointer = fgets(b__pointer,no__of__char,f__pointer);

Definitions : s__pointer—This variable is defined as a character pointer and will given the return value of the fgets function. This return will be the memory address of the first character read from the file or a NULL if an end of file or error condition is found.

b__pointer—This variable is defined as a character pointer and contains the address in which the retrieved string should be placed.

no__of__char—This parameter may be an integer variable or constant and contains the number of characters to be read from the file.

f__pointer—The file pointer is a pointer to an open data file. This variable must have obtained its pointer value from the return of the file open function fopen.

Examples :
```
FILE *f__pointer;
int no__of__char = 10;
char *s__pointer, *b__pointer;
f__pointer = (fopen ("data.dat","r");
. . .
s__pointer = fgets(b__pointer,no__of__char,f__pointer);
```

Rules :
1) The stdio.h header file must be included in the program using the #include compiler directive.
2) The file pointer must be a valid file pointer associated with an open file opened with read access privileges.
3) fgets reads the file until it finds a new line indicator or one character less then the specified number of bytes (or characters) to be read. This last byte is reserved for a null terminator ('\0').
4) Caution, some compilers will read the file until it finds a new line indicator and truncate all characters placed after the number specified in the fgets second parameter, hence, data may be lost.

floor

Name : floor

Long Name : floor of a number

Library/Header : math.h

Function : The floor function receives double-precision value and returns its floor value.

Syntax : ret__value = floor(double__value);

Definition : ret__value—This double precision variable will contain the parameter's floor value returned by the function.
double__value—This variable contains the value being passed to the function.

Example Setup : double ret__value;
double double__value;

Examples : double__value = 10;
ret__value = abs(double__value);
printf("\n First example = %f",ret__value);

double__value = 25;
ret__value = floor(double__value);
printf("\n Second example = %f",ret__value);

Rules : 1) The math.h header file must be included using the # include compiler directive.
2) The variable being passed to the function, as well as the variable receiving the function's return value, must be defined using the double data type.

Name : fopen

Long Name : file open

Library/Header : stdio.h

Function : The fopen function opens a data file for access and establishes the appropriate file buffers.

Syntax : file__pointer = fopen(filename,mode);

Definitions : file__pointer—The file pointer will contain the address of related file information. This pointer address must be saved because it is referenced by all file related functions.

filename—This may be a string variable pointer or a string constant and contains the file's directory name as shown when using the DOS dir function.

mode—The mode specifies the file type and the access privileges that should established.

Example : FILE *f__pointer;
char *file__name, *file__mode;
f__pointer = (fopen ("data.dat","r");

Rules : 1) The stdio.h header file must be included in the program using the #include compiler directive.
2) A file must be opened before it may be accessed by any other function.
3) Files may be opened in many modes (read, write, read binary, etc.). Refer to your particular compiler documentation for a list of all possible mode options.
4) Most compilers return a null pointer value if the file did not open properly.

for

Name : for

Long Name : for statement

Function : This statement facilitates the reiteration of source code based on a while condition and an incremental counter.

Syntax : for (*initialization; while-test; increment*)
statement or statement block

Examples : 1) int count;
for (x=0; x<5; count++)
    printf("\ncount is : %d",count);
2) int count;
for (x=0; x<5; count++)
    { printf("\nThis is the first statement");
      printf("\nThis is the second statement");
    }

Rules : 1) The initialization section is the first expression performed when the for statement is executed.
2) If more than one value must be initialized, the following techniques can be used:

a) x=1;
    for (y=0; x<5; x++)
b) for (x=1,y=2; x<5; x++)
c) for (x=y=0; x<5; x++)

3) The for statement is executed in the following order:
a) initialization
b) evaluate while test condition
c) statement or statement block
d) incrementation
4) The initialization section, while section, and incrementation section are mandatory. However, if any of these sections are not logically required in your particular application, you can signify that section with a blank statement. A blank statement is just a semicolon with no statement before it. In the example which follows, no initialization was needed. Note the stand-alone semicolon.
for (; x<10; x++)
5) Caution, if the while expression is placeheld with just a semicolon, then an endless loop condition is created that must be ended with a break statement, goto, or other means.

fprintf

Name : fprintf

Long Name : file—print function

Library/Header : stdio.h

Function : This function is used to print formatted data to a specified data file.

Syntax : printf(f__pointer, format__control, arguments);

Definitions : f__pointer—The file pointer is a pointer to an open data file. This variable must have obtained its pointer value from the return of the file open function fopen.

format__control—This string explains the output format.

arguments—This is a list of the variables to be printed.

Example Setup : int i__variable;
char c__variable[ ] = {"hello there"};
FILE *f__pointer;
char f__control[ ] = {"integer is %d, text is %s");

Example : f__pointer = fopen ("data.dat","w");
. . .
fprintf(f__pointer,f__control,i__variable,c__variable");
. . .
fprintf(f__pointer,"\nThe int value = %d",i__variable");

Rules : 1) The fprintf file pointer must be associated with a data file opened in output mode.
2) The print types listed in the format control must identically match the printing argument list.
3) Each variable has a coinciding print type identifier. For example, %d is integer, %s is character string and "%lf" is long float (double). Refer to your compiler documentation for a complete list of these identifiers. Note however, that these identifiers are all prefixed with a percent sign.

fputc

Name : fputc

Long Name : file—put character

Library/Header : stdio.h

Function : The "fputc" function is used to write a single character from a specified data file.

Syntax : ret__code = fputc(character,f__pointer);

Definitions : ret__code—This variable is defined as an int and will given the return value of the fputc function. This return will be the ASCII value of of the character written to the file or a −1 if an error condition is found.

character—This parameter is a character variable or constant containing the character to be printed in the file.

f__pointer—The file pointer is a pointer to an open data file. This variable must have obtained its pointer value from the return of the file open function fopen

Example : FILE *f__pointer;
int ret__code;
char c__variable;
f__pointer = (fopen ("data.dat","r");
. . .
c__variable = 'x';
ret__code = fputc(c__variable,f__pointer);
. . .
ret__code = fputc('x',f__pointer);

Rules : 1) The stdio.h header file must be included in the program using the #include compiler directive.
2) The file pointer must be a valid file pointer associated with a file open in output mode.
3) fputc is a function. Its define macro equivalent is the "putc" function.

Name : fputs

Long Name : file—put ASCII string

Library/Header : stdio.h

Function : The fputs function writes an ASCII character string to a specified data file.

Syntax : fputs(s__pointer,f__pointer);

Definitions : s__pointer—This variable is defined as a character pointer and contains the address of the character string that is to be written to the file.

f__pointer—The file pointer is a pointer to an open data file. This variable must have obtained its pointer value from the return of the file open function "fopen"

Example :
```
FILE *f__pointer;
char *s__pointer;
f__pointer = (fopen("data.dat","w");
...
fputs(s__pointer,f__pointer);
```

Rules :
1) The stdio.h header file must be included in the program using the #include compiler directive.
2) The file pointer must be a valid file pointer associated with an open file opened with write access privileges.
3) fputs writes to the file until it encounters a null terminator ('\0') in the string being printed.

fread

Name : fread

Long Name : file read

Library/Header : stdio.h

Function : The "fread" function is used to read blocks of data from the file and place then in the memory buffer for further use.

Syntax : ret__code = fread(b__pointer, b__size,no__of__blocks, file__pointer);

Definitions : ret__code—This integer variable receives the function return code stating the actual number of blocks retrieved.

b__pointer—This variable contains the starting point of the first file block to be read.

no__of__blocks—This integer variable or constant specifies the number of blocks to be read.

b__size—This integer variable or constant specifies the size of the data blocks being read.

f__pointer—The file pointer is a pointer to an open data file. This variable must have obtained its pointer value from the return of the file open function fopen.

Example :
```
FILE *f__pointer;
char *b__pointer
int ret__code, b__number, b__size;
f__pointer = (fopen ("data.dat","r");

. . .
b__number = 50;
b__size = 512;
ret__code = fread(b__pointer,b__size,b__number,f__pointer);
```

Rules :
1) The stdio.h header file must be included in the program using the #include compiler directive.
2) The file pointer must be a valid file pointer associated with an open file opened with read access privileges.
3) Be careful not to overflow your file input buffer.
4) The function returns the actual number of blocks read. Therefore, a return of 0 or null may signify a file error or an end-of-file condition.

Name : fscanf

Long Name : file read

Library/Header : stdio.h

Function : The fscanf function is used to read data from a data file, convert it to the appropriate data type and place it into the specified variables.

Syntax : fscanf(f__pointer, conversion__mask, arguments)

Definitions : f__pointer—The file pointer is a pointer to an open data file. This variable must have obtained its pointer value from the return of the file open function fopen.

conversion__mask—This string explains the format of the data being input.

arguments—This is a list pointers to the variables that will be receiving the data.

Example Setup : int i__variable;
char c__variable[ ];
FILE *f__pointer;

Example : fscanf(f__pointer,"%4d%6s,i__variable,c__variable");

Rules : 1) The fscanf file pointer must be associated with a data file opened in input mode.
2) The data types listed in the conversion mask must identically match the argument list.

fseek

Name : fseek

Long Name : file—seek to specified file location

Library/Header : stdio.h

Function : The fseek function is used to move the file pointer's current position.

Syntax : ret__code = fseek(file__pointer,offset,mode);

Definitions : ret__code—This integer variable receives the function return code.

f__pointer—The file pointer is a pointer to an open data file. This variable must have obtained its pointer value from the return of the file open function fopen.

offset—This parameter specifies where the current file pointer should be placed, based on the current position and the mode specified in the third parameter.

mode—The mode states where the function should start seeking the current file position from. The modes are 0, 1 and 2 and are explained below within the rules section.

Example :
```
FILE *f__pointer;
long int offset;
int ret__code, mode;
f__pointer = (fopen ("data.dat","r");
...
ret__code = fseek(f__pointer,1l,0);
...
mode = 1;
offset = 10;
ret__code = fseek(f__pointer,offset,mode);
```

Rules :
1) The stdio.h header file must be included in the program using the #include compiler directive.
2) The file pointer must be a valid file pointer associated with an open file opened.
3) Do not try to seek before the beginning or after the end of the file. If this is attempted, unexpected results may occur.

4) The function may return either the new pointer position or a zero if successful. Refer to your compiler documentation for clarification.
5) If the seek was unsuccessful a -1 will be returned.
6) Remember that the offset parameter is a long integer. Therefore, if you use an integer, it must be defined as long int. If you are using a numeric constant it must be specified as a long by placing a lower case "l" after the number.
7) The three seek modes are:
   0—Start seeking from the beginning of the file
   1—Start seeking at the current file position
   2—Start seeking from the end of the file

ftell

Name :	ftell
Long Name :	file—tell current file pointer position
Library/Header :	stdio.h
Function :	The ftell function returns the current access position of the data file being referenced.
Syntax :	ret__code = ftell(file__pointer);
Definitions :	ret__code—This integer variable receives the function return code.
	f__pointer—The file pointer is a pointer to an open data file. This variable must have obtained its pointer value from the return of the file open function fopen.

Example :	FILE *f__pointer;
	long int ret__code;
	f__pointer = (fopen ("data.dat","r");
	
	. . .
	
	ret__code = ftell(f__pointer);

Rules :	1) The stdio.h header file must be included in the program using the #include compiler directive. 2) The file pointer must be a valid file pointer associated with an open file opened. 3) The value returned by the ftell function is the current position being referenced within the file. This value is the actual number of bytes from the beginning of the file. 4) In most compilers, a −1 is returned if the function call was unsuccessful. 5) The variable receiving the functions return code must be defined as a long integer data type.

fwrite

Name :	fwrite
Long Name :	file write
Library/Header :	stdio.h
Function :	The fwrite function is used to write blocks of data from the memory buffer to the file.
Syntax :	ret__code = fwrite(b__pointer,b__size,no__of__blocks,file__pointer);
Definitions :	ret__code—This integer variable receives the function return code stating the actual number of blocks written.
	b__pointer—This variable contains the starting point of the first file block to be written.
	no__of__blocks—This integer variable or constant specifies the number of blocks to be written.
	b__size—This integer variable or constant specifies the size of the data blocks being written.
	f__pointer—The file pointer is a pointer to an open data file. This variable must have obtained its pointer value from the return of the file open function fopen.

Examples :
```
FILE *f__pointer;
char *b__pointer
int ret__code, b__number, b__size;
f__pointer = (fopen ("data.dat","w");
. . .
b__number = 50;
b__size = 512;
ret__code = fwrite(b__pointer,b__size,b__number,f__pointer);
```

Rules :
1) The stdio.h header file must be included in the program using the #include compiler directive.
2) The file pointer must be a valid file pointer associated with an open file opened with write access privileges.
3) The buffer value must be a valid memory location.
4) The return code should be checked to assure that the correct number of blocks are written to disk. Note that fwrite returns the actual number of blocks that were written. Therefore, if the number of blocks returned is different from the number specified in the third parameter, then an error may have occurred. If an error is suspected, execute ferror or feer to determine actual file status.

getc

Name	:	getc
Long Name	:	get character
Library/Header	:	stdio.h
Function	:	The getc function is used to return a character from a specified data file.
Syntax	:	ret__code = getc(file__pointer);
Definitions	:	ret__code—This integer variable receives the function return code which is either the octal value of the retrieved character or a -1 if an error or end of file condition arose.
		f__pointer—The file pointer is a pointer to an open data file. This variable must have obtained its pointer value from the return of the file open function fopen
Example	:	FILE *f__pointer;
		int ret__code;
		f__pointer = (fopen("data.dat","r");
		. . .
		ret__code = getc(f__pointer);
		printf("\n Character is a %c",ret__code);

Rules :
1) The stdio.h header file must be included in the program using the #include compiler directive.
2) The file pointer must be a valid file pointer associated with an open file opened with read access privileges.
3) In many compilers, the single character retrieval procedures are implemented as define macros and not functions. This can be done, because these procedures are actually getting a character from the input buffer and not from the file directly.

Name : getch

Long Name : get character from the console

Library/Header : stdio.h

Function : The getch function is used to return a single character from the keyboard.

Syntax : ret__code = getch();

Definition : ret__code—This integer variable receives the function return code which is either the octal value of the retrieved character or a -1 if an error or end of file condition arose.

Example :
```
int ret__code;
ret__code = getch(f__pointer);
putch(ret__code);
```

Rules :
1) The stdio.h header file must be included in the program using the #include compiler directive.
2) This function does not echo the input character to the screen, this character may be echoed using the putch function.

getchar

Name : getchar

Long Name : get character

Library/Header : stdio.h

Function : The getchar function is used to return a character from the keyboard.

Syntax : ret__code = getchar();

Definition : ret__code—This integer variable receives the function return code which is either the octal value of the retrieved character or a -1 if an error occurs.

Example :
```
int ret__code;
ret__code = getchar(f__pointer);
printf(" \ n Character is a %c",ret__code);
```

Rules :
1) The stdio.h header file must be included in the program using the #include compiler directive.
2) In many compilers, the single character retrieved procedures are implemented as define macros and not functions. This can be done because these procedures are actually getting a character from the input buffer and not from the file directly.
3) Because getch returns a character from the input buffer, it must wait until the input buffer contains data. In many cases, data is only moved to the buffer when the return key is entered, thus delaying when getchar can receive its data. Note that getch retreives a character directly from the console and therefore does not have to wait for the return key.

Name : goto

Function : The goto statement allows you to transfer program control from the current line to a specified label identifier else where within the function.

Syntax : got *label-name;*

Definition : label-name—This is a user defined line identifier ending with a colon .

Example : int ×;

  . . .

  if (× = = 1) goto alabel;

  . . .

  alabel:

Rules : 1) The label name must follow standard C naming conventions.
2) The label being referenced must be within the same function as the goto.
3) To adhere to standard structured programming techniques, the goto statement should be used with care.
4) The goto is best used to exit from single and nested loops in search of specific data.

if

Name : if

Function : The if statement facilitates procedural branching based on specified test criteria.

Syntax : if (*test-condition*)
statement or statement block
if (*test-condition*)
statement or statement block
else
statement or statement block

Examples : 1) int ×;
if (× = = 1)
printf("\n × has a value or one");

2) int ×;
if (× = =1)
{ printf("\n × has a value of one");
printf("\n this is line two of the block");
}
else
printf("\n × does not have a value of 1");

Rules : 1) The else condition is optional and should only be used when needed.
2) A value of zero in an if test condition denotes false
3) A nonzero value is considered to be a true.
4) As shown above, statements should be properly indented to assist in program readability.

Name : isalnum

Long Name : is this character an alphanumeric

Library/Header : ctype.h

Function : The isalnum function checks to see whether or not a character is a valid alphanumeric value.

Syntax : ret__value = isalnum(char__value);

Definitions : ret__value—This integer variable will contain the functions return value. This value will be a zero if the passed character is not an alphanumeric and a nonzero if it is within the alphanumeric character set.

char__value—This character variable contains the character being tested by the isalnum function.

Example :
```
char char__value;
int ret__value;
. . .
ret__value = isalnum(char__value);
```

Rules :
1) On some compilers this procedure is implemented as a define macro and not a function.
2) The ctype.h header file must be included using the #include compiler directive.
3) On some compilers, these procedures are defined as functions within the C runtime libraries and as macros within the ctype.h header file. Therefore, if you include the ctype.h header file you access the macros and if you do not include the ctype.h header file than you call the functions. Refer to your compiler documentation for clarification.
4) Some compilers return a 1 if the tested character meets the test requirements, other compilers return the octal value of the tested character. In both cases however, a zero is considered false and a nonzero is considered true.

isalpha

Name : isalpha

Long Name : is this character a valid alpha character

Library/Header : ctype.h

Function : The isalpha function checks to see whether or not a character is a valid alpha value.

Syntax : ret__value = isalpha(char__value);

Definitions : ret__value—This integer variable will contain the functions return value. This value will be a zero if the passed character is not an alpha and a nonzero if it is within the alpha character set.

char__value—This character variable contains the character being tested by the isalpha function.

Example : char char__value;
int ret__value;
. . .
ret__value = isalpha(char__value);

Rules : 1) On some compilers this procedure is implemented as a define macro and not a function.
2) The ctype.h header file must be included using the #include compiler directive.
3) On some compilers, these procedures are defined as functions within the C runtime libraries and as macros within the ctype.h header file. Therefore, if you include the ctype.h header file you access the macros and if you do not include the ctype.h header file than you call the functions. Refer to your compiler documentation for clarification.
4) Some compilers return a 1 if the tested character meets the test requirements, other compilers return the octal value of the tested character. In both cases however, a zero is considered false and a nonzero is considered true.

Name : isascii

Long Name : is this character a valid ASCII character

Library/Header : ctype.h

Function : The isascii function checks to see whether or not a character is a valid ASCII value.

Syntax : ret__value = isascii(char__value);

Definitions : ret__value—This integer variable will contain the functions return value. This value will be a zero if the passed character is not an ASCII and a nonzero if it is within the ASCII character set.

char__value—This character variable contains the character being tested by the isascii function.

Example : char char__value;
int ret__value;
. . .
ret__value = isascii(char__value);

Rules :
1) On some compilers this procedure is implemented as a define macro and not a function.
2) The ctype.h header file must be included using the #include compiler directive.
3) On some compilers, these procedures are defined as functions within the C runtime libraries and as macros within the ctype.h header file. Therefore, if you include the ctype.h header file you access the macros and if you do not include the ctype.h header file than you call the functions. Refer to your compiler documentation for clarification.
4) Some compilers return a 1 if the tested character meets the test requirements, other compilers return the octal value of the tested character. In both cases however, a zero is considered false and a nonzero is considered true.

iscntrl

Name : iscntrl

Long Name : is this character a control character

Library/Header : ctype.h

Function : The iscntrl function checks to see whether or not a character is a valid control value.

Syntax : ret__value = iscntrl(char__value);

Definitions : ret__value—This integer variable will contain the functions return value. This value will be a zero if the passed character is not a control and a nonzero if it is within the control character set.

char__value—This character variable contains the character being tested by the iscntrl function.

Example : char char__value;
int ret__value;
. . .
ret__value = iscntrl(char__value);

Rules :
1) On some compilers this procedure is implemented as a define macro and not a function.
2) The ctype.h header file must be included using the #include compiler directive.
3) On some compilers, these procedures are defined as functions within the C runtime libraries and as macros within the ctype.h header file. Therefore, if you include the ctype.h header file you access the macros and if you do not include the ctype.h header file than you call the functions. Refer to your compiler documentation for clarification.
4) Some compilers return a 1 if the tested character meets the test requirements, other compilers return the octal value of the tested character. In both cases however, a zero is considered false and a nonzero is considered true.

Name : isdigit

Long Name : is this character a numeric character

Library/Header : ctype.h

Function : The "isdigit" function checks to see whether or not a character is a valid numeric value.

Syntax : ret__value = isdigit(char__value);

Definitions : ret__value—This integer variable will contain the functions return value. This value will be a zero if the passed character is not a numeric and a nonzero if it is within the numeric character set.

char__value—This character variable contains the character being tested by the "isdigit" function.

Example :
```
char char__value;
int ret__value;
. . .
ret__value = isdigit(char__value);
```

Rules :
1) On some compilers this procedure is implemented as a define macro and not a function.
2) The ctype.h header file must be included using the #include compiler directive.
3) On some compilers, these procedures are defined as functions within the C runtime libraries and as macros within the ctype.h header file. Therefore, if you include the ctype.h header file you access the macros and if you do not include the ctype.h header file than you call the functions. Refer to your compiler documentation for clarification.
4) Some compilers return a 1 if the tested character meets the test requirements, other compilers return the octal value of the tested character. In both cases however, a zero is considered false and a nonzero is considered true.

islower

Name : islower

Long Name : is this character a lower case character

Library/Header : ctype.h

Function : The islower function checks to see whether or not a character is a valid lower case value.

Syntax : ret__value = islower(char__value);

Definitions : ret__value—This integer variable will contain the functions return value. This value will be a zero if the passed character is not a lower case and a nonzero if it is within the lower case character set.

char__value—This character variable contains the character being tested by the islower function.

Example :
```
char char__value;
int ret__value;
. . .
ret__value = islower(char__value);
```

Rules :
1) On some compilers this procedure is implemented as a define macro and not a function.
2) The ctype.h header file must be included using the #include compiler directive.
3) On some compilers, these procedures are defined as functions within the C runtime libraries and as macros within the ctype.h header file. Therefore, if you include the ctype.h header file you access the macros and if you do not include the ctype.h header file than you call the functions. Refer to your compiler documentation for clarification.
4) Some compilers return a 1 if the tested character meets the test requirements, other compilers return the octal value of the tested character. In both cases however, a zero is considered false and a nonzero is considered true.

Name : isprint

Long Name : is this character a printable character

Library/Header : ctype.h

Function : The isprint function checks to see whether or not a character is a valid printable value.

Syntax : ret__value = isprint(char__value);

Definitions : ret__value—This integer variable will contain the functions return value. This value will be a zero if the passed character is not printable and a nonzero if it is within the printable character set.

char__value—This character variable contains the character being tested by the isprint function.

Example :
```
char char__value;
int ret__value;
. . .
ret__value = isprint(char__value);
```

Rules :
1) On some compilers this procedure is implemented as a define macro and not a function.
2) The ctype.h header file must be included using the #include compiler directive.
3) On some compilers, these procedures are defined as functions within the C runtime libraries and as macros within the ctype.h header file. Therefore, if you include the ctype.h header file you access the macros and if you do not include the ctype.h header file than you call the functions. Refer to your compiler documentation for clarification.
4) Some compilers return a 1 if the tested character meets the test requirements, other compilers return the octal value of the tested character. In both cases however, a zero is considered false and a nonzero is considered true.

ispunct

Name : ispunct

Long Name : is this character a punctuation character

Library/Header : ctype.h

Function : The ispunct function checks to see whether or not a character is a valid punctuation value.

Syntax : ret__value = ispunct(char__value);

Definitions : ret__value—This integer variable will contain the functions return value. This value will be a zero if the passed character is not a punctuation character and a nonzero if it is within the punctuation character set.

char__value—This character variable contains the character being tested by the ispunct function.

Example :
```
char char__value;
int ret__value;
. . .
ret__value = ispunct(char__value);
```

Rules :
1) On some compilers this procedure is implemented as a define macro and not a function.
2) The ctype.h header file must be included using the #include compiler directive.
3) On some compilers, these procedures are defined as functions within the C runtime libraries and as macros within the ctype.h header file. Therefore, if you include the ctype.h header file you access the macros and if you do not include the ctype.h header file then you call the functions. Refer to your compiler documentation for clarification.
4) Some compilers return a 1 if the tested character meets the test requirements, other compilers return the octal value of the tested character. In both cases however, a zero is considered false and a nonzero is considered true.

Name : isspace

Long Name : is this character a white space character

Library/Header : ctype.h

Function : The isspace function checks to see whether or not a character is a valid white space value.

Syntax : ret__value = isspace(char__value);

Definitions : ret__value—This integer variable will contain the functions return value. This value will be a zero if the passed character is not a white space character and a nonzero if it is within the white space character set.

char__value—This character variable contains the character being tested by the isspace function.

Example :
```
char char__value;
int ret__value;
   . . .
ret__value = isspace(char__value);
```

Rules :
1) On some compilers this procedure is implemented as a define macro and not a function.
2) The ctype.h header file must be included using the #include compiler directive.
3) On some compilers, these procedures are defined as functions within the C runtime libraries and as macros within the ctype.h header file. Therefore, if you include the ctype.h header file you access the macros and if you do not include the ctype.h header file than you call the functions. Refer to your compiler documentation for clarification.
4) Some compilers return a 1 if the tested character meets the test requirements, other compilers return the octal value of the tested character. In both cases however, a zero is considered false and a nonzero is considered true.

isupper

Name : isupper

Long Name: is this character an upper case character

Library/Header : ctype.h

Function : The isupper function checks to see whether or not a character is a valid upper case value.

Syntax : ret__value = isupper(char__value);

Definitions : ret__value—This integer variable will contain the functions return value. This value will be a zero if the passed character is not an upper case character and a nonzero if it is within the upper case character set.

char__value—This character variable contains the character being tested by the isupper function.

Example : char char__value;
int ret__value;
. . .
ret__value = isupper(char__value);

Rules :
1) On some compilers this procedure is implemented as a define macro and not a function.
2) The ctype.h header file must be included using the #include compiler directive.
3) On some compilers, these procedures are defined as functions within the C runtime libraries and as macros within the ctype.h header file. Therefore, if you include the ctype.h header file you access the macros and if you do not include the ctype.h header file than you call the functions. Refer to your compiler documentation for clarification.
4) Some compilers return a 1 if the tested character meets the test requirements, other compilers return the octal value of the tested character. In both cases however, a zero is considered false and a nonzero is considered true.

Name : itoa

Long Name : integer to ASCII conversion

Library/Header : string.h

Function : The itoa is used to convert an integer number to its ASCII character string equivalent.

Syntax : itoa(int__value,char__pointer);

Definitions : int__value—This integer variable contains the number that is to be converted to a character string.

char__pointer—This parameter is the character pointer stating where in memory the converted number should be placed.

Example : int i__variable;
char *c__pointer;
. . .
itoa(i__variable,c__pointer);

Rules : 1) The character pointer must be associated with an area that is large enough to accommodate the converted integer number.
2) The character pointer may be either a defined character pointer associated with a character string or a character string name without the array brackets.

malloc

Name : malloc

Long Name : character allocation

Function : The malloc function is used to allocate a specified amount of contiguous CPU memory.

Syntax : c__pointer = malloc(no__of__units,unit__size);

Definitions : c__pointer—This is a character pointer that will contain the address of the first allocated memory location.

no__of__units—This is the number of data units you wish to allocate.

unit__size—This is the actual memory size in bytes of the data type, structure or union being allocated space.

Examples : 1) char *c__pointer;
char c__variable;
c__pointer = malloc (250, sizeof(c__variable);

2) char *c__pointer;
struct name {
char last[10];
char first[10];
char middle[10];
};
struct name *n__pointer;
n__pointer = (struct *)malloc(10,sizeof(struct name);

Rules : 1) The malloc function returns the address of the first allocated memory location. This address, must be saved to use as the base address for accessing the allocated memory.
2) The cfree and free functions use the memory address returned by malloc to free space originally reserved by malloc.
3) A null value is returned by malloc if the function cannot allocate the requested amount of space.
4) General industry standards suggest that the malloc size parameter should be stated using the sizeof function as shown in the above example.

5) This function always allocated contiguous memory space. Therefore, the reserved memory area can be acceded through arrays or pointer arithmetic.

6) Many compilers require that when allocating memory space, non char data types, such as integers, structures and union, that the returned malloc value should be cast into the appropriate pointer type. An example of this casting is shown above in the second example.

7) The malloc function is very similar to the calloc function. The main distinction being that calloc can allocate memory for structures of varying date types while malloc generally requires that all allocated space be of one data type.

printf

Name	:	printf
Long Name	:	print function
Library/Header	:	stdio.h
Function	:	This function is used to print formatted data to the screen or other specified output.
Syntax	:	printf(format__control, *arguments*);
Definitions	:	format__control—This string explains the output format.
		arguments—This is a list of the variables to be printed.
Example Setup	:	int i__variable; char c__variable[ ] = {"hello there"}; char f__control[ ] = {"integer is %d, text is %s");

Example	:	printf(i__variable,c__variable");
		. . .
		printf("\ nThe int value = %d",i__variable");

Rules	:	1) The print types listed in the format control must identically match the printing argument list. 2) Each variable has a coinciding print type identifier. For example, %d is integer, %s is character string and %lf is long float (double). Refer to your compiler documentation for a complete list of these identifiers. Note that these identifiers are all prefixed with a percent sign.

Name : putc

Long Name : put character

Library/Header : stdio.h

Function : The putc function is used to write a character from a specified data file.

Syntax : ret_code = putc(file_pointer);

Definitions : ret_code—This integer variable receives the function return code which is either the octal value of the written character or a −1 if an error condition was encountered.

f_pointer—The file pointer is a pointer to an open data file. This variable must have obtained its pointer value from the return of the file open function fopen.

Example :
```
FILE *f_pointer;
int ret_code;
f_pointer = (fopen("data.dat","w");
. . .
ret_code = putc(f_pointer);
```

Rules :
1) The stdio.h header file must be included in the program using the #include compiler directive.
2) The file pointer must be a valid file pointer associated with an open file opened with write access privileges.
3) In many compilers, the single character write procedures are implemented as define macros and not functions. This can be done, because these procedures are actually putting characters into the output buffer and not into the file directly.

putch

Name	:	putch
Long Name	:	put character to the screen
Library/Header	:	stdio.h
Function	:	The putch function is used to send a single character to the screen.
Syntax	:	putch(int__value);
Definition	:	int__value—This variable contains the octal value of the character to be printed on the screen.

Example	:	int int__value;
		int__value = getch();
		putch(int__value);

Rules	:	1) The stdio.h header file must be included in the program using the #include compiler directive. 2) This function is very commonly used in conjunction with getch which reads a character directly from the keyboard without printing it on the screen.

Name : putchar

Long Name : put character

Library/Header : stdio.h

Function : The putchar function is used to place a character in the output screen buffer (for file stdout the screen output file area).

Syntax : ret__code = putchar(char__variable);

Definition : ret__code—This integer variable receives the function return code which is either the octal value of the retrieved character or a −1 if an error occurs.

Example :
```
int ret__code;
char c__variable;
ret__code = putchar(c__variable);
```

Rules :
1) The stdio.h header file must be included in the program using the #include compiler directive.
2) In many compilers, the single character write procedures are implemented as define macros and not functions. This can be done, because these procedures are actually putting characters in the output buffer and not directly into the file.
3) Because putch writes a character into the output buffer, data is not immediately written to the file. Thus, delaying the actual writing to the file.

rand

Name : rand

Long Name : random number generation

Function : The rand function is used to generate a somewhat random number.

Syntax : ret_value = rand( );

ret_value—This integer variable will contain the returned random number.

Example : int ret_value;
ret_value = rand( );
printf("\n Random number = %d",ret_value);

Rules :
1) The rand function generates a somewhat random number because the default random seed is always 1. Therefore, the same random numbers are always generated.
2) The srand function can be used to change the random number seed and generate a different set of random numbers.
3) For truly random numbers, use the srand function to set the random seed based on the PC clock's hours, minute and seconds and hundreths of seconds.

realloc

Name :	realloc
Long Name :	character reallocation
Function :	The realloc function is used to reallocate a specified amount of contiguous CPU memory.
Syntax :	c__pointer = realloc(no__of__units,unit__size);
Definitions :	c__pointer—This is a character pointer that will contain the address of the first allocated memory location.
	no__of__units—This is the number of data units you wish to allocate.
	unit__size—This is the actual memory size in bytes of the data type, structure or union being allocated space.

Examples :

1)
```
char *c__pointer;
char c__variable;
c__pointer = realloc ( 250, sizeof(c__variable);
```

2)
```
char *c__pointer;
struct name {
   char last[10];
   char first[10];
   char middle[10];
   };
struct name *n__pointer;
n__pointer = ( struct *)realloc(10,sizeof(struct name);
```

Rules :

1) The "realloc" function returns the address of the first allocated memory location. This address, must be saved to use as the base address for accessing the allocated memory.

2) The cfree and free functions use the memory address returned by "realloc" to free space originally reserved by realloc.

3) A null value is returned by realloc if the function cannot allocate the requested amount of space.

4) General industry standards suggest that the realloc size parameter should be stated using the sizeof function as shown in the above example.

5) This function always allocated contiguous memory space. Therefore, the reserved memory area can be accessed through arrays or pointer arithmetic.

6) Many compilers require that when allocating memory space, non char data types, such as integers, structures and union, that the returned "realloc" value should be cast into the appropriate pointer type. An example of this casting is shown above in the second example.

7) The realloc function is very similar to the calloc and malloc functions, except that this function is used to reallocate space that has previously been allocated. For example, if you originally allocated memory for 50 integers and now require room for 75 integers. You would reallocate the 50 memory locations into 75 memory locations. By using realloc to reserve the additional 25 memory spaces you are guaranteed that all 75 integers are stored in contiguous memory space. If you just allocated 25 new spaces using calloc or malloc, there would be no guarantee that all 75 memory locations would be contiguous.

Name : remove

Long Name : remove a file from disk

Library/Header : stdio.h

Function : The "remove" function is used to delete a file from disk.

Syntax : ret__code = remove(file__name);

Definitions : ret__code—This integer variable will contain the functions return code. This code will be a 0 if the deletion was successful and a −1 if an error occurred.

file__name—The parameter names the file to be deleted.

Examples :
1) int ret__code;
   ret__code = remove("data.dat");
2) int ret__code;
   char file__name[12];
   strcpy("file__name,data.dat");
   ret__code = remove(file__name);

Rules :
1) If your compiler does not support the remove function, this task can easily be performed using the system function.
2) As shown above, the file that is to be deleted may be specified using either a constant character string or a character string containing the file name.
3) The file name being specified for deletion must contain valid DOS file name.

rename

Name : rename

Long Name : rename a disk file

Library/Header : stdio.h

Function : The rename function is used to rename a disk file.

Syntax : ret__code = rename(old__name,new__name);

Definitions : ret__code—This integer variable will contain the functions return code. This code will be a 0 if the rename was successful and a −1 if an error occurred.

old__name—This parameter is the name of the data file as it currently resides on disk.

new__name—This parameter contains the data file's new name.

Examples :
1) ```
   int ret__code;
   ret__code = rename("data.old,data.new");
   ```
2) ```
   int ret__code;
   char old__name[12];
   char new__name[12];
   strcpy("old__name,data.old");
   srecpy("new__name,data.new");
   ret__code = rename(file__name);
   ```

Rules :
1) If your compiler does not support the rename function, this task can easily be performed using the system function.
2) As shown above, the file that is to be deleted may be specified using either a constant character string or a character string containing the file name.
3) The file name being specified for deletion must contain valid DOS file name.

Name : rewind

Long Name : a file—rewind data file

Library/Header : stdio.h

Function : The rewind function is used to move the current file pointer to the beginning of the file.

Syntax : rewind(f__pointer);

Definition : f__pointer—The file pointer is a pointer to an open data file. This variable must have obtained its pointer value from the return of the file open function fopen.

Examples :
```
FILE *f__pointer;
f__pointer = (fopen("data.dat","r");
. . .
rewind(f__pointer);
```

Rules :
1) The stdio.h header file must be included in the program using the #include compiler directive.
2) The file pointer must be a valid file pointer associated with an open file.
3) If your compiler does not support the rewind function then the following fseek function will perform the same function.

```
ret__code = fseek(f__pointer,0l,0);
```

scanf

Name :	scanf
Long Name :	scan function
Library/Header :	stdio.h
Function :	The scanf function is used to read data from a standard input, convert it to the appropriate data type and place it into the specified variables.
Syntax :	scanf(conversion__mask, *arguments*)
Definitions :	conversion__mask—This string explains the format of the data being input.
	arguments—This is a list pointers to the variables that will be receiving the data.
Example Setup :	int i__variable; char c__variable[ ];
Example :	scanf("%4d%6s",i__variable,c__variable);
Rules :	1) The data types listed in the conversion mask must identically match the argument list. 2) Each variable has a coinciding data type identifier. For example, %d is integer, %s is character string and %lf is long float. Refer to your compiler documentation for a complete list of these identifiers. Note however, that these identifiers are all prefixed with a percent sign.

Name : sin

Long Name : sine

Library/Header : math.h

Function : The sin function receives a variable defined as a double and returns its corresponding sine value.

Syntax : ret__value = sin(double__value);

Definition : ret__value—This double variable will contain the returned value of the sin function.

double__value—This variable contains the value being passed to the function.

Example Setup : double ret__value;
double double__value;

Examples : double__value = 10;
ret__value = sin(double__value);
printf("\n First example = %d",ret__value);

double__value = −5;
ret__value = sin(double__value);
printf("\n Second example = %d",ret__value);

Rules : 1) The math.h header file must be included using the #include compile directive.
2) The variable being passed to the function, as well as the variable receiving the function's return value must be defined using the double data type.

sinh

Name :	sinh
Long Name :	sin hyperbolic
Library/Header :	math.h
Function :	The sinh function receives a variable defined as a double and returns its corresponding sine hyperbolic value.
Syntax :	ret__value = sinh(double__value);
Definitions :	ret__value—This double variable will contain the returned value of the "sinh" function.
	double__value—This variable contains the value being passed to the function.
Example Setup :	double ret__value; double double__value;

Examples :	double__value = 10;
	 ret__value = sinh(double__value);
	 printf("\n First example = %d",ret__value);
	
	 double__value = −5;
	 ret__value = sinh(double__value);
	 printf("\n Second example = %d",ret__value);

Rules :	1) The math.h header file must be include using the # include compile directive. 2) The variable being passed to the function, as well as the variable receiving the function's return value must be defined using the double data type.

Name : sprintf

Long Name : string print function

Library/Header : stdio.h

Function : This function is used to place formatted data to a specified memory location.

Syntax : sprintf(s__pointer, format__control, *arguments*);

Definitions : s__pointer—This parameter is the pointer that specifies where in memory the formatted string should be placed. format control—This string explains the output format. arguments—This is a list of the variables to be printed.

Example Setup : int i__variable;
char *c__pointer;
char c__variable[ ] = {"hello there"};
char f__control[ ] = {"integer is %d, text is %s"});

Example : printf(c__pointer,f__control,i__variable,c__variable);

. . .

printf(c__pointer,"\nThe int value = %d",i__variable);

Rules : 1) The string character pointer must point to a valid memory location with the appropriate amount of memory locations reserved for the output string.
2) The print types listed in the format control must identically match the printing argument list.
3) Each variable has a coinciding print type identifier. For example, %d is integer, %s is character string and %lf is long float (double). Refer to your compiler documentation for a complete list of these identifiers. Note however, that these identifiers are all prefixed with a percent sign.

srand

Name : srand

Long Name : random number seed

Function : The srand function provides the ability to change the seed number used in the random number generation process.

Syntax : srand(int__variable);

Definition : int__variable—This is the unsigned integer that will become the seed used in future random number generation.

Examples : unsigned int int__variable = 50;
srand(int__variable);

Rules : 1) The srand function generally has no return code.
2) The function's input parameter must be defined as an unsigned integer.
3) srand may be called at any time to change the random seed.
4) To assist in generating true random numbers you may wish to use the PC clock time as the seed.

Name : sscanf

Long Name : string scan function

Library/Header : stdio.h

Function : The sscanf function is used to convert data in memory from a character string data type to another specified data type.

Syntax : scanf(memory__pointer,conversion__mask, *argument*)

Definitions : memory__string—This pointer contains the first memory address of the character string to be converted.

conversion__mask—This string explains the data type of the variables receiving the converted data.

arguments—This is a list pointers to the variables that will be receiving the converted data.

Example Setup : int i__variable;
char c__variable[ ];
char old__string[ ];

Example : scanf(old__string,"*%4d%6s*",i__variable,c__variable);

Rules : 1) The data types listed in the conversion mask must identically match the argument list.
2) Each variable has a coinciding data type identifier. For example, %d is integer, %s is character string and %lf is long float. Refer to your compiler documentation for a complete list of these identifiers. Note that these identifiers are all prefixed with a percent sign.

strcat

Name : strcat

Long Name : string concatenation

Library/Header : string.h

Function : This function is used to add one string to the end of another string, thus concatenating the two values.

Syntax : ret__code = strcat(to__pointer,from__pointer);

Definitions : ret__code—This is the variable receiving the functions return value. This value will be a character pointer to the string receiving the additional data. Therefore, this variable must be defined as a pointer to a character.

to__pointer—This parameter must be defined as a character pointer and contains the address of the string receiving the new data.

from__pointer—This parameter must be defined as a character pointer and contains the address of the string that is to be added to the first parameter.

Example : char *ret__code;
char to__pointer[20] = {"hello"};
char from__pointer[ ] = {"there"};
ret__code = strcat(to__pointer,from__pointer);

Rules : 1) The two passed parameters must be character pointers defined as char * or as the unsubscripted name of a string array. Remember, the default pointer to char to__pointer[20] is the word "to__pointer" with no subscript brackets.
2) The string receiving the concatenated data must be large enough to contain that data. Otherwise, the function will write over, thus destroying, what ever happens to be in the next memory location.
3) The return pointer contains the address of the string receiving the concatenated data.

Name : strcmp

Long Name : string comparison

Library/Header : string.h

Function : This function is used to compare the value of two strings.

Syntax : ret__code = strcmp(first__pointer,second__pointer);

Definitions : ret__code—This is the variable that receives the functions return code. These return codes will be discussed below in the rules section.

first__pointer—This parameter must be defined as a character pointer and contains the address of the first string being compared.

second__pointer—This parameter must be defined as a character pointer and contains the address of the second string to be compared.

Example :
```
char *ret__code;
char *f__pointer;
char *s__pointer;
ret__code = strcmp(f__pointer,s__pointer);
```

Rules :
1) The two passed parameters must be character pointers defined as char * or as the unsubscripted name of a string array. Remember, the default pointer to char to__pointer[20] is the word "to__pointer" with no subscript brackets.
2) The integer value returned by the function will fall into one of the following three categories:
   equal to 0—the strings are equal
   less than 0—first string is less than second
   greater than 0—first string is greater than first
3) The return code variable must be defined as an integer int.

strcpy

Name : strcpy

Long Name : string copy

Library/Header : string.h

Function : This function is used to copy the value of one string to another string.

Syntax : ret__code = strcpy(to__pointer,from__pointer);

Definitions : ret__code—This is the variable receiving the functions return value. This value will be a character pointer to the string receiving the data. Therefore, this variable must be defined as a pointer to a character.

to__pointer—This parameter must be defined as a character pointer and contains the address of the string receiving the new data.

from__pointer—This parameter must be defined as a character pointer and contains the address of the string that is to be copied to the first parameter.

Example : char *ret__code;
char to__pointer[10];
char from__pointer[ ] = {"there"};
ret__code = strcpy(to__pointer,from__pointer);

Rules : 1) The two passed parameters must be character pointers defined as char * or as the unsubscripted name of a string array. Remember, the default pointer to char to__pointer[10] is the word "to__pointer" with no subscript brackets.
2) The string receiving the concatenated data must be large enough to contain that data. Otherwise, the function will write over, thus destroying, whatever happens to be in the next memory location.
3) The return pointer contains the address of the string receiving the new data.

strlen

Name :	strlen
Long Name :	string length
Library/Header :	string.h
Function :	This function is used to measure the length of a string.
Syntax :	ret__code = strlen(char__pointer,);
Definitions :	ret__code—This is the variable receiving the functions return value. This value will be an integer value stating the length of the string in characters.
	c__pointer—This parameter must be defined as a character pointer and contains the address of the string being measured.
Example :	char *ret__code; char c__pointer[ ] = {"I am 23 characters long"}; ret__code = strlen(c__pointer);

Rules :
1) The passed parameter must be character pointers defined as char * or as the unsubscripted name of a string array. Remember, the default pointer to char c__pointer[ ] is the word "c__pointer" with no subscript brackets.
2) The return code must be defined as an integer.
3) The null terminator at the end of the string is not included as part of its length.

strncat

Name : strncat

Long Name : string concatenation to a specified length

Library/Header : string.h

Function : This function is used to add a specified number of characters from one string to the end of another string, thus concatenating the two values.

Syntax : ret__code = strncat(to__pointer,from__pointer,max);

Definitions : ret__code—This is the variable receiving the functions return value. This value will be a character pointer to the string receiving the additional data. Therefore, this variable must be defined as a pointer to a character.

to__pointer—This parameter must be defined as a character pointer and contains the address of the string receiving the new data.

from__pointer—This parameter must be defined as a character pointer and contains the address of the string that is to be added to the first parameter.

max—This is an integer variable or constant that specifies the maximum number of characters to be concatenated.

Example :
```
char *ret__code;
int max = 10;
char to__pointer[20] = {"hello"};
char from__pointer[ ] = {"there"};
ret__code = strncat(to__pointer,from__pointer,max);
. . .
ret__code = strncat(to__pointer,from__pointer,7);
```

Rules : 1) The two passed parameters must be character pointers defined as char * or as the unsubscripted name of a string array. Remember, the default pointer to char to__pointer[20] is the word "to__pointer" with no subscript brackets.

2) The string receiving the concatenated data must be large enough to contain that data. Otherwise, the function will write over, thus destroying, whatever happens to be in the next memory location.

3) The return pointer contains the address of the string receiving the concatenated data.

4) The max parameter specifies the maximum number of characters that may be moved, not the exact amount. Therefore, if max has a value of 10 and the string being concatenated only has 6 characters, then only 6 characters are moved.

strncmp

Name : strncmp

Long Name : string comparison for a specified number of characters.

Library/Header : string.h

Function : This function is used to compare the value of a specified number of characters within two strings.

Syntax : ret__code = strncmp(f__pointer,s__pointer,length);

Definitions : ret__code—This is the variable that receives the functions return code. These return codes will be discussed below in the rules section.

f__pointer—This parameter must be defined as a character pointer and contains the address of the first string being compared.

s__pointer—This parameter must be defined as a character pointer and contains the address of the second string to be compared.

length—This integer value specifies the number of characters within the two strings that should be compared.

Example :
```
char *ret__code;
char *f__pointer;
char *s__pointer;
int length = 10;
ret__code = strncmp(f__pointer,s__pointer,length);
. . .
ret__code = strncmp(f__pointer,s__pointer,8);
```

Rules : 1) The two passed parameters must be character pointers defined as char * or as the unsubscripted name of a string array. Remember, the default pointer to char to__pointer[20] is the word "to__pointer" with no subscript brackets.

2) The integer value returned by the function will fall into one of the following three categories:

   equal to 0—the strings are equal
   less than 0—first string is less than second
   greater than 0—first string is greater than first

3) The return code variable must be defined as an integer.

4) The length parameter must be defined as an integer. It specifies the maximum number of characters to be compared.

Name : strncpy

Long Name : string copy a specified number of characters

Library/Header : string.h

Function : This function is used to copy a specified number of characters from one string to another string.

Syntax : ret__code = strncpy(to__pointer,from__pointer,max);

Definitions : ret__code—This is the variable receiving the functions return value. This value will be a character pointer to the string receiving the data. Therefore, this variable must be defined as a pointer to a character.

to__pointer—This parameter must be defined as a character pointer and contains the address of the string receiving the new data.

from__pointer—This parameter must be defined as a character pointer and contains the address of the string that is to be copied to the first parameter.

max—This is an integer variable or constant that specifies the maximum number of characters to be copied.

Example :
```
char *ret__code;
int max = 10;
char to__pointer[10];
char from__pointer[ ] = {"hello"};
ret__code = strncpy(to__pointer,from__pointer,max);
. . .
ret__code = strncpy(to__pointer,from__pointer,7);
```

Rules : 1) The two passed parameters must be character pointers defined as char * or as the unsubscripted name of a string array. Remember, the default pointer to char to__pointer[10] is the word "to__pointer" with no subscript brackets.

2) The string receiving the data must be large enough to contain that data. Otherwise, the function will write over, thus destroying, whatever happens to be in the next memory location.

3) The return pointer contains the address of the string receiving the copied data.

4) The max parameter specifies the maximum number of characters that may be moved, not the exact amount. Therefore, if max has a value of 10 and the string being copied only has 6 characters, then only 6 characters are moved.

switch

Name : switch

Function : The switch statement is used to execute selected statements based on specified selection criteria.

Syntax :
```
switch ( test-criteria )
    { case test-character:
        statement or statements
    case test-character:
        statement or statements
    . . .
    default:
        statement or statements
```

Example :
```
char c__variable;
c__variable = 'y';

switch (c__variable)
    { case 'x':
        printf("\n c__variable has a value of x");
        break;
    case 'y':
        printf("\n c__variable has a value of y");
        break;
    case 'z':
        printf("\n c__variable has a value of z");
        break;
    default:
        printf("\n c__variable in not x,y, or z ");
        break;
    }
```

Rules :
1) The test character being evaluated in the case statement must be an integer or a character data type.
2) Within a switch statement, no two case statements should contain the same test character value.
3) The default: label is not required to be the last switch option. However, general industry conventions suggest that it should always be used and be placed last.

4) C does not guarantee that the case statements will be evaluated in the order specified within the source code. They may be reordered if you are using an optimizing compiler. Therefore, if the order of evaluation is important, turn optimization off with the appropriate compilation command or use consecutive if/else statements instead of switch.

5) The default: label shown in the above example is a label that has a special meaning to the switch statement. This label instructs the switch statement to execute the statements after that label if no case statement conditions are met.

6) The break statement should be used to signify the end of the statements associated with a case statement. Refer to the above example for clarification.

tolower

Name : tolower

Long Name : convert character to lowercase

Library/Header : ctype.h

Function : The tolower function is used to convert the specified alphabetic character to lowercase.

Syntax : tolower(char__value);

Definition : char__value—This character variable contains the character being converted by the tolower function.

Example :
```
char char__value;
char__value = 'X';
. . .
tolower(char__value);
```

Rules :
1) On some compilers this procedure is implemented as a define macro and not a function.
2) The ctype.h header file must be included using the #include compiler directive.
3) On some compilers, these procedures are defined as functions within the C runtime libraries and as macros within the ctype.h header file. Therefore, if you include the ctype.h header file you access the macros and if you do not include the ctype.h header file then you call the functions. Refer to your compiler documentation for clarification.
4) A conversion will only take place if the character received by the function is an uppercase alphabetic. All other characters, including lowercase alpha's, numerics, white space, punctuation and control bytes will be returned unchanged.

Name : toupper

Long Name : convert character to uppercase

Library/Header : ctype.h

Function : The toupper function is used to convert the specified alphabetic character to uppercase.

Syntax : toupper(char__value);

Definition : char__value—This character variable contains the character being converted by the toupper function.

Example :
```
char char__value;
char__value = 'X';
. . .
toupper(char__value);
```

Rules :
1) On some compilers this procedure is implemented as a define macro and not a function.
2) The ctype.h header file must be included using the #include compiler directive.
3) On some compilers, these procedures are defined as functions within the C runtime libraries and as macros within the ctype.h header file. Therefore, if you include the ctype.h header file you access the macros and if you do not include the ctype.h header file then you call the functions. Refer to your compiler documentation for clarification.
4) A conversion will only take place if the character received by the function is an uppercase alphabetic. All other characters, including uppercase alpha's, numerics, white space, punctuation and control bytes will be returned unchanged.

ungetc

Name : ungetc

Long Name : unget a character from a file

Library/Header : stdio.h

Function : The ungetc function is used to return to the file the last character read for that file allowing it to be read again later.

Syntax : ret__code = ungetc(char__variable,f__pointer);

Definitions : ret__code—This variable is defined as an int and will give the return value of the ungetc function. This return will be the ASCII value of the character returned to the file or a −1 if an error condition occurred.

char__variable—This parameter contains the character that is to be returned to the file.

f__pointer—The file pointer is a pointer to an open data file. This variable must have obtained its pointer value from the return of the file open function fopen

Example : FILE *f__pointer;
int ret__code;
c__variable;
f__pointer = (fopen ("data.dat","r");
. . .
c__variable = getc(f__pointer);
int__variable = ungetc(f__pointer);

Rules : 1) The stdio.h header file must be included in the program using the #include compiler directive.
2) The file pointer must be a valid file pointer associated with an open file.
3) The character returned to the file must be the last character retrieved from that file.

Name : unlink

Long Name : unlink a file from disk

Library/Header : stdio.h

Function : The unlink function is used to delete a file from disk.

Syntax : ret__code = unlink(file__name);

Definitions : ret__code—This integer variable will contain the functions return code. This code will be a 0 if the deletion was successful and a −1 if an error occurred.

file__name—The parameter names the file to be deleted.

Examples : 1)   int ret__code;
            ret__code = unlink("data.dat");

         2)   int ret__code;
            char file__name[12];
            strcpy("file__name,"data.dat");
            ret__code = unlink(file__name);

Rules : 1)   If your compiler does not support the unlink function, this task can easily be performed using the system function.
         2)   As shown above, the file that is to be deleted may be specified using either a constant character string or a character string containing the file name.
         3)   The file name being specified for deletion must contain valid DOS file name.
         4)   The remove function is an equivalent function.

while

Name : while

Function : The while clause is used to repeat the execution of a selected group of statements based on test criteria within the while statement.

Syntax : while (test-expression)
    statement or statement block

Definitions : statement—A single C instruction may be repeated by placing it after the key while.

statement block—A statement block is a group of one or more C statements contained within block control brackets all of which will repeat execution while the while test criteria is met.

test-expression—The test expression is the criteria used to test if looping should be continued.

Examples :
1)
```
int x = 0;
while ( x < 5 );
    printf("\nLets count to 5 : %d",x + +);
```

2)
```
char answer[2];
answer[0] = 'N';
while (answer[0] != 'Y' && answer[0] != 'N');
  { printf(\nEnter Y for yes or N for no: ");
    gets(answer);
  }
```

Rules :
1) The statement or statement block within the while loop will only be executed if the while test criteria is met (unlike the do statement where they are always executed at least once).
2) The while condition is evaluated before each execution of the statement or statement block.
3) The statements will continue to execute until the while test expression returns a zero value.

Name : __exit

Function : The __exit statement if used to terminate program execution without closing any open data files or purging any input/output buffers.

Syntax : __exit(int__variable);

Definition : int__variable—This integer variable contains the value to be passed back to the calling program should one exist.

Example : 1) int int__variable = 1;
        __exit(int__variable);

    2) __exit(1);

Rules : 1) Returning a value of zero generally implies a normal program termination.
    2) A return code of other than zero generally indicates an abnormal termination.
    3) The return value may be expressed as either the value of an integer variable or as a numeric constant.

PART III

THE
C TOOLBOX
LIBRARY

16

Printer Output Functions

comp__off	—	compression off
comp__on	—	compression on
ds__off	—	double strike off
ds__on	—	double strike on
emph__off	—	emphasis off
emph__on	—	emphasis on
exp1__off	—	single expand mode off
exp1__on	—	single expand mode on
exp__off	—	expand mode off
exp__on	—	expand mode on
ital__off	—	italics off
ital__on	—	italics on
prop__off	—	proportional mode off
prop__on	—	proportional mode on
reset	—	reset printer
sub__off	—	subscript mode off
sub__on	—	subscript mode on
super__off	—	superscript mode off
super__on	—	superscript mode on
under__off	—	underline mode off
under__on	—	underline mode on

comp__off

Function Name: comp__off (compression off)

Description: This function instructs the printer to turn compressed mode off. This function works in conjunction with comp__on(). comp__on causes all characters to be printed in compressed format. This smaller type font allows 132 column reports to be printed on 80 column paper.

Variables: string — The string (octal 22) is sent to the screen to instruct the printer to enter compressed print format.

*prn__file — This variable is the file pointer used to open, define and close the file.

Example: comp__off();

Rules: The function is not passed any variables and is called to negate the comp__on() function.

Special Notes: This function is designed to work only on EPSON FX printers. If you are using a printer made by another manufacturer, you may have to send a different control string to the printer. If this is the case, you only must change the fprintf() file print line function.

If you will be using many of these special calls in conjunction with report printing, it may be to your advantage to open the printer as a file once at the beginning of your report and close it after all your printing is complete. If you take this plan of action, comment out the file calls used in this function.

```
#include <stdio.h>
comp_off()
{ FILE *prn_file, *fopen();
  prn_file = fopen("prn","w");
  fprintf(prn_file,"%c",'\022');
  fprintf(prn_file,"\nthis should not be compressed\n");
  fclose(prn_file);
}
```

Function Name: comp__on (compression on)

Description: This function instructs the printer to turn compressed mode on. This function works in conjunction with comp__off( ). comp__off turns compression mode off. Compression mode prints using a smaller font allowing 132 column reports to be printed on 80 column paper.

Variables: string — The string (octal 17) is sent to the screen to instruct the printer to enter compressed print format.

*prn__file — This variable is the file pointer used to open, define and close the file.

Example: comp__on( );

Rules: The function is not passed any variables and is called to initiate compression mode.

Special Notes: This function is designed to work only on EPSON FX printers. If you are using a printer made by another manufacturer, you may have to send a different control string to the printer. If this is the case, you only must change the fprintf( ) file print line function.

If you will be using many of these special calls in conjunction with report printing, it may be to your advantage to open the printer as a file once at the beginning of your report and close it after all your printing is complete. If you take this plan of action, comment out the file calls used in this function.

```
comp_on()
{ FILE *prn_file, *fopen();
  prn_file = fopen("prn","w");
  fprintf(prn_file,"%c",'\017');
  fprintf(prn_file,"\nthis should be compressed\n");
  fclose(prn_file);
}
```

ds__off

Function Name: ds__off (turn double strike off)

Description: This function instructs the printer to turn double strike mode off. This function works in conjunction with ds__on(). ds__on causes all characters to be printed twice (overstrike). This double striking produces a much darker copy because it actually prints the same character twice in the same place.

Variables: string   — A string of ESCAPE (octal 33) followed by the ASCII string "H" is sent to the screen to instruct the printer to enter double strike mode.

              *prn__file — This variable is the file pointer used to open, define and close the file.

Example: ds__off( );

Rules: The function is not passed any variables and is called to negate the ds__on( ) function.

Special Notes: This function is designed to work only on EPSON FX printers. If you are using a printer made by another manufacturer, you may have to send a different control string to the printer. If this is the case, you only must change the fprintf( ) file print line function.

If you will be using many of these special calls in conjunction with report printing, it may be to your advantage to open the printer as a file once at the beginning of your report and close it after all your printing is complete. If you take this plan of action, comment out the file calls used in this function.

```
ds_off()
{ FILE *prn_file, *fopen();
  prn_file = fopen("prn","w");
  fprintf(prn_file,"%cH",'\033');
  fprintf(prn_file,"\ndouble strike off\n");
  fclose(prn_file);
}
```

Function Name: ds__on (double strike on)

Description: This function instructs the printer to turn double strike mode on. This function works in conjunction with ds__off(). ds__off turns double strike mode off. Double strike mode prints each character twice. As a result, the printed output is much darker.

Variables: string — The string ESCAPE (octal 33) followed by the string "G" is sent to the screen to instruct the printer to enter double strike mode.

*prn__file — This variable is the file pointer used to open, define and close the file.

Example: ds__on( );

Rules: The function is not passed any variables and is called to initiate double strike mode.

Special Notes: This function is designed to work only on EPSON FX printers. If you are using a printer made by another manufacturer, you may have to send a different control string to the printer. If this is the case, you only must change the fprintf( ) file print line function.

If you will be using many of these special calls in conjunction with report printing, it may be to your advantage to open the printer as a file once at the beginning of your report and close it after all your printing is complete. If you take this plan of action, comment out the file calls used in this function.

```
ds_on()
{ FILE *prn_file, *fopen();
  prn_file = fopen("prn","w");
  fprintf(prn_file,"%cG",'\033');
  fprintf(prn_file,"\ndouble strike on\n");
  fclose(prn_file);
}
```

emph__off

Function Name: emph__off (turn emphasis off)

Description: This function instructs the printer to turn emphasis mode off. This function works in conjunction with emph__on( ). emph__on causes all characters to be printed twice, the second strike being slightly to the right of the first. This double striking produces a wider and darker copy because it actually prints the same character twice.

Variables: string   — A string of ESCAPE (octal 33) followed by the ASCII string "F" is sent to the screen to instruct the printer to exit emphasis mode.

           *prn__file — This variable is the file pointer used to open, define and close the file.

Example: emph__off( );

Rules: The function is not passed any variables and is called to negate the emph__on( ) function.

Special Notes: This function is designed to work only on EPSON FX printers. If you are using a printer made by another manufacturer, you may have to send a different control string to the printer. If this is the case, you only must change the fprintf( ) file print line function.

If you will be using many of these special calls in conjunction with report printing, it may be to your advantage to open the printer as a file once at the beginning of your report and close it after all your printing is complete. If you take this plan of action, comment out the file calls used in this function.

```
emph_off()
{ FILE *prn_file, *fopen();
  prn_file = fopen("prn","w");
  fprintf(prn_file,"%cF",'\033');
  fprintf(prn_file,"\nemphasis off\n");
  fclose(prn_file);
}
```

Function Name: emph__on (turn emphasis on)

Description: This function instructs the printer to turn emphasis mode on. This function works in conjunction with emph__off( ). emph__on( ) causes all characters to be printed twice, the second strike being slightly to the right of the first. This double striking produces a wider and darker copy because it actually prints the same character twice.

Variables: string — A string of ESCAPE (octal 33) followed by the ASCII string "E" is sent to the screen to instruct the printer to enter emphasis mode.

*prn__file — This variable is the file pointer used to open, define and close the file.

Example: emph__on( );

Rules: The function is not passed any variables and is called to turn emphasis mode on.

Special Notes: This function is designed to work only on EPSON FX printers. If you are using a printer made by another manufacturer, you may have to send a different control string to the printer. If this is the case, you only must change the fprintf( ) file print line function.

If you will be using many of these special calls in conjunction with report printing, it may be to your advantage to open the printer as a file once at the beginning of your report and close it after all your printing is complete. If you take this plan of action, comment out the file calls used in this function.

```
emph_on()
{ FILE *prn_file, *fopen();
  prn_file = fopen("prn","w");
  fprintf(prn_file,"%cE",'\033');
  fprintf(prn_file,"\nenphasis on\n");
  fclose(prn_file);
}
```

exp1__off

Function Name: exp1__off (single line expanded mode off)

Description: This function instructs the printer to turn single line expanded mode off. This function works in conjunction with exp1__on( ). exp1__on causes all characters to be printed in expanded format. This larger type font prints letters twice as wide as regular printed characters.

Variables: string   — The string (octal 24) is sent to the screen to instruct the printer to exit single line expanded print format.

            *prn__file — This variable is the file pointer used to open, define and close the file.

Example: exp1__off( );

Rules: The function is not passed any variables and is called to negate the exp1__on( ) function.

Special Notes: This function is designed to work only on EPSON FX printers. If you are using a printer made by another manufacturer, you may have to send a different control string to the printer. If this is the case, you only must change the fprintf( ) file print line function.

If you will be using many of these special calls in conjunction with report printing, it may be to your advantage to open the printer as a file once at the beginning of your report and close it after all your printing is complete. If you take this plan of action, comment out the file calls used in this function.

```
exp1_off()
{ FILE *prn_file, *fopen();
  prn_file = fopen("prn","w");
  fprintf(prn_file,"%c",'\024');
  fprintf(prn_file,"\nsingle line exanded on\n");
  fclose(prn_file);
}
```

Function Name: exp1__on (single line expanded mode on)

Description: This function instructs the printer to turn single line expanded mode on. This function works in conjunction with exp1__off( ). exp1__on causes all characters to be printed in expanded format. This larger type font prints letters twice as wide as regular printed characters.

Variables: string — The string (octal 16) is sent to the screen to instruct the printer to enter single line expanded print format.

*prn__file — This variable is the file pointer used to open, define and close the file.

Example: exp1__on( );

Rules: The function is not passed any variables and is called to turn single line expanded mode on.

Special Notes: This function is designed to work only on EPSON FX printers. If you are using a printer made by another manufacturer, you may have to send a different control string to the printer. If this is the case, you only must change the fprintf( ) file print line function.

If you will be using many of these special calls in conjunction with report printing, it may be to your advantage to open the printer as a file once at the beginning of your report and close it after all your printing is complete. If you take this plan of action, comment out the file calls used in this function.

```
exp1_on( )
{ FILE *prn_file, *fopen( );
  prn_file = fopen("prn","w");
  fprintf(prn_file,"%c",'\016');
  fprintf(prn_file,"\nsingle line expanded off\n");
  fclose(prn_file);
}
```

exp__off

Function Name: exp__off (expanded mode off)

Description: This function instructs the printer to turn expanded mode off. This function works in conjunction with exp__on( ). exp__on causes all characters to be printed in expanded format. This larger type font prints letters twice as wide as regular printed characters.

Variables: string — The string ESCAPE (octal 33) followed by the ASCII characters "W0" is sent to the screen to instruct the printer to exit expanded print format.

*prn__file — This variable is the file pointer used to open, define and close the file.

Example: exp__off( );

Rules: The function is not passed any variables and is called to negate the exp__on( ) function.

Special Notes: This function is designed to work only on EPSON FX printers. If you are using a printer made by another manufacturer, you may have to send a different control string to the printer. If this is the case, you only must change the fprintf( ) file print line function.

If you will be using many of these special calls in conjunction with report printing, it may be to your advantage to open the printer as a file once at the beginning of your report and close it after all your printing is complete. If you take this plan of action, comment out the file calls used in this function.

```
exp_off()
{ FILE *prn_file, *fopen();
  prn_file = fopen("prn","w");
  fprintf(prn_file,"%cW0",'\033');
  fprintf(prn_file,"\ncontinuous expanded off\n");
  fclose(prn_file);
}
```

Function Name: exp__on (expanded mode on)

Description: This function instructs the printer to turn expanded mode on. This function works in conjunction with exp__off( ). exp__on causes all characters to be printed in expanded format. This larger type font prints letters twice as wide as regular printed characters.

Variables: string — The string ESCAPE (octal 33) followed by the ASCII characters "W1" is sent to the screen to instruct the printer to enter expanded print format.

*prn__file — This variable is the file pointer used to open, define and close the file.

Example: exp__on( );

Rules: The function is not passed any variables and is called to turn expanded mode on.

Special Notes: This function is designed to work only on EPSON FX printers. If you are using a printer made by another manufacturer, you may have to send a different control string to the printer. If this is the case, you only must change the fprintf( ) file print line function.

If you will be using many of these special calls in conjunction with report printing, it may be to your advantage to open the printer as a file once at the beginning of your report and close it after all your printing is complete. If you take this plan of action, comment out the file calls used in this function.

```
exp_on()
{ FILE *prn_file, *fopen();
  prn_file = fopen("prn","w");
  fprintf(prn_file,"%cW1",'\033');
  fprintf(prn_file,"\ncontinuous expanded on\n");
  fclose(prn_file);
}
```

ital__off

Function Name: ital__off (italics mode off)

Description: This function instructs the printer to turn italics mode off. This function works in conjunction with ital__on( ). ital__on causes all characters to be printed in italics format. This fancy font type prints letters at a slight right angle.

Variables: string — The string ESCAPE (octal 33) followed by the ASCII characters "5" is sent to the screen to instruct the printer to exit italics print format.

*prn__file — This variable is the file pointer used to open, define and close the file.

Example: ital__off( );

Rules: The function is not passed any variables and is called to negate the ital__on( ) function.

Special Notes: This function is designed to work only on EPSON FX printers. If you are using a printer made by another manufacturer, you may have to send a different control string to the printer. If this is the case, you only must change the fprintf( ) file print line function.

If you will be using many of these special calls in conjunction with report printing, it may be to your advantage to open the printer as a file once at the beginning of your report and close it after all your printing is complete. If you take this plan of action, comment out the file calls used in this function.

```
ital_off()
{ FILE *prn_file, *fopen();
  prn_file = fopen("prn","w");
  fprintf(prn_file,"%c5",'\033');
  fprintf(prn_file,"\nitalics off\n");
  fclose(prn_file);
}
```

Function Name: ital__on (italics mode on)

Description: This function instructs the printer to turn italics mode off. This function works in conjunction with ital__off( ). ital__on causes all characters to be printed in italics format. This fancy font type prints letters at a slight right angle.

Variables: string — The string ESCAPE (octal 33) followed by the ASCII characters "4" is sent to the screen to instruct the printer to exit italics print format.

*prn__file — This variable is the file pointer used to open, define and close the file.

Example: ital__on( );

Rules: The function is not passed any variables and is called to turn italics mode on.

Special Notes: This function is designed to work only on EPSON FX printers. If you are using a printer made by another manufacturer, you may have to send a different control string to the printer. If this is the case, you only must change the fprintf( ) file print line function.

If you will be using many of these special calls in conjunction with report printing, it may be to your advantage to open the printer as a file once at the beginning of your report and close it after all your printing is complete. If you take this plan of action, comment out the file calls used in this function.

```
ital_on()
{ FILE *prn_file, *fopen();
  prn_file = fopen("prn","w");
  fprintf(prn_file,"%c4",'\033');
  fprintf(prn_file,"\nitalics on\n");
  fclose(prn_file);
}
```

prop__off

Function Name: prop__off (proportional mode off)

Description: This function instructs the printer to turn proportional mode off. This function works in conjunction with prop__on( ). prop__on causes all characters to be printed in proportional format. This print mode effects the space between printed characters. With proportional printing, the letters are printed close together, based on the size of the letters being printed.

Variables: string — The string ESCAPE (octal 33) followed by the ASCII characters "p0" is sent to the screen to instruct the printer to exit proportional print format.
*prn__file — This variable is the file pointer used to open, define and close the file.

Example: prop__off( );

Rules: The function is not passed any variables and is called to negate the "prop__on( ) function.

Special Notes: This function is designed to work only on EPSON FX printers. If you are using a printer made by another manufacturer, you may have to send a different control string to the printer. If this is the case, you only must change the fprintf( ) file print line function.
If you will be using many of these special calls in conjunction with report printing, it may be to your advantage to open the printer as a file once at the beginning of your report and close it after all your printing is complete. If you take this plan of action, comment out the file calls used in this function.

```
prop_off()
{ FILE *prn_file, *fopen();
  prn_file = fopen("prn","w");
  fprintf(prn_file,"%cp0",'\033');
  fprintf(prn_file,"\nproportional off\n");
  fclose(prn_file);
}
```

Function Name: prop__on (proportional mode on)

Description: This function instructs the printer to turn proportional mode on. This function works in conjunction with prop__off( ). prop__on causes all characters to be printed in proportional format. This print mode effects the space between printed characters. With proportional printing, the letters are printed close together, based on the size of the letters being printed.

Variables: string — The string ESCAPE (octal 33) followed by the ASCII characters "p1" is sent to the screen to instruct the printer to exit proportional print format.

           *prn__file — This variable is the file pointer used to open, define and close the file.

Example: prop__on( );

Rules: The function is not passed any variables and is called to enter proportional mode.

Special Notes: This function is designed to work only on EPSON FX printers. If you are using a printer made by another manufacturer, you may have to send a different control string to the printer. If this is the case, you only must change the fprintf( ) file print line function.

If you will be using many of these special calls in conjunction with report printing, it may be to your advantage to open the printer as a file once at the beginning of your report and close it after all your printing is complete. If you take this plan of action, comment out the file calls used in this function.

```
prop_on()
{ FILE *prn_file, *fopen();
  prn_file = fopen("prn","w");
  fprintf(prn_file,"%cp1",'\033');
  fprintf(prn_file,"\nproportional on\n");
  fclose(prn_file);
}
```

reset

Function Name: reset (reset printer)

Description: This function instructs the printer to cancel all programmed settings and return to the settings that were in place when the printer was first turned on. These settings will be a combination of the manufacturers defaults and the position of the printer dip switches.

Variables: string   — The string ESCAPE (octal 33) followed by the ASCII character "@" is sent to the screen to instruct the printer to reset settings.

            *prn__file — This variable is the file pointer used to open, define and close the file.

Example: reset( );

Rules: The function is not passed any variables and is called to reset the printer.

Special Notes: This function is designed to work only on EPSON FX printers. If you are using a printer made by another manufacturer, you may have to send a different control string to the printer. If this is the case, you only must change the fprintf( ) file print line function.

If you will be using many of these special calls in conjunction with report printing, it may be to your advantage to open the printer as a file once at the beginning of your report and close it after all your printing is complete. If you take this plan of action, comment out the file calls used in this function.

```
reset()
{ FILE *prn_file, *fopen();
  prn_file = fopen("prn","w");
  fprintf(prn_file,"%c@",'\033');
  fprintf(prn_file,"\nprinter reset\n");
  fclose(prn_file);
}
```

Function Name: sub__off (subscript mode off)

Description: This function instructs the printer to turn subscript mode off. This function works in conjunction with sub__on( ). sub__on causes all characters to be printed in subscript format. This type font prints letters in a footnote type fashion, being lower and shorter than the regular printed characters.

Variables: string   — The string ESCAPE (octal 33) followed by the ASCII characters "T" is sent to the screen to instruct the printer to exit subscript print format.

*prn__file — This variable is the file pointer used to open, define and close the file.

Example: sub__off( );

Rules: The function is not passed any variables and is called to negate the sub__on( ) function.

Special Notes: This function is designed to work only on EPSON FX printers. If you are using a printer made by another manufacturer, you may have to send a different control string to the printer. If this is the case, you only must change the fprintf( ) file print line function.

If you will be using many of these special calls in conjunction with report printing, it may be to your advantage to open the printer as a file once at the beginning of your report and close it after all your printing is complete. If you take this plan of action, comment out the file calls used in this function.

```
sub_off()
{ FILE *prn_file, *fopen();
  prn_file = fopen("prn","w");
  fprintf(prn_file,"%cT",'\033');
  fprintf(prn_file,"\nsubscript off\n");
  fclose(prn_file);
}
```

sub__on

Function Name: sub__on (subscript mode on)

Description: This function instructs the printer to turn subscript mode on. This function works in conjunction with sub__off( ). sub__on causes all characters to be printed in subscript format. This type font prints letters in a footnote type fashion, being lower and shorter than the regular printed characters.

Variables: string   — The string ESCAPE (octal 33) followed by the ASCII characters "S1" is sent to the screen to instruct the printer to exit subscript print format.

*prn__file — This variable is the file pointer used to open, define and close the file.

Example: sub__on( );

Rules: The function is not passed any variables and is called to enter subscript mode.

Special Notes: This function is designed to work only on EPSON FX printers. If you are using a printer made by another manufacturer, you may have to send a different control string to the printer. If this is the case, you only must change the fprintf( ) file print line function.

If you will be using many of these special calls in conjunction with report printing, it may be to your advantage to open the printer as a file once at the beginning of your report and close it after all your printing is complete. If you take this plan of action, comment out the file calls used in this function.

```
sub_on()
{ FILE *prn_file, *fopen();
  prn_file = fopen("prn","w");
  fprintf(prn_file,"%cS1",'\033');
  fprintf(prn_file,"\nsubscript on\n");
  fclose(prn_file);
}
```

Function Name: super__off (superscript mode off)

Description: This function instructs the printer to turn superscript mode off. This function works in conjunction with super__on( ). super__on causes all characters to be printed in superscript format. This type font prints letters in a footnote type fashion, being lower and shorter than the regular printed characters.

Variables: string — The string ESCAPE (octal 33) followed by the ASCII characters "T" is sent to the screen to instruct the printer to exit superscript print format.

*prn__file — This variable is the file pointer used to open, define and close the file.

Example: super__off( );

Rules: The function is not passed any variables and is called to negate the super__on( ) function.

Special Notes: This function is designed to work only on EPSON FX printers. If you are using a printer made by another manufacturer, you may have to send a different control string to the printer. If this is the case, you only must change the fprintf( ) file print line function.

If you will be using many of these special calls in conjunction with report printing, it may be to your advantage to open the printer as a file once at the beginning of your report and close it after all your printing is complete. If you take this plan of action, comment out the file calls used in this function.

```
super_off()
{ FILE *prn_file, *fopen();
  prn_file = fopen("prn","w");
  fprintf(prn_file,"%cT",'\033');
  fprintf(prn_file,"\nsuperscript off\n");
  fclose(prn_file);
}
```

super__on

Function Name: super__on (superscript mode on)

Description: This function instructs the printer to turn superscript mode on. This function works in conjunction with super__off( ). super__on causes all characters to be printed in superscript format. This type font prints letters in a footnote type fashion, being higher and shorter than the regular printed characters.

Variables: string — The string ESCAPE (octal 33) followed by the ASCII characters "T" is sent to the screen to instruct the printer to exit superscript print format.

*prn__file — This variable is the file pointer used to open, define and close the file.

Example: super__on( );

Rules: The function is not passed any variables and is called to enter SuperScript mode.

Special Notes: This function is designed to work only on EPSON FX printers. If you are using a printer made by another manufacturer, you may have to send a different control string to the printer. If this is the case, you only must change the fprintf( ) file print line function.

If you will be using many of these special calls in conjunction with report printing, it may be to your advantage to open the printer as a file once at the beginning of your report and close it after all your printing is complete. If you take this plan of action, comment out the file calls used in this function.

```
super_on()
{ FILE *prn_file, *fopen();
  prn_file = fopen("prn","w");
  fprintf(prn_file,"%cS0",'\033');
  fprintf(prn_file,"\nsuperscript on\n");
  fclose(prn_file);
}
```

Function Name: under__off (underline mode off)

Description: This function instructs the printer to turn underline mode off. This function works in conjunction with under__on( ). under__on causes all characters to be printed with an underline.

Variables: string — The string ESCAPE (octal 33) followed by the ASCII characters "O" is sent to the screen to instruct the printer to exit underline print format.
*prn__file — This variable is the file pointer used to open, define and close the file.

Example: under__off( );

Rules: The function is not passed any variables and is called to negate the under__on( ) function.

Special Notes: This function is designed to work only on EPSON FX printers. If you are using a printer made by another manufacturer, you may have to send a different control string to the printer. If this is the case, you only must change the fprintf( ) file print line function.
If you will be using many of these special calls in conjunction with report printing, it may be to your advantage to open the printer as a file once at the beginning of your report and close it after all your printing is complete. If you take this plan of action, comment out the file calls used in this function.

```
under_off()
{ FILE *prn_file, *fopen();
  prn_file = fopen("prn","w");
  fprintf(prn_file,"%c-0",'\033');
  fprintf(prn_file,"\nunderline off\n");
  fclose(prn_file);
}
```

under__on

Function Name: under__on (underline mode on)

Description: This function instructs the printer to turn underline mode off. This function works in conjunction with under__off( ). under__on causes all characters to be printed with an underline.

Variables: string   — The string ESCAPE (octal 33) followed by the ASCII characters "I" is sent to the screen to instruct the printer to exit underline print format.

             *prn__file — This variable is the file pointer used to open, define and close the file.

Example: under__on( );

Rules: The function is not passed any variables and is called to turn on underline mode.

Special Notes: This function is designed to work only on EPSON FX printers. If you are using a printer made by another manufacturer, you may have to send a different control string to the printer. If this is the case, you only must change the fprintf( ) file print line function.

If you will be using many of these special calls in conjunction with report printing, it may be to your advantage to open the printer as a file once at the beginning of your report and close it after all your printing is complete. If you take this plan of action, comment out the file calls used in this function.

```
under_on()
{ FILE *prn_file, *fopen();
  prn_file = fopen("prn","w");
  fprintf(prn_file,"%c-1",'\033');
  fprintf(prn_file,"\nunderline on\n");
  fclose(prn_file);
}
```

CALLING THE PRINTER OUTPUT FUNCTIONS

The code on the following pages will sequentially call each of the functions in this chapter, demonstrating their effects and how they can be used in actual programs.

```c
#include <math.h>
#include <stdio.h>

main()
{ ex2();
  ex1();
  ex4();
  ex3();
  ex6();
  ex5();
  ex8();
  ex7();
  ex10();
  ex9();
  ex12();
  ex11();
  ex14();
  ex13();
  ex15();
  ex17();
  ex16();
  ex19();
  ex18();
  ex21();
  ex20();
  ex15();
}

ex1()
{
  /****************************************************************
   ***************** calls to comp_off function *****************
   ***************************************************************/

  comp_off();

}

ex2()
{
  /****************************************************************
   *************** calls to comp_on function *************
   ***************************************************************/

  comp_on();

}

ex3()
{
  /****************************************************************
   *************** calls to ds_off function *************
```

```
**************************************************************/
ds_off();
}

ex4()
{
  /***************************************************************
   **************** calls to ds_on function ****************
   ***************************************************************/

  ds_on();

}

ex5()
{
  /***************************************************************
   **************** calls to emph_off function *****************
   ***************************************************************/

  emph_off();

}

ex6()
{
  /***************************************************************
   **************** calls to emph_on function *****************
   ***************************************************************/

  emph_on();

}

ex7()
{
  /***************************************************************
   **************** calls to exp1_off function *****************
   ***************************************************************/

  exp1_off();

}

ex8()
{
  /***************************************************************
   **************** calls to exp1_on function ***************
   ***************************************************************/

  exp1_on();

}

ex9()
{
```

```c
    /****************************************************************
     ************* calls to exp_off function **************
     ***************************************************************/

    exp_off();

}

ex10()
{
    /****************************************************************
     ****************** calls to exp_on function ***************
     ***************************************************************/

    exp_on ();

}

ex11()
{
    /****************************************************************
     ************ calls to ital_off function *************
     ***************************************************************/

    ital_off();

}

ex12()
{
    /****************************************************************
     ***************** calls to ital_on function ****************
     ***************************************************************/

    ital_on();

}

ex13()
{
    /****************************************************************
     ****************** calls to prop_off function ***************
     ***************************************************************/

    prop_off();

}

ex14()
{
    /****************************************************************
     **************** calls to prop_on function ***************
     ***************************************************************/

    prop_on();

}
```

```
ex15()
{
  /**************************************************************
   ***************** calls to reset function ***************
   **************************************************************/

  reset();

}

ex16()
{
  /**************************************************************
   ***************** calls to sub_off function ***************
   **************************************************************/

  sub_off();

}

ex17()
{
  /**************************************************************
   ***************** calls to sub_on function ***************
   **************************************************************/

  sub_on();

}

ex18()
{
  /**************************************************************
   ***************** calls to super_off function ***************
   **************************************************************/

  super_off();

}

ex19()
{
  /**************************************************************
   ***************** calls to super_on function ***************
   **************************************************************/

  super_on();

}

ex20()
{
  /**************************************************************
   ***************** calls to under_off function ***************
   **************************************************************/
```

```
    under_off();

}

ex21()
{
  /****************************************************************
    ****************** calls to under_on function ****************
    ****************************************************************/

  under_on();

}
```

17

String
Manipulation Functions

str_convert	—	convert upper and lowercase
str_count	—	count string size
str_delete	—	string characters delete
str_lindex	—	string left index
str_lower	—	convert to lowercase
str_lpad	—	string left space pad
str_rindex	—	string right index
str_rpad	—	string right space pad
str_swap	—	string swap
str_upper	—	convert to uppercase

Function Name: str__convert(string)

Description: This function is used to convert lowercase alpha characters to uppercase and uppercase alpha characters to lowercase.

Variables: string — This parameter is a character pointer to the string that is to be modified.

Example:
strcpy(str,"ABC");
output = str__convert(str);   returns the string abc
strcpy(str,"abC");
output = str__convert(str);   returns the string ABc

Rules:
1) The function must be passed a character pointer containing the address of the character string to be converted.
2) This function does not use a return value. Therefore it may be defined using the void data type if it is supported by your compiler.

```
str_convert(string)
 char string[];
{ int count;
  count = 0;
  while ( string[count] != '\0' )
     { if ( string[count] >= 'A' && string[count] <= 'Z' )
        string[count] = string[count] + 'a' - 'A';
       else
        if ( string[count] >= 'a' && string[count] <= 'z' )
           string[count] = string[count] - 'a' + 'A';
       count++;
     }
}
```

str__count

Function Name: str__count(string)

Description: This function counts the number of characters contained within a specified character string.

Variables: string — This parameter is a character pointer to the string that is to be counted.

Example: str__count("abcd");   returns a 4
str__count("ab");   returns a 2

Rules:
1) The function must be passed a character pointer containing the address of the character string being analyzed.
2) The return value must be passed to an integer variable.
3) The string being analyzed must be followed by a null terminator value.

```
str_count(string,sub_string)
 char string[];
 char sub_string;
{ int count, index;
  count = index = 0;
  while ( string[count] != '\0' )
    {   if ( string[count++] == sub_string ) index++;
    }
  return(index);
}
```

str__lindex

Function Name: str__lindex(string, sub)

Description: This function returns an integer value, indicating the first location of the specified sub-string character within the string being analyzed.

Variables: string — This parameter is a character pointer to the string that is to be counted.

sub — This parameter contains the character being searched.

Example:

output = str__lindex("abcde," 'c');	returns a 3
output = str__lindex("abcd," 'd');	returns a 4
output = str__lindex("abcd," 'b');	returns a 2

Rules:
1) The function must be passed a character pointer containing the address of the character string being analyzed.
2) The return value of this function must be passed to an integer variable.
3) The string being analyzed must be followed by a null terminator value.

```
str_lindex(string,sub_string)
 char string[];
 char sub_string;
{ int index;
  index = 0;

  while ( string[index] != '\0' && string[index] != sub_string)
    ++index;

  return(index);
}
```

str__delete

Function Name: str__delete(string, start, no__char)

Description: This function deletes a specified group of characters from within a character string as defined by the second and third parameter.

Variables: string   — This parameter is a character pointer to the string that is to be counted.

start   — This parameter specifies the location of the first character to be deleted.

no__char — This parameter specifies how many characters should be deleted.

Example: str__delete("abcdefg," 3, 1);   returns "abdeg"
str__delete("abcdefg," 2, 5);   returns "ag"

Rules: 1) The function must be passed a character pointer containing the address of the character string being analyzed.
2) The second and third parameters must be integers.
3) The string being analyzed must be followed by a null terminator value.

```
str_delete(string,start,no_char)
 char string[];
 int start, no_char;
{ int index1, index2;
  index1 = index2 = 0;
  index2 = start + no_char;
  for ( index1 = start; string[index1] = string[index2]; index1++)
    index2++;
}
```

Function Name: str__lower(string)

Description: This function is used to convert all uppercase characters within the passed string to lowercase.

Variables: string — This parameter is a character pointer to the string that is to be modified.

Example: strcpy(str,"ABC");
output = str__lower(str);   returns the string abc
strcpy(str,"Abcde");
output = str__lower(str);   returns the string abcde

Rules:
1) The function must be passed a character pointer containing the address of the character string to be converted.
2) This function does not use a return value. Therefore it may be defined using the void data type if it is supported by your compiler.

```
str_lower(string)
 char string[];
{ int count;
  count = 0;
  while ( string[count] != '\0' )
    { if ( string[count] >= 'A' && string[count] <= 'Z' )
      string[count] = string[count] + 'a' - 'A';
      count++;
    }
}
```

str__lpad

Function Name: str__lpad(string, no__char)

Description: This function places a specified number of spaces at the beginning of the passed character string.

Variables: string   — This parameter is a character pointer to the string that is to be modified.

no__char — This parameter specifies how many characters should be placed at the beginning of the passed character string.

Example: str__lpad("ab," 2);   returns " ab"
str__lpad("ab," 5);   returns "   ab"

Rules:
1) The function must be passed a character pointer containing the address of the character string being analyzed.
2) The second parameter must be an integer.
3) The string being modified must be followed by a null terminator value.

```
str_lpad(string,no_char)
 char *string;
 int no_char;
{ char temp;
  int count;
  count = 0;
  strcpy(temp,"");

  for ( count = 0; count < no_char; count++)
    strcat(temp," ");

  strcat(temp,string);
  strcpy(string,temp);
}
```

Function Name: str__rindex(string)

Description: This function returns an integer value indicating the last oc-
currence of the specified sub-string character within the string
being analyzed.

Variables: string — This parameter is a character pointer
to the string that is to be counted.

sub — This parameter contains the character
being searched.

Example: output = str__rindex("abcda," 'a');   returns a 5
output = str__rindex("abcde," 'd');   returns a 4
output = str__rindex("abccd," 'c');   returns a 4

Rules:
1) The function must be passed a character pointer containing the address of the character string to be
analyzed.
2) The return value of this function must be passed to an
integer variable.
3) The string being analyzed must be followed by a null
terminator value.

```
str_rindex(string,sub_string)
 char string[];
 char sub_string;
{ int index1, index2;
  index1 = index2 = 0;

  while ( string[index1] != '\0')
    { if ( string[index1] == sub_string )  index2 = index1;
      ++index1;
    }

  return(index2);
}
```

str__rpad

Function Name: str__rpad(string, no__char)

Description: This function places a specified number of spaces at the end of the passed character string.

Variables: string — This parameter is a character pointer to the string that is to be modified.

no__char — This parameter specifies how many characters should be placed at the end of the passed character string.

Example: str__lpad("ab," 2);   returns "ab "
str__lpad("ab," 5);   returns "ab   "

Rules: 1) The function must be passed a character pointer containing the address of the character string being analyzed.
2) The second parameter must be an integer.
3) The string being modified must be followed by a null terminator value.

```
str_rpad(string,no_char)
 char *string;
 int no_char;
{ int count;
  count = 0;

  for ( count = 0; count < no_char; count++)
    strcat(string," ");

}
```

Function Name: str__swap(string1, string2)

Description: This function exchanges the contents of two character variables.

Variables: string1 — This parameter is a character pointer to the first string being exchanged.

string2 — This parameter is a character pointer the second string being exchanged.

Example: strcpy(a__string,"AAAAA"   returns: a__string is "BBBB"
strcpy(b__string,"BBBBB"   b__string is "AAAAA"
str__swap(a__string, b__string)

Rules:
1) The function must be passed character pointers containing the addresses of the character strings being swapped.
2) The character strings must be defined large enough to contain each other's values.
3) The string being modified must be followed by a null terminator value.

```
str_swap(string1, string2)
 char *string1, *string2;
{ char temp;
  strcpy(temp,string1);
  strcpy(string1,string2);
  strcpy(string2,temp);
}
```

str__upper

Function Name: str__upper(string)

Description: This function is used to convert all lowercase characters within the passed string to uppercase.

Variables: string — This parameter is a character pointer to the string that is to be modified.

Example:
```
strcpy(str,"Abc");
output = str__upper(str);              returns the string ABC
strcpy(str,"ABCde");
output = str__upper(str);              returns the string ABCDE
```

Rules:
1) The function must be passed a character pointer containing the address of the character string to be converted.
2) This function does not use a return value. Therefore it may be defined using the void data type if it is supported by your compiler.

```
str_upper(string)
 char string[];
{ int count;
  count = 0;
  while ( string[count] != '\0' )
     { if ( string[count] >= 'a' && string[count] <= 'z' )
         string[count] = string[count] + 'A' - 'a';
       count++;
     }
}
```

CALLING THE STRING MANIPULATION FUNCTIONS

The code on the following pages will sequentially call each of the functions in this chapter, demonstrating their effects and how they can be used in actual programs.

```c
#include <math.h>
#include <stdio.h>

main()
{ ex1();
  ex2();
  ex3();
  ex4();
  ex5();
  ex6();
  ex7();
  ex8();
  ex9();
  ex10();
}

ex1()
{
  /************************************************************
   *********** calls to str_convert function ****************
   ************************************************************/
  char input;
  printf("\n\nstr_convert value function");

      strcpy(input,"Hello There");
      str_convert(input);
      printf("\n      str_convert value is == %s",input);

      strcpy(input,"Eric P. Bloom");
      str_convert(input);
      printf("\n      str_convert value is == %s",input);
}

ex2()
{
  /************************************************************
   *********** calls to str_count function ****************
   ************************************************************/
  char input, sub_input;
  int output;
  printf("\n\nstr_count value function");

      strcpy(input,"Hello There");
      output = str_count(input,'l');
      printf("\n      str_count value is == %d",output);

      strcpy(input,"Eric P. Bloom");
      sub_input = 'i';
      output = str_count(input,sub_input);
      printf("\n      str_count value is == %d",output);
}
```

345

```
ex3()
{
  /***************************************************************
   *********** calls to str_delete function *****************
   **************************************************************/
  char input;
  printf("\n\nstr_delete value function");

    strcpy(input,"Hello There");
    str_delete(input,2,2);
    printf("\n      str_delete value is == %s",input);

    strcpy(input,"Eric P. Bloom");
    str_delete(input,5,3);
    printf("\n      str_delete value is == %s",input);
}

ex4()
{
  /***************************************************************
   *********** calls to str_lindex function ****************
   **************************************************************/
  char input, sub_input;
  int output;
  printf("\n\nstr_lindex value function");

    strcpy(input,"Hello There");
    output = str_lindex(input,'l');
    printf("\n      str_lindex value is == %d",output);

    strcpy(input,"Eric P. Bloom");
    sub_input = 'c';
    output = str_lindex(input,sub_input);
    printf("\n      str_lindex value is == %d",output);
}

ex5()
{
  /***************************************************************
   *********** calls to str_lower function *****************
   **************************************************************/
  char input;
  printf("\n\nstr_lower value function");

    strcpy(input,"Hello There");
    str_lower(input);
    printf("\n      str_lower value is == %s",input);

    strcpy(input,"Eric P. Bloom");
    str_lower(input);
    printf("\n      str_lower value is == %s",input);
}

ex6()
{
  /***************************************************************
   *********** calls to str_lpad function *****************
   **************************************************************/
```

```
    char input[20];
    printf("\n\nstr_lpad value function");

        strcpy(input,"Hello");
        str_lpad(input,2);
        printf("\n      str_lpad value is == %s",input);

        strcpy(input,"Eric P. Bloom");
        str_lpad(input,5);
        printf("\n      str_lpad value is == %s",input);
}

ex7()
{
  /***************************************************************
   ************ calls to str_rindex function *****************
   ***************************************************************/
  char input, sub_input;
  int output;
  printf("\n\nstr_rindex value function");

        strcpy(input,"Hello There");
        output = str_rindex(input,'e');
        printf("\n      str_rindex value is == %d",output);

        strcpy(input,"Eric P. Bloom");
        sub_input = 'c';
        output = str_rindex(input,sub_input);
        printf("\n      str_rindex value is == %d",output);
}

ex8()
{
  /***************************************************************
   ************ calls to str_rpad function *****************
   ***************************************************************/
  char input[20];
  printf("\n\nstr_rpad value function");

        strcpy(input,"Hello");
        str_rpad(input,2);
        printf("\n      str_rpad value is == %s---",input);

        strcpy(input,"Eric P. Bloom");
        str_rpad(input,5);
        printf("\n      str_rpad value is == %s---",input);
}

ex9()
{
  /***************************************************************
   ************ calls to str_swap function *****************
   ***************************************************************/
  char input1[10], input2[10];
  printf("\n\nstr_swap value function");
  strcpy(input1,"Hello");
  strcpy(input2,"There");
```

```
        str_swap(input1, input2);
        printf("\n      str_swap values are == %s , %s",input1, input2);

        strcpy(input1,"Eric P.");
        strcpy(input2,"Bloom");
        str_swap(input1, input2);
        printf("\n      str_swap values are == %s , %s",input1, input2);
}

ex10()
{
   /***********************************************************
    *********** calls to str_upper function ****************
    ***********************************************************/
   char input;
   printf("\n\nstr_upper value function");

        strcpy(input,"Hello There");
        str_upper(input);
        printf("\n      str_upper value is == %s",input);

        strcpy(input,"Eric P. Bloom");
        str_upper(input);
        printf("\n      str_upper value is == %s",input);
}
```

18

Data Input Functions

d__convert

Function Name: d__convert(string)

Description: This function converts a character string number into the actual numerical value. This value then is placed in a double floating point variable.

Variables: string — This variable is the vehicle used to receive the character string sent by the calling function.

count — This variable is used to assist in loop control.

sign — This variable is set to 1 at the beginning of the function. Then, if a negative sign is encountered in the number, sign is set to a value of −1. Finally, just prior to returning a numeric value, this value is multiplied by sign. Thus, if a negative sign was encountered, then the multiplication by −1 would make the returned value negative.

digit — This variable contains the individual character values to be converted.

period — This variable tracks the location of the decimal point.

Examples: char ascii__number[ ] = "123.45";
double output, d__convert( );
output = d__convert(ascii__number);

Rules: Nonnumeric values are ignored, thus the value 12z3 is converted as 123.
The negative sign may be at either the beginning or ending of the input number.
The function name d__convert must be defined as a double within the calling function.

```
double d_convert(string)
 char string[];
{ int count, sign, digit, period;
  double amount, point;
  count = 0;
   sign = 1;
  while (string[count] )
    if (string[count++] == '-' )  sign = -1;

  count = amount = period = 0;
   point = 1;
   while ( string[count] )
```

```
        { if ( string[count] == '.' ) period = 1;
          if ( string[count] >= '0' && string[count] <= '9' )
            { digit = string[count] - '0';
              amount *= 10;
              amount += digit;
              if ( period == 1 ) point *= .1;
            }
          count++;
      }
    amount *= point;
    amount *= sign;
    return(amount);
}
```

f__convert

Function Name: f__convert(string)

Description: This function converts a character string number into the actual numerical value. This value is then placed in a floating point variable.

Variables: string — This variable is the vehicle used to receive the character string sent by the calling function.

             count — This variable is used to assist in loop control.

             sign — This variable is set to 1 at the beginning of the function. Then, if a negative sign is encountered in the number, sign is set to a value of -1. Finally, just prior to returning a numeric value, this value is multiplied by sign. Thus, if a negative sign was encountered, then the multiplication by -1 would make the returned value negative.

             digit — This variable contains the individual character values to be converted.

             period — This variable tracts the location of the decimal point.

Examples: char ascii__number[ ] = "123.45";

             float output, f__convert( );

             output = f__convert(ascii__number);

Rules: Nonnumeric values are ignored, thus the value 12z3 is converted as 123.

The negative sign may be at either the beginning or ending of the input number.

The function name f__convert must be defined as a float within the calling function.

```
float f_convert(string)
  char string[];
{ int count, sign, digit, period;
  float amount, point;
  count = 0;
  sign = 1;
```

```
    while (string[count] )
      if (string[count++] == '-' )  sign = -1;

    count = amount = period = 0;
    point = 1;
    while ( string[count] )
    { if ( string[count] == '.' ) period = 1;
       if ( string[count] >= '0' && string[count] <= '9' )
         { digit = string[count] - '0';
            amount *= 10;
            amount += digit;
            if ( period == 1 ) point *= .1;
         }
      count++;
    }
    amount *= point;
    amount *= sign;
    return(amount);
}
```

i__convert

Description: This function converts a character string number into the actual numerical value. This value then is placed in an integer variable.

Variables: string — This variable is the vehicle used to receive the character string sent by the calling function.

count — This variable is used to assist in loop control.

sign — This variable is set to 1 at the beginning of the function. Then, if a negative sign is encountered in the number, sign is set to a value of −1. Finally, just prior to returning a numeric value, this value is multiplied by sign. Thus, if a negative sign was encountered, then the multiplication by −1 would make the returned value negative.

digit — This variable contains the individual character values to be converted.

Examples: char ascii__number[] = "123.45";

int output, f__convert( );

output = i__convert(ascii__number);

Rules: Nonnumeric values are ignored, thus the value 12z3 is converted as 123.
The negative sign may be at either the beginning or ending of the input number.
The function name i__convert may optionally be defined as an integer within the calling function.
Decimal points are ignored.

```
i_convert(string)
 char string[];
{ int count, sign, amount, digit;
  count = 0;
  sign = 1;
  while (string[count] )
    if (string[count++] == '-' ) sign = -1;
```

```
    count = amount = 0;
    while ( string[count] )
     { if ( string[count] >= '0' && string[count] <= '9' )
          { digit = string[count] - '0';
            amount *= 10;
            amount += digit;
          }
       count++;
     }
    amount *= sign;
    return(amount);
}
```

i__to__a

Function Name: i__to__a(in__number, out__number)

Description: This function converts an integer number to an ASCII character string.

Variables: in__number — This variable is the integer number passed to the function to be converted to a string.

out__number — This is the character string into which the character string is placed.

Examples: char ascii__number[6];

int int__variable;

i__convert(int__variable, ascii__number);

Rules: The second parameter function must be passed a pointer associated with a character field. They may be in the format of defined character pointers or as the name of character arrays with no array brackets.
The variable passed must be defined as an int.

```
i_to_a(in_number,out_number)
 int in_number;
 char *out_number;
{ int r, count, length;
  char work_number[10];

  for ( count=0; in_number > 0; count++)
   { r = ( in_number % 10 );
     *(work_number + count) = r + '0';
     in_number /= 10;
   }
  *(work_number + count) = '\0';

  length = strlen(work_number);
  for ( count=0; count < length; count++ )
     *(out_number + length - count - 1 ) = *(work_number + count);
  *(out_number + length ) = '\0';
}
```

Function Name: lpr__char(x, y, string, outstring)

Description: This function facilitates the input of ASCII character strings. Additionally, prior to the actual input, the cursor is placed at a specified screen location and a prompt is displayed.

Variables: string   — This variable is the vehicle used to receive the prompt that is displayed on the screen.

        x   — This parameter defines the horizontal row on which the cursor will be placed.

        y   — This parameter defines the vertical column on which the cursor will be placed.

     outstring — This variable contains the ASCII character string input by the user.

Examples: char ascii__value[10];

lpr__char(10,5,"Enter employee name : ",ascii__value);

Rules: Any ASCII characters can be entered.
The x value must be between 1 and 24
The y value must be between 1 and 80

```
lpr_char(x,y,string,out_string)
 int x,y;
 char string[], *out_string;

{ printf("%c[%d;%dH",'\33',x,y);
  printf("%s",string);
  gets(out_string);
}
```

lpr__double

Function Name: lpr__double(x, y, string)

Description: This function facilitates the input of double floating point number. Additionally, prior to the actual input, the cursor is placed at a specified screen location and a prompt is displayed.

Variables: string — This variable is the vehicle used to receive the prompt that is displayed on the screen.

x — This parameter defines the horizontal row on which the cursor will be placed.

y — This parameter defines the vertical column on which the cursor will be placed.

Examples: double output, lpr__double( );

output = lpr__double(10,5,"Enter employee name : ");

Rules: Nonnumeric values are ignored, thus the value 12z3 is converted as 123.
The negative sign may be at either the beginning or ending of the input number.
The function name lpr__double must be defined as a double floating point number within the calling function.
The x value must be between 1 and 24
The y value must be between 1 and 80

```
double lpr_double(x,y,string)
 int x,y;
 char string[];

{ double out_num, d_convert();
  char in_num[15];
  printf("%c[%d;%dH",'\33',x,y);
  printf("%s",string);
  gets(in_num);
  out_num = d_convert(in_num);
  return(out_num);
}
```

lpr__float

Function Name: lpr__float(x, y, string)

Description: This function facilitates the input of floating point numbers. Additionally, prior to the actual input, the cursor is placed at a specified screen location and a prompt is displayed.

Variables: string — This variable is the vehicle used to receive the prompt that is displayed on the screen.

x — This parameter defines the horizontal row on which the cursor will be placed.

y — This parameter defines the vertical column on which the cursor will be placed.

Examples: float output, lpr__float( );

output = lpr__float(10,5,"Enter employee name : ");

Rules: Nonnumeric values are ignored, thus the value 12z3 is converted as 123.
The negative sign may be at either the beginning or ending of the input number.
The function name lpr__float must be defined as a double floating point number within the calling function.
The x value must be between 1 and 24
The y value must be between 1 and 80

```
float lpr_float(x,y,string)
 int x,y;
 char string[];

{ float out_num, f_convert();
  char in_num[15];
  printf("%c[%d;%dH",'\33',x,y);
  printf("%s",string);
  gets(in_num);
  out_num = f_convert(in_num);
  return(out_num);
}
```

lpr__g__response

Function Name: lpr__g__response(x, y, string)

Description: This function facilitates the input of a keyboard response. Additionally, prior to the actual input, the cursor is placed at a specified screen location and a prompt is displayed.

Variables: string — This variable is the vehicle used to receive the prompt that is displayed on the screen.

x — This parameter defines the horizontal row on which the cursor will be placed.

y — This parameter defines the vertical column on which the cursor will be placed.

Examples: lpr__g__response(10,5,"Hit any key to continue : ");

Rules: The value input is ignored.
The function returns control to the calling module as soon as any keyboard character is pressed.
The x value must be between 1 and 24
The y value must be between 1 and 80

```
lpr_g_response(x,y,string)
 int x,y;
 char string[];

{ char *out_string;
  printf("%c[%d;%dH",'\33',x,y);
  printf("%s",string);
  getch(out_string);
}
```

Function Name: lpr__g__yes__no(x, y, x__error, y__error, string, e__string, out__string)

Description: This function facilitates the input of a yes or no value. Prior to the actual input, the cursor is placed at a specified screen location and a prompt is displayed. Also, if an invalid response is entered, an error message is displayed at a user defined screen location.

Variables: string   — This variable is the vehicle used to receive the prompt that is displayed on the screen.

x   — This parameter defines the horizontal row on which the cursor will be placed.

y   — This parameter defines the vertical column on which the cursor will be placed.

x__error   — This parameter defines the horizontal row at which the error message is displayed.

y__error   — This parameter defines the vertical column at which the error message is displayed.

e__string   — This variable is used to pass the error message that will be displayed if an invalid response is entered.

out__string — This variable contains the yes or no response that is returned to the calling function.

Examples: char reply[2];

lpr__g__yes__no(5,5,25,5,"Enter Y or N","ERROR, reenter",out__string);

Rules: The reply must be "y," "n," "Y," or "N"
The x and x__error values must be between 1 and 24
The y and y__error values must be between 1 and 80

```
lpr_g_yes_no(x,y,x_error,y_error,string,e_string,out_string)
int x,y,x_error,y_error;
char string[], e_string[], *out_string;
```

```
{ do
   {  printf("%c[%d;%dH",'\33',x,y);
      printf("%s",string);
      gets(out_string);
      if ( *out_string != 'n' && *out_string != 'N' &&
           *out_string != 'y' && *out_string != 'Y' )
              {  printf("%c[%d;%dH",'\33',x_error,y_error);
                 printf("%s",e_string);
              }
   } while ( *out_string != 'n' && *out_string != 'N' &&
             *out_string != 'y' && *out_string != 'Y' );

}
```

Function Name: lpr__integer(x, y, string)

Description: This function facilitates the input of integer numbers. Additionally, prior to the actual input, the cursor is placed at a specified screen location and a prompt is displayed.

Variables: string — This variable is the vehicle used to receive the prompt that is displayed on the screen.

x — This parameter defines the horizontal row on which the cursor will be placed.

y — This parameter defines the vertical column on which the cursor will be placed.

Examples: int output, lpr__integer;

output = lpr__integer(10,5,"Enter employee name : ");

Rules: Nonnumeric values are ignored, thus the value 12z3 is converted as 123.
The negative sign may be at either the beginning or ending of the input number.
The function name lpr__integer may be optionally defined as an integer number within the calling function.
The x value must be between 1 and 24
The y value must be between 1 and 80
Decimal points are ignored.

```
lpr_integer(x,y,string)
 int x,y;
 char string[];

{ int out_num, i_convert();
  char in_num[15];
  printf("%c[%d;%dH",'\33',x,y);
  printf("%s",string);
  gets(in_num);
  out_num = i_convert(in_num);
  return(out_num);
}
```

l__char

Function Name: l__char(x, y, out__string)

Description: This function facilitates the input of ASCII character strings. Additionally, prior to the actual input, the cursor is placed at a specified screen location.

Variables: x — This parameter defines the horizontal row on which the cursor will be placed.

y — This parameter defines the vertical column on which the cursor will be placed.

out__string — This variable contains the ASCII character string input by the user.

Examples: char ascii__value[10];

l__char(10,5,ascii__value);

Rules: Any ASCII characters can be entered.
The x value must be between 1 and 24
The y value must be between 1 and 80

```
l_char(x,y,out_string)
 int x,y;
 char  *out_string;

{ printf("%c[%d;%dH",'\33',x,y);
  gets(out_string);
}
```

Function Name: l__double(x,y)

Description: This function facilitates the input of double floating point numbers. Additionally, prior to the actual input, the cursor is placed at a specified screen location.

Variables: x — This parameter defines the horizontal row on which the cursor will be placed.

y — This parameter defines the vertical column on which the cursor will be placed.

Examples: double output, l__double( );

output = l__double(10,5);

Rules: Nonnumeric values are ignored, thus the value 12z3 is converted as 123.
The negative sign may be at either the beginning or ending of the input number.
The function name l__double must be defined as a double floating point number within the calling function.
The x value must be between 1 and 24
The y value must be between 1 and 80

```
double l_double(x,y)
 int x,y;

{ double out_num, d_convert();
  char in_num[15];
  printf("%c[%d;%dH",'\33',x,y);
  gets(in_num);
  out_num = d_convert(in_num);
  return(out_num);
}
```

l__float

Function Name: l__float(x,y)

Description: This function facilitates the input of floating point numbers. Additionally, prior to the actual input, the cursor is placed at a specified screen location.

Variables: x — This parameter defines the horizontal row on which the cursor will be placed.

y — This parameter defines the vertical column on which the cursor will be placed.

Examples: float output, l__float( );
output = l__float(10,5);

Rules: Nonnumeric values are ignored, thus the value 12z3 is converted as 123.
The negative sign may be at either the beginning or ending of the input number.
The function name l__float must be defined as a double floating point number within the calling function.
The x value must be between 1 and 24
The y value must be between 1 and 80

```
float l_float(x,y)
 int x,y;

{ float out_num, f_convert();
  char in_num[15];
  printf("%c[%d;%dH",'\33',x,y);
  gets(in_num);
  out_num = f_convert(in_num);
  return(out_num);
}
```

l__g__response

Function Name: l__g__response(x,y)

Description: This function facilitates the input of a keyboard response. Additionally, prior to the actual input, the cursor is placed at a specified screen location.

Variables: x — This parameter defines the horizontal row on which the cursor will be placed.

y — This parameter defines the vertical column on which the cursor will be placed.

Examples: l__g__response(10,5);

Rules: The value input is ignored.
The function returns control to the calling module as soon as any keyboard character is pressed.
The x value must be between 1 and 24
The y value must be between 1 and 80

```
l_g_response(x,y)
 int x,y;

{ char *out_string;
  printf("%c[%d;%dH",'\33',x,y);
  getch(out_string);
}
```

l__g__yes__no

Function Name: l_g__yes__no(x, y, x__error, y__error, e__string, out__string)

Description: This function facilitates the input of a yes or no value. Prior to the actual input, the cursor is placed at a specified screen location and a prompt is displayed. Also, if an invalid response is entered, an error message is displayed.

Variables: x — This parameter defines the horizontal row on which the cursor will be placed.

y — This parameter defines the vertical column on which the cursor will be placed.

x__error — This parameter defines the horizontal row at which the error message is displayed.

y__error — This parameter defines the vertical column at which the error message is displayed.

e__string — This variable is used to pass the error message that will be displayed if an invalid response is entered.

out__string — This variable contains the yes or no response that is returned to the calling function.

Examples: char reply[2];
l_g__yes__no(5,5,25,5,"ERROR, reenter", out__string);

Rules: The reply must be "y," "n," "Y," or "N"
The x and x__error values must be between 1 and 24
The y and y__error values must be between 1 and 80

```
l_g_yes_no(x, y, x_error, y_error, e_string, out_string)
 int x,y,x_error,y_error;
 char e_string[], *out_string;

{ do
   {  printf("%c[%d;%dH",'\33',x,y);
   gets(out_string);
   if ( *out_string != 'n' && *out_string != 'N' &&
       *out_string != 'y' && *out_string != 'Y' )
       {  printf("%c[%d;%dH",'\33',x_error,y_error);
          printf("%s",e_string);
       }
} while ( *out_string != 'n' && *out_string != 'N' &&
         *out_string != 'y' && *out_string != 'Y' );

}
```

Function Name: I__integer(x,y)

Description: This function facilitates the input of integer numbers. Additionally, prior to the actual input, the cursor is placed at a specified screen location.

Variables: x   — This parameter defines the horizontal row on which the cursor will be placed.

           y   — This parameter defines the vertical column on which the cursor will be placed.

Examples:
```
int output, I__integer;
output = I__integer(10,5);
```

Rules: Nonnumeric values are ignored, thus the value 12z3 is converted as 123.
The negative sign may be at either the beginning or ending of the input number.
The function name I__integer may be optionally defined as an integer number within the calling function.
The x value must be between 1 and 24
The y value must be between 1 and 80
Decimal points are ignored.

```
l_integer(x,y,)
 int x,y;

{ int out_num, i_convert();
  char in_num[15];
  printf("%c[%d;%dH",'\33',x,y);
  gets(in_num);
  out_num = i_convert(in_num);
  return(out_num);
}
```

pr__char

Function Name: pr__char(string, outstring)

Description: This function facilitates the input of ASCII character strings. Additionally, prior to the actual input, a specified prompt is displayed.

Variables: string — This variable is the vehicle used to receive the prompt that is displayed on the screen.

outstring — This variable contains the ASCII character string input by the user.

Examples: char ascii__value[10];

pr__char("Enter employee name : ",ascii__value);

Rules: Any ASCII characters can be entered.

```
pr_char(string,out_string)
 char string[], *out_string;

{ printf("%s",string);
  gets(out_string);
}
```

Function Name: pr__double(string)

Description: This function facilitates the input of double floating point numbers. Additionally, prior to the actual input, a specified prompt is displayed.

Variables: string — This variable is the vehicle used to receive the prompt that is displayed on the screen.

Examples: double output, pr__double( );

output = lpr__double("Enter employee name : ");

Rules: Nonnumeric values are ignored, thus the value 12z3 is converted as 123.

The negative sign may be at either the beginning or ending of the input number.

The function name pr__double must be defined as a double floating point number within the calling function.

```
double pr_double(string)
 char string[];

{ double out_num, d_convert();
  char in_num[15];
  printf("%s",string);
  gets(in_num);
  out_num = d_convert(in_num);
  return(out_num);
}
```

pr__float

Function Name: pr__float(string)

Description: This function facilitates the input of floating point numbers. Additionally, prior to the actual input, a specified prompt is displayed.

Variables: string — This variable is the vehicle used to receive the prompt that is displayed on the screen.

Examples: float output, pr__float( );
output = pr__float("Enter employee name : ");

Rules: Nonnumeric values are ignored, thus the value 12z3 is converted as 123.
The negative sign may be at either the beginning of ending of the input number.
The function name pr__float must be defined as a double floating point number within the calling function.

```
float pr_float(string)
 char string[];

{ float out_num, f_convert();
  char in_num[15];
  printf("%s",string);
  gets(in_num);
  out_num = f_convert(in_num);
  return(out_num);
}
```

Function Name: pr__g__response(string)

Description: This function facilitates the input of a keyboard response. Additionally, prior to the actual input, a specified prompt is displayed.

Variables: string — This variable is the vehicle used to receive the prompt that is displayed on the screen.

Examples: pr__g__response("Hit any key to continue : ");

Rules: The value input is ignored.
The function returns control to the calling module as soon as any keyboard character is pressed.

```
pr_g_response(string)
 char string[];

{ char *out_string;
  printf("%s",string);
  getch(out_string);
}
```

pr__g__yes__no

Function Name: pr__g__yes__no(string, e__string, out__string)

Description: This function facilitates the input of a yes or no value. Prior to the actual input, a specified prompt is displayed. Also, if an invalid response is entered, an error message is displayed.

Variables: string — This variable is the vehicle used to receive the prompt that is displayed on the screen.

e__string — This variable is used to pass the error message that will be displayed if an invalid response is entered.

out__string — This variable contains the yes or no response that is returned to the calling function.

Examples: char reply[2];

pr__g__yes__no("Enter Y or N","ERROR, reenter",out__string);

Rules: The reply must be "y," "n," "Y," or "N"

```
pr_g_yes_no(string,e_string,out_string)
 char string[], e_string[], *out_string;

{ do
   {  printf("%s",string);
      gets(out_string);
      if ( *out_string != 'n' && *out_string != 'N' &&
           *out_string != 'y' && *out_string != 'Y' )
           {  printf("\n%s",e_string);
           }
   } while ( *out_string != 'n' && *out_string != 'N' &&
             *out_string != 'y' && *out_string != 'Y' );

}
```

Function Name: pr__integer(string)

Description: This function facilitates the input of integer numbers. Additionally, prior to the actual input, a specified prompt is displayed.

Variables: string — This variable is the vehicle used to receive the prompt that is displayed on the screen.

Examples: int output, pr__integer;

output = pr__integer("Enter employee name : ");

Rules: Nonnumeric values are ignored, thus the value 12z3 is converted as 123.
The negative sign may be at either the beginning of ending of the input number.
The function name pr__integer may be optionally defined as an integer number within the calling function.
Decimal points are ignored.

```
pr_integer(string)
 char string[];

{ int out_num, i_convert();
  char in_num[15];
  printf("%s",string);
  gets(in_num);
  out_num = i_convert(in_num);
  return(out_num);
}
```

CALLING THE DATA INPUT FUNCTIONS

The code on the following pages will sequentially call each of the functions in this chapter, demonstrating their effects and how they can be used in actual programs.

```c
#include <stdio.h>

main()
{ ex1();
  ex2();
  ex3();
  ex4();
  ex5();
  ex6();
  ex7();
  ex8();
  ex9();
  ex10();
  ex11();
  ex12();
  ex13();
  ex14();
  ex15();
  ex16();
  ex17();
  ex18();
  ex19();
  ex20();
  ex21();
}

ex1()
{
  /**************************************************************
    **************** calls to d_convert function **************
    **************************************************************/

  char in_string[10];
  double output, d_convert();

  printf("\nd_convert function");

  strcpy(in_string,"123.45");
  output = d_convert(in_string);
  printf("\n      d_convert value is == %f",output);

  strcpy(in_string,"1000.50");
  output = d_convert(in_string);
  printf("\n      d_convert value is == %f",output);
}


ex2()
{
  /**************************************************************
    **************** calls to f_convert function **************
    **************************************************************/
```

```
    char in_string[10];
    float output, f_convert();
    printf("\nf_convert function");

    strcpy(in_string,"123.45");
    output = f_convert(in_string);
    printf("\n     f_convert value is == %f",output);

    strcpy(in_string,"1000.50");
    output = f_convert(in_string);
    printf("\n     f_convert value is == %f",output);
}


ex3()
{
  /*************************************************************
   *************** calls to i_convert function **************
   *************************************************************/

    char in_string[10];
    int output, i_convert();

    printf("\ni_convert function");

    strcpy(in_string,"123");
    output = i_convert(in_string);
    printf("\n     i_convert value is == %d",output);

    strcpy(in_string,"1000");
    output = i_convert(in_string);
    printf("\n     i_convert value is == %d",output);
}


ex4()
{
  /*************************************************************
   *************** calls to lpr_char  function *************
   *************************************************************/

    char output[20];
    lpr_char(10,10,"enter employee name : ",output);
    printf("\n name is: %s",output);
}


ex5()
{
  /*************************************************************
   *************** calls to lpr_double function *************
   *************************************************************/

    double lpr_double(), output;
    output = lpr_double(15,15,"enter gross salary");
    printf("\n salry is: %f",output);
}
```

```
ex6()
{
   /***************************************************************
    ************** calls to lpr_float  function **************
    ***************************************************************/

   float lpr_float(), output;
   output = lpr_float(15,15,"enter gross salary");
   printf("\n salry is: %f",output);
}


ex7()
{
   /***************************************************************
    ************* calls to lpr_g_response  function **********
    ***************************************************************/

  lpr_g_response(5,5,"enter a response : ");
}


ex8()
{
   /***************************************************************
    ************* calls to lpr_g_yes_no function **************
    ***************************************************************/

   char reply[2];

   lpr_g_yes_no(10,5,24,5,"enter Y or N : ","answer must by Y or N",reply);
   printf("reply is : %s",reply);
}


ex9()
{
   /***************************************************************
    ************* calls to lpr_integer function **************
    ***************************************************************/

   int lpr_int(), output;
   output = lpr_integer(15,15,"enter gross salary");
   printf("\n salry is: %d",output);
}


ex10()
{
   /***************************************************************
    *************** calls to l_char  function **************
    ***************************************************************/

   char output[20];
   l_char(10,10,output);
   printf("\n name is: %s",output);
}
```

```
ex11()
{
  /*****************************************************************
   *************** calls to l_double function **************
   ****************************************************************/

  double l_double(), output;
  output = l_double(15,15);
  printf("\n salry is: %f",output);
}


ex12()
{
  /*****************************************************************
   *************** calls to l_float  function **************
   ****************************************************************/

  float l_float(), output;
  output = l_float(15,15);
  printf("\n salry is: %f",output);
}


ex13()
{
  /*****************************************************************
   ************* calls to l_g_response  function **********
   ****************************************************************/

  l_g_response(5,5);
}


ex14()
{
  /*****************************************************************
   ************* calls to l_g_yes_no function *************
   ****************************************************************/

  char reply[2];

  l_g_yes_no(10,5,24,5,"answer must by Y or N",reply);
  printf("reply is : %s",reply);
}


ex15()
{
  /*****************************************************************
   ************* calls to l_integer function *************
   ****************************************************************/

  int l_int(), output;
  output = l_integer(15,15);
  printf("\n salry is: %d",output);
}
```

```
ex16()
{
  /***************************************************************
   *************** calls to pr_char  function **************
   ***************************************************************/

  char output[20];
  pr_char("enter employee name : ",output);
  printf("\n name is: %s",output);
}


ex17()
{
  /***************************************************************
   ************** calls to pr_double function *************
   ***************************************************************/

  double pr_double(), output;
  output = pr_double("enter gross salary");
  printf("\n salry is: %f",output);
}


ex18()
{
  /***************************************************************
   ************** calls to pr_float  function *************
   ***************************************************************/

  float pr_float(), output;
  output = pr_float("enter gross salary");
  printf("\n salry is: %f",output);
}


ex19()
{
  /***************************************************************
   ************* calls to pr_g_response  function **********
   ***************************************************************/

 pr_g_response("enter a response : ");
}


ex20()
{
  /***************************************************************
   ************* calls to pr_g_yes_no function *************
   ***************************************************************/

  char reply[2];

  pr_g_yes_no("enter Y or N : ","answer must by Y or N",reply);
  printf("reply is : %s",reply);
}
```

```
ex21()
{
   /***************************************************************
    ************* calls to pr_integer function **************
    ***************************************************************/

   int pr_int(), output;
   output = pr_integer("enter gross salary");
   printf("\n salry is: %d",output);
}
```

19

Array
Manipulation Functions

ad__ave	—	array double average
ai__ave	—	array integer average
ad__found	—	array double found
ai__found	—	array integer found
ad__max	—	array double maximum value
ai__max	—	array integer maximum value
ad__mean	—	array double mean value
ai__mean	—	array integer mean value
ad__min	—	array double minimum value
ai__min	—	array integer minimum value
ad__search	—	array double search
ai__search	—	array integer search
ad__sum	—	array double sum
ai__sum	—	array integer sum

Function Name : ad__ave(start,size)

Description : This function receives an array starting location and the number of elements in that array and calculates a numeric average of its contents.

Variables : start — This pointer to a double specifies the memory address of the first array element.

size — This integer number specifies the number of array members.

Example : ave = ad__ave(d__array,50)

Rules : This function must be passed a variable defined as a pointer to a double. Additionally, the calling program must define the function ad__ave( ) and the function's return value as doubles. The size parameter denoting the number of elements contained within the array must be defined as an integer.

Calling Ex. :
```
double a__array[50];
double out__average;
int a__size;
double ad__ave( );
a__size = 50;
out__average = ad__ave(a__array,a__size);
```

```
double ad_ave(start,size)
 double *start;
 int size;
{ int count;
  double sum = 0;
  double average = 0;
  for ( count=0; count < size; count++ )
    {    sum += (*start++);
    }
  average = sum / count;
  return(average);
}
```

ai__ave

Function Name : ai__ave(start,size)

Description : This function receives an array starting location and the number of elements in that array and calculates a numeric average of its contents.

Variables : start — This pointer to an int specifies the memory address of the first array element.

           size — This integer number specifies the number of array members.

Example : ave = ai__ave(d__array,50)

Rules : This function must be passed a variable defined as a pointer to a int. Additionally, the calling program must define the function ai__ave( ) and the function's return value as an integer. The size parameter denoting the number of elements contained within the array must be defined as an integer.

Calling Ex. :
```
int a__array[50];
int out__average;
int a__size;
int ai__ave( );
a__size = 50;
out__average = ai__ave(a__array,a__size);
```

```
ai_ave(start,size)
 int *start, size;
{ int count;
  int sum = 0;
  int average = 0;
  for ( count=0; count < size; count++ )
    {   sum += (*start++);
    }
  average = sum / count;
  return(average);
}
```

Function Name : ad__found(start,size,value)

Description : This function receives an array starting location, the number of elements in that array and the appropriate search value and returns the number of times that that value appears in the array.

Variables : start — This pointer to a double specifying the memory address of the first array element.

size — This integer number specifies the number of array members.

value — This parameter contains the value to be searched for within the array.

Example : ave = ad__found(d__array,50,20.0l)

Rules : This function must be passed a variable defined as a pointer to a double. However, the calling program must define the function ad__found( ) and the function's return value as an integer.

The size parameter denoting the number of elements contained within the array must be defined as an integer.

The value parameter must be defined as a double.

Calling Ex. :
```
double a__array[50];
double d__value;
int output;
int a__size;
int ad__found( );
a__size = 50;
d__value = 25.1;
output = ad__found(a__array,a__size);
```

```
ad_found(start,size,value)
 double *start, value;
 int size;
{ int count;
  int found = 0;
  for ( count=0; count < size; count++ )
    {    if ( (*start++) == value ) found++;
    }
  return(found);
}
```

ai__found

386

Function Name : ai__found(start,size,value)

Description : This function receives an array starting location, the number of elements in that array and the appropriate search value and returns the number of times that that value appears in the array.

Variables : start — This pointer to an int specifying the memory address of the first array element.

size — This integer number specifies the number of array members.

value — This parameter contains the value to be searched for within the array.

Example : ave = ai__found(d__array,50,20)

Rules : This function must be passed a variable defined as a pointer to an int. Additionally, the calling program must define the function ai__found( ) and the function's return value as an integer.

The size parameter denoting the number of elements contained within the array must be defined as an integer.

The value parameter must be defined as a int.

```
ai_found(start,size,value)
 int *start, value;
 int size;
{ int count;
  int found = 0;
  for ( count=0; count < size; count++ )
    {   if ( (*start++) == value ) found++;
    }
  return(found);
}
```

Function Name : ad__max(start,size)

Description : This function receives an array starting location and the number of elements in that array and returns the largest value contained within that array.

Variables : start — This pointer to a double specifies the memory address of the first array element.

size — This integer number specifies the number of array members.

Example : maximum = ad__max(d__array,50)

Rules : This function must be passed a variable defined as a pointer to a double. Additionally, the calling program must define the function ad__max( ) and the function's return value as a double. The size parameter denoting the number of elements contained within the array must be defined as an integer.

```
double ad_max(start,size)
 double *start;
 int size;

{ int count;
  double max_value;

  max_value = (*start);
  for ( count=0; count < size; count++ )
    {   if ( (*start) > max_value ) max_value = (*start);
        start++;
    }
  return(max_value);
}
```

ai__max

Function Name : ai__max(start,size)

Description : This function receives an array starting location and the number of elements in that array and returns the largest value contained within that array.

Variables : start — This pointer to a int specifies the memory address of the first array element.

size — This integer number specifies the number of array members.

Example : maximum = ai__max(d__array,50)

Rules : This function must be passed a variable defined as a pointer to a int. Additionally, the calling program must define the function ai__max() and the function's return value as an integer.

The size parameter denoting the number of elements contained within the array must be defined as an integer.

```
ai_max(start,size)
 int *start, size;

{ int count;
  int max_value;

  max_value = (*start);
  for ( count=0; count < size; count++ )
    {   if ( (*start) > max_value ) max_value = (*start);
        start++;
    }
  return(max_value);
}
```

Function Name : ad__mean(start,size)

Description : This function receives an array starting location and the number of elements in that array and calculates a numeric mean of its contents.

Variables : start — This pointer to a double specifies the memory address of the first array element.

size — This integer number specifies the number of array members.

Example : mean = ad__mean(d__array,50)

Rules : This function must be passed a variable defined as a pointer to a double. Additionally, the calling program must define the function ad__mean( ) and the function's return value as a double. The size parameter denoting the number of elements contained within the array must be defined as an integer.

```
double ad_mean(start,size)
 double *start;
 int size;

{ int count;
  double max_value, min_value, mean_value;

  max_value = (*start);
  min_value = (*start);
  for ( count=0; count < size; count++ )
    {   if ( (*start) > max_value ) max_value = (*start);
        if ( (*start) < min_value ) min_value = (*start);
        start++;
    }
  mean_value = ( max_value + min_value ) / 2;
  return(mean_value);
}
```

ai__mean

Function Name : ai__mean(start,size)

Description : This function receives an array starting location and the number of elements in that array and calculates a numeric mean of its contents.

Variables : start — This pointer to an int specifies the memory address of the first array element.

size — This integer number specifies the number of array members.

Example : ave = ai__mean(d__array,50)

Rules : This function must be passed a variable defined as a pointer to a int. Additionally, the calling program must define the function ai__mean() and the function's return value as an integer.

The size parameter denoting the number of elements contained within the array must be defined as an integer.

```
ai_mean(start,size)
 int *start;
 int size;

{ int count;
  int max_value, min_value, mean_value;

  max_value = (*start);
  min_value = (*start);
  for ( count=0; count < size; count++ )
     {   if ( (*start) > max_value ) max_value = (*start);
         if ( (*start) < min_value ) min_value = (*start);
         start++;
     }
  mean_value = ( max_value + min_value ) / 2;
  return(mean_value);
}
```

Function Name : ad__min(start,size)

Description : This function receives an array starting location and the number of elements in that array and return the minimum array value.

Variables : start — This pointer to a double specifies the memory address of the first array element.

size — This integer number specifies the number of array members.

Example : minimum = ad__min(d__array,50)

Rules : This function must be passed a variable defined as a pointer to a double. Additionally, the calling program must define the function ad__mean( ) and the function's return value as a double. The size parameter denoting the number of elements contained within the array must be defined as an integer.

```
double ad_min(start,size)
 double *start;
 int size;

{ int count;
  double min_value;

  min_value = (*start);
  for ( count=0; count < size; count++ )
    {   if ( (*start) < min_value ) min_value = (*start);
        start++;
    }
  return(min_value);
}
```

ai__min

Function Name : ai__min(start,size)

Description : This function receives an array starting location and the number of elements in that array and returns the smallest value contained within that array.

Variables : start — This pointer to an int specifies the memory address of the first array element.

size — This integer number specifies the number of array members.

Example : minimum = ai__min(d__array,50)

Rules : This function must be passed a variable defined as a pointer to a int. Additionally, the calling program must define the function ai__mean() and the function's return value as an integer.

The size parameter denoting the number of elements contained within the array must be defined as an integer.

```
ai_min(start,size)
 int *start, size;

{ int count;
  int min_value;

  min_value = (*start);
  for ( count=0; count < size; count++ )
    {   if ( (*start) < min_value ) min_value = (*start);
        start++;
    }
  return(min_value);
}
```

Function Name : ad__search(start,size,value)

Description : This function receives an array starting location and the number of elements in that array and the appropriate search value and returns the location of the first occurence of that value.

Variables : start — This pointer to a double specifying the memory address of the first array element.

size — This integer number specifies the number of array members.

value — This parameter contains the value to be searched for within the array.

Example : location = ad__search(d__array,50,20.01)

Rules : This function must be passed a variable defined as a pointer to a double. However, the calling program must define the function ad__search( ) and the function's return value as an integer.

The size parameter denoting the number of elements contained within the array must be defined as an integer.

The value parameter must be defined as a double.

```
ad_search(start,size,value)
 double *start;
 int size;
 double value;
{ int count;
  int location = -1;
  for ( count=0; count < size; count++ )
     {   if ( (*start++) == value )
           { location = count;
              break;
           }
     }
  return(location);
}
```

ai__search

Function Name : ai__search(start,size,value)

Description : This function receives an array starting location, the number of elements in that array and the appropriate search value and returns the location of the first occurence of that value.

Variables :
start — This pointer to a int specifying the memory address of the first array element.

size — This integer number specifies the number of array members.

value — This parameter contains the value to be searched for within the array.

Example : location = ai__search(d__array,50,20)

Rules : This function must be passed a variable defined as a pointer to a int. However, the calling program must define the function ai__search( ) and the function's return value as an integer. The size parameter denoting the number of elements contained within the array must be defined as an integer. The value parameter must be defined as a int.

```
ai_search(start,size,value)
 int *start;
 int size;
 int value;
{ int count;
  int location = -1;
  for ( count=0; count < size; count++ )
     {   if ( (*start++) == value )
           { location = count;
              break;
           }
     }
  return(location);
}
```

Function Name : ad__sum(start,size)

Description : This function receives an array starting location and the number of elements in that array and calculates the sum of its contents.

Variables : start — This pointer to a double specifies the memory address of the first array element.

size — This integer number specifies the number of array members.

Example : sum = ad__sum(d__array,50)

Rules : This function must be passed a variable defined as a pointer to a double. Additionally, the calling program must define the function ad__sum( ) and the function's return value as a double. The size parameter denoting the number of elements contained within the array must be defined as an integer.

```
double ad_sum(start,size)
 double *start;
 int size;
{ int count;
  double sum = 0;
  for ( count=0; count < size; count++ )
    {   sum += (*start++);
    }
  return(sum);
}
```

ai__sum

Function Name : ai__sum(start,size)

Description : This function receives an array starting location and the number of elements in that array and calculates the sum of its contents.

Variables : start — This pointer to a int specifies the memory address of the first array element.

size — This integer number specifies the number of array members.

Example : sum = ai__sum(d__array,50)

Rules : This function must be passed a variable defined as a pointer to a int. Additionally, the calling program must define the function ai__sum( ) and the function's return value as an int. The size parameter denoting the number of elements contained within the array must be defined as an integer.

```
ai_sum(start,size)
 int *start, size;
{ int count;
  int sum = 0;
  for ( count=0; count < size; count++ )
    {   sum += (*start++);
    }
  return(sum);
}
```

CALLING THE ARRAY MANIPULATION FUNCTIONS

The code on the following pages will sequentially call each of the functions in this chapter, demonstrating their effects and how they can be used in actual programs.

```c
#include <stdio.h>

double da_array[] = {3,4,5,1,2,9,8,7,6};
double db_array[] = {10,11,12,13,14,15,16,17,18,19,20};

int ia_array[] = {3,4,5,1,2,9,8,7,6};
int ib_array[] = {10,11,12,13,14,15,16,17,18,19,20};


main()
{ ex1();
  ex2();
  ex3();
  ex4();
  ex5();
  ex6();
  ex7();
  ex8();
  ex9();
  ex10();
  ex11();
  ex12();
  ex13();
  ex14();
}


ex1()
{
  /***************************************************************
   **************** calls to ad_ave function *****************
   ***************************************************************/
  double ad_ave();
  double output;
  printf("\n\nad_ave value function");

     output = ad_ave(da_array,9);
     printf("\n      ad_ave value is == %f",output);

     output = ad_ave(db_array,10);
     printf("\n      ad_ave value is == %f",output);
}


ex2()
{
  /***************************************************************
   *********** calls to ai_ave function *****************
   ***************************************************************/
  int ai_ave();
  int output;
  printf("\n\nai_ave value function");
```

```
        output = ai_ave(ia_array,9);
        printf("\n     ai ave value is == %d",output);
        output = ai_ave(ib_array,10);
        printf("\n     ai_ave value is == %d",output);
}


ex3()
{
  /***************************************************************
   *************** calls to ad_found function ***************
   ***************************************************************/
  int ad_found();
  double output;
  printf("\n\nad_found value function");

        output = ad_found(da_array,9,4.0);
        printf("\n     ad_found value is == %d",output);

        output = ad_found(db_array,10,50.0);
        printf("\n     ad_found value is == %d",output);
}


ex4()
{
  /***************************************************************
   *********** calls to ai_found function ****************
   ***************************************************************/
  int ai_found();
  int output;
  printf("\n\nai_found value function");

        output = ai_found(ia_array,9,16);
        printf("\n     ai_found value is == %d",output);

        output = ai_found(ib_array,10,14);
        printf("\n     ai_found value is == %d",output);
}


ex5()
{
  /***************************************************************
   *************** calls to ad_max function ****************
   ***************************************************************/
  double ad_max();
  double output;
  printf("\n\nad_max value function");

        output = ad_max(da_array,9);
        printf("\n     ad_max value is == %f",output);

        output = ad_max(db_array,10);
        printf("\n     ad_max value is == %f",output);
}
```

```
ex6()
{
  /****************************************************************
   *********** calls to ai_max function *****************
   ****************************************************************/
  int ai_max();
  int output;
  printf("\n\nai_max value function");

     output = ai_max(ia_array,9);
     printf("\n     ai_max value is == %d",output);

     output = ai_max(ib_array,10);
     printf("\n     ai_max value is == %d",output);
}


ex7()
{
  /****************************************************************
   *************** calls to ad_mean function *****************
   ****************************************************************/
  double ad_mean();
  double output;
  printf("\n\nad_mean value function");

     output = ad_mean(da_array,9);
     printf("\n     ad_mean value is == %f",output);

     output = ad_mean(db_array,10);
     printf("\n     ad_mean value is == %f",output);
}


ex8()
{
  /****************************************************************
   *************** calls to ai_mean function *****************
   ****************************************************************/
  int ai_mean();
  int output;
  printf("\n\nai_mean value function");

     output = ai_mean(ia_array,9);
     printf("\n     ai_mean value is == %d",output);

     output = ai_mean(ib_array,10);
     printf("\n     ai_mean value is == %d",output);
}


ex9()
{
  /****************************************************************
   *************** calls to ad_min function *****************
   ****************************************************************/
```

```c
    double ad_min();
    double output;
    printf("\n\nad_min value function");

        output = ad_min(da_array,9);
        printf("\n        ad_min value is == %f",output);

        output = ad_min(db_array,10);
        printf("\n        ad_min value is == %f",output);
}


ex10()
{
  /****************************************************************
   *************** calls to ai_min function ******************
   ****************************************************************/
  int ai_min();
  int output;
  printf("\n\nai_min value function");

        output = ai_min(ia_array,9);
        printf("\n        ai_min value is == %d",output);

        output = ai_min(ib_array,10);
        printf("\n        ai_min value is == %d",output);
}


ex11()
{
  /****************************************************************
   *************** calls to ad_search function ***************
   ****************************************************************/
  int ad_search();
  double output;
  printf("\n\nad_search value function");

        output = ad_search(da_array,9,4.0);
        printf("\n        ad_search value is == %d",output);

        output = ad_search(db_array,10,50.0);
        printf("\n        ad_search value is == %d",output);
}


ex12()
{
  /****************************************************************
   *********** calls to ai_search function *****************
   ****************************************************************/
  int ai_search();
  int output;
  printf("\n\nai_search value function");

        output = ai_search(ia_array,9,16);
        printf("\n        ai_search value is == %d",output);
```

```
        output = ai_search(ib_array,10,14);
        printf("\n      ai_search value is == %d",output);
}


ex13()
{
  /***************************************************************
   *************** calls to ad_sum function ******************
   ***************************************************************/
  double ad_sum();
  double output;
  printf("\n\nad_sum value function");

      output = ad_sum(da_array,9);
      printf("\n      ad_sum value is == %f",output);

      output = ad_sum(db_array,10);
      printf("\n      ad_sum value is == %f",output);
}


ex14()
{
  /***************************************************************
   *************** calls to ai_sum function ******************
   ***************************************************************/
  int ai_sum();
  int output;
  printf("\n\nai_sum value function");

      output = ai_sum(ia_array,9);
      printf("\n      ai_sum value is == %d",output);

      output = ai_sum(ib_array,10);
      printf("\n      ai_sum value is == %d",output);
}
```

20

Measurement
Conversion Functions

cmet__feet	—	centimeters to feet
cmet__inch	—	centimeters to inches
feet__cmet	—	feet to centimeters
gal__liter	—	gallons to liters
gram__ounce	—	grams to ounces
inch__cmet	—	inches to centimeters
inch__met	—	inches to meters
kgram__ounce	—	kilograms to ounces
kgram__pound	—	kilograms to pounds
kmet__mile	—	kilometers to miles
liter__gal	—	liters to gallons
liter__quart	—	liters to quarts
met__inch	—	meters to inches
met__yards	—	meters to yards
mile__kmet	—	miles to kilometers
ounce__gram	—	ounces to grams
ounce__kgram	—	ounces to kilograms
pound__kgram	—	pounds to kilograms
quart__liter	—	quarts to liters
yards__met	—	yards to meters

Function Name : cmet__feet(cmet)

Description : This function converts centimeters to feet.

Variables : cmet — This variable is the input parameter and contains the number of centimeters to be converted.

feet — This variable is the function's return value and contains the number of feet corresponding to the centimeter value in cmet.

Example : output = cmet__feet(5) returns value .164
output = cmet__feet(10) returns value .328

Rules : This function must be passed a variable defined as a double. Additionally, the calling program must define the function cmet__feet( ) and the function's return value as a double. An example of these calling requirements is shown below.

```
double cmet_feet(cmet)
 double cmet;

{ double feet;
  feet = cmet * .0328;
  return(feet);
}
```

cmet__inch

Function Name : cmet__inch(cmet)

Description : This function converts centimeters to inches.

Variables : cmet — This variable is the input parameter and contains the number of centimeters to be converted.

inch — This variable is the function's return value and contains the number of inches corresponding to the centimeter value in cmet.

Example : output = cmet__inch(5)   returns value 1.97
output = cmet__inch(10)   returns value 3.94

Rules : This function must be passed a variable defined as a double. Additionally, the calling program must define the function cmet__inch( ) and the function's return value as a double. An example of these calling requirements is shown below.

```
double cmet_inch(cmet)
 double cmet;

{ double inch;
  inch = cmet * .394;
  return(inch);
}
```

Function Name : feet__cmet(feet)

Description : This function converts feet to centimeters.

Variables : feet — This variable is the input parameter and contains the number of feet to be converted.

                cmet — This variable is the function's return value and contains the number of centimeters corresponding to the feet value in feet.

Example : output = feet__cmet(5)   returns value 152.4

            output = feet__cmet(10)   returns value 304.8

Rules : This function must be passed a variable defined as a double. Additionally, the calling program must define the function feet__cmet( ) and the function's return value as a double. An example of these calling requirements is shown below.

```
double feet_cmet(feet)
 double feet;

{ double cmet;
  cmet = feet * 30.48;
  return(cmet);
}
```

gal__liter

Function Name : gal__liter(gal)

Description : This function converts gallons to liters.

Variables : gal — This variable is the input parameter and contains the number of gallons to be converted.

liter — This variable is the function's return value and contains the number of centimeters corresponding to the liters value in gal.

Example :

output = gal__liter(5)	returns value 18.925
output = gal__liter(10)	returns value 37.85

Rules : This function must be passed a variable defined as a double. Additionally, the calling program must define the function gal__liter( ) and the function's return value as a double. An example of these calling requirements is shown below.

```
double gal_liter(gal)
 double gal;

{ double liter;
  liter = gal * 3.785;
  return(liter);
}
```

Function Name : gram__ounce(gram)

Description : This function converts grams to ounces.

Variables : gram — This variable is the input parameter and contains the number of grams to be converted.

ounce — This variable is the function's return value and contains the number of ounces corresponding to the value in gram.

Example :

output = gram__ounce(5)	returns value .175
output = gram__ounce(10)	returns value .35

Rules : This function must be passed a variable defined as a double. Additionally, the calling program must define the function gram__ounce( ) and the function's return value as a double. An example of these calling requirements is shown below.

```
double gram_ounce(gram
 double gram;

{ double ounce;
  ounce = gram * .035;
  return(ounce);
}
```

inch__cmet

Function Name : inch__cmet(inch)

Description : This function converts inches to centimeters.

Variables : inch — This variable is the input parameter and contains the number of inches to be converted.

cmet — This variable is the function's return value and contains the number of centimeters corresponding to the value in inch.

Example : output = inch__cmet(5)   returns value 12.7
output = inch__cmet(10)   returns value 25.4

Rules : This function must be passed a variable defined as a double. Additionally, the calling program must define the function inch__cmet( ) and the function's return value as a double. An example of these calling requirements is shown below.

```
double inch_cmet(inch)
 double inch;

{ double cmet;
  cmet = inch * 2.54;
  return(cmet);
}
```

Function Name : inch__met(inch)

Description : This function converts inches to meters.

Variables : inch — This variable is the input parameter and contains the number of inches to be converted.

met — This variable is the function's return value and contains the number of centimeters corresponding to the value in inch.

Example : output = inch__met(5)   returns value .127
output = inch__met(10)   returns value .254

Rules : This function must be passed a variable defined as a double. Additionally, the calling program must define the function inch__met( ) and the function's return value as a double. An example of these calling requirements is shown below.

```
double inch_met(inch)
 double inch;

{ double met;
  met = inch / 39.37;
  return(met);
}
```

kgram__ounce

Function Name : kgram__ounce(kgram)

Description : This function converts kilograms to ounces.

Variables : kgram — This variable is the input parameter and contains the number of kilograms to be converted.

ounce — This variable is the function's return value and contains the number of ounces corresponding to the value in kgram.

Example : output = kgram__ounce(5)   returns value 176.36
output = kgram__ounce(10)   returns value 352.72

Rules : This function must be passed a variable defined as a double. Additionally, the calling program must define the function kgram__ounce( ) and the function's return value as a double. An example of these calling requirements is shown below.

```
double kgram_ounce(kgram)
 double kgram;

{ double ounce;
  ounce = kgram * 35.272;
  return(ounce);
}
```

kgram__pound

Function Name : kgram__pound(kgram)

Description : This function converts kilograms to ounces.

Variables : kgram — This variable is the input parameter and contains the number of kilograms to be converted.

pound — This variable is the function's return value and contains the number of pounds corresponding to the value in kgram.

Example : output = kgram__pound(5)   returns value 11.025
output = kgram__pound(10)   returns value 22.05

Rules : This function must be passed a variable defined as a double. Additionally, the calling program must define the function kgram__pound( ) and the function's return value as a double. An example of these calling requirements is shown below.

```
double kgram_pound(kgram)
 double kgram;

{ double pound;
  pound = kgram * 2.205;
  return(pound);
}
```

kmet__mile

Function Name : kmet__mile(kmet)

Description : This function converts kilometers to miles.

Variables : kmet — This variable is the input parameter and contains the number of kilometers to be converted.

         mile — This variable is the function's return value and contains the number of miles corresponding to the value in kmet.

Example : output = kmet__mile(5)   returns value 3.105

            output = kmet__mile(10)   returns value 6.21

Rules : This function must be passed a variable defined as a double. Additionally, the calling program must define the function kmet__mile( ) and the function's return value as a double. An example of these calling requirements is shown below.

```
double kmet_mile(kmet)
 double kmet;

{ double mile;
  mile = kmet * .621;
  return(mile);
}
```

liter__gal

Function Name : liter__gal(liter)

Description : This function converts liters to gallons.

Variables : liter — This variable is the input parameter and contains the number of liters to be converted.

gal — This variable is the function's return value and contains the number of gallons corresponding to the value in liter.

Example :
output = liter__gal(5)   returns value 1.32
output = liter__gal(10)   returns value 2.64

Rules : This function must be passed a variable defined as a double. Additionally, the calling program must define the function liter__gal( ) and the function's return value as a double. An example of these calling requirements is shown below.

```
double liter_gal(liter)
 double liter;

{ double gal;
  gal = liter * .264;
  return(gal);
}
```

liter__quart

Function Name : liter__quart(liter)

Description : This function converts liters to quarts.

Variables : liter — This variable is the input parameter and contains the number of liters to be converted.

quart — This variable is the function's return value and contains the number of quarts corresponding to the value in liter.

Example : output = liter__quart(5)   returns value 5.285
output = liter__quart(10)   returns value 10.57

Rules : This function must be passed a variable defined as a double. Additionally, the calling program must define the function liter__quart() and the function's return value as a double. An example of these calling requirements is shown below.

```
double liter_quart(liter)
 double liter;

{ double quart;
  quart = liter * 1.057;
  return(quart);
}
```

Function Name : met__inch(met)

Description : This function converts meters to inches.

Variables : met — This variable is the input parameter and contains the number of meters to be converted.

inches — This variable is the function's return value and contains the number of inches corresponding to the value in met.

Example : output = met__inch(5)   returns value 196.85

output = met__inch(10)   returns value 393.7

Rules : This function must be passed a variable defined as a double. Additionally, the calling program must define the function met__inch( ) and the function's return value as a double. An example of these calling requirements is shown below.

```
double met_inch(met)
 double met;

{ double inch;
  inch = met * 39.37;
  return(inch);
}
```

met__yards

Function Name : met__yards(yards)

Description : This function converts meters to yards.

Variables : met   —   This variable is the input parameter and contains the number of meters to be converted.

            yards   —   This variable is the function's return value and contains the number of yards corresponding to the value in met.

Example : output = met__yards(5)   returns value 5.465

              output = met__yards(10)   returns value 10.93

Rules : This function must be passed a variable defined as a double. Additionally, the calling program must define the function met__yards( ) and the function's return value as a double. An example of these calling requirements is shown below.

```
double met_yards(met)
 double met;

{ double yards;
  yards = met * 1.093;
  return(yards);
}
```

Function Name : mile__kmet(mile)

Description : This function converts miles to kilometers.

Variables : mile — This variable is the input parameter and contains the number of miles to be converted.

kmet — This variable is the function's return value and contains the number of kilometers corresponding to the value in mile.

Example : output = mile__kmet(5)   returns value 8.045
output = mile__kmet(10)   returns value 16.09

Rules : This function must be passed a variable defined as a double. Additionally, the calling program must define the function mile__kmet() and the function's return value as a double. An example of these calling requirements is shown below.

```
double mile_kmet(mile)
 double mile;

{ double kmet;
  kmet = mile * 1.609;
  return(kmet);
}
```

ounce__gram

Function Name : ounce__gram(ounce)

Description : This function converts miles to kilometers.

Variables : ounce — This variable is the input parameter and contains the number of ounces to be converted.

gram — This variable is the function's return value and contains the number of grams corresponding to the value in ounce.

Example : output = ounce__gram(5)   returns value 141.75

output = ounce__gram(10)   returns value 283.50

Rules : This function must be passed a variable defined as a double. Additionally, the calling program must define the function ounce__gram( ) and the function's return value as a double. An example of these calling requirements is shown below.

```
double ounce_gram(ounce)
 double ounce;

{ double gram;
  gram = ounce * 28.35;
  return(gram);
}
```

Function Name : ounce__kgram(ounce)

Description : This function converts ounces to kilograms.

Variables : ounce — This variable is the input parameter and contains the number of ounces to be converted.

kgram — This variable is the function's return value and contains the number of kilograms corresponding to the value in ounce.

Example : output = ounce__kgram(5)   returns value .14
output = ounce__kgram(10)   returns value .28

Rules : This function must be passed a variable defined as a double. Additionally, the calling program must define the function ounce__kgram( ) and the function's return value as a double. An example of these calling requirements is shown below.

```
double ounce_kgram(ounce)
 double ounce;

{ double kgram;
  kgram = ounce * .028;
  return(kgram);
}
```

pound__kgram

Function Name : pound__kgram(ounce)

Description : This function converts pounds to kilograms.

Variables : pound — This variable is the input parameter and contains the number of pounds to be converted.

kgram — This variable is the function's return value and contains the number of kilograms corresponding to the value in pound.

Example :
output = pound__kgram(5)   returns value 2.27
output = pound__kgram(10)   returns value 4.54

Rules : This function must be passed a variable defined as a double. Additionally, the calling program must define the function pound__kgram( ) and the function's return value as a double. An example of these calling requirements is shown below.

```
double pound_kgram(pound)
 double pound;

{ double kgram;
  kgram = pound * .454;
  return(kgram);
}
```

Function Name : quart__liter(quart)

Description : This function converts quarts to liters.

Variables : quart — This variable is the input parameter and contains the number of quarts to be converted.

liter — This variable is the function's return value and contains the number of liters corresponding to the value in quart.

Example : output = quart__liter(5)   returns value 4.73

output = quart__liter(10)   returns value 9.46

Rules : This function must be passed a variable defined as a double. Additionally, the calling program must define the function quart__liter( ) and the function's return value as a double. An example of these calling requirements is shown below.

```
double quart_liter(quart)
 double quart;

{ double liter;
  liter = quart * .946;
  return(liter);
}
```

yards__met

Function Name : yards__met(quart)

Description : This function converts yards to meters.

Variables : yards — This variable is the input parameter and contains the number of yards to be converted.

meter — This variable is the function's return value and contains the number of meters corresponding to the value in yards.

Example : output = yards__met(5)   returns value 4.57
output = yards__met(10)   returns value 9.14

Rules : This function must be passed a variable defined as a double. Additionally, the calling program must define the function yards__met( ) and the function's return value as a double. An example of these calling requirements is shown below.

```
double yards_met(yards)
 double yards;

{ double met;
  met = yards * .914;
  return(met);
}
```

CALLING THE MEASUREMENT CONVERSION FUNCTIONS

The code on the following pages will sequentially call each of the functions in this chapter, demonstrating their effects and how they can be used in actual programs.

```c
#include <math.h>
#include <stdio.h>


main()
{ ex1();
  ex2();
  ex3();
  ex4();
  ex5();
  ex6();
  ex7();
  ex8();
  ex9();
  ex10();
  ex11();
  ex12();
  ex13();
  ex14();
  ex15();
  ex16();
  ex17();
  ex18();
  ex19();
  ex20();
}

ex1()
{
  /**************************************************************
   *********** calls to cmet_feet function ****************
   **************************************************************/
  double cmet_feet();
  double input, output;
  printf("\n\ncmet_feet value function");

    input = 5;
    output = cmet_feet(input);
    printf("\n    cmet_feet value is == %f",output);

    input = 10;
    output = cmet_feet(input);
    printf("\n    cmet_feet value is == %f",output);
}

ex2()
{
  /**************************************************************
   *********** calls to cmet_inch function ****************
   **************************************************************/
  double cmet_inch();
```

```
    double input, output;
    printf("\n\ncmet_inch value function");

    input = 5;
    output = cmet_inch(input);
    printf("\n     cmet_inch value is == %f",output);

    input = 10;
    output = cmet_inch(input);
    printf("\n     cmet_inch value is == %f",output);
}

ex3()
{
  /****************************************************************
   ************ calls to feet_cmet function ******************
   ****************************************************************/
  double feet_cmet();
  double input, output;
  printf("\n\nfeet_cmet value function");

    input = 5;
    output = feet_cmet(input);
    printf("\n     feet_cmet value is == %f",output);

    input = 10;
    output = feet_cmet(input);
    printf("\n     feet_cmet value is == %f",output);
}

ex4()
{
  /****************************************************************
   ************ calls to gal_liter function ******************
   ****************************************************************/
  double gal_liter();
  double input, output;
  printf("\n\ngal_liter value function");

    input = 5;
    output = gal_liter(input);
    printf("\n     gal_liter value is == %f",output);

    input = 10;
    output = gal_liter(input);
    printf("\n     gal_liter value is == %f",output);
}

ex5()
{
  /****************************************************************
   ************ calls to gram_ounce function ******************
   ****************************************************************/
  double gram_ounce();
  double input, output;
  printf("\n\ngram_ounce value function");

    input = 5;
```

```
        output = gram_ounce(input);
        printf("\n      gram_ounce value is == %f",output);

        input = 10;
        output = gram_ounce(input);
        printf("\n      gram_ounce value is == %f",output);
}

ex6()
{
   /*************************************************************
    *********** calls to inch_cmet function ****************
    *************************************************************/
   double inch_cmet();
   double input, output;
   printf("\n\ninch_cmet value function");

        input = 5;
        output = inch_cmet(input);
        printf("\n      inch_cmet value is == %f",output);

        input = 10;
        output = inch_cmet(input);
        printf("\n      inch_cmet value is == %f",output);
}

ex7()
{
   /*************************************************************
    *********** calls to inch_met function ****************
    *************************************************************/
   double inch_met();
   double input, output;
   printf("\n\ninch_met value function");

        input = 5;
        output = inch_met(input);
        printf("\n      inch_met value is == %f",output);

        input = 10;
        output = inch_met(input);
        printf("\n      inch_met value is == %f",output);
}

ex8()
{
   /*************************************************************
    *********** calls to kgram_ounce function ****************
    *************************************************************/
   double kgram_ounce();
   double input, output;
   printf("\n\nkgram_ounce value function");

        input = 5;
        output = kgram_ounce(input);
        printf("\n      kgram_ounce value is == %f",output);
        input = 10;
        output = kgram_ounce(input);
```

```
        printf("\n     kgram_ounce value is == %f",output);
}

ex9()
{
  /***************************************************************
   ************ calls to kgram_pound function *****************
   ***************************************************************/
  double kgram_pound();
  double input, output;
  printf("\n\nkgram_pound value function");

     input = 5;
     output = kgram_pound(input);
     printf("\n     kgram_pound value is == %f",output);

     input = 10;
     output = kgram_pound(input);
     printf("\n     kgram_pound value is == %f",output);
}

ex10()
{
  /***************************************************************
   ************ calls to kmet_mile function *****************
   ***************************************************************/
  double kmet_mile();
  double input, output;
  printf("\n\nkmet_mile value function");

     input = 5;
     output = kmet_mile(input);
     printf("\n     kmet_mile value is == %f",output);

     input = 10;
     output = kmet_mile(input);
     printf("\n     kmet_mile value is == %f",output);
}

ex11()
{
  /***************************************************************
   ************ calls to liter_gal function *****************
   ***************************************************************/
  double liter_gal();
  double input, output;
  printf("\n\nliter_gal value function");

     input = 5;
     output = liter_gal(input);
     printf("\n     liter_gal value is == %f",output);
     input = 10;
     output = liter_gal(input);
     printf("\n     liter_gal value is == %f",output);
}

ex12()
{
```

426

```
   /****************************************************************
    *********** calls to liter_quart function ****************
    ****************************************************************/
   double liter_quart();
   double input, output;
   printf("\n\nliter_quart value function");

      input = 5;
      output = liter_quart(input);
      printf("\n      liter_quart value is == %f",output);

      input = 10;
      output = liter_quart(input);
      printf("\n      liter_quart value is == %f",output);
}

ex13()
{
   /****************************************************************
    *********** calls to met_inch function ****************
    ****************************************************************/
   double met_inch();
   double input, output;
   printf("\n\nmet_inch value function");

      input = 5;
      output = met_inch(input);
      printf("\n      met_inch value is == %f",output);

      input = 10;
      output = met_inch(input);
      printf("\n      met_inch value is == %f",output);
}

ex14()
{
   /****************************************************************
    *********** calls to met_yards function ****************
    ****************************************************************/
   double met_yards();
   double input, output;
   printf("\n\nmet_yards value function");

      input = 5;
      output = met_yards(input);
      printf("\n      met_yards value is == %f",output);

      input = 10;
      output = met_yards(input);
      printf("\n      met_yards value is == %f",output);
}

ex15()
{
   /****************************************************************
    *********** calls to mile_kmet function ****************
    ****************************************************************/
   double mile_kmet();
```

```
    double input, output;
    printf("\n\nmile_kmet value function");

    input = 5;
    output = mile_kmet(input);
    printf("\n     mile_kmet value is == %f",output);

    input = 10;
    output = mile_kmet(input);
    printf("\n     mile_kmet value is == %f",output);
}

ex16()
{
  /**************************************************************
   *********** calls to ounce_gram function *****************
   **************************************************************/
  double ounce_gram();
  double input, output;
  printf("\n\nounce_gram value function");

    input = 5;
    output = ounce_gram(input);
    printf("\n     ounce_gram value is == %f",output);

    input = 10;
    output = ounce_gram(input);
    printf("\n     ounce_gram value is == %f",output);
}

ex17()
{
  /**************************************************************
   *********** calls to ounce_kgram function *****************
   **************************************************************/
  double ounce_kgram();
  double input, output;
  printf("\n\nounce_kgram value function");

    input = 5;
    output = ounce_kgram(input);
    printf("\n     ounce_kgram value is == %f",output);

    input = 10;
    output = ounce_kgram(input);
    printf("\n     ounce_kgram value is == %f",output);
}

ex18()
{
  /**************************************************************
   *********** calls to pound_kgram function *****************
   **************************************************************/
  double pound_kgram();
  double input, output;
  printf("\n\npound_kgram value function");

    input = 5;
```

```
       output = pound_kgram(input);
       printf("\n      pound_kgram value is == %f",output);

       input = 10;
       output = pound_kgram(input);
       printf("\n      pound_kgram value is == %f",output);
}

ex19()
{
  /*************************************************************
   ************ calls to quart_liter function ****************
   *************************************************************/
  double quart_liter();
  double input, output;
  printf("\n\nquart_liter value function");

       input = 5;
       output = quart_liter(input);
       printf("\n      quart_liter value is == %f",output);

       input = 10;        .
       output = quart_liter(input);
       printf("\n      quart_liter value is == %f",output);
}

ex20()
{
  /*************************************************************
   ************ calls to yards_met function *****************
   *************************************************************/
  double yards_met();
  double input, output;
  printf("\n\nyards_met value function");

       input = 5;
       output = yards_met(input);
       printf("\n      yards_met value is == %f",output);

       input = 10;
       output = yards_met(input);
       printf("\n      yards_met value is == %f",output);
}
```

429

21

Date Functions

date__1	—	MM/DD/YYYY to DD-MMM-YYYY
date__2	—	MM/DD/YYYY to YYYYMMDD
date__3	—	MM/DD/YYYY to DDMMMYYYY
date__4	—	MM/DD/YYYY to Julian date
date__5	—	MM/DD/YYYY to day in year
date__6	—	MM/DD/YYYY for leap year test
date__7	—	MM/DD/YYYY to day of the week
date__8	—	MM/DD/YYYY to Day., Mon. DD, YYYY
date__9	—	MM/DD/YYYY to Dayyyyyy, Monthhhhh DD, YYYY
date__10	—	MM/DD/YYYY dates to inclusive days between
date__11	—	MM/DD/YYYY dates to exclusive days between
date__12	—	MM/DD/YYYY and no. of days for new date
date__13	—	DD-MM-YYYY to MM/DD/YYYY
date__14	—	DD-MM-YYYY to YYYYYMMDD
date__15	—	DD-MM-YYYY to DDMMMYYYY
date__16	—	DD-MM-YYYY to Julian date
date__17	—	DD-MM-YYYY to day in year
date__18	—	DD-MM-YYYY for leap year test
date__19	—	DD-MM-YYYY to day of the week
date__20	—	DD-MM-YYYY to Day., Mon. DD, YYYY
date__21	—	DD-MM-YYYY to Dayyyyyy, Monthhhhh DD, YYYY
date__22	—	DD-MM-YYYY dates to inclusive days between
date__23	—	DD-MM-YYYY dates to exclusive days between
date__24	—	DD-MM-YYYY and no. of days for new date
date__25	—	YYYYMMDD to DD-MM-YYYY
date__26	—	YYYYMMDD to MM/DD/YYYY

date__1

Function Name : date__1

Description : This function converts the date from a format of MM/DD/YYYY to a format of DD-MMM-YYYY.

Variables : d__in — This variable contains the date that is passed to the function for reformatting.

d__out — This variable contains the reformatted date field that is passed back to the calling module.

Rules : This function must be passed the pointer associated with a character field. This may be in the format of defined character pointer or as the name of a character array with no array brackets.

The date must be passed in the correct format or unexpected results may be returned.

The reformatted date will be returned by way of the second parameter. Therefore, no actual return code is used. The field into which the reformatted date is returned must be large enough to hold the output character string.

On this and all other date functions, all four digits of the year field are required. For example, 1986 is valid and 86 is not valid.

```
date_1(d_in, d_out)

char *d_in, *d_out;

{ int int_month;
  char months[37];
  *(d_out)    = *(d_in+3);
  *(d_out+1) = *(d_in+4);
  *(d_out+2) = '-';
  *(d_out+3) = 'X';
  *(d_out+4) = 'X';
  *(d_out+5) = 'X';
  *(d_out+6) = '-';
  *(d_out+7) = *(d_in+6);
  *(d_out+8) = *(d_in+7);
  *(d_out+9) = *(d_in+8);
  *(d_out+10) = *(d_in+9);
  *(d_out+11) = '\0';
  strcpy(months,"JANFEBMARAPRMAYJUNJULAUGSEPOCTNOVDEC");
  int_month = *(d_in+1) - '0';
  if ((*d_in) == '1' ) int_month +=10;
  if ( int_month >= 1 && int_month <= 12 )
    { *(d_out+3) = *(months+((int_month-1)*3));
      *(d_out+4) = *(months+1+((int_month-1)*3));
      *(d_out+5) = *(months+2+((int_month-1)*3));
    }
}
```

Function Name : date___2

Description : This function converts the date from a format of MM/DD/YYYY to a format of YYYYMMDD.

Variables : d__in — This variable contains the date that is passed to the function for reformatting.

d__out — This variable contains the reformatted date field that is passed back to the calling module.

Rules : This function must be passed the pointer associated with a character field. This may be in the format of defined character pointer or as the name of a character array with no array brackets.

The date must be passed in the correct format or unexpected results may be returned.

The reformatted date will be returned by way of the second parameter. Therefore, no actual return code is used. The field into which the reformatted date is returned must be large enough to hold the output character string.

On this and all other date functions, all four digits of the year field are required. For example, 1986 is valid and 86 is not valid.

```
date_2(d_in, d_out)

char *d_in, *d_out;

{ int int_month;
  char months[37];
  *(d_out)   = *(d_in+6);
  *(d_out+1) = *(d_in+7);
  *(d_out+2) = *(d_in+8);
  *(d_out+3) = *(d_in+9);
  *(d_out+4) = *(d_in);
  *(d_out+5) = *(d_in+1);
  *(d_out+6) = *(d_in+3);
  *(d_out+7) = *(d_in+4);
  *(d_out+8) = '\0';
}
```

433

date___3

Function Name : date___3

Description : This function converts the date from a format of MM/DD/YYYY to a format of DDMMMYYYY.

Variables : d__in — This variable contains the date that is passed to the function for reformatting.

d__out — This variable contains the reformatted date field that is passed back to the calling module.

Rules : This function must be passed the pointer associated with a character field. This may be in the format of defined character pointer or as the name of a character array with no array brackets.

The date must be passed in the correct format or unexpected results may be returned.

The reformatted date will be returned by way of the second parameter. Therefore, no actual return code is used. The field into which the reformatted date is returned must be large enough to hold the output character string.

On this and all other date functions, all four digits of the year field are required. For example, 1986 is valid and 86 is not valid.

```
date_3(d_in, d_out)

char *d_in, *d_out;

{ int int_month;
  char months[37];
  *(d_out)   = *(d_in+3);
  *(d_out+1) = *(d_in+4);
  *(d_out+2) = 'X';
  *(d_out+3) = 'X';
  *(d_out+4) = 'X';
  *(d_out+5) = *(d_in+6);
  *(d_out+6) = *(d_in+7);
  *(d_out+7) = *(d_in+8);
  *(d_out+8) = *(d_in+9);
  *(d_out+9) = '\0';
  strcpy(months,"JANFEBMARAPRMAYJUNJULAUGSEPOCTNOVDEC");
  int_month = *(d_in+1) - '0';
  if ((*d_in) == '1' ) int_month +=10;
  if ( int_month >= 1 && int_month <= 12 )
    { *(d_out+2) = *(months+((int_month-1)*3));
      *(d_out+3) = *(months+1+((int_month-1)*3));
      *(d_out+4) = *(months+2+((int_month-1)*3));
    }
}
```

Function Name : date__4

Description : This function converts the date from a format of MM/DD/YYYY to its julian equivalent.

Variables : d__in — The variables contain the date that is passed to the function for conversion to its julian date.

julian — This long integer variable contains the numeric julian value that is returned to the calling function.

Rules : This function must be passed the pointer associated with a character field. This may be in the format of defined character pointer or as the name of a character array with no array brackets.

The date must be passed in the correct format or unexpected results may be returned.

The reformatted date will be returned via a long integer. Therefore, the function must be defined as a long integer and the variable receiving the returned value must also be a long integer.

On this and all other date functions, all four digits of the year field are required. For example, 1986 is valid and 86 is not valid.

```
long int date_4(d_in)
 char *d_in;
{ int in_year, in_month, in_day;
  int cent, cent_y, month, year, out_day;
  long int long_day, temp_long;
  *(d_in+2) = '\0';
  *(d_in+5) = '\0';
  in_year  = i_convert(d_in+6);
  in_month = i_convert(d_in);
  in_day   = i_convert(d_in+3);

  if ( in_month > 2 )
    { month = in_month - 3;
      year  = in_year;
    }
  else
    { month = in_month + 9;
      year = in_year - 1;
    }
  temp_long = 146097;
  cent  = year / 100;
  cent_y = year - ( cent * 100 );
  long_day = temp_long * cent / 4;
  long_day = long_day + 1461.0 * cent_y / 4;
  long_day = long_day  + ( 153 * month + 2 ) / 5;
  long_day = long_day + in_day;

  return(long_day);
}
```

date__5

Function Name : date__5

Description : This function converts a date in the format of MM/DD/YYYY and returns its daily position within the year. For example, February 5th is the 36th day of the year.

Variables : d__in   — The variables contain the date that is passed to the function for conversion to its julian date.

out__day — This long integer variable contains the numeric value that is returned to the calling function.

Rules : This function must be passed the pointer associated with a character field. This may be in the format of defined character pointer or as the name of a character array with no array brackets.

The date must be passed in the correct format or unexpected results may be returned.

The converted date will be returned via an integer. Therefore, the function must be defined as an integer and the variable receiving the returned value must also be an integer. On this and all other date functions, all four digits of the year field are required. For example, 1986 is valid and 86 is not valid.

```
date_5(d_in)
 char *d_in;
{ int in_year, in_month, in_day;
  int cent, cent_y, month, year, out_day, leap_year;
  long int long_day;
  *(d_in+2) = '\0';
  *(d_in+5) = '\0';
  in_year   = i_convert(d_in+6);
  in_month  = i_convert(d_in);
  in_day    = i_convert(d_in+3);

  long_day = ( 3055.0 * ( in_months + 2 ) / 100 ) -91;
  out_day = long_day;

  if ( in_month > 2 )
    { leap_year = 0;
      if (( in_year % 4 )   == 0 ) leap_year = 1;
      if (( in_year % 100 ) == 0 ) leap_year = 0;
      if (( in_year % 400 ) == 0 ) leap_year = 1;
      out_day = out_day - 2 + leap_year;
    }
  out_day += in_day;
  return(out_day);
}
```

date__6

Function Name : date__6

Description : This function converts a date in the format of MM/DD/YYYY and returns a 0 if the year is not a leap year and a 1 if the year is a leap year.

Variables : d__in   — The variables contain the date that is passed to the function for conversion to its julian date.

leap-year — This integer variable contains the numeric value that is returned to the calling function.

Rules : This function must be passed the pointer associated with a character field. This may be in the format of defined character pointer or as the name of a character array with no array brackets.

The date must be passed in the correct format or unexpected results may be returned.

The reformatted date will be returned via an integer. Therefore, the function must be defined as an integer and the variable receiving the returned value must also be an integer. The converted date will be returned via an integer. Therefore, the function must be defined as an integer and the variable receiving the returned value must also be an integer. On this and all other date functions, all four digits of the year field are required. For example, 1986 is valid and 86 is not valid.

```
date_6(d_in)
 char *d_in;
{ int in_year, in_month, in_day;
  int leap_year;
  *(d_in+2) = '\0';
  *(d_in+5) = '\0';
  in_year   = i_convert(d_in+6);
  in_month  = i_convert(d_in);
  in_day    = i_convert(d_in+3);

  leap_year = 0;
  if (( in_year % 4 )   == 0 ) leap_year = 1;
  if (( in_year % 100 ) == 0 ) leap_year = 0;
  if (( in_year % 400 ) == 0 ) leap_year = 1;
  return(leap_year);
}
```

date__7

Function Name : date__7

Description : This function receives a date in the format MM/DD/YYYY and returns its daily position within the week. For example, Dec. 5, 1986 fell on a friday, therefore this function will return a 5. (0 = Sun, 1 = Mon, 2 = Tue, 3 = Wed, 4 = Thu, 5 = Fri, 6 = Sat).

Variables : d__in   — The variables contains the date that is passed to the function for conversion to its julian date.

out__day — This integer variable contains the numeric value standing for the day of the week that is returned to the calling function.

Rules : This function must be passed the pointer associated with a character field. This may be in the format of defined character pointer or as the name of a character array with no array brackets.

The date must be passed in the correct format or unexpected results may be returned.

The numeric value will be returned via an integer. Therefore, the function must be defined as an integer and the variable receiving the returned value must also be an integer. On this and all other date functions, all four digits of the year field are required. For example, 1986 is valid and 86 is not valid.

```
date_7(d_in)
 char *d_in;
{ int in_year, in_month, in_day;
  int cent, cent_y, month, year, out_day;
  long int long_day;
  *(d_in+2) = '\0';
  *(d_in+5) = '\0';
  in_year  = i_convert(d_in+6);
  in_month = i_convert(d_in);
  in_day   = i_convert(d_in+3);
  if ( in_month > 2 )
    { month = in_month - 2;
      year  = in_year;
    }
  else
    { month = in_month + 10;
      year = in_year - 1;
    }
  cent   = year / 100;
  cent_y = year - ( cent * 100 );
  long_day = ( 13 * month - 1 ) / 5;
  long_day = long_day + in_day + cent_y + ( cent_y/4 );
  long_day = long_day  + ( cent/4 ) - cent - cent + 77;
  long_day = long_day - 7 * ( long_day / 7 );
  out_day = long_day;
  return(out_day);
}
```

438

Function Name : date___8

Description : This function converts the date from a format of MM/DD/YYYY to a format of "Day. Mon. DD, YYYY".

Variables : d__in — The variables contains the date that is passed to the function for reformatting.

d__out — This variable contains the reformatted date field that is passed back to the calling module.

Rules : This function must be passed the pointer associated with a character field. This may be in the format of defined character pointer or as the name of a character array with no array brackets.

The date must be passed in the correct format or unexpected results may be returned.

The reformatted date value will be returned by way of the second parameter. Therefore, no actual return code is used.

The field into which the reformatted date is returned must be large enough to hold the output character string.

On this and all other date functions, all four digits of the year field are required. For example, 1986 is valid and 86 is not valid.

```
date_8(d_in, d_out)

char *d_in, *d_out;

{ int int_month, int_day;
  char months[37];
  char days[22];
  *(d_out)    = 'X';
  *(d_out+1) = 'X';
  *(d_out+2) = 'X';
  *(d_out+3) = '.';
  *(d_out+4) = ' ';
  *(d_out+5) = 'X';
  *(d_out+6) = 'X';
  *(d_out+7) = 'X';
  *(d_out+8) = '.';
  *(d_out+9) = ' ';
  *(d_out+10) = *(d_in+3);
  *(d_out+11) = *(d_in+4);
  *(d_out+12) = ',';
  *(d_out+13) = ' ';
  *(d_out+14) = *(d_in+6);
  *(d_out+15) = *(d_in+7);
  *(d_out+16) = *(d_in+8);
  *(d_out+17) = *(d_in+9);
  *(d_out+18) = '\0';
  strcpy(months,"JanFebMarAprMayJunJulAugSepOctNovDec");
```

```
int_month = *(d_in+1) - '0';
if ((*d_in) == '1' ) int_month +=10;
if ( int_month >= 1 && int_month <= 12 )
  { *(d_out+5) = *(months+((int_month-1)*3));
    *(d_out+6) = *(months+1+((int_month-1)*3));
    *(d_out+7) = *(months+2+((int_month-1)*3));
  }

strcpy(days,"SunMonTueWedThuFriSat");
int_day = date_7(d_in) + 1;
if ((*d_in) == '1' ) int_day +=10;
if ( int_day >= 1 && int_day <= 7 )
  { *(d_out) = *(days+((int_day-1)*3));
    *(d_out+1) = *(days+1+((int_day-1)*3));
    *(d_out+2) = *(days+2+((int_day-1)*3));
  }
}
```

date__9

Function Name : date__9

Description : This function converts the date from a format of MM/DD/YYYY to a format of "Dayyyyy Monthhhhh. DD, YYYY".

Variables : d__in — This variable contains the date that is passed to the function for reformatting.

d__out — This variable contains the reformatted date field that is passed back to the calling module.

Rules : This function must be passed the pointer associated with a character field. This may be in the format of defined character pointer or as the name of a character array with no array brackets.

The date must be passed in the correct format or unexpected results may be returned.

The reformatted date value will be returned by way of the second parameter. Therefore, no actual return code is used. The field into which the reformatted date is returned must be large enough to hold the output character string.

On this and all other date functions, all four digits of the year field are required. For example, 1986 is valid and 86 is not valid.

```
date_9(d_in, d_out)

char *d_in, *d_out;

{ int int_month, int_day;
  char months[109];
  char days[64];
  *(d_out+9)  = ',';
  *(d_out+10) = ' ';
  *(d_out+20) = ' ';
  *(d_out+21) = *(d_in+3);
  *(d_out+22) = *(d_in+4);
  *(d_out+23) = ',';
  *(d_out+24) = ' ';
  *(d_out+25) = *(d_in+6);
  *(d_out+26) = *(d_in+7);
  *(d_out+27) = *(d_in+8);
  *(d_out+28) = *(d_in+9);
  *(d_out+29) = '\0';
  strcpy(months,"January  February March    April    May      Jun      ");
  strcat(months,"July     August   SeptemberOctober  November December ");
  int_month = *(d_in+1) - '0';
  if ((*d_in) == '1' ) int_month +=10;
  if ( int_month >= 1 && int_month <= 12 )
    { *(d_out+11) = *(months+((int_month-1)*9));
      *(d_out+12) = *(months+1+((int_month-1)*9));
```

```
            *(d_out+13) = *(months+2+((int_month-1)*9));
            *(d_out+14) = *(months+3+((int_month-1)*9));
            *(d_out+15) = *(months+4+((int_month-1)*9));
            *(d_out+16) = *(months+5+((int_month-1)*9));
            *(d_out+17) = *(months+6+((int_month-1)*9));
            *(d_out+18) = *(months+7+((int_month-1)*9));
            *(d_out+19) = *(months+8+((int_month-1)*9));
      }

   strcpy(days,"Sunday   Monday   Tuesday wednesdayThursday Friday   ");
   strcat(days,"Sunday   ");
   int_day = date_7(d_in) + 1;
   if ( int_day >= 1 && int_day <= 7 )
      { *(d_out) = *(days+((int_day-1)*9));
        *(d_out+1) = *(days+1+((int_day-1)*9));
        *(d_out+2) = *(days+2+((int_day-1)*9));
        *(d_out+3) = *(days+3+((int_day-1)*9));
        *(d_out+4) = *(days+4+((int_day-1)*9));
        *(d_out+5) = *(days+5+((int_day-1)*9));
        *(d_out+6) = *(days+6+((int_day-1)*9));
        *(d_out+7) = *(days+7+((int_day-1)*9));
        *(d_out+8) = *(days+8+((int_day-1)*9));
      }
}
```

Function Name : date___10

Description : This function calculates the number of days between two dates including the days passed in the format MM/DD/YYYY.

Variables : s__date — The variable contains the starting date to be calculated from.

e__date — This variable contains the ending date to which the days should be counted.

no__days — This long integer variable will contain the number of days that is returned to the calling function.

Rules : This function must be passed the pointer associated with a character fields. They may be in the format of defined character pointer or as the name of a character array with no array brackets.

The dates must be passed in the correct format or unexpected results may be returned.

On this and all other date functions, all four digits of the years field are required.

The calculated value will be returned via a long integer. Therefore, the function must be defined as a long integer and the variable receiving the returned value must also be a long integer.

```
long int date_10(s_date, e_date)
char *s_date, *e_date;
{ long int no_days;
  no_days = date_4(e_date) - date_4(s_date) + 1;
  return(no_days);
}
```

date___11

Function Name : date___11

Description : This function calculates the number of days between two dates including the days passed in the format MM/DD/YYYY.

Variables : s___date — The variable contains the starting date to be calculated from.

e___date — This variable contains the ending date to which the days should be counted.

no___days — This long integer variable will contain the number of days that is returned to the calling function.

Rules : This function must be passed the pointers associated with a character fields. They may be in the format of defined character pointer or as the name of a character array with no array brackets.

The date must be passed in the correct format or unexpected results may be returned.

On this and all other date functions, all four digits of the year field are required. For example, 1986 is valid and 86 is not valid.

The calculated value will be returned via a long integer. Therefore, the function must be defined as a long integer and the variable receiving the returned value must also be a long integer.

```
long int date_11(s_date, e_date)
char *s_date, *e_date;
{ long int no_days;
  no_days = date_4(e_date) - date_4(s_date) - 1;
  return(no_days);
}
```

Function Name : date__12

Description : This function calculates what the date will be in a specified number of days, given the stating date in the format MM/DD/YYYY and the number of days to count..

Variables : d__in — This variable contains the starting date to be calculated from.

d__out — This variable contains the ending date after the appropriate number of days have been counted.

no__days — This long integer variable contains the number of days that must be counted to calculate the ending date.

Rules : This function must be passed the pointers associated with a character fields. They may be in the format of defined character pointers or as the name of character arrays with no array brackets.

The dates must be passed in the correct format or unexpected results may be returned.

On this and all other date functions, all four digits of the year field are required. For example, 1986 is valid and 86 is not valid.

```
date_12(d_in,d_out,no_days)
 char *d_in, *d_out;
 int no_days;
{ long int s_julian, e_julian;
  s_julian = date_4(d_in);
  e_julian = s_julian + no_days;
  date_49(e_julian,d_out);
}
```

date__13

Function Name : date__13

Description : This function converts the date from a format of DD-MMM-YYYY to a format of MM/DD/YYYY.

Variables : d__in — This variable contains the date that is passed to the function for reformatting.

d__out — This variable contains the reformatted date field that is passed back to the calling module.

Rules : This function must be passed the pointer associated with a character field. This may be in the format of defined character pointer (*) or as the name of a character array with no array brackets "[ ]".

The date must be passed in the correct format or unexpected results may be returned.

The reformatted date will be returned by way of the second parameter, therefore, no actual return code is used.

On this and all other date functions, all four digits of the year field are required. For example, 1986 is valid and 86 is not valid.

```c
date_13(d_in, d_out)

char *d_in, *d_out;

{ int int_month;
  char months[37];
  *(d_out)    = 'X';
  *(d_out+1)  = 'X';
  *(d_out+2)  = '/';
  *(d_out+3)  = *(d_in);
  *(d_out+4)  = *(d_in+1);
  *(d_out+5)  = '/';
  *(d_out+6)  = *(d_in+7);
  *(d_out+7)  = *(d_in+8);
  *(d_out+8)  = *(d_in+9);
  *(d_out+9)  = *(d_in+10);
  *(d_out+10) = '\0';
  strcpy(months,"JANFEBMARAPRMAYJUNJULAUGSEPOCTNOVDEC");
  for(int_month=0; int_month < 37; int_month+=3 )
   { if ( *(d_in+3) == *(months+int_month) &&
          *(d_in+4) == *(months+int_month+1) &&
          *(d_in+5) == *(months+int_month+2)
      )
       { int_month = (int_month+3) / 3;
         *(d_out) = '0';
         if ( int_month >= 10 )
           { *(d_out) = '1';
             int_month -= 10;
           }
         *(d_out+1) = int_month + '0';
         break;
       }
   }
}
```

date__14

Function Name : date__14

Description : This function converts the date from a format of DD-MMM-YYYY to a format of YYYYMMDD.

Variables : d__in — This variable contains the date that is passed to the function for reformatting.

d__out — This variable contains the reformatted date field that is passed back to the calling module.

Rules : This function must be passed the pointer associated with a character field. This may be in the format of defined character pointer or as the name of a character array with no array brackets.

The date must be passed in the correct format or unexpected results may be returned.

The reformatted date will be returned by way of the second parameter. Therefore, no actual return code is used. The field into which the reformatted date is returned must be large enough to hold the output character string.

On this and all other date functions, all four digits of the year field are required. For example, 1986 is valid and 86 is not valid.

```
date_14(d_in, d_out)

char *d_in, *d_out;

{ int int_month;
  char months[37];
  *(d_out)     = *(d_in+7);
  *(d_out+1) = *(d_in+8);
  *(d_out+2) = *(d_in+9);
  *(d_out+3) = *(d_in+10);
  *(d_out+4) = 'X';
  *(d_out+5) = 'X';
  *(d_out+6) = *(d_in);
  *(d_out+7) = *(d_in+1);
  *(d_out+8) = '\0';
  strcpy(months,"JANFEBMARAPRMAYJUNJULAUGSEPOCTNOVDEC");
  for(int_month=0; int_month < 37; int_month+=3 )
    { if ( *(d_in+3) == *(months+int_month) &&
         *(d_in+4) == *(months+int_month+1) &&
         *(d_in+5) == *(months+int_month+2)
      )
        { int_month = (int_month+3) / 3;
          *(d_out+4) = '0';
          if ( int_month >= 10 )
            { *(d_out+4) = '1';
              int_month -= 10;
            }
          *(d_out+5) = int_month + '0';
          break;
        }
    }
}
```

date___15

Function Name : date___15

Description : This function converts the date from a format of DD-MMM-YYYY to a format of DDMMMYYYY.

Variables : d__in — This variable contains the date that is passed to the function for reformatting.

d__out — This variable contains the reformatted date field that is passed back to the calling module.

Rules : This function must be passed the pointer associated with a character field. This may be in the format of defined character pointer or as the name of a character array with no array brackets.

The date must be passed in the correct format or unexpected results may be returned.

The reformatted date will be returned by way of the second parameter, therefore, no actual return code is used.

The field into which the reformatted date is returned must be large enough to hold the output character string.

On this and all other date functions, all four digits of the year field are required. For example, 1986 is valid and 86 is not valid.

```
date_15(d_in, d_out)

char *d_in, *d_out;

{ int int_month;
  char months[37];
  *(d_out)   = *(d_in);
  *(d_out+1) = *(d_in+1);
  *(d_out+2) = *(d_in+3);
  *(d_out+3) = *(d_in+4);
  *(d_out+4) = *(d_in+5);
  *(d_out+5) = *(d_in+7);
  *(d_out+6) = *(d_in+8);
  *(d_out+7) = *(d_in+9);
  *(d_out+8) = *(d_in+10);
  *(d_out+9) = '\0';
}
```

Function Name : date__16

Description : This function converts the date from a format of DD-MMM-YYYY to its julian equivalent.

Variables : d__in — The variables contain the date that is passed to the function for conversion to its julian date.

julian — This long integer variable contains the numeric julian value that is returned to calling function.

Rules : This function must be passed the pointer associated with a character field. This may be in the format of defined character pointer or as the name of a character array with no array brackets.

The date must be passed in the correct format or unexpected results may be returned.

The converted date will be returned via a long integer. Therefore, the function must be defined as a long integer and the variable receiving the returned value must also be a long integer.

On this and all other date functions, all four digits of the year field are required. For example, 1986 is valid and 86 is not valid.

```
long int date_16(d_in)
 char *d_in;
{ int in_year, in_month, in_day;
  int cent, cent_y, month, year, out_day;
  long int long_day, temp_long;
  char months[37];
  *(d_in+2) = '\0';
  in_year  = i_convert(d_in+7);
  in_day   = i_convert(d_in);
  strcpy(months,"JANFEBMARAPRMAYJUNJULAUGSEPOCTNOVDEC");
  for(in_month=0; in_month < 37; in_month+=3 )
    { if ( *(d_in+3) == *(months+in_month) &&
           *(d_in+4) == *(months+in_month+1) &&
           *(d_in+5) == *(months+in_month+2)
           )
         { in_month = (in_month+3) / 3;
           break;
         }
    }

    if ( in_month > 2 )
      { month = in_month - 3;
        year  = in_year;
      }
```

```
    else
      { month = in_month + 9;
        year = in_year - 1;
      }
    temp_long = 146097;
    cent   = year / 100;
    cent_y = year - ( cent * 100 );
    long_day = temp_long * cent / 4;
    long_day = long_day + 1461.0 * cent_y / 4;
    long_day = long_day  + ( 153 * month + 2 ) / 5;
    long_day = long_day + in_day;

    return(long_day);
}
```

date__17

Function Name : date__17

Description : This function receives a date in the format DD-MMM-YYYY and returns its daily position within the year. For example, February 5th is the 36th day of the year.

Variables : d__in — The variables contain the date that is passed to the function for conversion to its julian date.

out__day — This long integer variable contains the numeric value that is returned to calling function.

Rules : This function must be passed the pointer associated with a character field. This may be in the format of defined character pointer or as the name of a character array with no array brackets.

The date must be passed in the correct format or unexpected results may be returned.

The converted date will be returned via an integer. Therefore, the function must be defined as an integer and the variable receiving the returned value must also be an integer. On this and all other date functions, all four digits of the year field are required. For example, 1986 is valid and 86 is not valid.

```
date_17(d_in)
 char *d_in;
{ int in_year, in_month, in_day;
  int cent, cent_y, month, year, out_day, leap_year;
  long int long_day;
  char months[37];
  *(d_in+2) = '\0';
  in_year  = i_convert(d_in+7);
  in_day   = i_convert(d_in);
  strcpy(months,"JANFEBMARAPRMAYJUNJULAUGSEPOCTNOVDEC");
  for(in_month=0; in_month < 37; in_month+=3 )
   { if ( *(d_in+3) == *(months+in_month) &&
          *(d_in+4) == *(months+in_month+1) &&
          *(d_in+5) == *(months+in_month+2)
        )
      { in_month = (in_month+3) / 3;
        break;
      }
   }

  long_day = ( 3055.0 * ( in_months + 2 ) / 100 ) -91;
  out_day = long_day;
```

```
   if ( in_month > 2 )
     { leap_year = 0;
       if (( in_year % 4 )   == 0 ) leap_year = 1;
       if (( in_year % 100 ) == 0 ) leap_year = 0;
       if (( in_year % 400 ) == 0 ) leap_year = 1;
       out_day = out_day - 2 + leap_year;
     }
   out_day += in_day;
   return(out_day);
}
```

Function Name : date__18

Description : This function receives a date in the format DD-MMM-YYYY and returns a 0 if the year is not a leap year and a 1 if the year is a leap year.

Variables : d__in — The variables contain the date that is passed to the function for conversion to its julian date.

leap__year— This integer variable contains the numeric value that is returned to the calling function.

Rules : This function must be passed the pointer associated with a character field. This may be in the format of defined character pointer or as the name of a character array with no array brackets.

The date must be passed in the correct format or unexpected results may be returned.

The converted date will be returned via an integer. Therefore, the function must be defined as an integer and the variable receiving the returned value must also be an integer. On this and all other date functions, all four digits of the year field are required. For example, 1986 is valid and 86 is not valid.

```
date_18(d_in)
 char *d_in;
{ int in_year, in_month, in_day;
  int leap_year;
  char months[37];
  *(d_in+2) = '\0';
  *(d_in+5) = '\0';
  in_year   = i_convert(d_in+7);
  strcpy(months,"JANFEBMARAPRMAYJUNJULAUGSEPOCTNOVDEC");
  for(in_month=0; in_month < 37; in_month+=3 )
    { if ( *(d_in+3) == *(months+in_month) &&
           *(d_in+4) == *(months+in_month+1) &&
           *(d_in+5) == *(months+in_month+2)
           )
         { in_month = (in_month+3) / 3;
           break;
         }
    }
  in_day    = i_convert(d_in);

  leap_year = 0;
  if (( in_year % 4 )   == 0 ) leap_year = 1;
  if (( in_year % 100 ) == 0 ) leap_year = 0;
  if (( in_year % 400 ) == 0 ) leap_year = 1;
  return(leap_year);
}
```

date___19

Function Name : date___19

Description : This function receives a date in the format DD-MMM-YYYY and returns its daily position within the week. For example, Dec. 5, 1986 fell on a friday, therefore this function will return a 5. (0 = Sun, 1 = Mon, 2 = Tue, 3 = Wed, 4 = Thu, 5 = Fri, 6 = Sat)

Variables : d__in   — The variables contain the date that is passed to the function for conversion to its julian date.

out__day — This integer variable contains the numeric value standing for the day of the week that is returned to the calling function.

Rules : This function must be passed the pointer associated with a character field. This may be in the format of defined character pointer or as the name of a character array with no array brackets.

The date must be passed in the correct format or unexpected results may be returned.

The numeric value will be returned via an integer. Therefore, the function must be defined as an integer and the variable receiving the returned value must also be an integer. On this and all other date functions, all four digits of the year field are required. For example, 1986 is valid and 86 is not valid.

```
date_19(d_in)
 char *d_in;
{ int in_year, in_month, in_day;
  int cent, cent_y, month, year, out_day;
  long int long_day;
  char months[37];
  *(d_in+2) = '\0';
  in_year   = i_convert(d_in+7);
  strcpy(months,"JANFEBMARAPRMAYJUNJULAUGSEPOCTNOVDEC");
  for(in_month=0; in_month < 37; in_month+=3 )
    { if ( *(d_in+3) == *(months+in_month) &&
           *(d_in+4) == *(months+in_month+1) &&
           *(d_in+5) == *(months+in_month+2)
         )
      { in_month = (in_month+3) / 3;
        break;
      }
    }
  in_day    = i_convert(d_in);

  if ( in_month > 2 )
    { month = in_month - 2;
      year  = in_year;
    }
```

```
        else
          { month = in_month + 10;
            year = in_year - 1;
          }
        cent   = year / 100;
        cent_y = year - ( cent * 100 );
        long_day = ( 13 * month - 1 ) / 5;
        long_day = long_day + in_day + cent_y + ( cent_y/4 );
        long_day = long_day  + ( cent/4 ) - cent - cent + 77;
        long_day = long_day - 7 * ( long_day / 7 );
        out_day = long_day;

        return(out_day);
}
```

date__20

Function Name : date__20

Description : This function converts the date from a format of DD-MMM-YYYY to a format of Day. Mcn. DD, YYYY.

Variables : d__in — This variable contains the date that is passed to the function for reformatting.

d__out — This variable contains the reformatted date field that is passed back to the calling module.

Rules : This function must be passed the pointer associated with a character field. This may be in the format of defined character pointer or as the name of a character array with no array brackets.

The date must be passed in the correct format or unexpected results may be returned.

The reformatted date will be returned by way of the second parameter. Therefore, no actual return code is used.

The field into which the reformatted date is returned must be large enough to hold the output character string.

On this and all other date functions, all four digits of the year field are required. For example, 1986 is valid and 86 is not valid.

```
date_20(d_in, d_out)

char *d_in, *d_out;

{ int int_month, int_day;
  char months[37];
  char days[22];
  *(d_out)    = 'X';
  *(d_out+1) = 'X';
  *(d_out+2) = 'X';
  *(d_out+3) = '.';
  *(d_out+4) = ' ';
  *(d_out+5) = *(d_in+3);
  *(d_out+6) = *(d_in+4);
  *(d_out+7) = *(d_in+5);
  *(d_out+8) = '.';
  *(d_out+9) = ' ';
  *(d_out+10) = *(d_in);
  *(d_out+11) = *(d_in+1);
  *(d_out+12) = ',';
  *(d_out+13) = ' ';
  *(d_out+14) = *(d_in+7);
  *(d_out+15) = *(d_in+8);
```

```
        *(d_out+16) = *(d_in+9);
        *(d_out+17) = *(d_in+10);
        *(d_out+18) = '\0';

        strcpy(days,"SunMonTueWedThuFriSat");
        int_day = date_19(d_in) + 1;
        if ((*d_in) == '1' ) int_day +=10;
        if ( int_day >= 1 && int_day <= 7 )
          { *(d_out) = *(days+((int_day-1)*3));
            *(d_out+1) = *(days+1+((int_day-1)*3));
            *(d_out+2) = *(days+2+((int_day-1)*3));
          }
}
```

date__21

Function Name : date__21

Description : This function converts the date from a format of DD-MMM-YYYY to a format of Dayyyy Monthhhhh. DD, YYYY.

Variables : d__in — This variable contains the date that is passed to the function for reformatting.

d__out — This variable contains the reformatted date field that is passed back to the calling module.

Rules : This function must be passed the pointer associated with a character field. This may be in the format of defined character pointer or as the name of a character array with no array brackets.

The date must be passed in the correct format or unexpected results may be returned.

The reformatted date will be returned by way of the second parameter. Therefore, no actual return code is used. The field into which the reformatted date is returned must be large enough to hold the output character string.

On this and all other date functions, all four digits of the year field are required. For example, 1986 is valid and 86 is not valid.

```
date_21(d_In, d_out)

char *d_in, *d_out;

{ int int_month, int_day;
  char months[109];
  char days[64];
  *(d_out+9)  = ',';
  *(d_out+10) = ' ';
  *(d_out+20) = ' ';
  *(d_out+21) = *(d_in);
  *(d_out+22) = *(d_in+1);
  *(d_out+23) = ',';
  *(d_out+24) = ' ';
  *(d_out+25) = *(d_in+7);
  *(d_out+26) = *(d_in+8);
  *(d_out+27) = *(d_in+9);
  *(d_out+28) = *(d_in+10);
  *(d_out+29) = '\0';
  strcpy(months,"JANFEBMARAPRMAYJUNJULAUGSEPOCTNOVDEC");
  for(int_month=0; int_month < 37; int_month+=3 )
    { if ( *(d_in+3) == *(months+int_month) &&
           *(d_in+4) == *(months+int_month+1) &&
           *(d_in+5) == *(months+int_month+2)
         )
      { int_month = (int_month+3) / 3;
        break;
      }
```

```
    }
    strcpy(months,"January  February March    April    May      Jun      ");
    strcat(months,"July     August   SeptemberOctober  November December ");
    if ((*d_in) == '1' ) int_month +=10;
    if ( int_month >= 1 && int_month <= 12 )
    { *(d_out+11) = *(months+((int_month-1)*9));
      *(d_out+12) = *(months+1+((int_month-1)*9));
      *(d_out+13) = *(months+2+((int_month-1)*9));
      *(d_out+14) = *(months+3+((int_month-1)*9));
      *(d_out+15) = *(months+4+((int_month-1)*9));
      *(d_out+16) = *(months+5+((int_month-1)*9));
      *(d_out+17) = *(months+6+((int_month-1)*9));
      *(d_out+18) = *(months+7+((int_month-1)*9));
      *(d_out+19) = *(months+8+((int_month-1)*9));
    }

    strcpy(days,"Sunday   Monday   Tuesday  wednesdayThursday Friday   ");
    strcat(days,"Saterday ");
    int_day = date_19(d_in) + 1;
    if ( int_day >= 1 && int_day <= 7 )
    { *(d_out) = *(days+((int_day-1)*9));
      *(d_out+1) = *(days+1+((int_day-1)*9));
      *(d_out+2) = *(days+2+((int_day-1)*9));
      *(d_out+3) = *(days+3+((int_day-1)*9));
      *(d_out+4) = *(days+4+((int_day-1)*9));
      *(d_out+5) = *(days+5+((int_day-1)*9));
      *(d_out+6) = *(days+6+((int_day-1)*9));
      *(d_out+7) = *(days+7+((int_day-1)*9));
      *(d_out+8) = *(days+8+((int_day-1)*9));
    }
}
```

459

date__22

Function Name : date__22

Description : This function calculates the number of days between two dates including the days passed in the format DD-MMM-YYYY.

Variables : s__date — This variable contains the starting date to be calculated from.

e__date — This variable contains the ending date to which the days should be counted.

no__days — This long integer variable will contain the number of days that is returned to the calling function.

Rules : This function must be passed the pointers associated with a character fields. They may be in the format of defined character pointers or as the name of a character array with no array brackets.

The dates must be passed in the correct format or unexpected results may be returned.

On this and all other date functions, all four digits of the year field are required. For example, 1986 is valid and 86 is not valid.

The calculated value will be returned via a long integer. Therefore, the function must be defined as a long integer and the variable receiving the returned value must also be a long integer.

```
long int date_22(s_date, e_date)
char *s_date, *e_date;
{ long int no_days;
  no_days = date_16(e_date) - date_16(s_date) + 1;
  return(no_days);
}
```

Function Name : date__23

Description : This function calculates the number of days between two dates not including the days passed in the format DD-MMM-YYYY.

Variables : s__date — This variable contains the starting date to be calculated from.

e__date — This variable contains the ending date to which the days should be counted.

no__days — This long integer variable will contain the number of days that is returned to the calling function.

Rules : This function must be passed the pointer associated with a character field. This may be in the format of defined character pointer or as the name of a character array with no array brackets " ".

The date must be passed in the correct format or unexpected results may be returned.

On this and all other date functions, all four digits of the year field are required. For example, 1986 is valid and 86 is not valid.

The calculated value will be returned via a long integer. Therefore, the function must be defined as a long integer and the variable receiving the returned value must also be a long integer.

```
long int date_23(s_date, e_date)
char *s_date, *e_date;
{ long int no_days;
  no_days = date_16(e_date) - date_16(s_date) - 1;
  return(no_days);
}
```

date__24

Function Name : date__24

Description : This function calculates what the date will be in a specified number of days, given the starting date in the format DD-MMM-YYYY and the number of days to count.

Variables : d__in   — This variable contains the starting date to be calculated from.

d__out — This variable contains the ending date after the appropriate number of days have been counted.

no__days — This integer variable contains the number of days that must be counted to calculate the ending date.

Rules : This function must be passed the pointers associated with a character fields. They may be in the format of defined character pointers or as the name of character array with no array brackets.

The dates must be passed in the correct format or unexpected results may be returned.

On this and all other date functions, all four digits of the year field are required. For example, 1986 is valid and 86 is not valid.

```
date_24(d_in,d_out,no_days)
 char *d_in, *d_out;
 int no_days;
{ long int s_julian, e_julian;
  s_julian = date_16(d_in);
  e_julian = s_julian + no_days;
  date_50(e_julian,d_out);
}
```

Function Name : date__25

Description : This function converts the date from a format of YY-YYMMDD to a format of DD-MMM-YYYY.

Variables : d__in — This variable contains the date that is passed to the function for reformatting.

d__out — This variable contains the reformatted date field that is passed back to the calling module.

Rules : This function must be passed the pointer associated with a character field. This may be in the format of defined character pointer or as the name of a character array with no array brackets.

The date must be passed in the correct format or unexpected results may be returned.

The reformatted date will be returned by way of the second parameter, therefore, no actual return code is used.

The field into which the reformatted date is returned must be large enough to hold the output character string.

On this and all other date functions, all four digits of the year field are required. For example, 1986 is valid and 86 is not valid.

```
date_25(d_in, d_out)

char *d_in, *d_out;

{ int int_month;
  char months[37];
  *(d_out)    = *(d_in+6);
  *(d_out+1) = *(d_in+7);
  *(d_out+2) = '-';
  *(d_out+3) = 'X';
  *(d_out+4) = 'X';
  *(d_out+5) = 'X';
  *(d_out+6) = '-';
  *(d_out+7) = *(d_in);
  *(d_out+8) = *(d_in+1);
  *(d_out+9) = *(d_in+2);
  *(d_out+10) = *(d_in+3);
  *(d_out+11) = '\0';
  strcpy(months,"JANFEBMARAPRMAYJUNJULAUGSEPOCTNOVDEC");
  int_month = *(d_in+5) - '0';
  if ((*d_in+4) == '1' ) int_month +=10;
  if ( int_month >= 1 && int_month <= 12 )
    { *(d_out+3) = *(months+((int_month-1)*3));
      *(d_out+4) = *(months+1+((int_month-1)*3));
      *(d_out+5) = *(months+2+((int_month-1)*3));
    }
}
```

date__26

Function Name : date__26

Description : This function converts the date from a format of YY-YYMMDD to a format of MM/DD/YYYY.

Variables : d__in   —   This variable contains the date that is passed to the function for reformatting.

           d__out — This variable contains the reformatted date field that is passed back to the calling module.

Rules : This function must be passed the pointer associated with a character field. This may be in the format of defined character pointer or as the name of a character array with no array brackets.

The date must be passed in the correct format or unexpected results may be returned.

The reformatted date will be returned by way of the second parameter, therefore, no actual return code is used.

The field into which the reformatted date is returned must be large enough to hold the output character string.

On this and all other date functions, all four digits of the year field are required. For example, 1986 is valid and 86 is not valid.

```
date_26(d_in, d_out)

char *d_in, *d_out;

{ int int_month;
  char months[37];
  *(d_out)    = *(d_in+4);
  *(d_out+1) = *(d_in+5);
  *(d_out+2) = '/';
  *(d_out+3) = *(d_in+6);
  *(d_out+4) = *(d_in+7);
  *(d_out+5) = '/';
  *(d_out+6) = *(d_in);
  *(d_out+7) = *(d_in+1);
  *(d_out+8) = *(d_in+2);
  *(d_out+9) = *(d_in+3);
  *(d_out+10) = '\0';
}
```

464

Function Name : date__27

Description : This function converts the date from a format of YY-YYMMDD to a format of DDMMMYYYY.

Variables : d__in — This variable contain the date that is passed to the function for reformatting.

d__out — This long integer variable contains the reformatted date field that is passed back to the calling module.

Rules : This function must be passed the pointer associated with a character field. This may be in the format of defined character pointer or as the name of a character array with no array brackets.

The date must be passed in the correct format or unexpected results may be returned.

The reformatted date will be returned by way of the second parameter, therefore, no actual return code is used.

The field into which the reformatted date is returned must be large enough to hold the output character string.

On this and all other date functions, all four digits of the year field are required. For example, 1986 is valid and 86 is not valid.

```
date_27(d_in, d_out)

char *d_in, *d_out;

{ int int_month;
  char months[37];
  *(d_out)    = *(d_in+6);
  *(d_out+1) = *(d_in+7);
  *(d_out+2) = 'X';
  *(d_out+3) = 'X';
  *(d_out+4) = 'X';
  *(d_out+5) = *(d_in);
  *(d_out+6) = *(d_in+1);
  *(d_out+7) = *(d_in+2);
  *(d_out+8) = *(d_in+3);
  *(d_out+9) = '\0';
  strcpy(months,"JANFEBMARAPRMAYJUNJULAUGSEPOCTNOVDEC");
  int_month = *(d_in+5) - '0';
  if ((*d_in+4) == '1' ) int_month +=10;
  if ( int_month >= 1 && int_month <= 12 )
    { *(d_out+2) = *(months+((int_month-1)*3));
      *(d_out+3) = *(months+1+((int_month-1)*3));
      *(d_out+4) = *(months+2+((int_month-1)*3));
    }
}
```

date__28

Function Name : date__28

Description : This function converts the date from a format of YY-YYMMDD to its julian equivalent.

Variables : d__in — The variables contain the date that is passed to the function for conversion to its julian date.

julian — This long integer variable contains the numeric julian value that is returned to calling function.

Rules : This function must be passed the pointer associated with a character field. This may be in the format of defined character pointer or as the name of a character array with no array brackets.

The date must be passed in the correct format or unexpected results may be returned.

The converted date will be returned via a long integer. Therefore, the function must be defined as a long integer and the variable receiving the returned value must also be a long integer data type.

On this and all other date functions, all four digits of the year field are required. For example, 1986 is valid and 86 is not valid.

```
long int date_28(d_in)
 char *d_in;
{ int in_year, in_month, in_day;
  int cent, cent_y, month, year, out_day;
  long int long_day, temp_long;
  char temp[10];
  strncpy(temp,d_in,4);
   in_year   = i_convert(temp);
  strncpy(temp,d_in+4,2);
   in_month  = i_convert(temp);
  in_day     = i_convert(d_in+6);

  if ( in_month > 2 )
    { month = in_month - 3;
      year  = in_year;
    }
  else
    { month = in_month + 9;
      year = in_year - 1;
    }
  temp_long = 146097;
  cent   = year / 100;
  cent_y = year - ( cent * 100 );
  long_day = temp_long * cent / 4;
  long_day = long_day + 1461.0 * cent_y / 4;
  long_day = long_day  + ( 153 * month + 2 ) / 5;
  long_day = long_day + in_day;

  return(long_day);
}
```

Function Name : date__29

Description : This function receives a date in the format YYYYMMDD and returns its daily position within the year. For example, February 5th is the 36th day of the year.

Variables : d__in — The variables contain the date that is passed to the function for conversion to its julian date.

julian — This long integer variable contains the numeric value that is returned to the calling function.

Rules : This function must be passed the pointer associated with a character field. This may be in the format of defined character pointer or as the name of a character array with no array brackets.

The date must be passed in the correct format or unexpected results may be returned.

The converted date will be returned via an integer. Therefore, the function must be defined as an integer and the variable receiving the returned value must also be an integer. On this and all other date functions, all four digits of the year field are required. For example, 1986 is valid and 86 is not valid.

```
date_29(d_in)
 char *d_in;
{ int in_year, in_month, in_day;
  int cent, cent_y, month, year, out_day, leap_year;
  long int long_day;
  char temp[10];
  strncpy(temp,d_in,4);
   in_year   = i_convert(temp);
  strncpy(temp,d_in+4,2);
   in_month  = i_convert(temp);
  in_day    = i_convert(d_in+6);
  long_day = ( 3055.0 * ( in_months + 2 ) / 100 ) -91;
  out_day = long_day;

  if ( in_month > 2 )
    { leap_year = 0;
      if (( in_year % 4 )   == 0 ) leap_year = 1;
      if (( in_year % 100 ) == 0 ) leap_year = 0;
      if (( in_year % 400 ) == 0 ) leap_year = 1;
      out_day = out_day - 2 + leap_year;
    }
  out_day += in_day;
  return(out_day);
}
```

date__30

Description : This function receives a date in the format YYYYMMDD and returns a 0 if the year is not a leap year and a 1 if the year is a leap year.

Variables : d__in — The variables contain the date that is passed to the function for conversion to its julian date.

leap__year— This integer variable contains the numeric value that is returned to the calling function.

Rules : This function must be passed the pointer associated with a character field. This may be in the format of defined character pointer or as the name of a character array with no array brackets.

The date must be passed in the correct format or unexpected results may be returned.

The converted date will be returned via an integer. Therefore, the function must be defined as an integer and the variable receiving the returned value must also be an integer. On this and all other date functions, all four digits of the year field are required. For example, 1986 is valid and 86 is not valid.

```
date_30(d_in)
 char *d_in;
{ int in_year, in_month, in_day;
  int leap_year;
  char temp[10];
  strncpy(temp,d_in,4);
   in_year    = i_convert(temp);
  strncpy(temp,d_in+4,2);
   in_month   = i_convert(temp);
  in_day     = i_convert(d_in+6);

  leap_year = 0;
  if (( in_year % 4 )   == 0 ) leap_year = 1;
  if (( in_year % 100 ) == 0 ) leap_year = 0;
  if (( in_year % 400 ) == 0 ) leap_year = 1;
  return(leap_year);
}
```

Function Name : date__31

Description : This function receives a date in the format YYYYMMDD and returns its daily position within the week. For example, Dec. 5, 1986 fell on a friday, therefore this function will return a 5. (0 = Sun, 1 = Mon, 2 = Tue, 3 = Wed, 4 = Thu, 5 = Fri, 6 = Sat).

Variables : d__in — The variables contain the date that is passed to the function for conversion to its julian date.

out__day — This integer variable contains the numeric value standing for the day of the week that is returned to the calling function.

Rules : This function must be passed the pointer associated with a character field. This may be in the format of defined character pointer or as the name of a character array with no array brackets.

The date must be passed in the correct format or unexpected results may be returned.

The numeric value will be returned via an integer. Therefore, the function must be defined as an integer and the variable receiving the returned value must also be an integer. On this and all other date functions, all four digits of the year field are required. For example, 1986 is valid and 86 is not valid.

```
date_31(d_in)
 char *d_in;
{ int in_year, in_month, in_day;
  int cent, cent_y, month, year, out_day;
  long int long_day;
  char temp[10];
  strncpy(temp,d_in,4);
   in_year  = i_convert(temp);
  strncpy(temp,d_in+4,2);
   in_month = i_convert(temp);
  in_day   = i_convert(d_in+6);
  if ( in_month > 2 )
    { month = in_month - 2;
      year  = in_year;
    }
  else
    { month = in_month + 10;
      year = in_year - 1;
```

```
        }
    cent    = year / 100;
    cent_y = year - ( cent * 100 );
    long_day = ( 13 * month - 1 ) / 5;
    long_day = long_day + in_day + cent_y + ( cent_y/4 );
    long_day = long_day  + ( cent/4 ) - cent - cent + 77;
    long_day = long_day - 7 * ( long_day / 7 );
    out_day = long_day;

    return(out_day);
}
```

date__32

Function Name : date__32

Description : This function converts the date from a format of YY-YYMMDD to a format of Day. Mon. DD, YYYY.

Variables : d__in — The variable contains the date that is passed to the function for reformatting.

d__out — This variable contains the reformatted date field that is passed back to the calling module.

Rules : This function must be passed the pointer associated with a character field. This may be in the format of defined character pointer or as the name of a character array with no array brackets.

The date must be passed in the correct format or unexpected results may be returned.

The reformatted date will be returned by way of the second parameter. Therefore, no actual return code is used. The field into which the reformatted date is returned must be large enough to hold the output character string.

On this and all other date functions, all four digits of the year field are required. For example, 1986 is valid and 86 is not valid.

```
date_32(d_in, d_out)

char *d_in, *d_out;

{ int int_month, int_day;
  char months[37];
  char days[22];
  *(d_out)    = 'X';
  *(d_out+1) = 'X';
  *(d_out+2) = 'X';
  *(d_out+3) = '.';
  *(d_out+4) = ' ';
  *(d_out+5) = 'X';
  *(d_out+6) = 'X';
  *(d_out+7) = 'X';
  *(d_out+8) = '.';
  *(d_out+9) = ' ';
  *(d_out+10) = *(d_in+6);
  *(d_out+11) = *(d_in+7);
  *(d_out+12) = ',';
  *(d_out+13) = ' ';
  *(d_out+14) = *(d_in);
  *(d_out+15) = *(d_in+1);
  *(d_out+16) = *(d_in+2);
  *(d_out+17) = *(d_in+3);
  *(d_out+18) = '\0';
  strcpy(months,"JanFebMarAprMayJunJulAugSepOctNovDec");
```

```
      int_month = *(d_in+5) - '0';
      if ((*d_in+4) == '1' ) int_month +=10;
      if ( int_month >= 1 && int_month <= 12 )
         { *(d_out+5) = *(months+((int_month-1)*3));
           *(d_out+6) = *(months+1+((int_month-1)*3));
           *(d_out+7) = *(months+2+((int_month-1)*3));
         }

      strcpy(days,"SunMonTueWedThuFriSat");
      int_day = date_31(d_in) + 1;
      if ( int_day >= 1 && int_day <= 7 )
         { *(d_out) = *(days+((int_day-1)*3));
           *(d_out+1) = *(days+1+((int_day-1)*3));
           *(d_out+2) = *(days+2+((int_day-1)*3));
         }
}
```

date__33

Function Name : date__33

Description : This function converts the date from a format of YY-YYMMDD to a format of Dayyyyy Monthhhh. DD, YYYY.

Variables : d__in — This variable contains the date that is passed to the function for reformatting.

d__out — This variable contains the reformatted date field that is passed back to the calling module.

Rules : This function must be passed the pointer associated with a character field. This may be in the format of defined character pointer or as the name of a character array with no array brackets.

The date must be passed in the correct format or unexpected results may be returned.

The reformatted date will be returned by way of the second parameter. Therefore, no actual return code is used. The field into which the reformatted date is returned must be large enough to hold the output character string.

On this and all other date functions, all four digits of the year field are required. For example, 1986 is valid and 86 is not valid.

```
date_33(d_in, d_out)

char *d_in, *d_out;

{ int int_month, int_day;
  char months[109];
  char days[64];
  *(d_out+9)  = ',';
  *(d_out+10) = ' ';
  *(d_out+20) = ' ';
  *(d_out+21) = *(d_in+6);
  *(d_out+22) = *(d_in+7);
  *(d_out+23) = ',';
  *(d_out+24) = ' ';
  *(d_out+25) = *(d_in);
  *(d_out+26) = *(d_in+1);
  *(d_out+27) = *(d_in+2);
  *(d_out+28) = *(d_in+3);
  *(d_out+29) = '\0';
  strcpy(months,"January  February March    April    May      Jun      ");
  strcat(months,"July     August   SeptemberOctober  November December ");
  int_month = *(d_in+5) - '0';
  if ((*d_in+4) == '1' ) int_month +=10;
  if ( int_month >= 1 && int_month <= 12 )
    { *(d_out+11) = *(months+((int_month-1)*9));
      *(d_out+12) = *(months+1+((int_month-1)*9));
      *(d_out+13) = *(months+2+((int_month-1)*9));
```

```
        *(d_out+14) = *(months+3+((int_month-1)*9));
        *(d_out+15) = *(months+4+((int_month-1)*9));
        *(d_out+16) = *(months+5+((int_month-1)*9));
        *(d_out+17) = *(months+6+((int_month-1)*9));
        *(d_out+18) = *(months+7+((int_month-1)*9));
        *(d_out+19) = *(months+8+((int_month-1)*9));
    }

    strcpy(days,"Sunday    Monday    Tuesday  wednesdayThursday Friday
    strcat(days,"Sunday   ");
    int_day = date_31(d_in) + 1;
    if ( int_day >= 1 && int_day <= 7 )
    { *(d_out) = *(days+((int_day-1)*9));
      *(d_out+1) = *(days+1+((int_day-1)*9));
      *(d_out+2) = *(days+2+((int_day-1)*9));
      *(d_out+3) = *(days+3+((int_day-1)*9));
      *(d_out+4) = *(days+4+((int_day-1)*9));
      *(d_out+5) = *(days+5+((int_day-1)*9));
      *(d_out+6) = *(days+6+((int_day-1)*9));
      *(d_out+7) = *(days+7+((int_day-1)*9));
      *(d_out+8) = *(days+8+((int_day-1)*9));
    }
}
```

Function Name : date__34

Description : This function calculates the number of days between two dates including the days passed in the format YY-YYMMDD.

Variables : s__date — The variable contains the starting date to be calculated from.

e__date — This variable contains the ending date to which the days should be counted.

no__days — This long integer variable will contain the number of days that is returned to the calling function.

Rules : This function must be passed the pointer associated with a character field. They may be in the format of defined character pointer or as the name of a character array with no array brackets.

The date must be passed in the correct format or unexpected results may be returned.

On this and all other date functions, all four digits of the year field are required. For example, 1986 is valid and 86 is not valid.

The calculated value will be returned via a long integer. Therefore, the function must be defined as a long integer and the variable receiving the returned value must also be a long integer.

```
long int date_34(s_date, e_date)
char *s_date, *e_date;
{ long int no_days;
  no_days = date_28(e_date) - date_28(s_date) + 1;
  return(no_days);
}
```

date__35

Function Name : date__35

Description : This function calculates the number of days between two dates including the days passed in the format YY-YYMMDD.

Variables : s__date — The variable contains the starting date to be calculated from.

e__date — This variable contains the ending date to which the days should be counted.

no__days — This long integer variable will contain the number of days that is returned to the calling function.

Rules : This function must be passed the pointers associated with a character field. They may be in the format of defined character pointer or as the name of a character array with no array brackets.

The dates must be passed in the correct format or unexpected results may be returned.

On this and all other date functions, all four digits of the year field are required. For example, 1986 is valid and 86 is not valid.

The calculated value will be returned via a long integer. Therefore, the function must be defined as a long integer and the variable receiving the returned value must also be a long integer.

```
long int date_35(s_date, e_date)
char *s_date, *e_date;
{ long int no_days;
  no_days = date_28(e_date) - date_28(s_date) - 1;
  return(no_days);
}
```

476

date__36

Function Name : date__36

Description : This function calculates what the date will be in a specified number of days, given the stating date in the format YY-YYMMDD and the number of days to count.

Variables : d__in   — This variable contains the starting date to be calculated from.

                 d__out — This variable contains the ending date after the appropriate number of days have been counted.

                 no__days — This integer variable contains the number of days that must be counted to calculate the ending date.

Rules : This function must be passed the pointers associated with a character field. They may be in the format of defined character pointers or as the name of a character array with no array brackets.

The dates must be passed in the correct format or unexpected results may be returned.

On this and all other date functions, all four digits of the year field are required. For example, 1986 is valid and 86 is not valid.

```
date_36(d_in,d_out,no_days)
 char *d_in, *d_out;
 int no_days;
{ long int s_julian, e_julian;
  s_julian = date_28(d_in);
  e_julian = s_julian + no_days;
  date_51(e_julian,d_out);
}
```

date__37

Function Name : date__37

Description : This function converts the date from a format of DDMMMYYYY to a format of MM/DD/YYYY.

Variables : d__in — This variable contains the date that is passed to the function for reformatting.

d__out — This variable contains the reformatted date field that is passed back to the calling module.

Rules : This function must be passed the pointer associated with a character field. This may be in the format of defined character pointer or as the name of a character array with no array brackets.

The date must be passed in the correct format or unexpected results may be returned.

The reformatted date will be returned by way of the second parameter, therefore, no actual return code is used.

The field into which the reformatted date is returned must be large enough to hold the output character string.

On this and all other date functions, all four digits of the year field are required. For example, 1986 is valid and 86 is not valid.

```
date_37(d_in, d_out)

char *d_in, *d_out;

{ int int_month;
  char months[37];
  *(d_out)   = 'X';
  *(d_out+1) = 'X';
  *(d_out+2) = '/';
  *(d_out+3) = *(d_in);
  *(d_out+4) = *(d_in+1);
  *(d_out+5) = '/';
  *(d_out+6) = *(d_in+5);
  *(d_out+7) = *(d_in+6);
  *(d_out+8) = *(d_in+7);
  *(d_out+9) = *(d_in+8);
  *(d_out+10) = '\0';
  strcpy(months,"JANFEBMARAPRMAYJUNJULAUGSEPOCTNOVDEC");
  for(int_month=0; int_month < 37; int_month+=3 )
    { if ( *(d_in+2) == *(months+int_month) &&
        *(d_in+3) == *(months+int_month+1) &&
        *(d_in+4) == *(months+int_month+2)
```

```
        )
          { int_month = (int_month+3) / 3;
            *(d_out) = '0';
            if ( int_month >= 10 )
              { *(d_out) = '1';
                int_month -= 10;
              }
            *(d_out+1) = int_month + '0';
            break;
          }
      }
    }
```

date__38

Function Name : date__38

Description : This function converts the date from a format of DDMMMYYYY to a format of YYYYMMDD.

Variables : d__in — This variable contains the date that is passed to the function for reformatting.

d__out — This variable contains the reformatted date field that is passed back to the calling module.

Rules : This function must be passed the pointer associated with a character field. This may be in the format of defined character pointer or as the name of a character array with no array brackets.

The date must be passed in the correct format or unexpected results may be returned.

The reformatted date will be returned by way of the second parameter. Therefore, no actual return code is used. The field into which the reformatted date is returned must be large enough to hold the output character string.

On this and all other date functions, all four digits of the year field are required. For example, 1986 is valid and 86 is not valid.

```
date_38(d_in, d_out)

char *d_in, *d_out;

{ int int_month;
  char months[37];
  *(d_out)   = *(d_in+5);
  *(d_out+1) = *(d_in+6);
  *(d_out+2) = *(d_in+7);
  *(d_out+3) = *(d_in+8);
  *(d_out+4) = 'X';
  *(d_out+5) = 'X';
  *(d_out+6) = *(d_in);
  *(d_out+7) = *(d_in+1);
  *(d_out+8) = '\0';
  strcpy(months,"JANFEBMARAPRMAYJUNJULAUGSEPOCTNOVDEC");
  for(int_month=0; int_month < 37; int_month+=3 )
  { if ( *(d_in+2) == *(months+int_month) &&
         *(d_in+3) == *(months+int_month+1) &&
         *(d_in+4) == *(months+int_month+2)
       )
       { int_month = (int_month+3) / 3;
         *(d_out+4) = '0';
         if ( int_month >= 10 )
           { *(d_out+4) = '1';
             int_month -= 10;
           }
         *(d_out+5) = int_month + '0';
         break;
       }
  }
}
```

480

Function Name : date__39

Description : This function converts the date from a format of DDMMMYYYY to a format of DD-MMM-YYYY.

Variables : d__in — This variable contains the date that is passed to the function for reformatting.

d__out — This variable contains the reformatted date field that is passed back to the calling module.

Rules : This function must be passed the pointer associated with a character field. This may be in the format of defined character pointer or as the name of a character array with no array brackets.

The date must be passed in the correct format or unexpected results may be returned.

The reformatted date will be returned by way of the second parameter, therefore, no actual return code is used.

The field into which the reformatted date is returned must be large enough to hold the output character string.

On this and all other date functions, all four digits of the year field are required. For example, 1986 is valid and 86 is not valid.

```
date_39(d_in, d_out)

char *d_in, *d_out;

{ int int_month;
  char months[37];
  *(d_out)    = *(d_in);
  *(d_out+1) = *(d_in+1);
  *(d_out+2) = '-';
  *(d_out+3) = *(d_in+2);
  *(d_out+4) = *(d_in+3);
  *(d_out+5) = *(d_in+4);
  *(d_out+6) = '-';
  *(d_out+7) = *(d_in+5);
  *(d_out+8) = *(d_in+6);
  *(d_out+9) = *(d_in+7);
  *(d_out+10) = *(d_in+8);
  *(d_out+11) = '\0';
}
```

date__40

Function Name : date__40

Description : This function converts the date from a format of
DDMMMYYYY to its julian equivalent.

Variables : d__in — The variables contain the date that is passed to
the function for conversion to its julian date.

julian — This long integer variable contains the numeric
julian value that is returned to calling function.

Rules : This function must be passed the pointer associated with
a character field. This may be in the format of defined
character pointer or as the name of a character array with
no array brackets.

The date must be passed in the correct format or unexpected
results may be returned.

The converted date will be returned via a long integer.
Therefore, the function must be defined as a long integer
and the variable receiving the returned value must also be
a long integer.

On this and all other date functions, all four digits of the
year field are required. For example, 1986 is valid and 86
is not valid.

```
long int date_40(d_in)
 char *d_in;
{ int in_year, in_month, in_day;
  int cent, cent_y, month, year, out_day;
  long int long_day, temp_long;
  char months[37];
  char temp[3];
  strncpy(temp,d_in,2);
  in_day    = i_convert(temp);
  in_year   = i_convert(d_in+5);
  strcpy(months,"JANFEBMARAPRMAYJUNJULAUGSEPOCTNOVDEC");
  for(in_month=0; in_month < 37; in_month+=3 )
    { if ( *(d_in+2) == *(months+in_month) &&
           *(d_in+3) == *(months+in_month+1) &&
           *(d_in+4) == *(months+in_month+2)
         )
       { in_month = (in_month+3) / 3;
         break;
       }
    }

  if ( in_month > 2 )
    { month = in_month - 3;
      year  = in_year;
    }
  else
    { month = in_month + 9;
```

```
         year = in_year - 1;
      }
   temp_long = 146097;
   cent    = year / 100;
   cent_y = year - ( cent * 100 );
   long_day = temp_long * cent / 4;
   long_day = long_day + 1461.0 * cent_y / 4;
   long_day = long_day  + ( 153 * month + 2 ) / 5;
   long_day = long_day + in_day;

   return(long_day);
}
```

date__41

Function Name : date__41

Description : This function receives a date in the format DDMMMYYYY and returns its daily position within the year. For example, February 5th is the 36th day of the year.

Variables : d__in — The variables contain the date that is passed to the function for conversion to its julian date.

julian — This long integer variable contains the numeric value that is returned to calling function.

Rules : This function must be passed the pointer associated with a character field. This may be in the format of defined character pointer or as the name of a character array with no array brackets.

The date must be passed in the correct format or unexpected results may be returned.

The converted date will be returned via an integer. Therefore, the function must be defined as an integer and the variable receiving the returned value must also be an integer. On this and all other date functions, all four digits of the year field are required. For example, 1986 is valid and 86 is not valid.

```
date_41(d_in)
 char *d_in;
{ int in_year, in_month, in_day;
  int cent, cent_y, month, year, out_day, leap_year;
  long int long_day;
  char months[37];
  char temp[3];
  strncpy(temp,d_in,2);
  in_day    = i_convert(temp);
  in_year   = i_convert(d_in+5);
  strcpy(months,"JANFEBMARAPRMAYJUNJULAUGSEPOCTNOVDEC");
  for(in_month=0; in_month < 37; in_month+=3 )
    { if ( *(d_in+2) == *(months+in_month) &&
           *(d_in+3) == *(months+in_month+1) &&
           *(d_in+4) == *(months+in_month+2)
         )
        { in_month = (in_month+3) / 3;
          break;
        }
    }

  long_day = ( 3055.0 * ( in_months + 2 ) / 100 ) -91;
```

```
        out_day = long_day;

    if ( in_month > 2 )
        { leap_year = 0;
          if (( in_year % 4 )   == 0 ) leap_year = 1;
          if (( in_year % 100 ) == 0 ) leap_year = 0;
          if (( in_year % 400 ) == 0 ) leap_year = 1;
          out_day = out_day - 2 + leap_year;
        }
    out_day += in_day;
    return(out_day);
}
```

date__42

Function Name : date__42

Description : This function receives a date in the format DDMMMYYYY and returns a 0 if the year is not a leap year and a 1 if the year is a leap year.

Variables : d__in — The variables contain the date that is passed to the function for conversion to its julian date.

leap__year— This integer variable contains the numeric value that is returned to the calling function.

Rules : This function must be passed the pointer associated with a character field. This may be in the format of defined character pointer or as the name of a character array with no array brackets.

The date must be passed in the correct format or unexpected results may be returned.

The converted date will be returned via an integer. Therefore, the function must be defined as an integer and the variable receiving the returned value must also be an integer. On this and all other date functions, all four digits of the year field are required. For example, 1986 is valid and 86 is not valid.

```
date_42(d_in)
 char *d_in;
{ int in_year, in_month, in_day;
  int leap_year;
  char months[37];
  char temp[3];
  strncpy(temp,d_in,2);
  in_day    = i_convert(temp);
  in_year   = i_convert(d_in+5);
  strcpy(months,"JANFEBMARAPRMAYJUNJULAUGSEPOCTNOVDEC");
  for(in_month=0; in_month < 37; in_month+=3 )
    { if ( *(d_in+2) == *(months+in_month) &&
           *(d_in+3) == *(months+in_month+1) &&
           *(d_in+4) == *(months+in_month+2)
         )
       { in_month = (in_month+3) / 3;
         break;
       }
    }
  in_day    = i_convert(d_in);

  leap_year = 0;
  if (( in_year % 4 )   == 0 ) leap_year = 1;
  if (( in_year % 100 ) == 0 ) leap_year = 0;
  if (( in_year % 400 ) == 0 ) leap_year = 1;
  return(leap_year);
}
```

Function Name : date__43

Description : This function receives a date in the format DDMMMYYYY and returns its daily position within the week. For example, Dec. 5, 1986 fell on a Friday, therefore this function will return a 5. (0 = Sun, 1 = Mon, 2 = Tue, 3 = Wed, 4 = Thu, 5 = Fri, 6 = Sat).

Variables : d__in — The variables contain the date that is passed to the function for conversion to its julian date.

out__day — This integer variable contains the numeric value standing for the day of the week that is returned to the calling function.

Rules : This function must be passed the pointer associated with a character field. This may be in the format of defined character pointer or as the name of a character array with no array brackets.

The date must be passed in the correct format or unexpected results may be returned.

The numeric value will be returned via an integer. Therefore, the function must be defined as an integer and the variable receiving the returned value must also be an integer. On this and all other date functions, all four digits of the year field are required. For example, 1986 is valid and 86 is not valid.

```
date_43(d_in)
 char *d_in;
{ int in_year, in_month, in_day;
  int cent, cent_y, month, year, out_day;
  long int long_day;
  char months[37];
  char temp[3];
  strncpy(temp,d_in,2);
  in_day     = i_convert(temp);
  in_year    = i_convert(d_in+5);
  strcpy(months,"JANFEBMARAPRMAYJUNJULAUGSEPOCTNOVDEC");
  for(in_month=0; in_month < 37; in_month+=3 )
    { if ( *(d_in+2) == *(months+in_month) &&
           *(d_in+3) == *(months+in_month+1) &&
           *(d_in+4) == *(months+in_month+2)
         )
        { in_month = (in_month+3) / 3;
          break;
        }
    }

  if ( in_month > 2 )
    { month = in_month - 2;
```

```
          year  = in_year;
      }
   else
      { month = in_month + 10;
        year = in_year - 1;
      }
   cent   = year / 100;
   cent_y = year - ( cent * 100 );
   long_day = ( 13 * month - 1 ) / 5;
   long_day = long_day + in_day + cent_y + ( cent_y/4 );
   long_day = long_day  + ( cent/4 ) - cent - cent + 77;
   long_day = long_day - 7 * ( long_day / 7 );
   out_day = long_day;

   return(out_day);
}
```

Function Name : date__44

Description : This function converts the date from a format of DDMMMYYYY to a format of Day. Mon. DD, YYYY.

Variables : d__in — The variable contains the date that is passed to the function for reformatting.

d__out — This variable contains the reformatted date field that is passed back to the calling module.

Rules : This function must be passed the pointer associated with a character field. This may be in the format of defined character pointer or as the name of a character array with no array brackets.

The date must be passed in the correct format or unexpected results may be returned.

The reformatted date will be returned by way of the second parameter. Therefore, no actual return code is used.

The field into which the reformatted date is returned must be large enough to hold the output character string.

On this and all other date functions, all four digits of the year field are required. For example, 1986 is valid and 86 is not valid.

```
date_44(d_in, d_out)

char *d_in, *d_out;

{ int int_month, int_day;
  char months[37];
  char days[22];
  *(d_out)    = 'X';
  *(d_out+1) = 'X';
  *(d_out+2) = 'X';
  *(d_out+3) = '.';
  *(d_out+4) = ' ';
  *(d_out+5) = *(d_in+2);
  *(d_out+6) = *(d_in+3);
  *(d_out+7) = *(d_in+4);
  *(d_out+8) = '.';
  *(d_out+9) = ' ';
  *(d_out+10) = *(d_in);
  *(d_out+11) = *(d_in+1);
  *(d_out+12) = ',';
  *(d_out+13) = ' ';
  *(d_out+14) = *(d_in+5);
  *(d_out+15) = *(d_in+6);
```

```
    *(d_out+16) = *(d_in+7);
    *(d_out+17) = *(d_in+8);
    *(d_out+18) = '\0';

    strcpy(days,"SunMonTueWedThuFriSat");
    int_day = date_43(d_in) + 1;
    if ( int_day >= 1 && int_day <= 7 )
      { *(d_out) = *(days+((int_day-1)*3));
        *(d_out+1) = *(days+1+((int_day-1)*3));
        *(d_out+2) = *(days+2+((int_day-1)*3));
      }
}
```

Function Name : date__45

Description : This function converts the date from a format of
DDMMMYYYY to a format of Dayyyyy Monthhhhh. DD,
YYYY.

Variables : d__in — This variable contains the date that is passed to
the function for reformatting.

d__out — This variable contains the reformatted date field
that is passed back to the calling module.

Rules : This function must be passed the pointer associated with
a character field. This may be in the format of defined
character pointer or as the name of a character array with
no array brackets.

The date must be passed in the correct format or unexpected
results may be returned.

The reformatted date will be returned by way of the second parameter. Therefore, no actual return code is used.

The field into which the reformatted date is returned must
be large enough to hold the output character string.

On this and all other date functions, all four digits of the
year field are required. For example, 1986 is valid and 86
is not valid.

```
date_45(d_in, d_out)

char *d_in, *d_out;

{ int int_month, int_day;
  char months[109];
  char days[64];
  *(d_out+9)  = ',';
  *(d_out+10) = ' ';
  *(d_out+20) = ' ';
  *(d_out+21) = *(d_in);
  *(d_out+22) = *(d_in+1);
  *(d_out+23) = ',';
  *(d_out+24) = ' ';
  *(d_out+25) = *(d_in+5);
  *(d_out+26) = *(d_in+6);
  *(d_out+27) = *(d_in+7);
  *(d_out+28) = *(d_in+8);
  *(d_out+29) = '\0';
  strcpy(months,"JANFEBMARAPRMAYJUNJULAUGSEPOCTNOVDEC");
  for(int_month=0; int_month < 37; int_month+=3 )
   { if ( *(d_in+2) == *(months+int_month) &&
          *(d_in+3) == *(months+int_month+1) &&
          *(d_in+4) == *(months+int_month+2)
        )
      { int_month = (int_month+3) / 3;
```

```
            break;
        }
    }
    strcpy(months,"January  February March    April    May      Jun      ");
    strcat(months,"July     August  SeptemberOctober  November December ");
    if ( int_month >= 1 && int_month <= 12 )
      { *(d_out+11) = *(months+((int_month-1)*9));
        *(d_out+12) = *(months+1+((int_month-1)*9));
        *(d_out+13) = *(months+2+((int_month-1)*9));
        *(d_out+14) = *(months+3+((int_month-1)*9));
        *(d_out+15) = *(months+4+((int_month-1)*9));
        *(d_out+16) = *(months+5+((int_month-1)*9));
        *(d_out+17) = *(months+6+((int_month-1)*9));
        *(d_out+18) = *(months+7+((int_month-1)*9));
        *(d_out+19) = *(months+8+((int_month-1)*9));
      }

    strcpy(days,"Sunday   Monday   Tuesday  wednesdayThursday Friday   ");
    strcat(days,"Saterday ");
    int_day = date_43(d_in) + 1;
    if ( int_day >= 1 && int_day <= 7 )
      { *(d_out) = *(days+((int_day-1)*9));
        *(d_out+1) = *(days+1+((int_day-1)*9));
        *(d_out+2) = *(days+2+((int_day-1)*9));
        *(d_out+3) = *(days+3+((int_day-1)*9));
        *(d_out+4) = *(days+4+((int_day-1)*9));
        *(d_out+5) = *(days+5+((int_day-1)*9));
        *(d_out+6) = *(days+6+((int_day-1)*9));
        *(d_out+7) = *(days+7+((int_day-1)*9));
        *(d_out+8) = *(days+8+((int_day-1)*9));
      }
}
```

Function Name : date__46

Description : This function calculates the number of days between two dates including the days passed in the format DDMMMYYYY.

Variables : s__date — This variable contains the starting date to be calculated from.

e__date — This variable contains the ending date to which the days should be counted.

no__days — This long integer variable will contain the number of days that is returned to the calling function.

Rules : This function must be passed the pointers associated with a character field. They may be in the format of defined character pointers or as the name of a character array with no array brackets.

The dates must be passed in the correct format or unexpected results may be returned.

On this and all other date functions, all four digits of the year field are required. For example, 1986 is valid and 86 is not valid.

The calculated value will be returned via a long integer. Therefore, the function must be defined as a long integer and the variable receiving the returned value must also be a long integer.

```
long int date_46(s_date, e_date)
char *s_date, *e_date;
{ long int no_days;
  no_days = date_40(e_date) - date_40(s_date) + 1;
  return(no_days);
}
```

date__47

Function Name : date__47

Description : This function calculates the number of days between two dates not including the days passed in the format DDMMMYYYY.

Variables : s__date — This variable contains the starting date to be calculated from.

e__date — This variable contains the ending date to which the days should be counted.

no__days — This long integer variable will contain the number of days that is returned to the calling function.

Rules : This function must be passed the pointer associated with a character field. This may be in the format of defined character pointer or as the name of a character array with no array brackets.

The dates must be passed in the correct format or unexpected results may be returned.

On this and all other date functions, all four digits of the year field are required. For example, 1986 is valid and 86 is not valid.

The calculated value will be returned via a long integer. Therefore, the function must be defined as a long integer and the variable receiving the returned value must also be a long integer.

```
long int date_47(s_date, e_date)
char *s_date, *e_date;
{ long int no_days;
  no_days = date_40(e_date) - date_40(s_date) - 1;
  return(no_days);
}
```

date__48

Function Name : date__48

Description : This function calculates what the date will be in a specified number of days, given the starting date in the format YY-YYMMDD and the number of days to count.

Variables : d__in — This variable contains the starting date to be calculated from.

d__out — This variable contains the ending date after the appropriate number of days have been counted.

no__days — This integer variable contains the number of days that must be counted to calculate the ending date.

Rules : This function must be passed the pointers associated with a character fields. They may be in the format of defined character pointers or as the name of character arrays with no array brackets.

The dates must be passed in the correct format or unexpected results may be returned.

On this and all other date functions, all four digits of the year field are required. For example, 1986 is valid and 86 is not valid.

```
date_48(d_in,d_out,no_days)
 char *d_in, *d_out;
 int no_days;
{ long int s_julian, e_julian;
  s_julian = date_40(d_in);
  e_julian = s_julian + no_days;
  date_52(e_julian,d_out);
}
```

date__49

Description : This function converts the date from a Julian to a format of MM/DD/YYYY.

Variables : julian — This long integer contains the julian value that is to be transformed to the value placed in "d__out".

d__out — This variable contains the reformatted date field that is passed back to the calling module.

Rules : The second parameter must be the pointer associated with a character field. This may be in the format of defined character pointer or as the name of a character array with no array brackets.

The first parameter must be a long integer containing the julian date value to be analyzed.

The reformatted date will be returned by way of the second parameter. Therefore, no actual return code is used.

The field into which the reformatted date is returned must be large enough to hold the output character string.

On this and all other date functions, all four digits of the year field are required. For example, 1986 is valid and 86 is not valid.

```
date_49(julian,d_out)
 long int julian;
 char *d_out;
{ long int out_year, out_month, out_day;
  long int long_day, temp_long, temp_julian;
  int year, month, day;
  char temp_char[5];
  *(d_out+2) = '/';
  *(d_out+5) = '/';
  *(d_out+10) = '\0';

  temp_long = 146097;
  temp_julian = julian;
  out_year = (4 * julian - 1 ) / temp_long;
  temp_julian = 4 * temp_julian - 1 - temp_long * out_year;
  out_day = temp_julian / 4;
  temp_julian = ( 4 * out_day + 3 ) / 1461;
  out_day = 4 * out_day + 3 - 1461 * temp_julian;
  out_day = ( out_day + 4) / 4;
  out_month = ( 5 * out_day - 3 ) / 153;
  out_day = 5 * out_day - 3 - 153 * out_month;
  out_day = ( out_day + 5 ) / 5;
  out_year = 100 * out_year + temp_julian;

  if ( out_month < 10 )
    { out_month = out_month + 3;
```

```
      }
  else
   { out_month = out_month - 9;
     out_year = out_year + 1;
   }

 year =  out_year;
 month = out_month;
 day = out_day;

 i_to_a(year,temp_char);
     *(d_out + 6) = *(temp_char);
     *(d_out + 7) = *(temp_char+1);
     *(d_out + 8) = *(temp_char+2);
     *(d_out + 9) = *(temp_char+3);

 i_to_a(month,temp_char);
 if ( out_month < 10 )
    { *(d_out)     = '0';
      *(d_out + 1) = *(temp_char);
    }
 else
    { *(d_out)     = *(temp_char);
      *(d_out + 1) = *(temp_char+1);
    }

 i_to_a(day,temp_char);
 if ( out_day < 10 )
    { *(d_out + 3) = '0';
      *(d_out + 4) = *(temp_char);
    }
 else
    { *(d_out + 3) = *(temp_char);
      *(d_out + 4) = *(temp_char+1);
    }
}
```

date__50

Function Name : date__50

Description : This function converts the date from a Julian to a format of DD-MMM-YYYY.

Variables : julian — This long integer contains the julian value that is to be transformed to a value placed in "d__out".

d__out — This variable contains the reformatted date field that is passed back to the calling module.

Rules : The second parameter must be the pointer associated with a character field. This may be in the format of defined character pointer or as the name of a character array with no array brackets.

The first parameter must be a long integer containing the julian date value to be analyzed.

The reformatted date will be returned by way of the second parameter. Therefore, no actual return code is used. The field into which the reformatted date is returned must be large enough to hold the output character string.

On this and all other date functions, all four digits of the year field are required. For example, 1986 is valid and 86 is not valid.

```
date_50(julian,d_out)
 long int julian;
 char *d_out;
{ long int out_year, out_month, out_day;
  long int long_day, temp_long, temp_julian;
  int year, month, day;
  char temp_char[5];
  char months[37];
  *(d_out+2) = '-';
  *(d_out+6) = '-';
  *(d_out+11) = '\0';

  temp_long = 146097;
  temp_julian = julian;
  out_year = (4 * julian - 1 ) / temp_long;
  temp_julian = 4 * temp_julian - 1 - temp_long * out_year;
  out_day = temp_julian / 4;
  temp_julian = ( 4 * out_day + 3 ) / 1461;
  out_day = 4 * out_day + 3 - 1461 * temp_julian;
  out_day = ( out_day + 4) / 4;
  out_month = ( 5 * out_day - 3 ) / 153;
  out_day = 5 * out_day - 3 - 153 * out_month;
  out_day = ( out_day + 5 ) / 5;
  out_year = 100 * out_year + temp_julian;

  if ( out_month < 10 )
```

```
              { out_month = out_month + 3;
              }
       else
          { out_month = out_month - 9;
            out_year = out_year + 1;
          }


       year =  out_year;
       month = out_month;
       day = out_day;

       i_to_a(year,temp_char);
            *(d_out + 7) = *(temp_char);
            *(d_out + 8) = *(temp_char+1);
            *(d_out + 9) = *(temp_char+2);
            *(d_out + 10) = *(temp_char+3);

       strcpy(months,"JANFEBMARAPRMAYJUNJULAUGSEPOCTNOVDEC");
       if ( month >= 1 && month <= 12 )
          { *(d_out+3) = *(months+((month-1)*3));
            *(d_out+4) = *(months+1+((month-1)*3));
            *(d_out+5) = *(months+2+((month-1)*3));
          }

       i_to_a(day,temp_char);
       if ( out_day < 10 )
          { *(d_out) = '0';
            *(d_out + 1) = *(temp_char);
          }
       else
          { *(d_out) = *(temp_char);
            *(d_out + 1) = *(temp_char+1);
          }

}
```

date__51

Function Name : date__51

Description : This function converts the date from a Julian to a format of YYYYMMDD.

Variables : julian — This long integer contains the julian value that is to be transformed to a value placed in "d__out".

d__out — This variable contains the reformatted date field that is passed back to the calling module.

Rules : The second parameter must be the pointer associated with a character field. This may be in the format of defined character pointer or as the name of a character array with no array brackets.

The first parameter must be a long integer containing the julian date value to be analyzed.

The reformatted date will be returned by way of the second parameter. Therefore, no actual return code is used. The field into which the reformatted date is returned must be large enough to hold the output character string.

On this and all other date functions, all four digits of the year field are required. For example, 1986 is valid and 86 is not valid.

```
date_51(julian,d_out)
 long int julian;
 char *d_out;
{ long int out_year, out_month, out_day;
  long int long_day, temp_long, temp_julian;
  int year, month, day;
  char temp_char[5];
  *(d_out+8) = '\0';

  temp_long = 146097;
  temp_julian = julian;
  out_year = (4 * julian - 1 ) / temp_long;
  temp_julian = 4 * temp_julian - 1 - temp_long * out_year;
  out_day = temp_julian / 4;
  temp_julian = ( 4 * out_day + 3 ) / 1461;
  out_day = 4 * out_day + 3 - 1461 * temp_julian;
  out_day = ( out_day + 4) / 4;
  out_month = ( 5 * out_day - 3 ) / 153;
  out_day = 5 * out_day - 3 - 153 * out_month;
  out_day = ( out_day + 5 ) / 5;
  out_year = 100 * out_year + temp_julian;


  if ( out_month < 10 )
    { out_month = out_month + 3;
    }
```

```
            else
              { out_month = out_month - 9;
                out_year = out_year + 1;
              }

            year =  out_year;
            month = out_month;
            day = out_day;

            i_to_a(year,temp_char);
                *(d_out) = *(temp_char);
                *(d_out + 1) = *(temp_char+1);
                *(d_out + 2) = *(temp_char+2);
                *(d_out + 3) = *(temp_char+3);

            i_to_a(month,temp_char);
            if ( out_month < 10 )
              { *(d_out + 4) = '0';
                *(d_out + 5) = *(temp_char);
              }
            else
              { *(d_out + 4) = *(temp_char);
                *(d_out + 5) = *(temp_char+1);
              }

            i_to_a(day,temp_char);
            if ( out_day < 10 )
              { *(d_out + 6) = '0';
                *(d_out + 7) = *(temp_char);
              }
            else
              { *(d_out + 6) = *(temp_char);
                *(d_out + 7) = *(temp_char+1);
              }
        }
```

date___52

Function Name : date___52

Description : This function converts the date from a Julian to a format of DDMMMYYYY.

Variables : julian — This long integer contains the julian value that is to be transformed to a value placed in "d__out".

julian — This variable contains the reformatted date field that is passed back to the calling module.

Rules : The second parameter must be the pointer associated with a character field. This may be in the format of defined character pointer or as the name of a character array with no array brackets.

The first parameter must be a long integer containing the julian date value to be analyzed.

The reformatted date will be returned by way of the second parameter. Therefore, no actual return code is used.

The field into which the reformatted date is returned must be large enough to hold the output character string.

On this and all other date functions, all four digits of the year field are required. For example, 1986 is valid and 86 is not valid.

```
date_52(julian,d_out)
 long int julian;
 char *d_out;
{ long int out_year, out_month, out_day;
  long int long_day, temp_long, temp_julian;
  int year, month, day;
  char temp_char[5];
  char months[37];
  *(d_out+9) = '\0';

  temp_long = 146097;
  temp_julian = julian;
  out_year = (4 * julian - 1 ) / temp_long;
  temp_julian = 4 * temp_julian - 1 - temp_long * out_year;
  out_day = temp_julian / 4;
  temp_julian = ( 4 * out_day + 3 ) / 1461;
  out_day = 4 * out_day + 3 - 1461 * temp_julian;
  out_day = ( out_day + 4) / 4;
  out_month = ( 5 * out_day - 3 ) / 153;
  out_day = 5 * out_day - 3 - 153 * out_month;
  out_day = ( out_day + 5 ) / 5;
  out_year = 100 * out_year + temp_julian;


  if ( out_month < 10 )
    { out_month = out_month + 3;
```

```
        }
    else
        { out_month = out_month - 9;
          out_year = out_year + 1;
        }

    year  =  out_year;
    month = out_month;
    day = out_day;

    i_to_a(year,temp_char);
        *(d_out + 5) = *(temp_char);
        *(d_out + 6) = *(temp_char+1);
        *(d_out + 7) = *(temp_char+2);
        *(d_out + 8) = *(temp_char+3);

    strcpy(months,"JANFEBMARAPRMAYJUNJULAUGSEPOCTNOVDEC");
    if ( month >= 1 && month <= 12 )
        { *(d_out+2) = *(months+((month-1)*3));
          *(d_out+3) = *(months+1+((month-1)*3));
          *(d_out+4) = *(months+2+((month-1)*3));
        }

    i_to_a(day,temp_char);
    if ( out_day < 10 )
        { *(d_out)     = '0';
          *(d_out + 1) = *(temp_char);
        }
    else
        { *(d_out)     = *(temp_char);
          *(d_out + 1) = *(temp_char+1);
        }
}
```

date__53

Function Name : date__53

Description : This function receives a date in a julian format and returns its daily position within the year. For example, February 5th is the 36th day of the year.

Variables : julian — This long integer contains the julian value that is to be transformed to a value placed in "d__out".

julian — This long integer variable contains the numeric value that is returned to the calling function.

Rules : The julian value which is passed to the function must be defined as a long integer.

The converted date will be returned via an integer. Therefore, the function must be defined as an integer and the variable receiving the returned value must also be an integer. On this and all other date functions, all four digits of the year field are required. For example, 1986 is valid and 86 is not valid.

```
date_53(julian)
 long int julian;
{ long int out_year, out_month, out_day;
  long int long_day, temp_long, temp_julian;
  int year, month, day, leap_year, no_days;
  char temp_char[5];
  char months[37];

  temp_long = 146097;
  temp_julian = julian;
  out_year = (4 * julian - 1 ) / temp_long;
  temp_julian = 4 * temp_julian - 1 - temp_long * out_year;
  out_day = temp_julian / 4;
  temp_julian = ( 4 * out_day + 3 ) / 1461;
  out_day = 4 * out_day + 3 - 1461 * temp_julian;
  out_day = ( out_day + 4) / 4;
  out_month = ( 5 * out_day - 3 ) / 153;
  out_day = 5 * out_day - 3 - 153 * out_month;
  out_day = ( out_day + 5 ) / 5;
  out_year = 100 * out_year + temp_julian;


  if ( out_month < 10 )
    { out_month = out_month + 3;
    }
  else
    { out_month = out_month - 9;
      out_year = out_year + 1;
    }

  year =  out_year;
```

```
      month = out_month;
      day = out_day;

      long_day = ( 3055.0 * ( month + 2 ) / 100 ) -91;
      no_days = long_day;

      if ( month > 2 )
         { leap_year = 0;
           if (( year % 4 )   == 0 ) leap_year = 1;
           if (( year % 100 ) == 0 ) leap_year = 0;
           if (( year % 400 ) == 0 ) leap_year = 1;
           no_days = no_days - 2 + leap_year;
         }
      no_days += day;
      return(no_days);
}
```

date__54

Function Name : date__54

Description : This function receives a date in julian format and returns
a 0 if the year is not a leap year and a 1 if the year is a leap
year.

Variables : julian   — This long integer contains the julian value that
is to be transformed to a value placed in
"d__out".

           leap__year— This integer variable contains the numeric value
that is returned to the calling function.

Rules : The julian value which is passed to the function must be
defined as a long integer.

The leap year indicator will be returned via an integer.
Therefore, the function must be defined as an integer and
the variable receiving the returned value must also be an
integer.

On this and all other date functions, all four digits of the
year field are required. For example, 1986 is valid and 86
is not valid.

```
date_54(julian)
 long int julian;
{ long int out_year, out_month, out_day;
  long int long_day, temp_long, temp_julian;
  int year, month, day, leap_year;
  char temp_char[5];
  char months[37];

  temp_long = 146097;
  temp_julian = julian;
  out_year = (4 * julian - 1 ) / temp_long;
  temp_julian = 4 * temp_julian - 1 - temp_long * out_year;
  out_day = temp_julian / 4;
  temp_julian = ( 4 * out_day + 3 ) / 1461;
  out_day = 4 * out_day + 3 - 1461 * temp_julian;
  out_day = ( out_day + 4) / 4;
  out_month = ( 5 * out_day - 3 ) / 153;
  out_day = 5 * out_day - 3 - 153 * out_month;
  out_day = ( out_day + 5 ) / 5;
  out_year = 100 * out_year + temp_julian;


  if ( out_month < 10 )
     { out_month = out_month + 3;
     }
```

```
    else
      { out_month = out_month - 9;
        out_year = out_year + 1;
      }

    year =  out_year;

    leap_year = 0;
    if (( year % 4 )   == 0 ) leap_year = 1;
    if (( year % 100 ) == 0 ) leap_year = 0;
    if (( year % 400 ) == 0 ) leap_year = 1;
    return(leap_year);
}
```

date___55

Function Name : date___55

Description : This function receives a date in julian format and returns its daily position within the week. For example, Dec. 5, 1986 fell on a friday, therefore this function will return a 5. (0 = Sun, 1 = Mon, 2 = Tue, 3 = Wed, 4 = Thu, 5 = Fri, 6 = Sat).

Variables : julian — This long integer contains the julian value that is to be transformed to a value placed in "d__out".

out__day — This integer variable contains the numeric value standing for the day of the week that is returned to the calling function.

Rules : The julian value which is passed to the function must be defined as a long integer.

The leap year indicator will be returned via an integer. Therefore, the function must be defined as an integer and the variable receiving the returned value must also be an integer.

On this and all other date functions, all four digits of the year field are required. For example, 1986 is valid and 86 is not valid.

```
date_55(julian)
 long int julian;
{ long int out_year, out_month, out_day;
  long int long_day, temp_long, temp_julian;
  int year, month, day, the_day, cent, cent_y;
  char temp_char[5];
  char months[37];

  temp_long = 146097;
  temp_julian = julian;
  out_year = (4 * julian - 1 ) / temp_long;
  temp_julian = 4 * temp_julian - 1 - temp_long * out_year;
  out_day = temp_julian / 4;
  temp_julian = ( 4 * out_day + 3 ) / 1461;
  out_day = 4 * out_day + 3 - 1461 * temp_julian;
  out_day = ( out_day + 4) / 4;
  out_month = ( 5 * out_day - 3 ) / 153;
  out_day = 5 * out_day - 3 - 153 * out_month;
  out_day = ( out_day + 5 ) / 5;
  out_year = 100 * out_year + temp_julian;

  year =  out_year;
  month = out_month;
  day = out_day;

  if ( month < 10 )
    { month = month + 3;
```

```
        }
    else
      { month = month - 9;
        year = year + 1;
      }


    if ( month > 2 )
      { month = month - 2;
        year  = year;
      }
    else
      { month = month + 10;
        year = year - 1;
      }
    cent    = year / 100;
    cent_y = year - ( cent * 100 );
    long_day = ( 13 * month - 1 ) / 5;
    long_day = long_day + day + cent_y + ( cent_y/4 );
    long_day = long_day  + ( cent/4 ) - cent - cent + 77;
    long_day = long_day - 7 * ( long_day / 7 );
    the_day = long_day;


    return(the_day);
}
```

date__56

Function Name : date__56

Description : This function converts the date from a julian to a format of Day. Mon. DD, YYYY.

Variables : julian   — This long integer contains the julian value that is to be transformed to a value placed in "d__out".

           d__out   — This variable contains the reformatted date field that is passed back to the calling module.

Rules : The second parameter must be passed the pointer associated with a character field. This may be in the format of defined character pointer or as the name of a character array with no array brackets.

The first parameter must be a long integer containing the julian date value to be analyzed.

The reformatted date will be returned by way of the second parameter. Therefore, no actual return code is used. The field into which the reformatted date is returned must be large enough to hold the output character string.

On this and all other date functions, all four digits of the year field are required. For example, 1986 is valid and 86 is not valid.

```
date_56(julian,d_out)
 long int julian;
 char *d_out;
{ long int out_year, out_month, out_day;
  long int long_day, temp_long, temp_julian;
  int year, month, day, temp_day;
  char temp_char[5];
  char months[37];
  char days[21];

  temp_long = 146097;
  temp_julian = julian;
  out_year = (4 * julian - 1 ) / temp_long;
  temp_julian = 4 * temp_julian - 1 - temp_long * out_year;
  out_day = temp_julian / 4;
  temp_julian = ( 4 * out_day + 3 ) / 1461;
  out_day = 4 * out_day + 3 - 1461 * temp_julian;
  out_day = ( out_day + 4) / 4;
  out_month = ( 5 * out_day - 3 ) / 153;
  out_day = 5 * out_day - 3 - 153 * out_month;
  out_day = ( out_day + 5 ) / 5;
  out_year = 100 * out_year + temp_julian;


  if ( out_month < 10 )
    { out_month = out_month + 3;
    }
```

```
    else
      { out_month = out_month - 9;
        out_year = out_year + 1;
      }


    year =  out_year;
    month = out_month;
    day = out_day;

    *(d_out+3) = ',';
    *(d_out+4) = ' ';
    *(d_out+8) = '.';
    *(d_out+9) = ' ';
    *(d_out+12) = ',';
    *(d_out+13) = ' ';
    *(d_out+18) = '\0';

    i_to_a(year,temp_char);
        *(d_out + 14) = *(temp_char);
        *(d_out + 15) = *(temp_char+1);
        *(d_out + 16) = *(temp_char+2);
        *(d_out + 17) = *(temp_char+3);

    strcpy(months,"JANFEBMARAPRMAYJUNJULAUGSEPOCTNOVDEC");
    if ( month >= 1 && month <= 12 )
      { *(d_out+5) = *(months+((month-1)*3));
        *(d_out+6) = *(months+1+((month-1)*3));
        *(d_out+7) = *(months+2+((month-1)*3));
      }

    i_to_a(day,temp_char);
    if ( out_day < 10 )
      { *(d_out + 10) = '0';
        *(d_out + 11) = *(temp_char);
      }
    else
      { *(d_out + 10) = *(temp_char);
        *(d_out + 11) = *(temp_char+1);
      }
    strcpy(days,"SunMonTueWedThuFriSat");
    temp_day = date_55(julian) + 1;
    if ( temp_day >= 1 && temp_day <= 7 )
      { *(d_out) = *(days+((temp_day-1)*3));
        *(d_out+1) = *(days+1+((temp_day-1)*3));
        *(d_out+2) = *(days+2+((temp_day-1)*3));
      }
}
```

date__57

Description : This function converts the date from a julian to a format
of Dayyyyyy Monthhhhh. DD, YYYY.

Variables : julian   — This long integer contains the julian value that
is to be transformed to a value placed in
"d__out".

d__out   — This variable contains the reformatted date field
that is passed back to the calling module.

Rules : The second parameter must be the pointer associated with
a character field. This may be in the format of defined
character pointer or as the name of a character array with
no array brackets.

The first parameter must be a long integer containing the
julian date to be analyzed.

The reformatted date will be returned by way of the second parameter. Therefore, no actual return code is used.
The field into which the reformatted date is returned must
be large enough to hold the output character string.

On this and all other date functions, all four digits of the
year field are required. For example, 1986 is valid and 86
is not valid.

```
date_57(julian,d_out)
 long int julian;
 char *d_out;
{ long int out_year, out_month, out_day;
  long int long_day, temp_long, temp_julian;
  int year, month, day, temp_day;
  char temp_char[5];
  char months[109];
  char days[64];

  temp_long = 146097;
  temp_julian = julian;
  out_year = (4 * julian - 1 ) / temp_long;
  temp_julian = 4 * temp_julian - 1 - temp_long * out_year;
  out_day = temp_julian / 4;
  temp_julian = ( 4 * out_day + 3 ) / 1461;
  out_day = 4 * out_day + 3 - 1461 * temp_julian;
  out_day = ( out_day + 4) / 4;
  out_month = ( 5 * out_day - 3 ) / 153;
  out_day = 5 * out_day - 3 - 153 * out_month;
  out_day = ( out_day + 5 ) / 5;
  out_year = 100 * out_year + temp_julian;


  if ( out_month < 10 )
    { out_month = out_month + 3;
    }
  else
    { out_month = out_month - 9;
```

```
          out_year = out_year + 1;
     }

    year =  out_year;
    month = out_month;
    day = out_day;

    *(d_out+9) = ',';
    *(d_out+10) = ' ';
    *(d_out+20) = ' ';
    *(d_out+23) = ',';
    *(d_out+24) = ' ';
    *(d_out+29) = '\0';

    i_to_a(year,temp_char);
        *(d_out + 25) = *(temp_char);
        *(d_out + 26) = *(temp_char+1);
        *(d_out + 27) = *(temp_char+2);
        *(d_out + 28) = *(temp_char+3);

    i_to_a(day,temp_char);
    if ( out_day < 10 )
      { *(d_out + 21) = '0';
        *(d_out + 22) = *(temp_char);
      }
    else
      { *(d_out + 21) = *(temp_char);
        *(d_out + 22) = *(temp_char+1);
      }
    strcpy(months,"January  February March    April    May      Jun       ");
    strcat(months,"July     August   SeptemberOctober  November December ");
    if ( month >= 1 && month <= 12 )
      { *(d_out+11) = *(months+((month-1)*9));
        *(d_out+12) = *(months+1+((month-1)*9));
        *(d_out+13) = *(months+2+((month-1)*9));
        *(d_out+14) = *(months+3+((month-1)*9));
        *(d_out+15) = *(months+4+((month-1)*9));
        *(d_out+16) = *(months+5+((month-1)*9));
        *(d_out+17) = *(months+6+((month-1)*9));
        *(d_out+18) = *(months+7+((month-1)*9));
        *(d_out+19) = *(months+8+((month-1)*9));
      }

    strcpy(days,"Sunday   Monday   Tuesday  WednesdayThursday Friday   ");
    strcat(days,"Saterday ");
    temp_day = date_55(julian) + 1;
    if ( temp_day >= 1 && temp_day <= 7 )
      { *(d_out) = *(days+((temp_day-1)*9));
        *(d_out+1) = *(days+1+((temp_day-1)*9));
        *(d_out+2) = *(days+2+((temp_day-1)*9));
        *(d_out+3) = *(days+3+((temp_day-1)*9));
        *(d_out+4) = *(days+4+((temp_day-1)*9));
        *(d_out+5) = *(days+5+((temp_day-1)*9));
        *(d_out+6) = *(days+6+((temp_day-1)*9));
        *(d_out+7) = *(days+7+((temp_day-1)*9));
        *(d_out+8) = *(days+8+((temp_day-1)*9));
      }
```

date__58

Function Name : date__58

Description : This function calculates the number of days between two dates including the days passed in a julian format.

Variables : s__julian — This long integer contains the julian value that is to be calculated from.

e__julian — This long integer variable contains the ending date to which the days should be counted.

no__days — This long integer variable will contain the number of days that is returned to the calling function.

Rules : The julian values which are passed to the function must be defined as a long integer.

The calculated value will be returned via an integer. Therefore, the function must be defined as an integer and the variable receiving the returned value must also be an integer.

```
long int date_58(s_julian, e_julian)
long int s_julian, e_julian;
{ long int no_days;
  no_days = e_julian - s_julian + 1;

  return(no_days);
}
```

date__59

Function Name : date__59

Description : This function calculates the number of days between two dates not including the days passed in a julian format.

Variables : s__julian — This long integer variable contains the julian date starting to be calculated from.

e__julian — This long integer variable contains the ending date to which the days should be counted.

no__days — This long integer variable will contain the number of days that is returned to the calling function.

Rules : The julian values which are passed to the function must be defined as a long integer.

The calculated value will be returned via an integer. Therefore, the function must be defined as an integer and the variable receiving the returned value must also be an integer.

```
long int date_59(s_julian, e_julian)
long int s_julian, e_julian;
{ long int no_days;
  no_days = e_julian - s_julian - 1;

  return(no_days);
}
```

date__60

Function Name : date__60

Description : This function calculates what the date will be in a specified number of days, given the starting date in the format YY-YYMMDD and the number of days to count.

Variables : s__julian — This long integer contains the starting julian date to be calculated from.

e__julian — This long integer variable contains the ending julian date that will be returned after the appropriate number of days have been counted.

no__days — This integer variable contains the number of days that must be counted to calculate the ending date.

Rules : The julian value that is passed to the function must be defined as a long integer.
The calculated julian date will be returned via an integer. Therefore, the function must be defined as an integer and the variable receiving the returned value must also be an integer.

```
long int date_60(s_julian, no_days)
long int s_julian;
int no_days;
{ long int e_julian;
  e_julian = s_julian + no_days;

  return(e_julian);
}
```

CALLING THE DATE FUNCTIONS

The code on the following pages will sequentially call each of the functions in this chapter, demonstrating their effects and how they can be used in actual programs.

```c
#include <stdio.h>

main()
{ ex1();
  ex2();
  ex3();
  ex4();
  ex5();
  ex6();
  ex7();
  ex8();
  ex9();
  ex10();
  ex11();
  ex12();
  ex13();
  ex14();
  ex15();
  ex16();
  ex17();
  ex18();
  ex19();
  ex20();
  ex21();
  ex22();
  ex23();
  ex24();
  ex25();
  ex26();
  ex27();
  ex28();
  ex29();
  ex30();
  ex31();
  ex32();
  ex33();
  ex34();
  ex35();
  ex36();
  ex37();
  ex38();
  ex39();
  ex40();
  ex41();
  ex42();
  ex43();
  ex44();
  ex45();
  ex46();
  ex47();
  ex48();
  ex49();
```

```
      ex50();
      ex51();
      ex52();
      ex53();
      ex54();
      ex55();
      ex56();
      ex57();
      ex58();
      ex59();
      ex60();

}

ex1()
{
  /****************************************************************
   ***************** call to date_1 function *****************
   ****************************************************************/

   char in_date[12];
   char out_date[40];

   strcpy(in_date,"03/02/1984");
   date_1(in_date, out_date);
   printf("\n Output date_1 ( DD-MMM-YYYY ) = %s",out_date);
}

ex2()
{
  /****************************************************************
   ***************** call to date_2 function *****************
   ****************************************************************/

   char in_date[12];
   char out_date[40];

   strcpy(in_date,"03/02/1984");
   date_2(in_date, out_date);
   printf("\n Output date_2 ( YYYYMMMDD ) = %s",out_date);
}

ex3()
{
  /****************************************************************
   ***************** call to date_3 function *****************
   ****************************************************************/

   char in_date[12];
   char out_date[40];

   strcpy(in_date,"03/02/1984");
   date_3(in_date, out_date);
   printf("\n Output date_3 ( DDMMMYYYY ) = %s",out_date);
}

ex4()
{
```

```
/*****************************************************************
 ****************** call to date_4 function ***************
 ****************************************************************/

  char in_date[12];
  long int long_days;
  long int date_4();

  strcpy(in_date,"03/02/1984");
  long_days = date_4(in_date);
  printf("\n Output date_4 ( DDDDDDDD ) = %ld",long_days);
}

ex5()
{
 /*****************************************************************
  ****************** call to date_5 function ***************
  ****************************************************************/

  char in_date[12];
  int out_days;

  strcpy(in_date,"03/02/1984");
  out_days = date_5(in_date);
  printf("\n Output date_5 ( DDDDD ) = %d",out_days);
}

ex6()
{
 /*****************************************************************
  ****************** call to date_6 function ***************
  ****************************************************************/

  char in_date[12];
  int out_days;

  strcpy(in_date,"03/02/1984");
  out_days = date_6(in_date);
  printf("\n Output date_6 ( DDDDD ) = %d",out_days);
}

ex7()
{
 /*****************************************************************
  ****************** call to date_7 function ***************
  ****************************************************************/

  char in_date[12];
  int out_days;

  strcpy(in_date,"03/02/1984");
  out_days = date_7(in_date);
  printf("\n Output date_7 ( DDDDD ) = %d",out_days);
}


ex8()
{
```

```
   /*************************************************************
    ***************** call to date_8 function ****************
    *************************************************************/

   char in_date[12];
   char out_date[40];

   strcpy(in_date,"03/02/1984");
   date_8(in_date, out_date);
   printf("\n Output date_8 = %s",out_date);
}

ex9()
{
   /*************************************************************
    ***************** call to date_9 function ****************
    *************************************************************/

   char in_date[12];
   char out_date[40];

   strcpy(in_date,"03/02/1984");
   date_9(in_date, out_date);
   printf("\n Output date_9 = %s",out_date);
}

ex10()
{
   /*************************************************************
    ***************** call to date_10 function ***************
    *************************************************************/

   char in_date[12];
   char end_date[12];
   long int long_days;
   long int date_10();

   strcpy(in_date,"03/02/1984");
   strcpy(end_date,"03/04/1984");
   long_days = date_10(in_date, end_date);
   printf("\n Output date_10 ( DDDDDDDD ) = %ld",long_days);
}

ex11()
{
   /*************************************************************
    ***************** call to date_11 function ***************
    *************************************************************/

   char in_date[12];
   char end_date[12];
   long int long_days;
   long int date_11();
   strcpy(in_date,"03/02/1984");
   strcpy(end_date,"03/04/1984");
   long_days = date_11(in_date, end_date);
   printf("\n Output date_11 ( DDDDDDDD ) = %ld",long_days);
}
```

```
ex12()
{
  /**************************************************************
   ****************** call to date_12 function ***************
   *************************************************************/

  char in_date[12];
  char out_date[40];

  strcpy(in_date,"03/02/1984");
  date_12(in_date, out_date, 10);
  printf("\n Output date_12 ( MM/DD/YYYY ) = %s",out_date);
}

ex13()
{
  /**************************************************************
   ****************** call to date_13 function ***************
   *************************************************************/

  char in_date[12];
  char out_date[40];

  strcpy(in_date,"05-DEC-1986");
  date_13(in_date, out_date);
  printf("\n Output date_13 ( MM/DD/YYYY ) = %s",out_date);
}

ex14()
{
  /**************************************************************
   ****************** call to date_14 function ***************
   *************************************************************/

  char in_date[12];
  char out_date[40];

  strcpy(in_date,"05-DEC-1986");
  date_14(in_date, out_date);
  printf("\n Output date_14 ( YYYYMMMDD ) = %s",out_date);
}

ex15()
{
  /**************************************************************
   ****************** call to date_15 function ***************
   *************************************************************/

  char in_date[12];
  char out_date[40];

  strcpy(in_date,"05-DEC-1986");
  date_15(in_date, out_date);
  printf("\n Output date_15 ( DDMMMYYYY ) = %s",out_date);
}

ex16()
{
```

```c
   /***************************************************************
    ****************** call to date_16 function ***************
    ***************************************************************/

   char in_date[12];
   long int long_days;
   long int date_16();

   strcpy(in_date,"05-DEC-1986");
   long_days = date_16(in_date);
   printf("\n Output date_16 ( DDDDDDDD ) = %ld",long_days);
}

ex17()
{
   /***************************************************************
    ****************** call to date_17 function ***************
    ***************************************************************/

   char in_date[12];
   int out_days;

   strcpy(in_date,"05-DEC-1986");
   out_days = date_17(in_date);
   printf("\n Output date_17 ( DDDDD ) = %d",out_days);
}

ex18()
{
   /***************************************************************
    ****************** call to date_18 function ***************
    ***************************************************************/

   char in_date[12];
   int out_days;

   strcpy(in_date,"05-DEC-1986");
   out_days = date_18(in_date);
   printf("\n Output date_18 ( DDDDD ) = %d",out_days);
}

ex19()
{
   /***************************************************************
    ****************** call to date_19 function ***************
    ***************************************************************/

   char in_date[12];
   int out_days;

   strcpy(in_date,"05-DEC-1986");
   out_days = date_19(in_date);
   printf("\n Output date_19 ( DDDDD ) = %d",out_days);
}

ex20()
{
   /***************************************************************
```

```
    ****************** call to date_20 function ***************
    **************************************************************/

  char in_date[12];
  char out_date[40];

  strcpy(in_date,"05-DEC-1986");
  date_20(in_date, out_date);
  printf("\n Output date_20 = %s",out_date);
}

ex21()
{
  /*************************************************************
    ****************** call to date_21 function ***************
    **************************************************************/

  char in_date[12];
  char out_date[40];

  strcpy(in_date,"05-DEC-1986");
  date_21(in_date, out_date);
  printf("\n Output date_21 = %s",out_date);
}

ex22()
{
  /*************************************************************
    ****************** call to date_22 function ***************
    **************************************************************/

  char in_date[12];
  char end_date[12];
  long int long_days;
  long int date_22();

  strcpy(in_date,"05-DEC-1986");
  strcpy(end_date,"23-DEC-1986");
  long_days = date_22(in_date, end_date);
  printf("\n Output date_22 ( DDDDDDDD ) = %ld",long_days);
}

ex23()
{
  /*************************************************************
    ****************** call to date_23 function ***************
    **************************************************************/

  char in_date[12];
  char end_date[12];
  long int long_days;
  long int date_23();

  strcpy(in_date,"05-DEC-1986");
  strcpy(end_date,"23-DEC-1986");
  long_days = date_23(in_date, end_date);
  printf("\n Output date_23 ( DDDDDDDD ) = %ld",long_days);
}
```

```
ex24()
{
  /***************************************************************
   ***************** call to date_24 function ***************
   **************************************************************/

  char in_date[12];
  char out_date[40];

  strcpy(in_date,"05-DEC-1986");
  date_24(in_date, out_date, 10);
  printf("\n Output date_24 ( DD-MMM-YYYY ) = %s",out_date);
}

ex25()
{
  /***************************************************************
   ***************** call to date_25 function ***************
   **************************************************************/

  char in_date[12];
  char out_date[40];

  strcpy(in_date,"19861205");
  date_25(in_date, out_date);
  printf("\n Output date_25 ( DD-MMM-YYYY ) = %s",out_date);
}

ex26()
{
  /***************************************************************
   ***************** call to date_26 function ***************
   **************************************************************/

  char in_date[12];
  char out_date[40];

  strcpy(in_date,"19861205");
  date_26(in_date, out_date);
  printf("\n Output date_26 ( MM/DD/YYYY ) = %s",out_date);
}

ex27()
{
  /***************************************************************
   ***************** call to date_27 function ***************
   **************************************************************/

  char in_date[12];
  char out_date[40];

  strcpy(in_date,"19861205");
  date_27(in_date, out_date);
  printf("\n Output date_27 ( DDMMMYYYY ) = %s",out_date);
}

ex28()
{
```

```
/******************************************************************
***************** call to date_28 function **************
*****************************************************************/

    char in_date[12];
    long int long_days;
    long int date_28();

    strcpy(in_date,"19861205");
    long_days = date_28(in_date);
    printf("\n Output date_28 ( DDDDDDDD ) = %ld",long_days);
}

ex29()
{
/******************************************************************
***************** call to date_29 function **************
*****************************************************************/

    char in_date[12];
    int out_days;

    strcpy(in_date,"19861205");
    out_days = date_29(in_date);
    printf("\n Output date_29 ( DDDDD ) = %d",out_days);
}

ex30()
{
/******************************************************************
***************** call to date_30 function **************
*****************************************************************/

    char in_date[12];
    int out_days;
    strcpy(in_date,"19861205");
    out_days = date_30(in_date);
    printf("\n Output date_30 ( DDDDD ) = %d",out_days);
}

ex31()
{
/******************************************************************
***************** call to date_31 function **************
*****************************************************************/

    char in_date[12];
    int out_days;

    strcpy(in_date,"19861205");
    out_days = date_31(in_date);
    printf("\n Output date_31 ( DDDDD ) = %d",out_days);
}

ex32()
{
/******************************************************************
***************** call to date_32 function **************
```

```
             ************************************************************/

   char in_date[12];
   char out_date[40];

   strcpy(in_date,"19861205");
   date_32(in_date, out_date);
   printf("\n Output date_32 = %s",out_date);
}

ex33()
{
   /***************************************************************
    ***************** call to date_33 function ***************
    ************************************************************/

   char in_date[12];
   char out_date[40];

   strcpy(in_date,"19861205");
   date_33(in_date, out_date);
   printf("\n Output date_33 = %s",out_date);
}

ex34()
{
   /***************************************************************
    ***************** call to date_34 function ***************
    ************************************************************/

   char in_date[12];
   char end_date[12];
   long int long_days;
   long int date_34();

   strcpy(in_date,"19861205");
   strcpy(end_date,"19861223");
   long_days = date_34(in_date, end_date);
   printf("\n Output date_34 ( DDDDDDDD ) = %ld",long_days);
}

ex35()
{
   /***************************************************************
    ***************** call to date_35 function ***************
    ************************************************************/

   char in_date[12];
   char end_date[12];
   long int long_days;
   long int date_35();

   strcpy(in_date,"19861205");
   strcpy(end_date,"19861223");
   long_days = date_35(in_date, end_date);
   printf("\n Output date_35 ( DDDDDDDD ) = %ld",long_days);
}
```

```
ex36()
{
  /*****************************************************************
   ***************** call to date_36 function **************
   *****************************************************************/

  char in_date[12];
  char out_date[40];

  strcpy(in_date,"19861205");
  date_36(in_date, out_date, 10);
  printf("\n Output date_36 ( YYYYMMDD ) = %s",out_date);
}

ex37()
{
  /*****************************************************************
   ***************** call to date_37 function **************
   *****************************************************************/

  char in_date[12];
  char out_date[40];

  strcpy(in_date,"05DEC1986");
  date_37(in_date, out_date);
  printf("\n Output date_37 ( MM/DD/YYYY ) = %s",out_date);
}

ex38()
{
  /*****************************************************************
   ***************** call to date_38 function **************
   *****************************************************************/

  char in_date[12];
  char out_date[40];

  strcpy(in_date,"05DEC1986");
  date_38(in_date, out_date);
  printf("\n Output date_38 ( YYYYMMMDD ) = %s",out_date);
}

ex39()
{
  /*****************************************************************
   ***************** call to date_39 function **************
   *****************************************************************/

  char in_date[12];
  char out_date[40];

  strcpy(in_date,"05DEC1986");
  date_39(in_date, out_date);
  printf("\n Output date_39 ( DD-MMM-YYYY ) = %s",out_date);
}

ex40()
{
```

```
  /******************************************************************
   ***************** call to date_40 function ***************
   ******************************************************************/

  char in_date[12];
  long int long_days;
  long int date_40();

  strcpy(in_date,"05DEC1986");
  long_days = date_40(in_date);
  printf("\n Output date_40 ( DDDDDDDD ) = %ld",long_days);
}

ex41()
{
  /******************************************************************
   ***************** call to date_41 function ***************
   ******************************************************************/

  char in_date[12];
  int out_days;

  strcpy(in_date,"05DEC1986");
  out_days = date_41(in_date);
  printf("\n Output date_41 ( DDDDD ) = %d",out_days);
}

ex42()
{
  /******************************************************************
   ***************** call to date_42 function ***************
   ******************************************************************/

  char in_date[12];
  int out_days;

  strcpy(in_date,"05DEC1986");
  out_days = date_42(in_date);
  printf("\n Output date_42 ( DDDDD ) = %d",out_days);
}

ex43()
{
  /******************************************************************
   ***************** call to date_43 function ***************
   ******************************************************************/

  char in_date[12];
  int out_days;

  strcpy(in_date,"05DEC1986");
  out_days = date_43(in_date);
  printf("\n Output date_43 ( DDDDD ) = %d",out_days);
}

ex44()
{
  /******************************************************************
```

```
                  ***************** call to date_44 function ***************
   *********************************************************************/

   char in_date[12];
   char out_date[40];

   strcpy(in_date,"05DEC1986");
   date_44(in_date, out_date);
   printf("\n Output date_44 = %s",out_date);
}

ex45()
{
   /********************************************************************
    ***************** call to date_45 function ***************
    *********************************************************************/

   char in_date[12];
   char out_date[40];

   strcpy(in_date,"05DEC1986");
   date_45(in_date, out_date);
   printf("\n Output date_45 = %s",out_date);
}

ex46()
{
   /********************************************************************
    ***************** call to date_46 function ***************
    *********************************************************************/

   char in_date[12];
   char end_date[12];
   long int long_days;
   long int date_46();

   strcpy(in_date,"05DEC1986");
   strcpy(end_date,"23DEC1986");
   long_days = date_46(in_date, end_date);
   printf("\n Output date_46 ( DDDDDDDD ) = %ld",long_days);
}

ex47()
{
   /********************************************************************
    ***************** call to date_47 function ***************
    *********************************************************************/

   char in_date[12];
   char end_date[12];
   long int long_days;
   long int date_47();

   strcpy(in_date,"05DEC1986");
   strcpy(end_date,"23DEC1986");
   long_days = date_47(in_date, end_date);
   printf("\n Output date_47 ( DDDDDDDD ) = %ld",long_days);
}
```

```
ex48()
{
  /**************************************************************
   ***************** call to date_48 function ***************
   *************************************************************/

  char in_date[12];
  char out_date[40];

  strcpy(in_date,"05DEC1986");
  date_48(in_date, out_date, 10);
  printf("\n Output date_48 ( DDMMMYYYY ) = %s",out_date);
}

ex49()
{
  /**************************************************************
   ***************** call to date_49 function ***************
   *************************************************************/

  char out_date[40];
  long int in_julian;

  in_julian  = 725651;
  date_49(in_julian, out_date);
  printf("\n Output date_49 ( MM/DD/YY ) = %s",out_date);
}

ex50()
{
  /**************************************************************
   ***************** call to date_50 function ***************
   *************************************************************/

  char out_date[40];
  long int in_julian;

  in_julian  = 725651;
  date_50(in_julian, out_date);
  printf("\n Output date_50 ( DD-MMM-YYYY ) = %s",out_date);
}

ex51()
{
  /**************************************************************
   ***************** call to date_51 function ***************
   *************************************************************/

  char out_date[40];
  long int in_julian;

  in_julian  = 725651;
  date_51(in_julian, out_date);
  printf("\n Output date_51 ( YYYYMMDD ) = %s",out_date);
}

ex52()
{
```

```
  /****************************************************************
   ***************** call to date_52 function **************
   ***************************************************************/

  char out_date[40];
  long int in_julian;

  in_julian  = 725651;
  date_52(in_julian, out_date);
  printf("\n Output date_52 ( DDMMMYYYY ) = %s",out_date);
}

ex53()
{
  /****************************************************************
   ***************** call to date_53 function **************
   ***************************************************************/

  int out_days;
  long int in_julian;

  in_julian  = 725651;
  out_days = date_53(in_julian);
  printf("\n Output date_53 ( DDD ) = %d",out_days);
}

ex54()
{
  /****************************************************************
   ***************** call to date_54 function **************
   ***************************************************************/

  int out_days;
  long int in_julian;

  in_julian  = 725651;
  out_days = date_54(in_julian);
  printf("\n Output date_54 ( DDD ) = %d",out_days);
}

ex55()
{
  /****************************************************************
   ***************** call to date_55 function **************
   ***************************************************************/

  int out_days;
  long int in_julian;

  in_julian  = 725651;
  out_days = date_55(in_julian);
  printf("\n Output date_55 ( DDD ) = %d",out_days);
}

ex56()
{
  /****************************************************************
   ***************** call to date 56 function **************
```

```
     ****************************************************************/

     char out_date[40];
     long int in_julian;

     in_julian  = 725651;
     date_56(in_julian,out_date);
     printf("\n Output date_56 = %s",out_date);
}

ex57()
{

   /****************************************************************
     ***************** call to date_57 function ***************
     ****************************************************************/

     char out_date[40];
     long int in_julian;

     in_julian  = 725651;
     date_57(in_julian,out_date);
     printf("\n Output date_57 = %s",out_date);
}

ex58()
{
   /****************************************************************
     ***************** call to date_58 function ***************
     ****************************************************************/

     long int long_days;
     long int in_julian;
     long int end_julian;
     long int date_58();

     in_julian  = 725651;
     end_julian = 725653;
     long_days = date_58(in_julian, end_julian);
     printf("\n Output date_58 ( DDD ) = %ld",long_days);
}

ex59()
{
   /****************************************************************
     ***************** call to date_59 function ***************
     ****************************************************************/

     long int long_days;
     long int in_julian;
     long int end_julian;
     long int date_59();

     in_julian  = 725651;
     end_julian = 725653;
     long_days = date_59(in_julian, end_julian);
     printf("\n Output date_59 ( DDD ) = %ld",long_days);
}
```

```
ex60()
{
  /****************************************************************
   ****************** call to date_60 function ****************
   ****************************************************************/

  long int long_days;
  long int in_julian;
  long int date_60();
  in_julian  = 725651;
  long_days = date_60(in_julian, 10);
  printf("\n Output date_60 ( DDD ) = %ld",long_days);
}
```

22

Screen Output Functions

bell	—	sound bell
blink_in	—	blink on
blink_off	—	blink off
box_1	—	print box with single lines
box_2	—	print box with double lines
box_3	—	print box with wide lines
e_line	—	erase line
e_screen	—	erase screen
hi_intensity	—	high intensity on
locate	—	locate on the screen
low_intensity	—	low intensity
rv_off	—	reverse video off
rv_on	—	reverse video on
srn_off	—	screen reverse video off
srn_on	—	screen reverse video on

Function Name: bell

Description: This function instructs the PC to sound (ring) the bell.

Variables: none — The string of ASCII 7 (octal 7) is displayed to the screen, thus sounding the bell.

Example: bell(); produces the computer bell sound

Rules: The function is not passed any variables and is called at the time the bell should be sounded.

```
bell()
{ printf("\7");
}
```

blink__on

Function Name: blink__on

Description: This function instructs the PC to blink all characters printed on the screen until the blink__off function is called. Note that even after the blink__off function is called, the characters printed with blink on will still blink. The only way to stop them from blinking is to reprint them with the blink off or remove them from the screen by a clear screen or natural screen scrolling.

Variables: none — The string of ESCAPE (octal 33) followed by "[5m" is sent to the screen instructing the screen to blink.

Example: blink__on( ); instructs the computer to turn blink mode on

Rules: The function is not passed any variables and is called prior to printing the characters you wish to blink.
Blink mode will stay on until it is turned off by calling the blink__off( ) function.

```
blink_on()
{ printf("%c[5m",'\33');
}
```

Function Name: blink__off

Description: This function instructs the PC to turn blink mode off. This function works in conjunction with blink__on( ). blink__on causes all characters printed to the screen to blink. This function turns this blink mode off. Note that this function will not stop previously printed characters from blinking, it only stops future characters from blinking.

Variables: none — The string of ESCAPE (octal 33) followed by "[0m" is sent to the screen instructing the screen to blink.

Example: blink__off( ); instructs the computer to turn blink mode off

Rules: The function is not passed any variables and is called to turn negate the blink__on function.
Blink mode will stay off until it is turned on by calling the blink__on( ) function.

Caution: The string used to turn blink mode off (escape [0m) is also used to turn off other functions such as hi__intensity( ) and rv__on( ). Therefore, after turning the blink off, if applicable, you may have to turn high intensity or reverse video back on.

```
blink_off()
{ printf("%c[0m",'\33');
}
```

box__1

box__1

Function Name: box__1

Description: This function instructs the PC to print a single line box on the screen. Note that its location on the screen and its size are defined by input parameters.

Variables: x — This parameter refers to the horizontal row on which the top line of the box will be placed.

y — This parameter refers to the vertical row on which the left line of the box will be placed.

w — This parameter refers to the width of the box being displayed in horizontal print positions.

h — This parameter refers to the height of the box being printed in vertical print lines.

Example: box__1(4,5,6,7); creates a single line box that in 6 rows wide and 7 lines high with the top left corner being at screen location (4,5)

Rules: The parameters passed must allow the box being created to fit on the screen. For example, on an 80 character screen, a box starting in column 60 cannot be 30 characters wide.

```
box_1(x,y,w,h)
 int x,y,w,h;

{ int w_count, h_count, left, right;

  locate(x,y);
  printf("%c",'\332');
  for ( w_count = 0; w_count <= w; ++w_count )  printf("\304");
  printf("%c",'\277');
  for ( h_count = 0; h_count <= h; ++h_count )
    { locate(x + h_count + 1, y );
      printf("%c",'\263');
      for ( w_count = 0; w_count <= w; ++w_count )  printf(" ");
      printf("%c",'\263');
    }

  locate(x + h + 1, y);
  printf("%c",'\300');
  for ( w_count = 0; w_count <= w; ++w_count )  printf("%c",'\304');
  printf("%c",'\331');

}
```

box__2

Function Name: box__2

Description: This function instructs the PC to print a double line box on the screen. Note that its location on the screen and its size are defined by input parameters.

Variables: x — This parameter refers to the horizontal row on which the top line of the box will be placed.

y — This parameter refers to the vertical row on which the left line of the box will be placed.

w — This parameter refers to the width of the box being displayed in horizontal print positions.

h — This parameter refers to the height of the box being printed in vertical print lines.

Example: box__2(4,5,6,7);   creates a double line box that in 6 rows wide and 7 lines high with the top left corner being at screen location (4,5)

Rules: The parameters passed must allow the box being created to fit on the screen. For example, on an 80 character screen, a box starting in column 60 cannot be 30 characters wide.

```
box_2(x,y,w,h)
 int x,y,w,h;

{ int w_count, h_count, left, right;

  locate(x,y);
  printf("%c",'\311');
  for ( w_count = 0; w_count <= w; ++w_count )  printf("\315");
  printf("%c",'\273');
  for ( h_count = 0; h_count <= h; ++h_count )
    { locate(x + h_count + 1, y );
      printf("%c",'\272');
      for ( w_count = 0; w_count <= w; ++w_count )  printf(" ");
      printf("%c",'\272');
    }

  locate(x + h + 1, y);
  printf("%c",'\310');
  for ( w_count = 0; w_count <= w; ++w_count )  printf("%c",'\315');
  printf("%c",'\274');

}
```

box__3

Function Name: box__3

Description: This function instructs the PC to print a wide line box on the screen. Note that its location on the screen and its size are defined by input parameters.

Variables: x — This parameter refers to the horizontal row on which the top line of the box will be placed.

y — This parameter refers to the vertical row on which the left line of the box will be placed.

w — This parameter refers to the width of the box being displayed in horizontal print positions.

h — This parameter refers to the height of the box being printed in vertical print lines.

Example: box__3(4,5,6,7); creates a double line box that in 6 rows wide and 7 lines high with the top left corner being at screen location (4,5)

Rules: The parameters passed must allow the box being created to fit on the screen. For example, on an 80 character screen, a box starting in column 60 cannot be 30 characters wide.

```
box_3(x,y,w,h)
 int x,y,w,h;

{ int w_count, h_count, left, right;

  locate(x,y);
  printf("%c",'\333');
  for ( w_count = 0; w_count <= w; ++w_count )  printf("\333");
  printf("%c",'\333');
  for ( h_count = 0; h_count <= h; ++h_count )
    { locate(x + h_count + 1, y );
      printf("%c",'\333');
      for ( w_count = 0; w_count <= w; ++w_count )  printf(" ");
      printf("%c",'\333');
    }

  locate(x + h + 1, y);
  printf("%c",'\333');
  for ( w_count = 0; w_count <= w; ++w_count )  printf("%c",'\333');
  printf("%c",'\333');

}
```

Function Name: e__line( )

Description: This function instructs the PC to blank out all characters residing on the line where the cursor is currently placed. When wishing to clear various lines on the screen, use this function in conjunction with the locate( ) function which can locate the cursor at any specified screen location.

Variables: none — The string of ESCAPE (octal 33) followed by "[k" is passed to the screen.

Example: e__line( );   instructs the computer to clear the specified line

Rules: The function is not passed any variables and is called after the cursor has been placed on the appropriate line.

```
e_line()
{ printf("%c[k",'\33');
}
```

e__screen

Function Name: e__screen( )

Description: This function instructs the PC to blank out all characters on the screen and places the cursor in screen location (1,1).

Variables: none — The string of ESCAPE (octal 33) followed by "[J" is passed to the screen.

Example: e__screen( ); instructs the computer to clear the screen

Rules: The function is not passed any variables and is called at the time the screen should be cleared.

Special Note: There are some screens that will place the cursor in a location other than (1,1). In this case, if desired, you may place the cursor in location (1,1) by calling the locate( )" function using parameters (1,1).

```
e_screen()
{ printf("%c[2J",'\33');
}
```

Function Name: hi__intensity

Description: This function instructs the PC to brighten all characters printed on the screen until the low__intensity function is called. Note that even after the low__intensity function is called, the characters printed with high intensity will still be bright. The only way to lower their intensity is to reprint them with the low intensity or remove them from the screen by a clear screen or natural screen scrolling.

Variables: none — The string of ESCAPE (octal 33) followed by "[1m" is sent to the screen instructing the screen to enter high intensity mode.

Example: hi__intensity( ); instructs the computer to turn high intensity

Rules: The function is not passed any variables and is called prior to printing the characters you wish to print brightly.
High intensity mode will stay on until it is turned off by calling the low__intensity( ) function.

```
hi_intensity()
{ printf("%c[1m",'\33');
}
```

locate

Function Name: locate

Description: This function instructs the PC to move the cursor to a specified location on the screen.

Variables: x — This parameter refers to the horizontal row on which the cursor will be placed.

y — This parameter refers to the vertical row on which the cursor will be placed.

Example: locate(5,10);   instructs the computer to move the cursor to locate 5,10

Rules: The passed parameters must be a valid screen location. The x value must be between 1 and 24 and the y value must be between 1 and 80.

```
locate(x, y)
    int x, y;
{ printf("%c[%d;%dH", '\33', x, y);
}
```

Function Name: low___intensity

Description: This function instructs the PC to turn high intensity mode off. This function works in conjunction with hi___intensity( ). hi___intensity causes all characters printed to the screen to print brightly. This function turns this high intensity mode off. Note that this function will not stop previously printed characters from being bright.

Variables: none — The string of ESCAPE (octal 33) followed by "[0m" is sent to the screen instructing the screen to blink.

Example: low___intensity( );   instructs the computer to turn high intensity off

Rules: The function is not passed any variables and is called to negate the hi___intensity function.
High intensity mode will stay off until it is turned on by calling the hi___intensity( ) function.

Caution: The string used to turn intensity mode off (escape [0m) is also used to turn off other functions such as blink___on( ) and rv___on( ). Therefore, after turning the high intensity off, if applicable, you may have to turn blink or reverse video back on.

```
low_intensity()
{ printf("%c[0m",'\33');
}
```

rv__off

Function Name: rv__off

Description: This function instructs the PC to turn reverse video mode off. This function works in conjunction with rv__on(). rv__on causes all characters printed to the screen to print in reverse screen color. This function turns this reverse video mode off. Note that this function will not stop previously printed characters from being in reverse.

Variables: none — The string of ESCAPE (octal 33) followed by "[0m" is sent to the screen instructing the screen to blink.

Example: rv__off();   instructs the computer to turn reverse video off

Rules: The function is not passed any variables and is called to negate the rv__on function.
High video mode will stay off until it is turned on by calling the rv__on() function.

Caution: The string used to turn video mode off (escape [0m) is also used to turn off other functions such as blink__on() and hi__intensity(). Therefore, after turning the reverse video off, if applicable, you may have to turn blink or high intensity back on.

```
rv_off()
{ printf("%c[0m",'\33');
}
```

Function Name: rv__on

Description: This function instructs the PC to reverse all characters printed on the screen until the rv__off function is called. Note that even after the rv__off function is called, the characters printed with reverse video will still be reversed. The only way to change their video is to reprint them with the regular video or remove them from the screen by a clear screen or natural screen scrolling.

Variables: none — The string of ESCAPE (octal 33) followed by "[7m" is sent to the screen instructing the screen to enter reverse video mode.

Example: rv__on(); instructs the computer to turn reverse video

Rules: The function is not passed any variables and is called prior to printing the characters you wish to print in reverse video. Reverse video mode will stay on until it is turned off by calling the rv__off() function.

```
rv_on()
{ printf("%c[7m",'\33');
}
```

srn__off

Function Name: srn__off( )

Description: This function instructs the PC to blank out all characters on the screen, turn reverse video off and place the cursor in screen location (1,1).

Variables: none — This function calls two other video functions: rv__off( ) to turn reverse video off and e__screen( ) to clear the screen.

Example: srn__off( ); instructs the computer to clear the screen and turn reverse video off

Rules: The function is not passed any variables and is called at the time the screen should be cleared and reverse video turned off.

Special Note: There are some screens that will place the cursor in a location other than (1,1). In this case, if desired, you may place the cursor in location (1,1) by calling the locate( ) function using parameters (1,1).

```
srn_off()
{ rv_off();
  e_screen();
}
```

Function Name: srn__on( )

Description: This function instructs the PC to blank out all characters on the screen, turn reverse video on and place the cursor in screen location (1,1).

Variables: none — This function calls two other video functions: rv__on( ) to turn reverse video on and e__screen( ) to clear the screen.

Example: srn__on( );   instructs the computer to clear the screen and turn reverse video on

Rules: The function is not passed any variables and is called at the time the screen should be cleared and reverse video turned on.

Special Note: There are some screens that will place the cursor in a location other than (1,1). In this case, if desired, you may place the cursor in location (1,1) by calling the locate( ) function using parameters (1,1).

```
srn_on()
{ rv_on();
  e_screen();
}
```

CALLING THE SCREEN OUTPUT FUNCTIONS

The code on the following pages will sequentially call each of the functions in this chapter, demonstrating their effects and how they can be used in actual programs.

```
#include <math.h>
#include <stdio.h>

main()
{ ex8();
  ex1();
  ex2();
  ex13();
  ex4();
  ex12();
  ex3();
  ex5();
  ex2();
  ex6();
  ex7();
  ex9();
  ex11();
  ex12();
  ex15();
  ex14();
}

ex1()
{
  /*****************************************************************
   ****************** calls to bell function ******************
   ****************************************************************/

  bell();

}

ex2()
{
  /*****************************************************************
   **************** calls to blink_off function **************
   ****************************************************************/

  blink_off();

}

ex3()
{
  /*****************************************************************
   **************** calls to blink_on function *************
   ****************************************************************/

  blink_on();
```

```
}

ex4()
{
  /*****************************************************************
   ***************** calls to box_1 function *****************
   ****************************************************************/

  box_1(5,5,15,15);

}

ex5()
{
  /*****************************************************************
   ***************** calls to box_2 function *****************
   ****************************************************************/

  box_2(7,7,10,10);

}

ex6()
{
  /*****************************************************************
   ***************** calls to box_3 function *****************
   ****************************************************************/

  box_3(9,9,5,5);

}

ex7()
{
  /*****************************************************************
   ***************** calls to e_line function *****************
   ****************************************************************/

  e_line();

}

ex8()
{
  /*****************************************************************
   ***************** calls to e_screen function *****************
   ****************************************************************/

  e_screen();

}

ex9()
{
  /*****************************************************************
   ************ calls to hi_intensity function ***************
```

```
    *************************************************************/

  hi_intensity();


}

ex10()
{
  /**************************************************************
   ***************** calls to locate function **************
   *************************************************************/

  int a,b;
  a = 5;
  b = 10;
  locate (a,b);

}

ex11()
{
  /**************************************************************
   *********** calls to low_intensity function *************
   *************************************************************/

  low_intensity();

}

ex12()
{
  /**************************************************************
   **************** calls to rv_off function ***************
   *************************************************************/

  rv_off();

}

ex13()
{
  /**************************************************************
   ***************** calls to rv_on function ***************
   *************************************************************/

  rv_on();

}

ex14()
{
  /**************************************************************
   ***************** calls to srn_off function **************
   *************************************************************/

  srn_off();
```

```
}

ex15()
{
  /****************************************************************
   ***************** calls to srn_on function ****************
   ****************************************************************/

  srn_on();

}
```

23

Mathematic Functions

absolute	—	absolute value
average	—	return average
cube	—	numeric cube
d__to__h	—	decimal to hex conversion
is__bin	—	is binary digit
is__even	—	is number even
is__hex	—	is hexadecimal digit
is__octal	—	is octal digit
is__odd	—	is odd number
max	—	return maximum value
min	—	return minimum value
is__remainder	—	is there a remainder
round	—	round off
square	—	numeric square
truncate	—	truncation

absolute

Function Name: d__absolute(value) / f__absolute(value) /i__absolute(value)

Description: These functions return the absolute value of the number contained in variable value

Variables: value — The number passed to the function and modified to contain the absolute value

Example:

output = d__absolute(10);	returns the value 10
output = f__absolute(−5);	returns the value 5
output = i__absolute(45);	returns the value 45

Rules: The function must be passed a numerically defined variable. Additionally, the calling program must define the absolute function in a manner consistent with the version of the function called. For example if you call d__absolute then the calling program must define d__absolute() as a double.

```
double d_absolute(value)
 double value;
 { if ( value < 0 ) return( 0 - value ); else return(value);
 }

float f_absolute(value)
 float value;
 { if ( value < 0 ) return( 0 - value ); else return(value);
 }

i_absolute(value)
 int value;
 { if ( value < 0 ) return( 0 - value ); else return(value);
 }
```

average

Function Name: d__average(a,b) / f__average(a,b) / i__average(a,b)

Description: This function returns the average values of the numbers contained in variables a and b

Variables: a,b — The numbers passed to the function are averaged, this average is passed back to the calling function

Example:

output = d__average(10,20);	returns the value 15
output = f__average(2,4);	returns the value 3
output = i__average(4,5);	returns the value 4.5

Rules: The function must be passed a numerically defined variable. Additionally, the calling program must define the average function in a manner consistent with the version of the function called. For example, if you call d__average then the calling program must define d__average( ) as a double.

```
double d_average(value1,value2)
 double value1, value2;
 { return( (value1 + value2) / 2 );
 }

float f_average(value1,value2)
 float value1, value2;
 { return( (value1 + value2) / 2 );
 }

i_average(value1,value2)
 int value1, value2;
 { return( (value1 + value2) / 2 );
 }
```

Function Name: d__cube(value) / f__cube(value) / i__cube(value)

Description: This function returns the cube value of the number contained in variable value

Variables: value — The number passed to the function and modified to contain the cube value

Example:

output = d__cube(2);	returns the value 8
output = f__cube(3);	returns the value 27
output = i__cube(4);	returns the value 64

Rules: The function must be passed a numerically defined variable. Additionally, the calling program must define the cube function in a manner consistent with the version of the function called. For example, if you call d__cube then the calling program must define d__cube( ) as a double.

```
double d_cube(value)
 double value;
 { return( value * value * value );
 }

float f_cube(value)
 float value;
 { return( value * value * value );
 }

i_cube(value)
 int value;
 { return( value * value * value );
 }
```

d__to__h

Function Name: d__to__h(value)

Description: This function converts the number passed from a decimal number to a hexadecimal number

Variables: dec — The number passed to the function that is converted to hexadecimal

hex — The variable that contains the calculated hexadecimal value passed back in the return statement

count — This variable is a counter used in the for loop

Example:
output = d__to__h(20);	returns the value 24
output = d__to__h(29);	returns the value 1D
output = d__to__h(42);	returns the value 2A

Rules: The function must be passed a variable defined as an integer.

```
d_to_h(dec)
 int dec;
{ int hex = 0;
  int count;

  for ( count=0; (dec / 16.0) != 0; count++ )
   { hex = hex + ( dec % 16 ) * i_to_power(10.0, count);
     dec = dec / 16;
   }
  return(hex);
}
```

Function Name: is__bin(value)

Description: This function returns a 1 if the value passed is a binary digit. If the value is not a binary digit then a 0 is returned

Variables: value — The number passed to the function that is tested as a binary digit

Example:

output = is__bin(0);	returns the value 1
output = is__bin(1);	returns the value 1
output = is__bin(2);	returns the value 0

Rules: The function must be passed a variable defined as a character.

```
is_bin(value)
 char value[];
 { if ( value[0] == '0' || value[0] == '1' ) return(1); else return(0);
 }
```

is__even

Function Name: is__even(value)

Description: This function returns a 1 if the value passed is an even. If the value is not an even number then a 0 is returned

Variables: value — The number passed to the function that is tested as an even number

Example:
output = is__even(10);   returns the value 1
output = is__even(11);   returns the value 0
output = is__even(12);   returns the value 1

Rules: The function must be passed a variable defined as an integer.

```
is_even(value)
 int value;
 { if ( remainder(value,2) == 0 ) return(1); else return(0);
 }
```

Function Name: is__hex(value)

Description: This function returns a 1 if the value passed is a hexadecimal digit. If the value is not a binary digit then a 0 is returned

Variables: value — The number passed to the function that is tested as a hexadecimal digit

Example:
output = is__hex(0);	returns the value 1
output = is__hex(1);	returns the value 1
output = is__hex(2);	returns the value 0

Rules: The function must be passed a variable defined as a character.

```
is_hex(value)
 int value;
 { if ( ( value >= '0' && value <= '9' ) ||
         ( value >= 'A' && value <= 'F' ) ||
         ( value <= 'a' && value <= 'f' ) )

            return(1);

    else return(0);
 }
```

is__octal

Function Name: is__octal(value)

Description: This function returns a 1 if the value passed is an octal digit. If the value is not an octal digit then a 0 is returned

Variables: value — The number passed to the function that is tested as an octal digit

Example:

output = is__octal(0);	returns the value 1
output = is__octal(6);	returns the value 1
output = is__octal(9);	returns the value 0

Rules: The function must be passed a variable defined as a character.

```
is_octal(value)
 int value;
 { if ( value >= '0' && value <= '7' ) return(1); else return(0);
 }
```

Function Name: is__odd(value)

Description: This function returns a 1 if the value passed is an odd. If the value is not an odd number, then a 0 is returned

Variables: value — The number passed to the function that is tested as an odd number

Example: output = is__odd(10); returns the value 1
output = is__odd(11); returns the value 0
output = is__odd(12); returns the value 1

Rules: The function must be passed a variable defined as an integer.

```
is_odd(value)
 int value;
 { if ( remainder(value,2) != 0 ) return(1); else return(0);
 }
```

max

Function Name: d__max(value1, value2) / f__max(value1, value2) / i__max(value1, value2)

Description: This function returns the number with the maximum value.

Variables: value1 — The numbers passed to the function and com-
value2 pared to assess the maximum value

Example:

output = d__max(10);	returns the value 10
output = f__max(− 5);	returns the value 5
output = i__max(45);	returns the value 45

Rules: The function must be passed a numerically defined variable. Additionally, the calling program must define the max function in a manner consistent with the version of the function called. For example if you call d__max then the calling program must define d__max( ) as a double.

```
double d_max(value1, value2)
 double value1, value2;
 { if ( value1 > value2 ) return( value1 ); else return(value2);
 }

float f_max(value1, value2)
 float value1, value2;
 { if ( value1 > value2 ) return( value1 ); else return(value2);
 }

i_max(value1, value2)
 int value1, value2;
 { if ( value1 > value2 ) return( value1 ); else return(value2);
 }
```

Function Name: d__min(value1, value2) / f__min(value1, value2) / i__min(value1, value2)

Description: This function returns the number with the minimum value.

Variables: value1 — The numbers passed to the function and com-
value2   pared to assess the minimum value

Example:
output = d__min(10);	returns the value 10
output = f__min(−5);	returns the value 5
output = i__min(45);	returns the value 45

Rules: The function must be passed a numerically defined variable. Additionally, the calling program must define the min function in a manner consistent with the version of the function called. For example, if you call d__min then the calling program must define d__min( ) as a double.

```
double d_min(value1, value2)
 double value1, value2;
 { if ( value1 < value2 ) return( value1 ); else return(value2);
 }

float f_min(value1, value2)
 float value1, value2;
 { if ( value1 < value2 ) return( value1 ); else return(value2);
 }

i_min(value1, value2)
 int value1, value2;
 { if ( value1 < value2 ) return( value1 ); else return(value2);
 }
```

is__remainder

Function Name: is__remainder(value1, value2)

Description: This function returns a 1 if the value passed is a remainder. If the value is not a remainder number then a 0 is returned

Variables: value — The number passed to the function that is tested as a remainder number

Example: output = is__remainder(10);   returns the value 1
output = is__remainder(11);   returns the value 0
output = is__remainder(12);   returns the value 1

Rules: The function must be passed a variable defined as an integer.

```
remainder(value1, value2)
 int value1, value2;
{ int remaind;
  remaind = value1 % value2;
  return (remaind);
}
```

Function Name: d__round(value) / f__round(value)

Description: This function returns the round value of the number contained in variable value

Variables: value — The number passed to the function and modified to contain the round value

Example: output = d__round(2);   returns the value 8
output = f__round(3);   returns the value 27

Rules: The function must be passed a numerically defined variable. Additionally, the calling program must define the round function in a manner consistent with the version of the function called. For example, if you call d__round, then the calling program must define d__round() as a double.

```
double d_round(value)
 double value;
 { int temp1;
   double temp2;
   temp1 = value + .5;
   temp2 = temp1;
   return( temp2);
 }

float f_round(value)
 float value;
 { int temp1;
   float temp2;
   temp1 = value + .5;
   temp2 = temp1;
   return( temp2);
 }
```

square

Function Name: d__square(value) / f__square(value) / i__square(value)

Description: This function returns the square value of the number contained in variable value

Variables: value — The number passed to the function and modified to contain the square value

Example:
output = d__square(2);	returns the value 8
output = f__square(3);	returns the value 27
output = i__square(4);	returns the value 64

Rules: The function must be passed a numerically defined variable. Additionally, the calling program must define the square function in a manner consistent with the version of the function called. For example, if you call d__square, then the calling program must define d__square( ) as a double.

```
double d_sqare(value)
 double value;
 { return( value * value );
 }

float f_sqare(value)
 float value;
 { return( value * value );
 }

i_sqare(value)
 int value;
 { return( value * value );
 }
```

truncate

Function Name: d__truncate(value) / f__truncate(value)

Description: This function returns the truncate value of the number contained in variable value

Variables: value — The number passed to the function and modified to contain the truncate value

Example:
output = d__truncate(2); returns the value 8
output = f__truncate(3); returns the value 27

Rules: The function must be passed a numerically defined variable. Additionally, the calling program must define the truncate function in a manner consistent with the version of the function called. For example, if you call d__truncate then the calling program must define d__truncate( ) as a double.

```
double d_truncate(value)
 double value;
 { int temp1;
   double temp2;
   temp1 = value;
   temp2 = temp1;
   return( temp2);
 }

float f_truncate(value)
 float value;
 { int temp1;
   float temp2;
   temp1 = value;
   temp2 = temp1;
   return( temp2);
 }
```

CALLING THE MATHEMATIC FUNCTIONS

The code on the following pages will sequentially call each of the functions in this chapter, demonstrating their effects and how they can be used in actual programs.

```c
#include <math.h>
#include <stdio.h>

/* double input, output; */

main()
{ ex1();
  ex2();
  ex3();
  ex4();
  ex5();
  ex6();
  ex7();
  ex8();
  ex9();
  ex10();
  ex11();
  ex12();
  ex13();
  ex14();
  ex15();
  ex16();
  ex17();
  ex18();
  ex19();
  ex20();
  ex21();
  ex22();
  ex23();
  ex24();
  ex25();
  ex26();
  ex27();
  ex28();
  ex29();
  ex30();
  ex31();
  ex32();
  ex33();
  ex34();
  ex35();
}

ex1()
{
  /***************************************************************
   *********** calls to d_absolute function *****************
   ***************************************************************/
  double d_absolute();
  double input, output;
  printf("\n\nd_absolute value function");
```

```
        input = 15;
        output = d_absolute(input);
        printf("\n     d_absolute value is == %f",output);
        input = -15;
        output = d_absolute(input);
        printf("\n     d_absolute value is == %f",output);
}

ex2()
{
  /****************************************************************
   *********** calls to f_absolute function *****************
   ***************************************************************/
.  float f_absolute();
   float input, output;
   printf("\n\nf_absolute value function");

        input = 15;
        output = f_absolute(input);
        printf("\n     f_absolute value is == %f",output);

        input = -15;
        output = f_absolute(input);
        printf("\n     f_absolute value is == %f",output);
}

ex3()
{
  /****************************************************************
   *********** calls to i_absolute function *****************
   ***************************************************************/
   int i_absolute();
   int input, output;
   printf("\n\ni_absolute value function");

        input = 15;
        output = i_absolute(input);
        printf("\n     i_absolute value is == %d",output);

        input = -15;
        output = i_absolute(input);
        printf("\n     i_absolute value is == %d",output);
}

ex4()
{
  /****************************************************************
   *********** calls to d_average function *****************
   ***************************************************************/
   double d_average();
   double input1, input2, output;
   printf("\n\nd_average value function");

        input1 = 10; input2 = 20;
        output = d_average(input1, input2);
        printf("\n     d_average value is == %f",output);
```

```
      input1 = 15; input2 = 20;
      output = d_average(input1, input2);
      printf("\n      d_average value is == %f",output);
}

ex5()
{
  /****************************************************************
   ************ calls to f_average function *****************
   ****************************************************************/
  float f_average();
  float input1, input2, output;
  printf("\n\nf_average value function");

      input1 = 10; input2 = 20;
      output = f_average(input1, input2);
      printf("\n      f_average value is == %f",output);

      input1 = 15; input2 = 20;
      output = f_average(input1, input2);
      printf("\n      f_average value is == %f",output);
}

ex6()
{
  /****************************************************************
   ************ calls to i_average function *****************
   ****************************************************************/
  int i_average();
  int input1, input2, output;
  printf("\n\ni_average value function");

      input1 = 10; input2 = 20;
      output = i_average(input1, input2);
      printf("\n      i_average value is == %d",output);

      input1 = 15; input2;
      output = i_average(input1, input2);
      printf("\n      i_average value is == %d",output);
}

ex7()
{
  /****************************************************************
   *************** calls to d_cube function *****************
   ****************************************************************/
  double d_cube();
  double input, output;
  printf("\n\nd_cube value function");

      input = 2;
      output = d_cube(input);
      printf("\n      d_cube value is == %f",output);

      input = 3;
      output = d_cube(input);
      printf("\n      d_cube value is == %f",output);
}
```

```
ex8()
{
  /****************************************************************
   **************** calls to f_cube function *****************
   ****************************************************************/
  float f_cube();
  float input, output;
  printf("\n\nf_cube value function");

     input = 2;
     output = f_cube(input);
     printf("\n      f_cube value is == %f",output);

     input = 3;
     output = f_cube(input);
     printf("\n      f_cube value is == %f",output);
}

ex9()
{
  /****************************************************************
   **************** calls to i_cube function *****************
   ****************************************************************/
  int i_cube();
  int input, output;
  printf("\n\ni_cube value function");

     input = 2;
     output = i_cube(input);
     printf("\n      i_cube value is == %d",output);

     input = 3;
     output = i_cube(input);
     printf("\n      i_cube value is == %d",output);
}

ex10()
{
  /****************************************************************
   **************** calls to d_to_h function *****************
   ****************************************************************/
  int input, output;
  printf("\n\nd_to_h value function");

     input = 29;
     output = d_to_h(input);
     printf("\n      d_to_h value is == %x",output);

     input = 42;
     output = d_to_h(input);
     printf("\n      d_to_h value is == %x",output);

}

ex11()
{
  /****************************************************************
```

```
    ****************** calls to is_bin function *****************
    ****************************************************************/
    char input[2];
    int output;
    printf("\n\nis_bin value function");

        strcpy(input,"1");
        output = is_bin(input);
        printf("\n      is_bin value is == %d",output);

        input[0] = '2';
        output = is_bin(input);
        printf("\n      is_bin value is == %d",output);
}

ex12()
{
    /****************************************************************
    ***************** calls to is_even function **************
    ****************************************************************/
    int input, output;
    printf("\n\nis_even value function");

        input = 10;
        output = is_even(input);
        printf("\n      is_even value is == %d",output);

        input = 11;
        output = is_even(input);
        printf("\n      is_even value is == %d",output);
}

ex13()
{
    /****************************************************************
    ***************** calls to is_hex function *****************
    ****************************************************************/
    int input, output;
    printf("\n\nis_hex value function");

        input = 'a';
        output = is_hex(input);
        printf("\n      is_hex value is == %d",output);

        input = 4;
        output = is_hex(input);
        printf("\n      is_hex value is == %d",output);

        input = 'x';
        output = is_hex(input);
        printf("\n      is_hex value is == %d",output);
}


ex14()
{
    /****************************************************************
    ***************** calls to is_octal function ***************
```

```
         *****************************************************************/
    int input, output;
    printf("\n\nis_octal value function");

       input = 'a';
       output = is_octal(input);
       printf("\n     is_octal value is == %d",output);

       input = '4';
       output = is_octal(input);
       printf("\n     is_octal value is == %d",output);

       input = 9;
       output = is_octal(input);
       printf("\n     is_octal value is == %d",output);
    }


ex15()
{
   /*****************************************************************
    *************** calls to is_odd function **************
    *****************************************************************/
    int input, output;
    printf("\n\nis_odd value function");

       input = 10;
       output = is_odd(input);
       printf("\n     is_odd value is == %d",output);

       input = 11;
       output = is_odd(input);
       printf("\n     is_odd value is == %d",output);
    }


ex16()
{
   /*****************************************************************
    *********** calls to d_max function *****************
    *****************************************************************/
    double d_max();
    double input1, input2, output;
    printf("\n\nd_max value function");

       input1 = 15; input2 = 18;
       output = d_max(input1, input2);
       printf("\n     d_max value is == %f",output);

       input1 = 6; input2 = 14;
       output = d_max(input1, input2);
       printf("\n     d_max value is == %f",output);
    }

ex17()
{
   /*****************************************************************
    *********** calls to f_max function *****************
```

```
    *****************************************************************/
    float f_max();
    float input1, input2, output;
    printf("\n\nf_max value function");

        input1 = 20; input2 = 7;
        output = f_max(input1, input2);
        printf("\n      f_max value is == %f",output);

        input1 = 15; input2 = 0;
        output = f_max(input1, input2);
        printf("\n      f_max value is == %f",output);
}

ex18()
{
  /*****************************************************************
    ************ calls to i_max function ******************
    *****************************************************************/
  int i_max();
  int input1, input2, output;
  printf("\n\ni_max value function");

        input1 = 15; input2 = 7;
        output = i_max(input1, input2);
        printf("\n      i_max value is == %d",output);

        input1 = 42; input2 = 36;
        output = i_max(input1, input2);
        printf("\n      i_max value is == %d",output);
}

ex19()
{
  /*****************************************************************
    ************ calls to d_min function ******************
    *****************************************************************/
  double d_min();
  double input1, input2, output;
  printf("\n\nd_min value function");

        input1 = 15; input2 = 18;
        output = d_min(input1, input2);
        printf("\n      d_min value is == %f",output);
        input1 = 6; input2 = 14;
        output = d_min(input1, input2);
        printf("\n      d_min value is == %f",output);
}

ex20()
{
  /*****************************************************************
    ************ calls to f_min function ******************
    *****************************************************************/
  float f_min();
  float input1, input2, output;
  printf("\n\nf_min value function");
```

```
        input1 = 20; input2 = 7;
        output = f_min(input1, input2);
        printf("\n      f_min value is == %f",output);

        input1 = 15; input2 = 0;
        output = f_min(input1, input2);
        printf("\n      f_min value is == %f",output);
}

ex21()
{
  /*****************************************************************
   ************ calls to i_min function ******************
   ****************************************************************/
  int i_min();
  int input1, input2, output;
  printf("\n\ni_min value function");

        input1 = 15; input2 = 7;
        output = i_min(input1, input2);
        printf("\n      i_min value is == %d",output);

        input1 = 42; input2 = 36;
        output = i_min(input1, input2);
        printf("\n      i_min value is == %d",output);
}

ex22()
{
  /*****************************************************************
   ************ calls to d_percent function ******************
   ****************************************************************/
  double d_percent();
  double input1, input2, output;
  printf("\n\nd_percent value function");

        input1 = 15; input2 = 18;
        output = d_percent(input1, input2);
        printf("\n      d_percent value is == %f",output);
        input1 = 6; input2 = 14;
        output = d_percent(input1, input2);
        printf("\n      d_percent value is == %f",output);
}

ex23()
{
  /*****************************************************************
   ************ calls to f_percent function ******************
   ****************************************************************/
  float f_percent();
  float input1, input2, output;
  printf("\n\nf_percent value function");

        input1 = 20; input2 = 7;
        output = f_percent(input1, input2);
        printf("\n      f_percent value is == %f",output);

        input1 = 15; input2 = 20;
```

```
        output = f_percent(input1, input2);
        printf("\n       f_percent value is == %f",output);
}


ex24()
{
  /***************************************************************
   *********** calls to i_percent function *****************
   ***************************************************************/
  int i_percent();
  int input1, input2, output;
  printf("\n\ni_percent value function");

        input1 = 5; input2 = 17;
        output = i_percent(input1, input2);
        printf("\n       i_percent value is == %d",output);

        input1 = 42; input2 = 36;
        output = i_percent(input1, input2);
        printf("\n       i_percent value is == %d",output);
}


ex25()
{
  /***************************************************************
   *********** calls to d_to_power function *****************
   ***************************************************************/
  double d_to_power();
  double input1, input2, output;
  printf("\n\nd_to_power value function");

        input1 = 5; input2 = 3;
        output = d_to_power(input1, input2);
        printf("\n       d_to_power value is == %f",output);
        input1 = 6; input2 = 2;
        output = d_to_power(input1, input2);
        printf("\n       d_to_power value is == %f",output);
}

ex26()
{
  /***************************************************************
   *********** calls to f_to_power function *****************
   ***************************************************************/
  float f_to_power();
  float input1, input2, output;
  printf("\n\nf_to_power value function");

        input1 = 3; input2 = 3;
        output = f_to_power(input1, input2);
        printf("\n       f_to_power value is == %f",output);

        input1 = 15; input2 = 2;
        output = f_to_power(input1, input2);
        printf("\n       f_to_power value is == %f",output);
}
```

```
ex27()
{
  /***************************************************************
   ************ calls to i_to_power function ******************
   ***************************************************************/
  int i_to_power();
  int input1, input2, output;
  printf("\n\ni_to_power value function");

     input1 = 5; input2 = 3;
     output = i_to_power(input1, input2);
     printf("\n     i_to_power value is == %d",output);

     input1 = 10; input2 = 3;
     output = i_to_power(input1, input2);
     printf("\n     i_to_power value is == %d",output);
}

ex28()
{
  /***************************************************************
   ************ calls to remainder function ******************
   ***************************************************************/
  int remainder();
  int input1, input2, output;
  printf("\n\nremainder value function");

     input1 = 15; input2 = 7;
     output = remainder(input1, input2);
     printf("\n     remainder value is == %d",output);

     input1 = 42; input2 = 36;
     output = remainder(input1, input2);
     printf("\n     remainder value is == %d",output);
}

ex29()
{
  /***************************************************************
   ************ calls to d_round function ******************
   ***************************************************************/
  double d_round();
  double input, output;
  printf("\n\nd_round value function");

     input = 15.4;
     output = d_round(input);
     printf("\n     d_round value is == %f",output);

     input = 9.9;
     output = d_round(input);
     printf("\n     d_round value is == %f",output);
}

ex30()
{
  /***************************************************************
   ************ calls to f_round function ******************
```

```
  ***********************************************************/
    float f_round();
    float input, output;
    printf("\n\nf_round value function");

    input = 17.2;
    output = f_round(input);
    printf("\n     f_round value is == %f",output);

    input = 3.9;
    output = f_round(input);
    printf("\n     f_round value is == %f",output);
}

ex31()
{
  /***********************************************************
   *************** calls to d_sqare function ****************
   ***********************************************************/
    double d_sqare();
    double input, output;
    printf("\n\nd_sqare value function");

    input = 2;
    output = d_sqare(input);
    printf("\n     d_sqare value is == %f",output);

    input = 3;
    output = d_sqare(input);
    printf("\n     d_sqare value is == %f",output);
}

ex32()
{
  /***********************************************************
   *************** calls to f_sqare function ****************
   ***********************************************************/
    float f_sqare();
    float input, output;
    printf("\n\nf_sqare value function");

    input = 2;
    output = f_sqare(input);
    printf("\n     f_sqare value is == %f",output);

    input = 3;
    output = f_sqare(input);
    printf("\n     f_sqare value is == %f",output);
}

ex33()
{
  /***********************************************************
   *************** calls to i_sqare function ****************
   ***********************************************************/
    int i_sqare();
    int input, output;
    printf("\n\ni_sqare value function");
```

```
        input = 2;
        output = i_sqare(input);
        printf("\n      i_sqare value is == %d",output);

        input = 3;
        output = i_sqare(input);
        printf("\n      i_sqare value is == %d",output);
}

ex34()
{
  /****************************************************************
   ************ calls to d_truncate function *****************
   ****************************************************************/
  double d_truncate();
  double input, output;
  printf("\n\nd_truncate value function");

        input = 15.4;
        output = d_truncate(input);
        printf("\n      d_truncate value is == %f",output);

        input = 9.9;
        output = d_truncate(input);
        printf("\n      d_truncate value is == %f",output);
}

ex35()
{
  /****************************************************************
   ************ calls to f_truncate function *****************
   ****************************************************************/
  float f_truncate();
  float input, output;
  printf("\n\nf_truncate value function");

        input = 17.2;
        output = f_truncate(input);
        printf("\n      f_truncate value is == %f",output);

        input = 3.9;
        output = f_truncate(input);
        printf("\n      f_truncate value is == %f",output);
}
```

Appendix A

Order of Precedence Among Operators
(Listed from Highest to Lowest)

```
-> [] . ->
* & - / ++ ! ~          (unary)
* / %
+ -
>> <<
< >  <= >=
= = !=
&
!
&&
!!
?!
= += -= *= /= %=
```

Appendix B

Data Type Conversions

Data Type	Outcome when moved to
double	truncates integers
	rounds floats
float	zero fills double
	truncates integers
int	zero fills floats and doubles
char	zero fills floats and doubles

Function Index

Index

Edited by Carl Aron

Other Bestsellers From TAB

☐ **C PROGRAMMING—WITH BUSINESS APPLICATIONS—Dr. Leon A. Wortman and Thomas O. Sidebottom**

This learn-by-doing guide puts its emphasis on actual programs that demonstrate the ways C code is entered, manipulated, and modified to achieve specific applications goals. Also included are sample runs for many of the programs and a disk containing all of the book's programs, for use on the IBM PC/XT/AT and compatibles with at least 256K. 260 pp., 95 illus.

Paper $18.95   **Hard $25.95**
Book No. 2857

☐ **BUILD YOUR OWN IBM® COMPATIBLE AND SAVE A BUNDLE—Aubrey Pilgrim**

Now you can build one of these computers yourself . . . and you can do it for hundreds, even thousands, of dollars less than comparable, factory-built systems. This book also includes instructions for upgrading an IBM computer. Why should you pay more than you have to when the computer you'll assemble using this book will completely fulfill your word processing, spreadsheet, database, games, graphics, educational, and other applications needs. And even if you can afford the high prices of big-name computer manufacturers, you'll benefit from customizing one to fit your own personal requirements and you'll gain valuable insight into how a computer works by assembling one yourself. 224 pp., 108 illus.

Paper $14.95   **Hard $22.95**
Book No. 2831

☐ **dBASE III® PLUS: ADVANCED APPLICATIONS FOR NONPROGRAMMERS—Richard H. Baker**

The new dBASE III PLUS makes all the advantages offered by dBASE as a programming language incredibly easy even for the non-programmer. And to make it even simpler for you to program like a pro; dBASE expert Richard Baker leads you painlessly through each programming step. Focusing on the practical rather than the theoretical aspects of programming, he explores dBASE III PLUS on three levels—entry level, intermediate, and experienced—showing that it's possible to use dBASE effectively no matter what your experience. 448 pp., 232 illus.

Paper $19.95   **Hard $27.95**
Book No. 2808

☐ **THE MULTIMATE ADVANTAGE™: Power for Professional Word Processing —Deborah Ritchie and Barbara Spear**

Discover insider tricks for getting maximum performance from MultiMate's most advanced word processing software! Using real-world business applications as models, the authors teach you how to format legal and accounting documents, charts, reports, forms, newsletters, and more—and then show you how to create documents to suit your own specific word processing needs. 208 pp., 60 illus.

Paper $16.95   **Hard $22.95**
Book No. 2793

☐ **C PROGRAMMER'S UTILITY LIBRARY —Frank Whitsell**

Here's a sourcebook that goes beyond simple programming techniques to focus on the efficient use of system resources to aid in the development of higher quality C programs! It's a unique collection of ready-to-use functions and utilities! There's also a ready-to-run disk available for use on the IBM PC/XT/AT and compatibles with at least 256K. 200 pp., 268 illus.

Paper $16.95   **Hard $24.95**
Book No. 2855

☐ **XYWRITE™ MADE EASIER —David H. Rothman**

"XyWrite is THE hot word processor right now and I think people should know about it . . . the most powerful word processor out there and . . . Rothman makes you understand how to use it." —From the Foreword by John C. Dvorak. Fully endorsed by XyQuest Corporation, developers and publishers of XyWrite word processing software, this guide makes learning to use XyWrite almost completely painless. 352 pp., 12 illus.

Paper $21.95   **Hard $27.95**
Book No. 2820

☐ **FRAMEWORK II™ APPLICATIONS —2nd Edition— Richard H. Baker**

This invaluable, revised edition shows you how to get the most out of Framework II's vastly improved communications facilities, its strengthened word processor, and its larger spreadsheet. And you'll learn how to do most of it by direct command using one of Framework's unique functions called "Idea Processing." This feature allows you to think about information as you do naturally, instead of trying to conform to the needs of your computer. 336 pp., 218 illus.

Paper $19.95   **Hard $26.95**
Book No. 2798

☐ **MAXIMUM PERFORMANCE WITH LOTUS® 1-2-3®, Versions 1.0 and 2.0—Robin Stark and Stuart Leitner**

Going far beyond the material covered in ordinary user's manuals, the authors provide expert techniques, shortcuts, and programming tips gleaned from their own experience and the experience of others who have reached "power-user" status in 1-2-3 operation. Included are "10 tricks every Lotus user should know" and "10 common worksheet problems and how to solve them"! 250 pp., 96 illus., Hardbound.

Paper $17.95   **Hard $25.95**
Book No. 2771

☐ **THE WORDPERFECT® BOOK (Covering Versions 4.0 and 4.1)—Leo J. Scanlon**

Whether you are writing letters, reports, articles, term papers, books, memoranda, legal documents, or financial summaries, this guide will show you how to use WordPerfect's many features to make them more professional. You'll learn to use its built-in Speller and thesaurus, how to draw lines on the screen for creating charts, how to perform mathematical operations, and more! 208 pp., 56 illus.

Paper $16.95   **Hard $24.95**
Book No. 2757

Other Bestsellers From TAB

The C Trilogy Software Available On Disk

If you are intrigued with the possibilities of the programs included in *The C Trilogy* (TAB Book No. 2890), you should definitely consider having the ready-to-run disk containing the functions from Part III. This software is guaranteed free of manufacturer's defects. (If you have any problems, return the disk within 30 days, and we'll send you a new one.) Not only will you save the time and effort of typing the programs, the disk eliminates the possibility of errors that can prevent the programs from functioning. Interested?

Available on DSDD disk for MS/PC DOS compatibles with 256 K and any C compiler at $24.95 for each disk plus $1.00 each shipping and handling.